Manitoba Stuc

Manitoba Studies in Native History publishes new scholarly interpretations of the historical experience of Native peoples in the western interior of North America. The series is under the editorial direction of a board representative of the scholarly and Native communities in Manitoba.

I *The New Peoples: Being and Becoming Métis in North America,* edited by Jacqueline Peterson and Jennifer S.H. Brown

II *Indian-European Trade Relations in the Lower Saskatchewan River Region to 1840,* by Paul Thistle

III *"The Orders of the Dreamed": George Nelson on Cree and Northern Ojibwa Religion and Myth, 1823,* by Jennifer S.H. Brown and Robert Brightman

IV *The Plains Cree: Trade, Diplomacy and War, 1790 to 1870,* by John S. Milloy

V *The Dakota of the Canadian Northwest: Lessons for Survival,* by Peter Douglas Elias

VI *Aboriginal Resource Use in Canada: Historical and Legal Aspects,* edited by Kerry Abel and Jean Friesen

VII *Severing the Ties that Bind: Government Repression of Indigenous Religious Ceremonies on the Prairies,* by Katherine Pettipas

VIII *The Ojibwa of Western Canada, 1780 to 1870,* by Laura Peers

IX *Women of the First Nations: Power, Wisdom, and Strength,* edited by Christine Miller and Patricia Chuchryk, with Marie Smallface Marule, Brenda Manyfingers, and Cheryl Deering

X *Night Spirits: The Story of the Relocation of the Sayisi Dene,* by Ila Bussidor and Üstün Bilgen-Reinart

XI *"A National Crime": The Canadian Government and the Residential School System, 1879 to 1986,* by John S. Milloy

XII *Muskekowuck Athinuwick: Original People of the Great Swampy Land,* by Victor P. Lytwyn

XIII *Preserving the Sacred: Historical Perspectives on the Ojibwa Midewiwin,* by Michael Angel

Albert Little Wolf (Main'ans), Ojibwa Mide from White Earth Reservation, and Frances Densmore, American ethnologist, who cooperated to preserve the "spiritual essence" of Ojibwa culture for future generations (1908). (Photograph courtesy The Smithsonian Institution)

Historical Perspectives on the Ojibwa Midewiwin

Preserving the Sacred

Michael Angel

The University of Manitoba Press

University of Manitoba Press
Winnipeg, Manitoba R3T 2N2
Canada
www.umanitoba.ca/uofmpress
Printed in Canada on acid-free paper by Friesens.

Cover Design: Steven Rosenberg, Doowah Design
Text Design: Karen Armstrong and Sharon Caseburg
Maps: Weldon Hiebert
Cover photograph: Midewiwin Lodge, Nett Lake, 1946. Courtesy Minnesota Historical Society.

Canadian Cataloguing in Publication Data

Angel, Michael, 1940-

Preserving the sacred : historical perspectives on the Ojibwa Midewiwin / Michael Angel.

(Manitoba studies in native history ; xiii)
Includes bibliographical references and index.
ISBN 0-88755-173-4 (bound).--ISBN 0-88755-657-4 (pbk.)

1. Midéwiwin. 2. Ojibwa Indians--Rites and ceremonies. 3. Ojibwa Indians--Religion. I. Title. II. Series.
E99.C6A63 2002 299'.783 C2002-911112-9

The University of Manitoba Press acknowledges the financial support for its publishing activities provided by the Canada Council for the Arts; the Manitoba Arts Council; and the Manitoba Department of Culture, Heritage and Tourism.

The University of Manitoba Press also acknowledges the financial assistance of the Government of Canada through the Book Publishing Industry Development Program (BPIDP).

The Manitoba Studies in Native History series is published with the financial support of the people of Manitoba, through the Department of Culture, Heritage and Tourism, the honourable Eric Robinson, Minister.

CONTENTS

List of Maps and Illustrations

Maps

Illustrations

Preface

Few issues provoke as much passion as the question of religious beliefs. Even though there would appear to be many contemporary people who either have never given a thought to the meaning of existence, or, having done so, believe it to be meaningless, most of us attempt to make some sense of existence and, to the best of our abilities, live our lives on the basis of these beliefs. Probably because these spiritual beliefs are at once so fundamental and, in many cases, so personal, communication with those who do not share our beliefs becomes difficult. We often fear they will not understand our behaviour, and thus will misconstrue, or, worse still, heap scorn on, our beliefs. Still others, believing so strongly in their own vision, will attempt to convince us that their views are the only correct views, and that ours are therefore false, or even evil.

Years ago, when I was a young Catholic boy growing up in a small, predominantly Protestant community, I remember trying to explain to my young friends what I did as an altar boy "serving mass." The Catholic service at that time took place entirely in Latin, and was accompanied by the wearing of vestments, the ringing of bells, and the use of incense. Each year, many members of a local Bible College would attend Midnight Mass on

Christmas Eve, and the Stations of the Cross on Good Friday, sitting in the back rows, in order to observe our strange rites and customs, which they believed to be the work of the Antichrist. How I hated this desecration of what was, for us, the holiest of times, and yet I knew equally little about their beliefs and ceremonies.

Years later (and no longer a Catholic), I have been invited from time to time by friends to participate in some of their religious ceremonies—Protestant, Jewish, Islamic, and Hindu—and, in turn, have shared some of mine with them. It has been an opportunity to witness their experience of faith and to realize that, beneath the external differences, we share a common belief in a transcendent reality, even though different traditions, conditioned by history and circumstance, may emphasize different means of acquiring knowledge of this ultimate truth.

Nevertheless, as history reveals, few religious groups have been consistently willing to grant that any beliefs other than their own are true. Christian groups have been particularly apt to adopt exclusivist positions and proselytize their neighbours, by force when persuasion failed. For this reason, and remembering my own experience as a youth, I've always been reluctant to attempt any study of North American Aboriginal religion and spirituality.

Yet, as I became more involved in my interdisciplinary studies program, I came to be increasingly fascinated by the extraordinary strength and resilience of Ojibwa religious beliefs and practices in the face of overwhelming odds during the past several centuries. Surely there was more to their belief system than was suggested by the partisan reports by Christian missionaries and the esoteric ethnographic studies of social scientists. Many Ojibwa are understandably reluctant to have others undertake to study them further. Nevertheless, I wanted to find out *for myself*; to give life to the "dry bones" of history from the perspective of a sympathetic outsider, who came not to judge, but to learn, and, having learned, to share this knowledge with others.

My main goal in this book is to undertake an historiographical study of an Ojibwa religious ceremony, the Midewiwin, as it was described by Euro-Americans during the nineteenth and twentieth centuries. This work brings together the major and some minor texts on the Midewiwin, and establishes their relationship to each other and the wider context within which they were written. I have attempted to identify the patterns that occur in the documents and synthesize the main themes (motifs), to identify and correct major misconceptions and instances of misinformation in the documents, and to trace the changing role played by the Midewiwin in Ojibwa society as portrayed by these documents. I have had to become conversant with postmodernism and post-structuralism insofar as they are used in anthropology, religion, and literary theory in order to analyze the documents. While I found this a useful exercise in helping to refine my own interpretations, the ahistorical approach of postmodernism is at odds with my basic premise. Moreover, I believe that the language used by many practitioners of these approaches would not facilitate understanding among a varied group of readers.

Therefore, while I certainly believe that interpretation of texts and artifacts is crucial to understanding all human beings, and while I may occasionally employ certain terms used in modern literary theory or discourse analysis, I do not profess to follow any specific approach or school. This book also uses some of the techniques of a post-colonial approach in that I am engaged in bringing voice to a subjugated people through an analysis of the colonial processes and constructions of knowledge that have muted their voices. However, while I am philosophically in agreement with the post-colonial approach, I do not employ it exclusively since my focus is primarily on the Midewiwin as an Ojibwa religious institution per se.

My own interpretation of the religious beliefs and practices described in the documents is that of a culturally sensitive outsider with a background in history and religious studies, endeavouring to understand a world view that is fundamentally different from my own. I agree with Ake Hultkrantz, who, in his essay on the study of Aboriginal American religions (1980), states, "It is essential that we try to understand Indian religions in their own right, as testimonies of the expression of the human spirit in existential issues." We may know the narratives, the rites, the outer shell, but we know little of their basic religious sentiments and beliefs. Insofar as it is possible, I have tried to let the narratives speak for themselves. In explaining religious beliefs and practices, I have tried to rely on the terminology and explanations of practitioners whenever possible, rather than to force them into other philosophical, religious, or anthropological structures. I am acutely aware of the sacred nature of the ceremonies, scrolls, songs, and objects that are described and analyzed in the documents, and have made every effort to treat them with the respect they deserve. For this reason, I have avoided dealing with some aspects entirely, and have used a minimum of illustrations, all of which have been used previously in other published works.

This work begins by attempting to place the Midewiwin within its historical context in order to determine how it changed over time as the Ojibwa developed, in relation to both their Aboriginal and Euro-American neighbours. The nineteenth century was a formative period for the development of the Ojibwa as a people, and the Midewiwin played a central role in this process. Moreover, this ethnogenesis did not take place in a vacuum, but was influenced by events and ideas that affected the Ojibwa and their Aboriginal and Euro-American neighbours alike. Since the Ojibwa were a geographically scattered and culturally diverse people, the changes and developments took a number of different forms. Moreover, no single Ojibwa leader arose to lead a religious or political protest movement, as happened with several other Aboriginal groups in northeastern North America during the nineteenth century. This has meant that Ojibwa socio-political and religious ideas and practices have not received the same attention as their neighbours, since most historians prefer to focus on key individuals whose impact can be readily traced. Evidence points to considerable religious and political ferment among the Ojibwa during the later eighteenth, the nineteenth, and early twentieth centuries, but with a few exceptions, it did not manifest itself in open rebellion. Euro-American observers often referred to the reputation of Ojibwa "medicine men" who were feared and respected by Aboriginal neighbours, just as they regularly cited Ojibwa bands that steadfastly refused to compromise their beliefs when they were negotiating with government officials or debating with Christian missionaries. Nevertheless, with some notable exceptions, Euro-Americans were mainly fascinated (and sometimes repelled) by those aspects of Ojibwa life that were, from a Euro-American perspective, esoteric or mysterious, and often could not be explained. Rather than trying to understand the Ojibwa world view, Euro-Americans attempted to make Ojibwa beliefs and actions fit into their own world view, and passed judgement on the Ojibwa accordingly. Although the individual perspectives of the Euro-Americans varied considerably, almost all believed themselves to be representatives of a superior culture, writing about a culture that would shortly be absorbed into Euro-American society.

Under such circumstances, it might be better to forget about documents that describe Midewiwin ceremonies and leaders. While I personally find many of the attitudes expressed in the sources I've examined to be repugnant, I do not feel that this is sufficient reason to ignore them. Even with their various biases and prejudices, the documents provide a convincing picture of a society that had developed an holistic cosmological system, which was embedded in their language and all aspects of their social structure. It is hardly surprising that Euro-Americans were easily confused when attempting to describe different aspects of the ceremonies and rituals, or the relationships among the different traditional religious figures, and the overlapping roles of political and social leaders. Nevertheless, certain commonalities do begin to emerge from the different accounts, and this has allowed me to make some speculations regarding the structure, history, and geographical distribution of the Midewiwin. Although I make no claim to providing an insider's perspective, I believe that an in-depth examination of the documents and of their historical and geographical settings provides a much fuller understanding of the historical role played by the Midewiwin among the different groups of Ojibwa than the usual view of it as an example of a revitalization movement. Secondly, by identifying a number of Ojibwa socio-political leaders as prominent members of the Midewiwin, I hope that I have succeeded in transforming an abstract study of religious beliefs and practices into something that is anchored in time and place—and which takes on a human face. Finally, I believe that the documents provide an excellent means of demonstrating how succeeding generations of Euro-Americans from various walks of life have viewed the Midewiwin. As such, they offer an interesting microcosm of changing Euro-American world views.

A word about orthography—because most practitioners of the Midewiwin have been Ojibwe speakers, I have used Ojibwe terms wherever possible in referring to different aspects of the Midewiwin. However, Ojibwe speakers are spread over a wide geographic area and speak a variety of related dialects. Moreover, because there is no standard orthography for the language, past and present writers have used a number of different systems in an attempt to represent Ojibwe sounds, a number of which are not present in English.

I have, therefore, employed Nichols's and Nyholm's *Concise Dictionary of Minnesota Ojibwe* as my guide in spelling Ojibwe terms used in the book. However, I have made a few exceptions to this rule. Thus, I have followed Laura Peers and others in using the term "Ojibwa" when referring to the people. Where other authors have used variant spellings, I have indicated the spelling they use, followed by Nichols's spelling in parentheses, when it is necessary to avoid confusion. A glossary of key Ojibwe terms precedes the bibliography.

Acknowledgements

This book has been a long time in the making, and its appearance in print form is the result of the support, the prodding, and the assistance of many different people. I would like to express special thanks to the following people. Wayne Moodie, Klaus Klostermaier, and Jennifer Brown saw to it that I received a solid multidisciplinary background and helped shape my research efforts. Leo Waisberg, Don Smith, Laura Peers, and Michael Pomedli, among many others, provided me with leads to new original sources, and used their own different backgrounds to offer valuable insights into my early efforts. John Nichols helped me to decipher Ojibwe words transcribed in numerous orthographies, while Eleanor Blain and Paul Voorhis provided assistance in producing the Ojibwe glossary. Over the years, Barb Bennell and her Interlibrary Loan staff at Elizabeth Dafoe Library performed great service in tracking down and obtaining obscure materials, as did the librarians and archivists at the Minnesota Historical Research Center, the Glenbow-Alberta Institute, the Provincial Archives of Manitoba, the National Archives of Canada, and various other institutions. While I confined my research to written accounts, discussions with Charlie Nelson, Peter Kinew, and other Ojibwa helped me to remember that the Midewiwin continues to exist as a living religion, despite the attempts of church and government officials to destroy it.

I would also like to thank the people at the University of Manitoba Press, who have been a pleasure to work with. Gerry Friesen's careful reading of my manuscript and his incisive comments gave me the courage to attempt putting it in book form. Dave Carr, Pat Sanders, Sharon Caseburg, and Weldon Hiebert have each, in their own way, contributed to making the book readable and visually attractive.

Finally, I must thank my family, who have put up with my obsessions over the years, whether it was constantly serving as a sounding board, or helping me to transport my computer, books, and files to a remote northwestern Ontario cabin by boat and back. Barbara, my wife, has been especially patient, and always helpful in turning scattered insights into readable prose. I would like to dedicate this book to her.

Preserving the Sacred

ONE

In Search of the Midewiwin

> "My grandson," said he, "the megis I spoke of, means the Me-da-we religion. Our forefathers, many string of lives ago, lived on the shores of the Great Salt Water in the east. Here it was, that while congregated in a great town, and while they were suffering the ravages of sickness and death, the Great Spirit, at the intercession of Man-ab-o-sho, the great common uncle of the An-ishin-aub-ag, granted them this rite wherewith life is restored and prolonged.... Our forefathers moved from the shores of the great water and proceeded westward.
>
> "This, my grandson, is the meaning of the words you did not understand; they have been repeated to us by our fathers for many generations."[1]

From time immemorial, during the long winter months, the Anishinaabeg had listened to their elders tell narratives such as this one, collected by historian William Warren in the early nineteenth century.[2] These *aadizookaanag*, or "sacred narratives," were passed on orally from generation to generation precisely in order that the Ojibwa would always know who they were, where they had come from, how they fitted into the world around them, and how they needed to behave in order to ensure a long life. Since theirs was a world view that prized stability over change, any appearance of change was interpreted as a repetition of old themes.[3] These themes formed the basis of the stories told by Anishinaabe elders.

The aadizookaanag explained the origin of the world, and the behaviour of all things, regardless of their outward form. They explained the birth of the mythic figure Nanabozho, the Ojibwa culture hero and trickster, and his role in helping to create a new earth.[4] The Anishinaabeg learned of the birth of the first people, and how their descendants had been taught many things by Nanabozho so that they would be able to survive. They learned of the power of visions and dreams by which they could communicate with the *manidoog,*[5] or spirits, and they learned to pay respect to their animal brethren with whom they shared their existence. Among the most important of Nanabozho's gifts to the Anishinaabeg was the institution of the Midewiwin, since practitioners were promised a long life if they followed its teachings and precepts as taught by the Mide elders.[6]

Other narratives told of their journey westward from the "shores of the great salt water," and of the separation of the original group at the Straits of Michilimackinac into the three tribes of Ojibwa, Ottawa, and Potawatomi. Still others told of the further division of the Ojibwa into two groups at Bowating (Sault Ste. Marie), one moving westward along the northern shores of Gichi Gami (Lake Superior), and the other southwest along the southern shores.[7] In these aadizookaanag, or formalized stories about the distant past in which the protagonists took both human and animal forms, what was important was not historical fact as conceived by Euro-Americans, but the truths that were implicit in the stories themselves. The Anishinaabeg distinguished the aadizookaanag from *dibaajimowin*, which were chronicles or anecdotes of personal experience involving human beings.[8] Examples of these can be found in the narratives that Warren collected of exploits of various Ojibwa leaders in their wars with the Sioux and the Fox. However, with the passage of time, the historical present and the distant past ultimately merged together, and historical facts were transformed into mythological truths.[9]

In his *History of the Ojibway People* (1885), William Warren sought to take the oral traditions of the Ojibwa people as told to him by their elders, and publish them in a format that would be understood by Euro-American readers. Of mixed Ojibwa and Euro-American heritage, Warren spoke Ojibwa and English fluently. Although a practising Episcopalian himself, he sincerely believed the Ojibwa people's religious traditions were worthy of respect, and that the religious movement he termed the *Me-da-we* (Midewiwin) was central to the Ojibwa world view. Unfortunately, Warren died before he was able to begin a projected book on the Midewiwin.

The exact nature of the Midewiwin was, and continues to be, shrouded in mystery and controversy. It is considered by contemporary Ojibwa scholars, such as Basil Johnston, Edward Benton-Banai, and Nicholas Deleary, to be the traditional religion of the Anishinaabeg.[10] Many Euro-American scholars, such as Harold Hickerson, have argued that it is a "crisis cult" or revitalization movement that originated as a reaction to the intrusion of Euro-Americans and the devastating effects of disease, alcohol, and social dislocation they brought with them.[11] Even the meaning of the name itself is unclear. Most commentators have concluded that the meaning has been lost in time, although some modern Ojibwa scholars such as Basil Johnston believe that the name refers to the sound resonance produced by the Mide drum.[12] The most common English equivalents are Medicine Society, Grand Medicine Dance, or some variation of these terms. These latter terms identify two features of the Midewiwin that Euro-Americans have paid particular attention to: the fact that participants were members of a structured society, and that gatherings of Midewiwin members featured a dance in which new members received the power to cure or harm. In focussing on these features, Euro-Americans ignored, or attached little importance to, the sacred narratives and the teachings that emanated from them. As a result, they often misinterpreted the role of the Midewiwin in Ojibwa society.

The version of the sacred narrative collected by Warren provides a succinct outline of the basic elements of the Midewiwin. The narrative begins with a brief description of the story of the migration from the land of their Anishinaabe forefathers, thus helping to situate the people in a larger universe. Secondly, there is mention of the quest for a long life, free from hunger, sickness, and enemies, which is the goal of all people. Thirdly, the role of Nanabozho in bringing the Midewiwin ceremonies, which conveyed "spirit power" to adherents, is made clear. Fourthly, the teaching function of the elders in passing on the beliefs and ceremonies of the Midewiwin is established. Not all versions of Midewiwin narratives contain all these elements. However, the foregoing is a good basic description of the role of the Midewiwin in Ojibwa society. Attempts to look for historical or geographical contexts of this and other particular narratives forget that every generation is faced with its own form of sickness and suffering, and thus requires help in seeking the good life. The specifics of the narrative might vary somewhat in the telling, but the eternal truths concerning the vulnerability of humans who needed assistance if they were to live a long and productive life remained constant, regardless of when or where the narrative was recited.

The Midewiwin has never attracted the attention of recent Euro-American scholars to the same extent as movements such as those of the Delaware Prophet and the Shawnee Prophet among the Algonquians, Handsome Lake among the Iroquois, or the Ghost Dance among several Plains groups. Yet, the Midewiwin came to exemplify "Indian Religion" to many nineteenth-century Euro-Americans. As a result of their selective emphasis on particular rituals, taken out of the broader context, the Midewiwin symbolized to Euro-Americans all that was strange, savage, evil, and potentially dangerous in Aboriginal people who had not become "civilized" and Christianized. Mide "priests," as they were normally portrayed in words and pictures by Euro-American observers, became the ultimate "other."[13] Even today, many religious scholars, anthropologists, and historians continue to cite uncritically nineteenth-century Euro-American reports as being authoritative descriptions of esoteric rites practised among the Ojibwa.

What was it about Ojibwa religious beliefs and practices that acquired such negative connotations in the minds of Euro-Americans? How could popular Euro-American conceptions of these beliefs and practices have been at such odds with Ojibwa conceptions? Before it is possible even to begin to answer such questions, it is essential that we listen to how the Ojibwa viewed themselves and the Midewiwin. At the same time, their versions need to be compared with the writings of various groups of Euro-Americans who have attempted to understand the Ojibwa and the Midewiwin.[14]

If pre-contact members of the Ojibwa had been asked how they identified themselves, they would have replied that they were Anishinaabeg, the "First or True People." As such, the many hunting bands and families shared not only a common linguistic base (Algonquian), but also many common beliefs and traditions, including a belief that, as Anishinaabeg, they were descendants of the original people, and therefore different from other human beings, to whom they gave specific, sometimes derogatory, names.[15]

If asked to identify themselves more narrowly, members of the Anishinaabeg would have referred to the small kinship or clan group to which they belonged, since this was the most significant social group in Anishinaabe society. Perhaps they would also have referred to the name of the socio-economic unit or band to which they belonged. This name might be taken from the name of the leader, from the geographical location, or perhaps from the name of the clan in cases where all members were from the same clan. At the time when larger groupings began to develop, bands that occupied a general geographic area were usually given a name related to the area in which they lived.[16] Thus, for instance, the

Anishinaabeg who occupied the northern shores of Lake Superior were known as "Sug-waun-dug-ah-win-in-e-wug" ("Men of the thick fir woods"), whom the French were to call "*Bois Forts.*"[17] The term "tribe," which came to describe the larger socio-political units, only began to be used following contact with Euro-Americans, and even then, decision making continued to take place at the band level. Nevertheless, by the nineteenth century, many Anishinaabeg were becoming aware of themselves as the Ojibwa tribe or nation, either as a result of internal or external forces. The formation of the tribes was explained in greater detail in the narrative recounted by Warren. According to this oral account, the Ojibwa, Ottawa (Odawa), and Potawatomi were said to have migrated from the shores of the great water (Atlantic Ocean) and to have separated into three groupings or tribes at the Straits of Michilimackinac at some time within the preceding several hundred years.[18]

Although they were one of the largest Aboriginal groups in North America during the nineteenth century,[19] the Ojibwa never achieved the recognition from the contemporary Euro-American public that was accorded their neighbours, the Iroquois and Sioux. However, as members of the Algonquian linguistic family, they formed part of a vast body of socio-political groups, which extended roughly from the Atlantic seaboard on the east to the eastern slopes of the Rocky Mountains on the west, and from the subarctic regions of the Canadian Shield to the Ohio Valley. Members of the northeastern divisions of this family, of whom the Ojibwa were part, shared not only a common language base but also a common culture, defined, to a large extent, by the geographical region they inhabited.

Owing to the vast area they came to occupy, coupled with the changing political structure of their society and changes in Euro-American terminology used to describe them, the Ojibwa, as they are generally known today, have been known in Euro-American society by a variety of names. Early commentators generally made reference to clan names used by particular bands, or used indigenous names for groupings of bands such as the Saulteurs or Mississaugas. Later, the name Ojibwa came to be more generally used, but in a variety of spellings: Ojibwa, Ojibway, Ojibwe, Otchipwe, or Chippewa. Moreover, subgroups in the nineteenth century and beyond continued to be known as the Mississaugas, Saulteurs or Saulteux, and Bungi.[20] To make matters more complicated, many present-day Ojibwa have begun once more to refer to themselves as Anishinaabeg, while others continue to prefer to use variants of the nineteenth-century name. Since there is a strong historical component to this present work, I have chosen

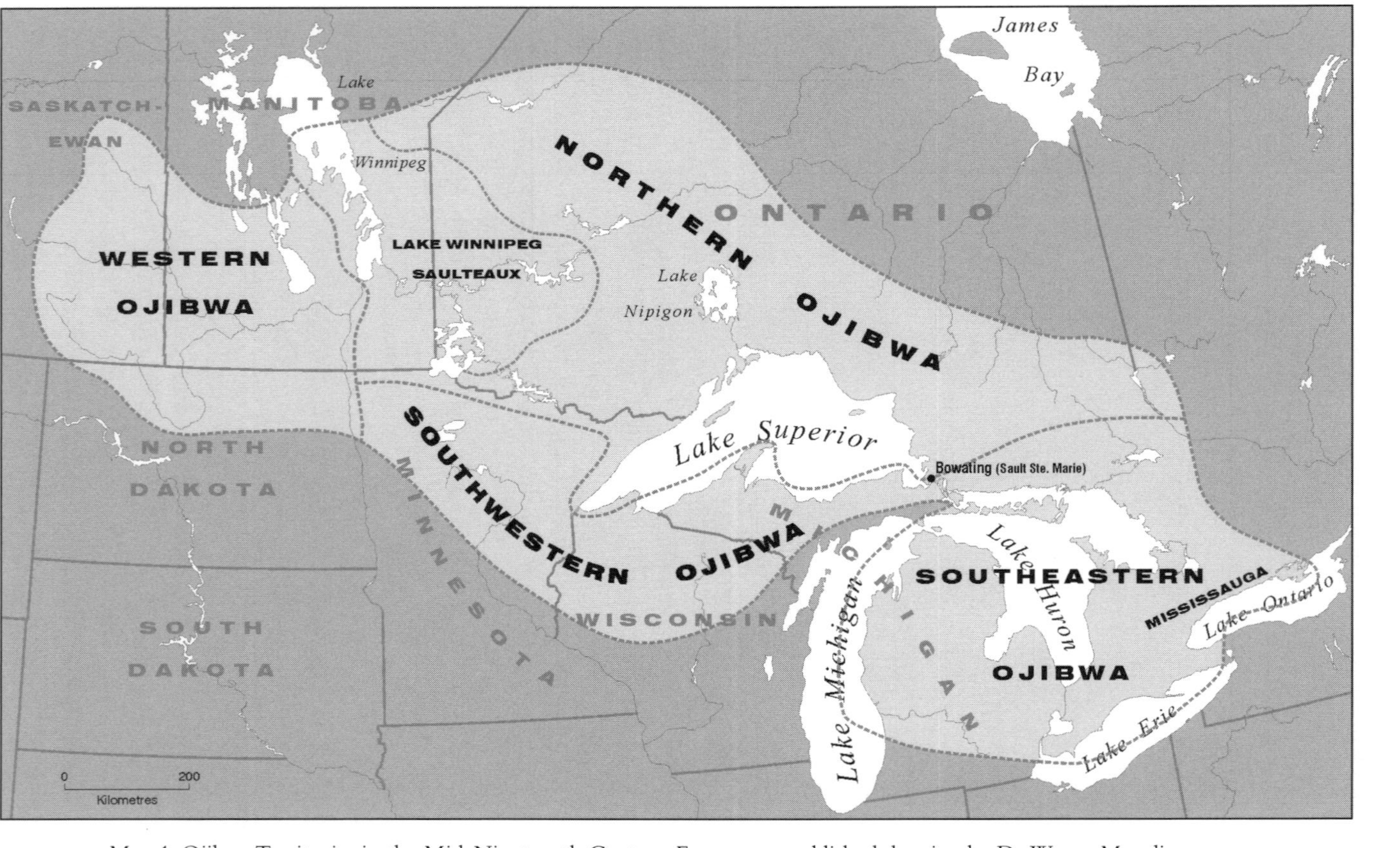

Map 1: Ojibwa Territories in the Mid-Nineteenth Century. From an unpublished drawing by Dr. Wayne Moodie.

to use the term "Ojibwa" for those sections of the work dealing with the nineteenth and twentieth centuries.

Of course, in an area as large as this, there were, and continue to be, numerous variations in language and culture. This has created difficulties in establishing a common terminology for various aspects of Anishinaabe religious life, since spelling and pronunciation of names vary considerably from region to region. Nevertheless, it gradually became accepted that the Ojibwa shared many aspects of what anthropologists have generally termed the "Woodlands culture," which was characterized by a hunting, fishing, food-gathering economy, with some horticultural practices. Like their more northerly neighbours, they lived in small kinship groups, assembling in larger groups at certain times of the year as part of the annual seasonal cycle. Similarly, they shared a common world view, which was expressed in the stories that their elders passed on to each generation, and which was lived in the rites of passage and ceremonies practised with some variations by most of the Algonquian-speaking peoples. Therefore, it is difficult to study the Ojibwa in isolation from their neighbours. In some respects, the Midewiwin may have been a specifically Ojibwa phenomenon. However, it grew out of a shared culture, and its Ojibwa manifestations were due, in large part, to the historical circumstances in which it emerged.

Euro-American scholars generally agree that the early Ojibwa were most closely related to the Ottawa and Potawatomi, with whom they shared a language, way of life, and geographic homeland in the region around the Great Lakes. However, the Ojibwa also had relatively close relations with the Winnebago, who spoke a Siouan language, and with the Huron, who spoke an Iroquoian language. The latter were particularly important to the Ojibwa in the seventeenth century, owing to their role in the trade with the early French settlers and their wars with other Iroquoian groups—wars in which the Ojibwa became involved. Later the Ojibwa participated in equally vicious wars with their Algonquian neighbours, the Fox (Mascoutens), and various groups of Sioux. With a few minor exceptions, however, they engaged in few wars with the French, the English, or the Americans and Canadians who first traded with them and who later occupied most of the lands that had been held by the Ojibwa. Owing to the crucial geographical location of their homeland in the unfolding of recent North American history, the Ojibwa have experienced numerous outward changes in their way of life during the past 300 years. Nevertheless, their traditions have proven far stronger than was ever anticipated by nineteenth- and early twentieth-century Euro-American observers, who predicted the quick demise of the Ojibwa as a distinct people, and the replacement of their religious beliefs and practices by Christian ones. Even many of those Ojibwa who have embraced Christianity continue to do so within the context of an Ojibwa world view, while an increasing number of other Ojibwa either continue to observe the tenets of the Midewiwin, or have returned to its practices.

Unlike William Warren, who was willing to accept the oral traditions of the Ojibwa regarding the Midewiwin, most Euro-American scholars have been reluctant to give credence to the historical veracity of these narratives. Instead, they have turned to the scanty historical accounts of earlier Euro-American observers in an effort to discover when the Midewiwin was first described, and thus could be said to have originated. Relying mainly on Euro-American sources, the majority have accepted ethnohistorian Harold Hickerson's conclusion that the Midewiwin was a nativistic movement, or "crisis cult," which emerged in reaction to European contact.[21]

Recently, anthropologist Karl Schlesier has challenged several of Hickerson's assertions, although he continues to accept the post-contact thesis.[22] Whereas Hickerson posited a harmonious period of change during which the Ojibwa profited from their middleman role in the fur trade, Schlesier sees the seventeenth century as a catastrophic age when Ojibwa and other Algonquian societies were shattered by Iroquois attacks and Euro-American diseases. The Midewiwin, he suggests, was primarily a response to these catastrophes.[23] According to Schlesier, the rise of the multi-clan villages was the result of depopulation, not the desire of the Ojibwa to be fur-trade middlemen. Moreover, villages such as Chequamegon were not simply multi-clan villages, they were multi-tribal refugee villages—an unlikely place for tribal identity or tribal religious ceremonies to develop. Finally, Schlesier suggests, the re-emergence of tribal villages in the latter part of the seventeenth century and the westward push of mixed multi-clan bands indicate that the Ojibwa had returned to previously existing patterns. In other words, the early Ojibwa whom Hickerson saw as being small, independent, clan-based units did, in fact, have a tribal identity, according to Schlesier. The question, therefore, is far from resolved.[24]

The Midewiwin has been viewed, in another context, as representing a major shift in Ojibwa world view. Most recent scholars believe that the rise of the Midewiwin reflected a change from a dependence on dreams and visions, to a reliance on inherited knowledge, as a means of acquiring power in Ojibwa society. Scholars of religion, such as Ake Hultkrantz and John Grim, have argued that the Midewiwin is part of a larger movement of North American Aboriginal groups in California, the Northwest Coast, and the Great Lakes regions to participate in cults and secret societies.[25] The rise of these societies represented one stage in the gradual transition of the role of "medicine men," from individual visionaries, to "shamans" who underwent formal training and initiation rites, to priests who ministered in permanent "cult" sites, using collectively preserved "cult" objects. Hultkrantz used the Midewiwin as an example of the "shamanistic" stage of development in his study of the religions of North American Aboriginal peoples.[26]

The majority of the aforementioned scholars have relied primarily on the written records of early missionaries, traders, government officials, and travellers to determine when the Midewiwin originated, when and where it spread, and to predict its decline and eventual disappearance. Such efforts underline the difficulties that arise when members of a literate culture attempt to understand an oral culture, particularly when they restrict their search for evidence to written materials. Many Euro-American commentators failed to take into account these differences.[27]

There are, of course, a variety of other tools by which an outside observer can attempt to understand a phenomenon such as the Midewiwin. The most obvious is to give more weight to the origin narratives of the Ojibwa. Following the groundbreaking work of historian Jan Vansina on oral tradition as history, some scholars have begun to make use of origin and migration narratives (aadizookaanag) as sources, while keeping in mind their limitations as chronologies.[28]

Although nineteenth-century observers were aware of the existence of these origin stories, they generally considered all Ojibwa narratives to be fables, and therefore not historically valid. Henry Schoolcraft, the earliest and most prolific nineteenth-century collector of Ojibwa narratives, failed to see in them anything more than interesting fables, which illustrated the "savage mind" of the Ojibwa and other northeastern Aboriginal people.[29] Even Warren, who did quote them, was careful to warn his readers that the narratives must not be taken literally, though he did give them limited historical credence. In fact, he appended the "historical narratives" of the Ojibwa battles with the Sioux to his accounts of earlier myths, thus bringing the story of the Ojibwa as a people up to the present for his readers, and perhaps unconsciously linking the two into a single history.[30] Twentieth-century scholars, with few exceptions, have been generally unwilling to accept the historical veracity of any of the Ojibwa narratives.

The origin and migration narratives also have visual and oral counterparts in the Mide *wiigwaas* (birchbark scrolls), and the Mide *nagamonan* (Midewiwin songs), which are sacred but, like the narratives, have both religious and secular significance. Nineteenth-century Euro-American observers such as Schoolcraft, Walter Hoffman, and Johann Kohl were all intrigued by the possibility of decoding the mysterious symbols contained on the birchbark scrolls. However, the real significance of the Mide songs was not understood until the early part of the twentieth century, with the work of Frances Densmore.[31] Only recently did Selwyn Dewdney and Fred Blessing begin to work on a theory that the pictographic symbols on the scrolls were a complex memory aid used by Mide officials.[32] Not only did they conclude that the scrolls and songs contained information regarding the Midewiwin ceremonies per se, but they also recognized that the scrolls were intimately connected with the Mide songs and Mide narratives. It remained for Thomas Vennum to bring together these components and illustrate how they contained historical and geographical information that could help to illuminate the Ojibwa past.[33] And, in so doing, Vennum has provided one more example of how the sacred and secular were intimately connected in the Ojibwa world view.

Whether precise "facts," dates, and places are totally verifiable is not as important as what these narratives, songs, and scrolls tell us about the Ojibwa conceptual system, and how these beliefs affected the lives of the Ojibwa people. "Myth," after all, is "an arrangement of the past, whether real or imagined, in patterns, that resonate with a culture's deepest values and aspirations.... They are the maps by which cultures navigate through time."[34]

Most nineteenth-century Euro-Americans who left written descriptions of the Midewiwin had at least fleeting first-hand knowledge of the ceremonies, which normally took place in the spring and fall of the year. While only members and initiates were allowed to attend the full range of events, some parts of the ceremony were open to the entire community as well as to outside observers. Nevertheless, most reports by casual observers provide only cursory descriptions. Midewiwin ceremonies were highly complex affairs, often lasting a week, and incorporating many different elements. Since many of these elements were common to other Ojibwa religious ceremonies, observers often had difficulty distinguishing them from one another. Dances, songs, and feasts looked and sounded similar, particularly to those who didn't speak the language, and who often believed that they were the work of the devil.

The majority of authors on the Midewiwin emphasize that its central ritual was a healing ceremony meant to protect the Ojibwa (and practitioners from neighbouring tribes) from disease and to promote long life. However, the ceremony clearly addressed not only the health needs of the community, but also its spiritual and social condition. In one sense, individual members of the society sought and received "blessings," which gave them power to ensure that their well-being would be guaranteed.[35] While individuals received special powers, the communal nature of Ojibwa society meant that these powers would normally be used to contribute to the welfare of the band in general. Thus, it was natural that individuals who had received considerable power through Midewiwin ceremonies would also be seen as people with socio-political power. It is no surprise, then, that Ojibwa political leaders, such as Eshkebugecoshe (Flat Mouth), Pizhiki (Buffalo), Shingwaukonse (Little Pine), Powasang (Powassan), Mawedopenais, and Ogimauwinini were also high-ranking Mideg, since the survival of the community depended upon the ability of these leaders to deal with the environmental and political challenges that faced them. Many Midewiwin rituals were concerned not only with the acquisition of blessings, but also with the use of these powers for the benefit of the people as a whole. Problems occurred when individual Mideg misused the powers for their own individual benefit.

The rituals were also meant to provide an alternative world view to that of the missionaries, which would permit the Ojibwa and other Aboriginal groups to once again enjoy the "good life." As such, the Midewiwin, as it developed in the nineteenth century, can be seen, in part, as one of the many "revitalization movements" that arose among Aboriginal peoples as a means of coming to terms with the effects of Euro-American expansion. Like many revitalization movements, the Midewiwin cut across tribal boundaries to offer a common resistance to Euro-American ideas and practices. At the same time, it sometimes intensified divisions within local groups, as followers of the Midewiwin vied with other traditional religious figures, such as the *Jiisakiiwininiwag* and *Waabanowag* (who practised other ceremonies), and with leaders of other revitalization movements, such as the Shawnee Prophet, for authority.[36]

The combative stance of the Ojibwa towards Christian missionaries and Christian Aboriginal people may have contributed to many Mide practitioners' adopting a code of secrecy vis-à-vis Euro-Americans. Secrecy codes normally surrounded dreams or visions, which could only be shared if they were purchased—thus ensuring that the manidoog were not insulted. However, secrecy about the Midewiwin went much further than this. Many of the early descriptions of Mide rituals were the work of Christian converts such as Peter Jones, George Copway, and Peter Jacobs, or of Christian missionaries, all of whom were anxious to paint the ceremonies in the blackest possible terms. This, in turn, may have led to renewed efforts on the part of Mide practitioners to keep their rituals and beliefs secret, in order to actively oppose the efforts of Christian missionaries. Of course, members of the Anishinaabeg were reluctant to share their visions with anyone, and the Ojibwa were particularly noted for being suspicious of strangers until they were certain that the newcomers could be trusted.

As Euro-Americans encroached further on Ojibwa lands, and with the signing of land treaties in the second half of the nineteenth century, many Ojibwa were forced to come to terms with a new and potentially greater catastrophe than the one related in Warren's rendition of the Midewiwin myth. Increasing numbers of Ojibwa again sought new ways of dealing with these threats to cultural survival; more elaborate Midewiwin ceremonies developed, many of them connected with what came to be known as "bad medicine," or "sorcery." Other Ojibwa turned to alternative religious practices such as the *Waabanowiwin*, or, later, to the Drum Dance adopted from their former enemies, the Sioux. Still others at least outwardly embraced Christianity, fitting its teachings and practices into the context of their traditional world view. Some members of the Midewiwin society began to reveal some of the rituals, songs, and stories of the Midewiwin to a succession of outside Euro-American observers.[37] Although a few of the informants were converts who were willing to share their former secrets, most were practising Mide members who were concerned that there were no new initiates to whom they could pass on their knowledge. This willingness to have the oral scriptures written down is a familiar theme, which has frequently occurred when the perception develops that a culture is threatened by outside forces.[38] Therefore, it should not be surprising that some Ojibwa religious leaders willingly shared their religious knowledge with outsiders in the hope that their descendants would once again be able to make use of the Mide teachings.[39] It is this written material that now serves as one of the principal sources of knowledge for non-Ojibwa and Ojibwa alike.

Although the collected printed materials reveal a considerable variation in practices and beliefs, there is an underlying consistency in structure, themes, and values. All the accounts look upon humans as spiritual beings who can and do communicate with the rest of creation. The chief Mide manidoog may vary from Bear, to Otter, to Nanabozho, to the *miigis* (a sacred shell), but in all cases, humans seek and receive assistance from manidoog through the medium of Midewiwin ceremonies. All the accounts present a ceremony composed of two elements, an initiation rite, which includes a ritual re-enactment, and a healing ceremony. Most ceremonies were public affairs in which new members were initiated, and which attracted large numbers of people over extended periods of time. Some were primarily healing ceremonies for ill or dying members.[40] Ghost

Midewiwin ceremonies were also held so that those who had already died could be initiated into the society or advance in it through the use of a proxy.[41] Initiates were taught about their common Anishinaabe ancestry, the requirements and rituals for living a good life, and the songs to be sung at healing ceremonies.

The number of historical accounts of the Midewiwin from the Ojibwa in present-day Minnesota gives further credence to the belief that this area became the heartland of the Midewiwin following the dispersal of many Ojibwa from the region around Bowating (now Sault Ste. Marie) and Chequamegon. Nevertheless, the existence of the Midewiwin is far more widespread and pervasive than scholars originally believed. It is possible that it was brought to Georgian Bay and Manitoulin Island, Walpole Island, and other locations by Ojibwa and Potawatomi from the lower Michigan peninsula who took up residence in Upper Canada following the War of 1812, but it probably existed even earlier in these regions. There are also frequent accounts of the Midewiwin among the Ojibwa in what is now southern Manitoba and northwestern Ontario. Adolph Greenberg and James Morrison make the intriguing suggestion that as the Midewiwin spread from Lake Winnipeg into the headwaters of the Albany River, many of the different groups in the region began to call themselves Ojibwa.[42] Just how far north the Midewiwin society extended is a matter of debate; it certainly existed at one time as far north as Berens River, though in Irving Hallowell's time (1930s) it was no longer practised by the Ojibwa in the region.[43] Likewise, the Plains Ojibwa or Bungi practised the Midewiwin (often alongside the Sun Dance) and records of it exist in various locations in southern Manitoba and Saskatchewan as well as Montana.[44]

As Euro-American society exerted increasing pressure on the Ojibwa to give up their "traditional" beliefs, practitioners were forced to go underground in their activities. Gradually, their numbers decreased as younger Ojibwa sought other means of taking control of their lives, and it became difficult to pass on the old lore. In many cases there was a blurring of boundaries between the Midewiwin and other Ojibwa ceremonies, particularly among groups living on the periphery of Ojibwa territory; there was also some evidence of a merging of Midewiwin and Christian beliefs and rituals. This latter practice often occurred when some Christian beliefs and practices were incorporated into the Midewiwin—a strategy of adaptation practised by many Aboriginal people.

The Midewiwin had become less important in many Ojibwa communities by the end of the nineteenth century. Numerous scrolls, religious ceremonial objects, and medicine bundles were either destroyed or lost during the Midewiwin's decline—largely as a result of the efforts of governments and Christian religious bodies to erase all traces of Aboriginal religion. Recently, however, there has been a revival in interest in the teachings and ceremonies of the Midewiwin among many younger Ojibwa who are searching for a positive sense of ethnic identity. The works of early recorders such as Hoffman, and the recent works of Basil Johnston[45] and Edward Benton-Banai[46] have contributed to the reconstruction of their tradition in different ways, since there are few surviving Mideg who were trained in the old ways.

Richard White and Bruce Greenfield have argued that nineteenth-century "Americans invented Indians and forced Indians to live with the consequences of this invention."[47] They go on to elaborate how the literate construction of Aboriginal people as "savages" or "wild men" continued among intellectuals long after Aboriginals and Euro-Americans had learned to live together as equals in the Great Lakes region. However, while Euro-Americans and Aboriginals were often able to engage in both complex and subtle communication at the local level, only literate Euro-Americans were able to create a written record of these communications and controversies. As Euro-American societies began to grow in strength, the oral nature of Ojibwa culture (and other Aboriginal cultures) began to be seen as inferior, especially by those Euro-Americans who were removed from personal contact. This was accentuated by the processes by which writers' works were edited for their Euro-American audiences in order to highlight the superiority of Euro-American culture and religion. Because Euro-Americans controlled the means of writing and publishing, their writings about Aboriginal religion remained largely unchallenged by the people they described.

Any understanding of the Midewiwin as it existed must incorporate an analysis of the Euro-American documents that describe it, so that by understanding the hidden messages implicit in the descriptions we can attempt to decipher what really was believed, or what was happening. While it is necessary to have at least a basic understanding of the socio-political events that led to this misrepresentation of Aboriginal identity, it is even more important to understand something of the world views of the Ojibwa and the Euro-Americans who depicted them.

TWO

Anishinaabe Religion and Society in the Pre- and Early Contact Period

Anishinaabe Narratives of Origin

The Anishinaabeg,[1] as they called themselves, had several different explanations of how the earth came to be, how human beings were created, and the origin of death. Sometimes the point of the story might be easy to comprehend, but often it was difficult to determine, and it would be only with repeated tellings, sometimes with additions, that the story would begin to make sense.[2]

Odinigun, an elder from the White Earth Reservation, offered the following account of the first earth to ethnologist Frances Densmore:

> The first earth was called Ca'ca. It was in this part of the country. The people who lived here were not wise. They had no clothing, but sat around and did nothing. Then the spirit of the creator sent a man to teach them. This man was called ockabe'wis ["messenger," according to Densmore].... The first thing he taught them was how to make a fire by means of a bow and stick and a bit of decayed wood. Then he taught them how to cook meat by the fire. They had no axes, but he took a pole and burned it over the fire.... This was long before Winabojo [Nanabozho].[3]

The above quote, while not pre-contact in nature, provides a good example of how the Anishinaabeg viewed their origin. In this version, the Aadizookaanag, or "original people" (often termed "Our Grandfathers"), in these narratives behaved like ordinary human beings, although in some instances they also performed extraordinary feats of spiritual power. In Odinigun's version, Nanabozho doesn't make an appearance until later to help the people, who by then had become subject to misfortunes and death. In many creation stories, Nanabozho *is* the messenger referred to by Odinigun.[4]

The next group of stories focusses on the creation of a new earth. Although there are many different versions of the earth-diver story, as it is sometimes known, most adhere to the following outline. In the first part of the story, Nanabozho went hunting with a group of wolves, one of whom was or became his grandson. The child, Chibiabos,[5] as he was called in many versions of this tale, stayed with him when the others went off. However, some evil serpents (water monsters) became jealous and decided to kill Chibiabos. Nanabozho had a dream, and tried to warn the young wolf not to cross a certain lake when he went hunting. However, Chibiabos did anyway, fell in, and was murdered by the serpents. Nanabozho blackened his face and fasted for several days in mourning, then set out in search of his grandson. A kingfisher told him where the evil serpents came out of the lake to sun themselves. He went there, and shot the leader of the serpents. The others began to pursue him, so he headed for the highest mountain, where he climbed a tall tree. To his horror he saw that waters had covered the land and were gradually rising. He told the tree to stretch itself, which it did, and finally the waters stopped, just as they reached his chin:

> He then cast his eyes around the illimitable expanse, and spied a loon. "Dive down, my brother," he said to him, "fetch up some earth, so that I can make a new earth." The bird obeyed, but rose up to the surface a lifeless form. He then saw a muskrat. "Dive!" said he, "and if you succeed, you may hereafter live either on land or water, as you please; or I will give you a chain of beautiful lakes, surrounded with rushes, to inhabit." He dove down, but he floated up senseless. He [Nanabozho] took the body and breathed in his nostrils, which restored him to life. "Try again," said he. The muskrat did so. He came up senseless the second time, but clutched a little earth in one of his paws, from which, together with the carcass of the dead loon, he created a new earth as large as the former had been, with all living animals, fowls, and plants.[6]

Although the particulars of these origin narratives varied according to the circumstances of the teller, the basic storyline, characters, and message of the narratives have remained remarkably constant to the present day. Many folklorists and ethnologists have spent a considerable amount of time searching for "authentic, traditional" narratives, "uncorrupted" by Euro-American influences, so that they can uncover a "pure" Anishinaabe world view. However, I would argue that all narratives told by elders are authentic, for the world view expressed by the narratives results from an oral tradition whose texts are not locked in time in the same way as are those belonging to religions "of the book." The Anishinaabe tradition was a living tradition, which adapted the incidentals of the narratives to new circumstances. The people adopted some versions from neighbouring groups of friendly Aboriginal people, and even from former enemies such as the Sioux. That they should adopt and adapt some Euro-American concepts (in the same way that they adopted and adapted material goods) into their world view is neither surprising, nor indicative that they were on the road to assimilation.

While few of the collected narratives of the Anishinaabeg predate the nineteenth century, it was clear to the early collectors such as American Indian Agent Henry Rowe Schoolcraft that such narratives were part of an oral tradition that had been handed down from previous generations of Anishinaabe elders. Passing references by earlier Euro-American observers to various Anishinaabe practices and beliefs also indicate that the beliefs exemplified by these narratives were an intrinsic part of the Anishinaabe world view long before they came to be collected in printed form by Euro-Americans. The problem is to distinguish the narratives that have a modicum of authenticity in the sense that they represent Anishinaabe beliefs, rather than the beliefs of their interpreters. While Schoolcraft's versions are usually considered to be among the most reliable of the early compilations, there can be little doubt that he reshaped them to conform to his own literary style, sometimes distorting Anishinaabe beliefs beyond recognition.[7]

Versions of the early narratives told by contemporary Ojibwa complicate the picture. Although they are received first-hand, they often will have changed over time. Nevertheless, a remarkable continuity of essential concepts exists in the world view of Anishinaabeg and their Ojibwa descendants. Thus, for instance, not only do we find correspondences between the world view of early twentieth-century Ojibwa at Berens River, Manitoba,[8] and mid-twentieth-century Chippewa (Ojibwa) in northern Minnesota,[9] but it is also possible to trace many of these concepts back to the earlier ethnographic work carried out in the nineteenth century in

Minnesota, Wisconsin, Michigan, and Ontario. Selwyn Dewdney found in his research that oral traditions could be similar as far apart as Lake Nipissing and Lac La Ronge, but might vary considerably in the same community.[10] The characters, locations, and terminology might differ, but the world view remained remarkably consistent.

Anishinaabe World View or Cosmology[11]

The world view described in these narratives is radically different from that of secularized North Americans today. The Anishinaabeg believed there was more to existence than the physical world of perception. Anishinaabe traditions, like the traditions of other religions, describe a reality that takes into account, but encompasses more than, the material world. It was, above all, a "peopled cosmos," which, as Irving Hallowell has emphasized, was controlled by the actions of persons, human or otherwise, and which could be verified by empirical means.[12]

The most important categorical distinction made by the Anishinaabeg, and illustrated not only in the narratives, but also in the grammatical structure of their language, was that between animate and inanimate, between living and non-living things. The Anishinaabeg (human beings), animals, and plants were alive, but so were *some* natural and created objects such as specific stones, locations, dolls, etc. All such beings or creatures, not just humans, were considered to have what in English is termed a soul, and thus to be alive, and have power.[13]

Also living in the universe was a group of spiritual beings, which the Anishinaabeg called "manidoog." The word "manidoo" has been the subject of considerable academic discussion and frequent misrepresentations, since, as American ethnologist William Jones long ago remarked, the term referred both to an object or spirit, and to a quality or property.[14] The Ojibwa, along with other Algonquians, appear to have used the term "manidoo" to refer to certain manifestations of humans, other creatures such as animals and birds, natural objects such as the sun and moon, geographical locations, and even some technological objects of the Euro-Americans, which appeared to be suffused with mystery, wonder, or power. This has led many Euro-American scholars to emphasize either the concept of spiritual beings, or the concept of manidoo as a type of "non-particularized form of power."[15] However, contemporary Ojibwa scholars such as Basil Johnston have continued to use the word "manidoo" to refer to both concepts.[16] As Catherine Albanese remarks in *Nature Religion in*

America, the problem occurs because scholars have tried to force Algonquian beliefs into European categories and definitions.[17]

Although the major world religions also acknowledged spiritual beings (in Hinduism spirits were known as *devas*, in Islam they were called *jinnee*, and in the Judeo-Christian tradition they were known as angels or devils), among the Anishinaabeg, and in the tradition of North American Aboriginal people generally, these manidoog or spirits usually took the outer form of animals rather than humans. Neither Catholic nor Protestant missionaries who worked among the Anishinaabeg during the early period of contact denied the existence of such spirits, or their powers. However, most Christians were convinced that spirits "worshipped" by the Ojibwa and other Anishinaabeg represented the "demonic" rather than the "angelic" forces of the Christian cosmology—partly at least, it could be argued, since the Anishinaabeg considered the angelic spirits to have animal forms. Nineteenth-century Christians, such as William Warren, compared the Ojibwa belief in spirits to spiritualism, which, he noted, was then "making such a stir in the midst of our most enlightened and civilized communities."[18] Many other nineteenth-century Euro-Americans adopted British anthropologist Edward Tylor's use of the term "animism" for the Anishinaabe belief (and that of other "primitive" groups) in a variety of forms of spirits, a belief that "more rational" and "evolutionarily advanced" societies had come to reject.

Certainly the Anishinaabeg had a more plural and more personal sense of the universe than did the increasingly mechanistic Euro-American vision. No less than their Euro-American neighbours, the Anishinaabeg elaborated a cosmology in which all things were named and ordered. This is illustrated in charts such as the one drawn by the informant of William Jones in conjunction with some notes on the "mystic rite" (Midewiwin).[19] In the accounts collected by Jones and Victor Barnouw,[20] the informants describe a multi-layered cosmos inhabited by manidoog. However, as religious scholar Theresa Smith has noted in her discussion of the subject, the hierarchy of layers was somewhat fluid.[21]

In Anishinaabe cosmology, some of the manidoog presided over the plants and animals as "masters" of the different species. Others dwelt at the four cardinal points of the earth and made their presence known in the form of brothers who were the Four Winds. In the sky above dwelt the *Animikiig*, often called the Thunderers; and in the waters below, particularly in turbulent water, were the *Mishibizhii (Misipisiwak)*, the Underwater Panther, and *Missipkinepi*, the Sea Serpents.[22] Anishinaabe narratives are full of accounts of the warfare of these two manidoog. The Thunderers represented

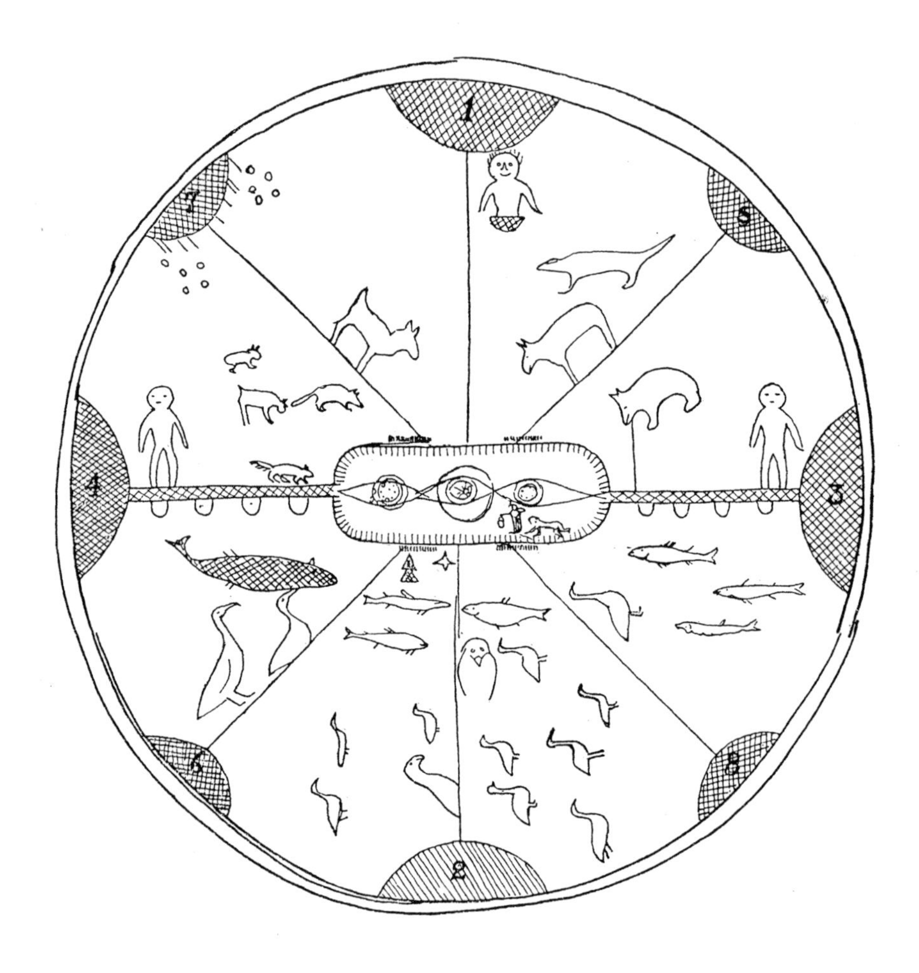

Illustration 1: Ojibwa Cosmological Chart. The chart helps place the Midewiwin in relation to the peopled universe of the Ojibwa. The outer circle (*aki*) is the earth or world. The rectangle in the centre represents the Midewiwin Lodge. The four half-circles under the paths leading to the east and west entrances represent sweat lodges used in conjunction with the Midewiwin ceremonies. The cross-hatched half-circles on the inner circumference represent the directions in the form of the winds. The wind most feared was the one from the northwest, for it brought strong winds, while the figure under the north wind represents *Wiindigoo,* who brought winter and often starvation. The two human-like figures may be manidoog connected with the Midewiwin, while the animal figures represent the spirit guardians or masters of the different species. Many of these, such as the bear, otter, and owl, played key roles in the Midewiwin ceremonies, while all were part of the Ojibwa world. (From Jones, *Ojibwa Texts,* Part II, plate I.)

the sky, light, and good, and the Underwater Panthers or Monsters represented the lower world, darkness, and evil. Euro-American observers were often quick to see this as a form of dualism, but the situation is not quite so simple. For instance, there was, for some time, no direct equivalent to the Christian dichotomy between God and Satan. While the Thunderers were generally considered to be good, and the Underwater Panthers were generally considered to be evil, this was not always the case. The Thunderers could, and often did, exhibit their destructive tendencies, while the Underwater Panthers provided knowledge of medicinal herbs and thereby functioned as the earliest patrons of the Midewiwin Society. In the Anishinaabe cosmology, the Thunderers and the Underwater Panthers represented the two sides of the whole, both of whom had to be placated so that things could be kept in balance. It could be argued that the Animikiig and Mishibizhii were closer to the Taoist concepts of *yin* and *yang* than to the Manichean or Christian concepts of good and evil. Nevertheless, following contact with Christian ideas, the Anishinaabeg approach to good and evil came to be represented by Gichi-Manidoo and Maji-Manidoo,[23] rather than the Animikiig and Mishibizhii.

In Anishinaabe traditions, a number of other manidoog took on terrifying forms, such as *Wiindigoo*, the winter cannibal monster that fed on human flesh, and *Paagak* (*Pahkack*), the flying skeleton. Neither was inherently evil, but they both played an important role in the lives of people for whom starvation was always a distinct possibility. Like many other North American Aboriginal people, the Anishinaabeg also believed in more benign manidoog, such as the hairy dwarf spirits who dwelt among the rocks or in the cut banks along rivers. These *Memegwesiwag*, or little people, were sometimes encountered by solitary travellers or by children, and tobacco offerings were left in places where they were said to dwell.

Central to a major cycle of Anishinaabe narratives was the person of Nanabozho, who figures prominently in the cosmology of various Algonquian peoples.[24] In most narratives Nanabozho was said to have been born of a human mother and a spirit, often the West or North Wind. As a result, he possessed greater powers than any human, but at the same time he had all the human frailties. Nanabozho was sometimes regarded as the messenger or helper (*oshkaabewis*) of Gichi-Manidoo, the Great Spirit or Master of Life. The narratives tell of early life with his older brothers and his grandmother, Nookomis. They tell of his marriage, his wife and children, of hunting, going to war—all normal activities for a member of the Anishinaabeg. They also tell of his titanic battles with his father and the Underwater Panthers, his survival of a great flood, and the creation of a new earth with the help of the muskrat. Still others tell of his capriciousness, his vain boasting, his deceitful tricks, and his sufferings. In the original, unexpurgated versions of the narratives, he appears to Euro-American audiences as a bawdy, lewd figure, for there are numerous references to faeces, anuses, penises, and other "private body parts." In actuality, Nanabozho represented the ambiguous nature of existence; he was capable of the most noble deeds, as well as the most stupid and base acts. As a trickster figure, particularly among the more northern Anishinaabeg, he was a buffoon-like figure, treated with a mixture of amused affection and respect. However, as a transformer figure, he was credited with helping to teach the Anishinaabeg how to use fire, to hunt, to practise horticulture, and to use medicinal plants, and, most significantly, he was usually credited with bringing them the powers of the Midewiwin.

It would appear that Nanabozho has played a more significant role in Anishinaabe cosmology than the more remote figure variously known as the Master of Life or Gichi-Manidoo. Unlike other Anishinaabe persons, such as Nanabozho, the Master of Life did not take an active role in human affairs, but was known only through his creations. While this has caused some scholars to assume Christian influences, John Cooper has noted in his thorough study, *The North Algonquian Supreme Being*, that the ideas and practices associated with the Master of Life concept conform to non-Christian patterns.[25] Moreover, there was, according to Cooper's old informants, a point in time at which Christian beliefs began to influence Algonquian beliefs. Thus, they explained that previously, when their ancestors had spoken of manidoog, they spoke of the Master of Life, but after the arrival of Christian missionaries, they began to speak of Gichi-Manidoo.

Cooper's statements are corroborated to a point by those of anthropologist Vernon Kinietz in his work on the Chippewa village of Katikitegan.[26] Kinietz relied on the statements of early Euro-Americans such as the fur trader Peter Grant,[27] whose 1804 account of the Ojibwa in the Boundary Waters region dealt at some length with Ojibwa religious beliefs, deities, and ceremonies. Grant stated that the Gichi-Manidoo, or the Master of Life, was considered to be the creator of the world, but he was a distant figure who was never worshipped. Although Grant also mentioned Maji-Manidoo, whom he described as being the source of all evil, Kinietz correctly asserts that this latter belief was the result of Christian influence, and does not reflect pre-contact beliefs. It was also only after the advent of Christian missionaries that the idea of future reward and punishment in a heaven and hell developed. Although Cooper's archival and field research was primarily concerned with the Cree, I believe that Kinietz's work shows that Cooper's conclusions can be extended to the ancestors of the present-day Ojibwa.[28]

Like the Christian God with whom he often came to be identified, Gichi-Manidoo was usually addressed through a host of lesser manidoog. Sometimes the sun symbolized the Master of Life, the four rays indicating "his" universal presence. At other times, the sun and the moon were seen as intermediaries between the Master of Life and the Anishinaabeg; while in still other cases, the sun was said to be the father of Nanabozho.[29] Although some scholars, notably Sam Gill,[30] have argued against a pre-contact concept of "Mother Earth" among North American Aboriginal people, there is some evidence that such beliefs may have been expressed by the Ojibwa during the late eighteenth century. In his story of his captivity, John Tanner (whose parents were Euro-American but who was culturally an Ottawa/ Ojibwa, having spent most of his youth and adulthood among them) described how songs used on occasions of "medicine hunts" were sung either to Nanabozho, or to "*Me-su-kum-mik-oakwi*," the earth, whom he terms the "great-grandmother of all."[31] There are valid questions regarding editor Edwin James's translation of the term, but the possibility cannot be totally discounted, given the fluidity of Anishinaabe belief (and the paucity of sources upon which to build a case either way).

The spiritual connection among all these living things created a universal bond, a kinship, which ethnologist Mary Black-Rogers termed *bimaadiziwad,* from the Ojibwe verb "it lives." But bimaadiziwad signifies more than simply "living." It also signifies that the person has "power." In other words, those things that have power are considered to be living.[32]

Through his work with Ojibwa informants near Berens River, anthropologist Irving Hallowell worked out a complex taxonomy of categories or classes that make up the Ojibwa world.[33] In creating this taxonomy, he attempted as far as possible to avoid Western categorization, although he was not entirely successful. In an effort to make sense of Ojibwa belief systems, Hallowell termed all living things "persons," some human, some other-than-human, even though the Ojibwa themselves have no such category of "persons." Similarly, his "other-than-human persons" category includes what in Western thought could be called spiritual beings, mythological characters, and the elements. In most world views, they would have been considered supernatural, but Hallowell did not believe that the Ojibwa made this distinction in their world view. Rather, the class in his taxonomy, while not human, was closer to human beings than to other parts of the universe. Unfortunately, he had to deal with numerous exceptions such as *some* animals, *some* trees, and *some* stones, which also fit into the category of "other-than-human persons." Mary Black-Rogers argued that "[Hallowell] avoided imposing Western categories ('as far as possible') by imposing the structure of taxonomic categorization that his Western preconceptions assumed to be universal."[34]

Hallowell's attempt to explain the Ojibwa world view was far more successful than the efforts of his predecessors and is now commonly accepted in the literature. Unfortunately, many scholars, and even some Ojibwa, speak of Hallowell's concepts of "human" and "other-than-human" beings as though these concepts were intrinsic to the Ojibwa world view, rather than an attempt to interpret this world view. Hallowell himself was aware of the difference between emic and etic viewpoints, and struggled to avoid the pitfalls that face outside observers, but he was unable to do so entirely. His description of the Ojibwa world view remains rational, lacking any sense of mystery, the spiritual, or the holy, since for him the supernatural did not exist. Yet, many others would argue that Ojibwa narratives are infused with a sense of mystery, of the spiritual. This clash of world views has been debated vigorously in the literature.[35]

In her own attempt to understand the Ojibwa world view, Black-Rogers points out that the "Ojibwa [have a] preoccupation with *appearance, form,* and *perceptibility itself*.... Outward appearance is only an incidental attribute of being." She goes on to state that "what is vital in defining living things is the soul" (the italics are Black-Rogers's, the underlining mine).[36] I would go even further to argue that the concept of soul or "life force" is the central concept in Anishinaabe cosmology, and that it plays a significant role in the Midewiwin.

Religious scholar Christopher Vecsey has further argued that if all living things share the same spiritual substance, and outward appearance is only an incidental attribute of being, then metamorphosis is possible—and does play an important part in the Anishinaabe world view.[37] Creatures with great power, such as Nanabozho, the aadizookaanag, and individual Anishinaabeg who have received power from a powerful manidoo, are believed to be able to change the outward manifestation of their bodily shape while retaining their essential being. As a result, the Anishinaabeg were and still are invariably suspicious of strangers, since there is no telling who the person might really be. Evil manidoog and evil humans were even said to take the shape of bears at night in order to wreak havoc on their victims, both living and dead.[38] Because these "bearwalks" were described by early observers of the Midewiwin, they have been commonly linked to Mide beliefs and practices, but beliefs involving metamorphosis into the form of bears were common among northern peoples in North America and

Siberia.[39] James Howard, an anthropologist, noted that the Turtle Mountain Métis believed in *Rúgarùs* (a possible corruption of the French *loup garou*), which Howard believed to be a European version of the "bearwalk."[40]

Since the Anishinaabeg had limited control over many aspects of their lives, it was important for them to seek the assistance of living creatures that had more power than they did. As Odinigun explained: "The ockabewis [messenger] told them that they must fast and find out things by dreams and that if they paid attention to these dreams they would learn how to heal the sick. The people listened and fasted and found in dreams how to teach their children and do everything. The young men were taught that they must regulate their lives by dreams."[41]

Dreams were of great importance in the life of individual Anishinaabeg, since they served as the vehicle by which the teachings were passed on or new teachings were revealed.[42] Moreover, as Odinigun's story suggests, visions seen in dreams, and messages received therein, were regarded as "blessings" from the manidoog, which gave them individually the power to survive in the world. The possibility of an ongoing communication with manidoog through visions and dreams ensured that the Anishinaabe cosmology was an extremely flexible one.

This is not to imply that the fundamental structure of their world view was constantly changing, but rather that Anishinaabeg were open to new beliefs and practices as revealed to them through dreams and visions. This openness allowed them also to incorporate a variety of beliefs and practices from their Aboriginal neighbours and from Euro-Americans. The Anishinaabeg found it impossible to completely adopt the exclusivist views of Christian missionaries who argued that only Christian beliefs were valid, and thus demanded the total dismemberment of Anishinaabe cosmology.

Instead, many Anishinaabeg adopted certain beliefs and religious figures from Christianity and placed them within the context of Anishinaabe cosmology. Other Anishinaabeg challenged Christian missionaries' exclusiveness, by developing their own vision of a segregated world view in which the cosmologies of Euro-American and Anishinaabe societies co-existed, but did not overlap. However, in protecting themselves from the aggressive proselytization of the Euro-American missionaries, the Anishinaabeg risked becoming exclusivist themselves, thereby relinquishing a fundamental tenet of their own world view.

Children were trained in methods of securing dreams in preparation for what has become known as the "vision quest," when a young man or woman reached the age of puberty. At this time the young person went into isolation, fasted, and meditated, while waiting for some manidoo to appear in a vision or induced dream.[43] If and when this happened, there was usually some kind of test the dreamer had to undergo. If the person was successful, the manidoo would explain what must be done to lead a good life. It would then serve throughout the person's life as a guardian or dream spirit, a *bawaagan*, providing power when it was needed. For this reason, many Anishinaabeg kept in their possession some form of representation of the dream subject, so that the manidoo could be called upon for guidance or assistance.[44]

Among the Anishinaabeg, anyone might seek out blessings bestowed by the manidoog. Most were successful in their quest, although some never secured dream visions, and were thus powerless for life. It is notable that some Christian converts reported not having received a visit from a manidoo during their vision quest, which could perhaps account for their willingness to accept the Christian god. Others, like nineteenth-century Ojibwa Methodist missionaries Peter Jacobs and Allen Salt, attributed their conversion to a vision in which the Christian spirit came to them, and thus incorporated their traditional beliefs into those of their new religion.[45]

Individual Anishinaabeg who sought and received "blessings" from the manidoog in the form of a dream or vision were recognized by their brethren as having received "power," a status made evident by the changes in their behaviour and their ritual obligations (the need to perform certain rituals and avoid taboos related to their tutelary spirit).[46] This power aided the individual to be "in control" or "self-sufficient" in his or her daily activities. The blessings of some were more plentiful or powerful than others, since their bawaaganag, or "spirit guardians," were of higher rank or greater in number. Some exceptional individuals were granted powers related to hunting, warfare, and curing; some individuals received knowledge about plants that could aid in the cure of various illnesses; others used their power to undo spells placed on individuals by evil "medicine men."[47] The vision/dream experience helped explain why some individuals were more powerful than others, and it could also serve as a means of sanctioning and encouraging actions that were used to benefit the group as a whole.

The Ojibwa leader Chingwauk (Shingwaukonse) explained this to Henry Schoolcraft at Mackinac in 1839:

> Chingwauk began by saying that the ancient Indians made a great merit of fasting.... What a young man sees and experiences during these dreams and fasts, is adopted by him as truth, and it becomes a principle to regulate his future life. If he has been much favoured in his fasts, and the

people believe that he has the art of looking into futurity, his path is open to the highest honors.

The prophet, he continued, begins to try his power in secret, with only one assistant, whose testimony is necessary should he succeed. As he goes on, he puts down the figures of his dreams or revelations by symbols, on bark or other material.... If what he predicts is verified, the assistant mentions it, and the record is then appealed to as proof of his prophetic power and skill. Time increases his fame. His kekkeenowin, or records are finally shown to the old people, who meet together and consult upon them, for the whole nation believe in these revelations. They, in the end, give their approval, and declare that he is gifted as a prophet—is inspired with wisdom, and is fit to lead the opinions of the nation.[48]

Normally, as the above quotation indicates, individuals never spoke of their visions, for such actions were considered boasting and would cause them to lose the power gained from the vision, although visions had to be validated by the spiritual elders before a person's power was recognized by the community.[49] Nevertheless, some Christian converts were willing to break tradition and speak of their vision experiences they had undergone before they became Christians. Catherine Wambose, whom Schoolcraft termed the "prophetess of Chequoimegon," was one such individual. Her story illustrates the role played by dreams in the acquisition of power. She explained in some detail to Schoolcraft's Ojibwa wife, Jane, daughter of John Johnston and Oshawguscoday-Wayqua (Susan Johnson), how at the time of her first menstruation her mother helped her build a lodge, and she blackened her face and began to fast. After several days she had a number of visions in which she was given a name, plus one for her first son, as well as instructions and songs to sing. After the seventh day of fasting, she was given the power of seeing into the future, which was to be used for her benefit and that of her relatives and fellow band members. The first time she utilized her new powers was in response to the requests of her family and friends, who were in danger of starvation and had asked for her assistance. The next day the hunters found and killed a moose where she had said it would be. "My reputation was established by this success," she concluded.[50]

Such individuals came to be recognized and respected for the power they possessed, since it often aided others. However, they were also feared, for the Anishinaabeg believed that this power could also be used for evil purposes. They were well aware that power corrupts. The first French and English who encountered the Anishinaabeg made no distinctions between individuals who used their power for good or evil purposes. They lumped all such people together as "jugglers," "sorcerers," or "conjurers," the terms reflecting their belief that these individuals were deceptive and evil, since their powers must have come from demonic forces. In the world view of Euro-American Christians, individuals who had such powers owed their allegiance to the devil, not to Jesus Christ.

In the nineteenth century, Euro-American observers such as Schoolcraft and French scientist Joseph Nicollet made an attempt to understand the world view of Aboriginal Americans, and began to use Anishinaabe terms, or English translations of them, to describe Anishinaabe concepts and institutions to the degree that they understood them. Gradually, the older terms for traditional healers began to give way to new Anishinaabe ones, while the general term "medicine men" came to refer to the group as a whole. Most Euro-Americans, nevertheless, continued to disparage the role and efficacy of these traditional healers, often treating all such individuals as charlatans, at best.[51]

Anishinaabe Religious Leaders and Traditional Healers

An examination of the earliest post-contact, Euro-American primary sources clearly indicates that at least from the period of contact, Anishinaabe society distinguished a number of different types of people who had received special powers from the manidoog through a dream vision. Among their fellow Anishinaabeg, these individuals were viewed as dreamers, as visionaries who used their power to heal others, and as ceremonial leaders who helped to keep the various forces of the universe in equilibrium. They were given a number of different names, depending upon the nature of their vision and the types of power they were given. Such names were not meant to be mutually exclusive, since some individuals received more than one type of power and could, therefore, be described in different ways. Moreover, these same individuals could also be described in numerous other ways, according to their particular skills as hunters or war leaders, or according to their roles in civil society.

Since individuals in Anishinaabe society were not distinguished primarily by their "occupation," but rather by the fact that they had received a vision in which they had been blessed by the manidoog with varying amounts and different kinds of power, which could be used for good or evil, it is possible to consider a number of ways in which this power was obtained and used. The most commonly reported traditional spiritual leader singled out by Euro-Americans was known to the Anishinaabeg as a Jiisakiiwinini.[52] Jiisakiiwininiwag summoned spirit helpers with whom they communicated by drumming and singing. The Jiisakiiwin, or, as it came to be known by

Euro-Americans, the "Shaking Tent" ceremony or "Conjuring Lodge" ceremony, has been well documented by Euro-American observers among northern Algonquian peoples.[53] Reports of this ceremony were mentioned by a variety of observers, going back to the time of Samuel de Champlain. One of the most complete early descriptions among the Anishinaabeg is by fur trader Alexander Henry the Elder, who devotes a whole chapter of his 1764 *Travels* to a description of what he terms "Consulting the GREAT TURTLE." His account is not only one of the earliest Euro-American accounts, but it also demonstrates many misconceptions Euro-Americans held regarding Aboriginal religious figures and ceremonies.

Henry was living with some Ojibwa who had just arrived at Sault Ste. Marie, shortly after the fall of Michilimackinac to Aboriginal followers of Pontiac in 1763. The occasion was an invitation by Sir William Johnson, the British Superintendent of Indian Affairs, to all Aboriginal people who were peacefully disposed towards the British to meet with him at Fort Niagara. As various bands of Ojibwa had recently joined Pontiac in opposing the English, wrote Henry, "the occasion was of too much magnitude not to call for more than human knowledge and discretion; and preparations were accordingly made for solemnly invoking and consulting the GREAT TURTLE."[54] Turtle, or Mikinaak the Turtle (as he was named by the Anishinaabeg), acted as a messenger between the Jiisakiiwinini and the spirits or manidoog. Like Nanabozho, Mikinaak is often portrayed as a figure of some derision (an old gossip, according to Schoolcraft), but at the same time he possessed unique powers of translation, which were vital to the Ojibwa, enabling them to speak with the manidoog. Perhaps it was this power that sometimes led the Ojibwa to portray him as a sinister figure, since he might literally hold their lives in his control.

The ceremony began with the preparation of the tent: "Five poles, or rather pillars, of five different species of timber, about ten feet in height, and eight inches in diameter were set in a circle of about four feet in diameter. The holes made to receive them were about two feet deep . . . the pillars were bound together by a circular hoop, or girder. Over this edifice were spread moose-skins. . . ."[55] The ceremonies, Henry explained, did not begin until nightfall, when several fires were kindled around the tent. Once the village had assembled, the Jiisakiiwinini's arms were bound and he crawled into the tent. The tent began to shake and there was a cacophony of animal sounds emanating from it, followed by a period of silence. Then Turtle was heard, followed by a half-hour of songs. Next, the Jiisakiiwinini addressed the multitude and declared the spirit's readiness to answer questions. The chief then took a quantity of tobacco and offered it to the spirit before he asked whether the English were preparing to make war on the Aboriginal people.

The tent instantly began to shake, and a terrible cry announced the departure of Turtle. After a quarter of an hour of silence, the voice of Turtle was heard again, so the Jiisakiiwinini translated. He explained that Turtle had visited Fort Niagara, where he had seen no troops, but on proceeding further towards Montreal, the river was covered with boats full of soldiers on their way up the river to make war. The chief asked again if Sir William Johnson would receive the Aboriginal people who came to Fort Niagara as friends. The answer was that he would fill their canoes with gifts and every man would be able to return home safely.

Henry related that after the questions of "public interest" had been answered, individuals were able to ask personal questions such as concerns about absent friends. Although Henry made no mention of it, the Shaking Tent ceremony was also used by individuals as a means of asking for a cure for themselves or others, as a means of finding game, and as a means of "finding" a mate. In a sense, then, the ceremony was a form of "divination," since the object was to gain insight into the future or the unknown through supernatural means. However, the power of the Jiisakiiwininiwag extended not only to providing such insights, but also to influencing events. Given the highly unpredictable nature of Ojibwa life, such ceremonies and their practitioners were useful in helping to make important decisions.

Henry himself took the opportunity to ask whether he would ever revisit his native country, and was reassured that he would—so he made an extra offering of tobacco. The private questions continued until about midnight, at which time everyone returned to their lodges. Henry concluded that he made every effort to "detect the particular contrivances by which the fraud was carried on; but such was the skill displayed . . . that I made no discoveries."[56]

Henry's description parallels other accounts: the brief 1804 description of an Ojibwa ceremony by North West Company fur trader Duncan Cameron[57] at Lake Nipigon; the more clinical description given by Joseph Nicollet[58] of a similar Ojibwa ceremony held at Leech Lake in 1836; and Hudson's Bay Company fur trader George Nelson's more sympathetic description of a Cree ceremony at Lac La Ronge in 1823.[59] The Shaking Tent ceremony continued to be described in some detail by a variety of ethnographers throughout the latter part of the nineteenth century and well into the twentieth.

Henry's testimony is important, for what it tells us about the ceremony, for what it omits, and for what it reveals about the world view of many

Euro-Americans during that time. The book was probably written years after the trader's experiences among the Ojibwa, but it has an immediacy lacking in many other travelogues, which were intended for the growing market of readers who longed for accounts of Aboriginal life. Henry made no attempt to understand the world view of his Ojibwa companions but, as befitting a Euro-American businessman, he stuck to the practical details, coloured with a few vivid descriptions that illustrate just how exotic the ceremony must have seemed. But what intrigued him, as it did Cameron and Nelson later, was that he could find no evidence of deception in the performance; all these observers were forced to admit that the answers given were correct, though they could not explain how they were obtained. Only the scientist and devout Roman Catholic Joseph Nicollet was not totally convinced, although in many other respects he was more sympathetic to the ways of the Ojibwa than were the fur traders.

Both Henry and Nelson describe some of the basic ingredients in the ceremony but Henry, in particular, illustrates the context. He recognized the role that the ceremony played in Ojibwa society. In a sense, his rough-hewn account is appropriate, for the proceedings were often carried out in a very ribald way, and the ceremony had an entertainment value as well as a serious intent. Nevertheless, as all the observers make clear, the Ojibwa believed implicitly in the power of the Jiisakiiwininiwag to do what they claimed to be able to do, although they were not uncritical of Jiisakiiwininiwag whose power failed them.

Although Henry did not make any attempt to explain the origin of this power, and in fact confused the messenger (Mikinaak the Turtle) with the manidoo source of the power, most other Euro-Americans were eager to provide explanations. Devout Christians who shared the Ojibwa belief in immaterial spiritual beings were convinced that it was the devil,[60] while more rationalist ethnographers such as W.J. Hoffman attributed any appearance of "power" to the deceptive practices of the Jiisakiiwininiwag.[61] Few observers appear to be aware that the power they were witnessing could be used not only for good but for evil purposes, depending upon the circumstances.[62]

The dramatic nature of the Jiisakiiwin and Jiisakiiwininiwag attracted the most attention of Euro-Americans, but Jiisakiiwininiwag were not the only Anishinaabeg who possessed power to heal. Individuals received a variety of different types of power in their vision quests that could be used for healing purposes. However, the difficulties in classifying such individuals is apparent in the confusion of terms applied to them. This is certainly the case with traditional healers, who were termed *Mashkikiiwininiwag* and, at other times, *Nenaandawiiwejig*. Both terms are listed in Baraga's 1878 Ojibwe dictionary: the first is clearly a derivative of the Ojibwe term *mashkiki,* translated as "medicine," while the derivation of the second is from the verb *nanandawia,* "to administer medicines." Baraga considers both of them doctors or physicians, and makes no distinctions.[63] However, many Euro-Americans considered Mashkikiiwininiwag strictly as herbalists, while Nenaandawiiwejig (or "sucking bone" doctors, as they were usually called) were considered to be shamans who relied on spirits or manidoog for their cures. Despite these purported distinctions, observers had difficulty being consistent in identifying specific classes of healers. Thus, for instance, while Hoffman mentioned the Mashkikiiwininiwag (whom he termed "herbalists") as "non-shamanistic" healers,[64] the illustration in his work is that of a Nenaandawiiwed. Later, he described a person whom he calls a Jiisakiiwinini performing a ceremony that is attributed in most cases to the Nenaandawiiwejig.[65]

Evidently, Mashkikiiwininiwag were individuals who had received the power to use certain herbs for the treatment of certain ailments. Since Euro-Americans believed such ills to be the result of "natural" causes, they more readily accepted herbal treatments. However, it can not be assumed that "spiritual" aspects were lacking in the treatment, as Hoffman and most others seem to contend. On the contrary, the healing properties of the specific herbs had been bestowed on them by the manidoog, and these powers had then been revealed to the individual Mashkikiiwinini. The use of herbs was also a "religious" ritual. Therefore, it was carried out in conjunction with appropriate offerings of tobacco and songs to the manidoog, along with dances. This is illustrated in the song used by Chiahba, described by John Tanner as a "celebrated Ojibbeway medicine man," as he cured a patient who had fallen victim to "bad medicine." He began by invoking the power of black snakes, and then he sang, "*Ne-man-i-to-we-tah hi-you-che-be-kun-na on-je-man-i-to-wee-yaun we-ug-usk*" ("I am Manito, the roots of shrubs and herbs make me Manito"). He went on to sing that the snakes and the Underwater Panther were his "friends," while exhibiting his medicines.[66] Following such a ceremony, gifts of food would be offered by the family of the ill person, in order to show proper deference and gratitude to the manidoog involved.

Moreover, powerful herbs, roots, and other mashkiki or medicines could be used for purposes other than treating the sick. Every Anishinaabe youth had a *biinjigoosan,* or "medicine bag," containing herbs, "charms," and an "effigy" of his bawaagan or guardian spirit, which he carried with him. Depending upon what powers the individual had received, his biinjigoosan might well include medicines that could be used during a *Nah-gitch-e-gumme* or "medicine hunt" when starvation was faced—or he might be able to purchase some from someone who had them. Tanner recounted such an instance in which medicines were to be applied to the images of the animals to be killed.[67] "Love potions" were also used in a similar way to gain the affections of some woman who had ignored the advances of her suitor.[68]

Nenaandawiiwejig received different powers from the manidoog for the treatment of ailments. Since Euro-Americans observed that Nenaandawiiwejig cured patients by sucking through a couple of small bones in order to draw the cause of the illness out of the patient, this group of healers was often called "sucking bone" doctors. This "act of deception," as Euro-Americans usually saw it, probably contributed to the Nenaandawiiwed's being considered one of "the class of conjurors," along with the Jiisakiiwinini and Mide, as opposed to the Mashkikiiwinini, who used medicines.[69]

Like many Aboriginal peoples in both North and South America, the Anishinaabeg believed that sicknesses were often caused by a foreign object in a person's body. The object may have entered by "natural" means, or, more often, as a result of the practices of evil "medicine men" who wished to harm the patient. In order to cure the patient, the cause of the illness had to be removed. Before attempting to cure patients, Nenaandawiiwejig fasted and, having purified themselves, beseeched the manidoog for help with an offering of smoke. This was followed by singing and drumming rituals, during which they again asked the manidoog for help in locating the source of the illness. Once this source was located, they symbolically removed the offending object by using the sucking bones, and placed it on a dish for everyone present to see. In the meantime, the family of the individual would prepare gifts of food for the manidoog who were being invoked. The success of the cure, where "bad medicine" was involved, depended upon the respective powers of the individual Nenaandawiiwed and of the person who had caused the illness.

Early Euro-American accounts of traditional Anishinaabe healers and religious leaders usually described Jiisakiiwininiwag, Mashkikiiwininiwag, and Nenaandawiiwejig, although they seldom used these terms. By the early nineteenth century, Euro-Americans began to make references to Mideg and Waabanowag, and what the writers termed these new and "esoteric" ceremonies. Precisely why they began to use Anishinaabe words to refer to these traditional healers is unclear, but it is highly debatable that they were describing entirely new religious ceremonies. The Waabanowiwin may have arisen as a reaction to the more institutionalized Midewiwin, which attracted the most attention from nineteenth-century Euro-Americans. Na'waji'bigo'kwe, an elderly female Mide from White Earth Reservation, explained to Frances Densmore that the Waabanowiwin had come into being when a young Ojibwa man had wished to join the Midewiwin, but was opposed by his father, who felt that the son did not have a sufficient appreciation for the solemn ritual. Therefore, the young man undertook a vision quest on his own and was visited by a manidoo from the East. Although Densmore's informant did not mention the name of the manidoo, the slight information that exists appears to indicate that Waabanowag gained their power from either the morning star or the sun.[70] The young man was promised a new medicine by the manidoo, which, it was said, would either cure or kill all those who took it. He and a group of young men accepted the medicine and used it in an unscrupulous fashion.[71]

The Waabanowiwin appears to have originated as a healing ritual in which Waabanowag received power (mashkiki) through a vision. During the ritual, which was held at night, they demonstrated that they possessed strong powers by juggling burning coals in their mouths, breathing fire from their mouths, or reaching into pots of boiling water to grasp pieces of meat. Their power could be used for good purposes, such as for healing the sick, or for locating game. However, popular Ojibwa tradition and Euro-American reports suggest that it was often, if not mainly, used for the evil purposes, such as harming or even killing people, or as a love potion to bring people under their control.

Most descriptions of the Waabanowiwin concentrate on the spectacular acts by which the Waabano demonstrated his power, rather than on the powers themselves. The earliest recorded Euro-American account was by North West Company fur trader David Thompson, who described a 1798 ceremony in the region between Lake of the Woods and Red River: "I learned that of late a superstition had sprung up, and was now the attention of all the Natives. It appeared that the old songs, Dances, and Ceremonies by frequent repetition had lost all their charms, and religious attention ... some novelty was required and called for. . . . Accordingly two, or three crafty chiefs, contrived to dream ... they saw a powerful Medicine . . . they were to call it the Wah-bin-no."[72] His account is reinforced by similar accounts made at roughly the same time by Thomas McKenney, head of the United States Bureau of Indian Affairs, and by John Tanner.

In 1826 McKenney recorded two versions of a Waabanowiwin ceremony, one at Sault Ste. Marie and the other at Fond du Lac. According to his account, the ceremony began in the evening with the beating of a drum, to which a large number of individuals began to dance. Suddenly, he recounted, "an unusually tall Indian with a cap of skins on, and a covering of the same, entered with a wild and fierce countenance, blowing, and looking around the tent, and uttering at every expiration of his breath, an *eh—eh—eh;*— when presently, a younger Indian entered, and seized him by the arms, and being disengaged by the force of the other, caught at his body, as if his object was to make him surrender something."[73] Presently, an older man took the drum and, after making a round of the tent with the drum, commenced to make a speech. Shortly after, he was approached by someone else begging for some whiskey, which was distributed to those present. McKenney went to bed at midnight but, upon rising at four o'clock the next morning, he found that the ceremony was still proceeding. At that point, two boiling kettles containing mush-like soup, one of which contained a dog, had been brought in. McKenney did not stay for the feast.

However, he did witness another Waabanowiwin ceremony at Fond du Lac. It commenced in like fashion:

> All at once, and by throwing dirt and ashes on them, the remains of the fires were extinguished, when for a moment everything was still. Then the drums beat louder and quicker, and the song broke out from a hundred mouths. . . . In the midst of this, three or four Indians went around the circle blowing fire from their mouths, emitting thousands of sparks, and lighting up, by means of them, their faces, whilst their distended cheeks looked like lanterns.[74]

McKenney's account focussed on the exotic, but it captured the essential elements of the ceremony, as can be seen by comparing it with Tanner's account.

Tanner's account is more matter-of-fact, although he too makes some judgements regarding the Waabanowag:

> At this time the Waw-be-no was fashionable among the Ojibbeways, but it has ever been considered by the older and more respectable men as a false and dangerous religion. The ceremonies of the Waw-be-no differ very essentially from those of the Metai, and are usually accompanied by much licentiousness and irregularity. The Ta-wae-e-gun used for a drum in this dance, differs from the Woin Ah-keek or Metikwaw-keek, used in the Me-tai, it being made of a hoop of bent wood like a soldier's drum, while the latter is a portion of the trunk of a tree, hollowed by fire, and having skin tied over it. The She-zhe-gwun, or rattle, differs also in its construction from that used in the Metai. In the Waw-be-no, men and women dance and sing together, and there is much juggling and playing with fire. The initiated take coals of fire, and red hot stones in their hands,

> and sometimes in their mouths.... Sometimes one of the principal performers at the Waw-be-no, has a kettle brought and set down before him, which is taken boiling from the fire, and before it has time to cool, he plunges his hands to the bottom, and brings up the head of the dog....[75]

Tanner explained that the Waabanowag apply the medicine from the yarrow plant to protect themselves from burns, but he provided no explanation of the purpose behind these ceremonies. Nevertheless, his explanatory details fill in some of the background left blank by Thompson and McKenney. Together with the oral narrative regarding the origin of the Waabanowiwin, they provide a brief introduction to the ceremony.

It is also possible that Warren was referring to Waabanowag rather than Mideg in his description of the dark days at Chequamegon in the early 1800s when the Ojibwa "fell entirely under the power of their Satanic medicine men."[76] Certainly, there does seem to have been a connection between the Midewiwin and the Waabanowiwin, in that the two ceremonies were celebrated at similar times of the year. There are frequent references to Waabanowag who were engaged in power struggles with other traditional healers, usually Mideg. Nevertheless, few accounts explain for what purposes Waabanowag used their power, although it appears they were diviners whose power to see into the future would have helped them in hunting and war.[77] Main Poc, who was one of the major supporters of Tecumseh, the Potawatomi military leader, was reported to have been a Waabano. However, it is likely that most Waabanowag simply used their powers for the same purposes as did other Anishinaabe traditional healers. An informant told Aboriginal ethnologist William Jones that they performed their Waabanowiwin ceremonies so that they might kill sufficient game for food, find plentiful amounts of berries to eat, and live a long life.[78]

No doubt the fact that the ceremonies took place at night and involved demonstrations of power involving fire heightened the belief among Euro-Americans that the Waabanowiwin was inherently evil. Many Ojibwa also appear to have feared the Waabano's capacity for evil. This has led some to suggest that the Waabanowiwin was essentially a society of evil "shamans."[79] However, other sources such as Hoffman claim that they functioned independently like Jiisakiiwininiwag, although both they and Jiisakiiwininiwag could and did become high-ranking members of the Midewiwin. The fact that they possessed great power appears to have been the reason that they were feared by some Ojibwa, since such power could be misused. However, there are recorded instances in which their powers were used for good in duels with evil Mideg.[80] Nothing was as it seemed in the Anishinaabe world.

While traditional healers were individuals who had received extraordinary amounts of power from the manidoog, every individual in Anishinaabe society had the potential to receive blessings during his or her vision quest, and almost all Anishinaabe actions had a ceremonial aspect to them. From the birth and naming of a child, to the ceremonies for the dead, individuals pleaded with the manidoog for "pity," and gave thanks for any blessings received. Like most other North American Aboriginal people, they fasted and cleansed themselves in a *madoodiswan* (sweat lodge) in order to purify their bodies and souls before attempting any special communication with the manidoog. Tobacco and music were two other essential elements in successful communication. Tobacco offerings were left when roots and herbs were collected for medicines. Such offerings were also left near places frequented by manidoog, and were thrown on the waters when wild rice was harvested. After kinnikinnick,[81] a blend of European tobacco and red willow bark, had been added in order to make it more pleasing to the manidoog, tobacco was smoked in pipes for ceremonial purposes connected with divination and curing ceremonies. It was also smoked during trade and political negotiations since it was important to have the support of the manidoog at these times. Music, in the form of drumming, singing, and dancing, also formed an essential part of Anishinaabe ceremonies. Dream songs acquired during a dream or vision were believed to assure the recipient of aid from the manidoog, and were used whenever communication with the manidoog was desired—for instance, in curing ceremonies or war preparations. Melody, not words, was the important element in ensuring the power of these songs and ultimately the power of the individual who owned them.[82]

Early Euro-American observers did not understand Anishinaabe ceremonies because they approached them with their own preconceptions. Most descriptions concentrated on the external aspects of these Anishinaabe ceremonies, because the authors believed the ceremonies to be deceptions on the part of charlatans, or devotions to false gods. While most members of both societies believed in the existence of spiritual beings, early Euro-Americans as a general rule understood them only in Christian terms. Thus, they often attributed any unexpected power exercised by Aboriginal participants to the devil, particularly since many of the ceremonies took place at night to the accompaniment of music they did not understand and secretly feared, especially the "incessant" beat of the drum. Nor did they initially understand the Anishinaabe ceremonial use of the pipe, or the concept of providing gifts to the manidoog in return for their assistance.[83] Moreover, in a society that made radical distinctions between the responsibilities and power of the clergy and of physicians, the apparent interrelationship between these two in the Aboriginal community was totally incomprehensible to Euro-American observers.[84]

Euro-Americans subsequently began to use the Anishinaabe term "mashkikiiwinini," or more often the English term "medicine man," to refer to a range of practitioners who made use of specialized "medicine" powers obtained through visions. While Euro-Americans tended to see "medicine power" as being a single entity, contrasting "good" and "bad" medicine men, the Anishinaabeg distinguished three major kinds of mashkiki: curing medicine, protection medicine, and bad medicine. Curing medicine helped the individual to regain control that had been lost, either as a result of an illness, an accident, a wound, or the effects of bad medicine used by an enemy. Protection medicine, as its name implies, was used to protect a person, whether from dangers in battle or as a defence against potential evil, such as being made helpless or out of control. Bad medicine was used to render other people helpless, or out of control, or to kill them.[85]

It might be thought that "good" medicine would be obtained only from "good" manidoog and vice versa, but this was not the case. The three types of medicine were parts of a single whole; the distinction was mainly on how the power was used. Even so-called "evil" manidoog such as the Underwater Panthers provided power that could be used for good as well as bad purposes. What each individual had to do was to ensure that the proper spirits were placated and kept in balance.

It was often difficult to tell from outward appearances whether a person might use power for good or evil purposes. Individuals who were believed to be selfish, uncooperative, or who in other ways threatened the corporate life of the community, were often suspected of practising bad medicine, as were strangers or members of other tribal groups. This sometimes resulted in power contests between "good" and "evil" medicine men—labels that often depended upon one's perspective. In other instances, community sanctions including banishment and, in the most extreme cases, even death might be applied against the offender or offenders. In some instances, such as the situation at Chequamegon described by Warren, evil practices might even take over an entire community for a period of time.[86] Warren suggests the problem was resolved when the Ojibwa once again resumed their migration.

It does not seem that pre- and early contact Ojibwa undertook the type of "witch hunts" that characterized some neighbouring groups such as the Iroquois, who often sought out and put to death suspected evil medicine men.[87] Anthony Wallace has argued in his studies of revitalization and religion that the fear of witchcraft ensured a level of individual compliance with community mores.[88] This, in turn, allowed leaders such as Handsome Lake to use "witch hunts" as an instrument of social control in communities where there had been a breakdown in traditional practices following a period of rapid, enforced acculturation.[89]

Since pre-contact Anishinaabeg lived in small groups or bands for the greater part of the year, individuals who had received power, and were able to "practise medicine," were important to the daily life of the band. The successful wielding of their power could mean the difference between starvation and plenty, particularly in times of adverse weather conditions. Dreams or visions—either unsolicited or as part of ceremonies such as the Jiisakiiwin (Shaking Tent)—were important to both individuals and band members as a whole. However, such power was two-edged in Anishinaabe terms, since individuals practised not only curing and protective medicine, but also bad medicine. In the latter case, their power could be disruptive, even dangerous to the community. Rather than a dualistic universe clearly divided between good and evil, as many Christian observers thought it to be, the Anishinaabe world was thus a more complex one in which good and evil were fused together, differing only in the form they took. Thus, "powerful" individuals were both respected and feared, because they could both help others to maintain their autonomy or cause them to lose control of their lives. It was natural, then, that powerful individuals would assume leadership roles beyond the spiritual or medical spheres.

Anishinaabe Socio-Political Organization and Leadership

Early in the seventeenth century, prior to contact with Europeans, the Anishinaabeg lived mainly in the area drained by lakes Huron and Superior.[90] Small groups ranged from the area around Georgian Bay west along Lake Huron and north to Lake Superior and the upper peninsula of present-day Michigan. Around this time, the Anishinaabeg around Bowating (which the French named Sault Ste. Marie) appear to have begun to move outside their original territory, according to their own narratives, such as those collected and written down by Warren, Hoffman, and Densmore.

Scholars are generally divided into two schools of thought as to what characterized the social organization of these "proto-Ojibwa," as the ancestors of present-day Ojibwa are often known to scholars. One school argues that, according to the evidence of early French missionaries and traders, Ojibwa clans had existed prior to contact with Europeans. Conversely, the other school maintains that Ojibwa clan structure was a post-contact phenomenon, brought about by a number of different factors.

Within each school, there are differences of opinion regarding the origin, nature, and significance of Ojibwa clans.

Harold Hickerson (in *The Southwestern Chippewa*) and Charles Bishop (in "The Indian Inhabitants of Northern Ontario," and "The Question of Ojibwa Clans") both support the pre-contact emergence of patrilocal totemic clans such as the *Noquet* (Bear), *Awasse* or *Marquet* (Catfish), and the *Amicoures* (Beaver). Hickerson, however, viewed Ojibwa clan structure as primarily egalitarian and communal in nature, whereas Bishop claimed that clan leaders functioned as lineage chiefs, particularly in inter-group relations, and that proto-Ojibwa social organization, therefore, was patently inegalitarian

James G.E. Smith, Edward Rogers, and Charles Callender disagreed with the claim that new patrilineal clans emerged among the proto-historical Ojibwa.[91] They argued that the proto-Ojibwa were, in fact, composed of egalitarian, patrilocal, and patrilineal migratory bands that returned seasonally to fish and plant gardens at Bowating. And, they refused to limit the proto-Ojibwa to the few named clan groups, arguing instead that they were part of a culturally and linguistically similar population in the upper Great Lakes region.

Callender was particularly insistent that clans did not exist among the Ojibwa prior to the 1600s. He speculated that they may have originated among the Ojibwa, Ottawa, and Potawatomi when they encountered the Menominee, who were already established in sedentary villages in what is now Wisconsin. Callender pointed out that while all three groups shared a common parent language, the Ojibwa clans had fewer corporate features than their neighbours. Supernatural power among the Ojibwa was an individual possession, comparable to private property, as were sacred bundles and sacred songs. Naming, which was a clan function among the Menominee, was carried out in connection with private visions among the Ojibwa.

According to Smith and Rogers, population movements among the proto-Ojibwa at the smallest social unit were common in the upper Great Lakes region in the 1600s and 1700s as a result of war with neighbouring Iroquois and Sioux, and the search for game. These movements increased as the proto-Ojibwa encountered Euro-Americans and engaged in the fur trade. As can be expected, there was some fission and fusion among these bands. Nevertheless, according to Smith and Rogers, there was little change in the essential makeup of these bands until the middle of the eighteenth century.

In a recent work on the socio-political organization of the Lake Superior Ojibwa, historian Theresa Schenck argues that the clan groups were not merely subgroups of the Ojibwa or proto-Ojibwa. Rather, they were equal and independent groups who shared the same language and culture. She revives an earlier argument that the Otchitchak identified in early Euro-American documents were, in reality, the Crane clan. Schenck discounts the influence of the Iroquois Wars and the fur trade as factors in the transformation of these independent clans into the people who, in the nineteenth century, had taken the corporate name of Ojibwa. She attributes the mixing process to such factors as the exogamous marriage practices, which were facilitated by the annual gatherings of the clans, and the gradual expansion into new regions. Throughout the eighteenth century, various totemic groups gradually came together in semi-permanent villages, and out of these groups were born the nineteenth-century clans described by Warren.[92]

It seems most probable that if clans arose, they did so as the Ojibwa moved south and west into an area of more diverse and abundant resources, and encountered related groups who already had clan structures. The rise of alliance chiefs at this time, as Bishop and Schenck suggest, would certainly have been an additional reason for clan development. Regardless of when the Ojibwa clan structure arose, it facilitated increased movement, since it provided a structure for friendship and support among fellow clan members in various villages throughout the region. Such movement among small groups of Ojibwa was common until they were confined to reserves (termed "reserves" in Canada and "reservations" in the United States). However, since they did not necessarily remain clan-based, the term "band" is probably more accurate during much of the contact period.

None of the above debates alters the generally agreed-upon fact that large, semi-permanent villages did develop at Bowating, Chequamegon and Michilimackinac, Green Bay, and elsewhere—probably as a result of a combination of climatic conditions and an abundance of natural resources. These settlements served important trade and ceremonial functions even prior to the coming of the Euro-Americans, and later became "service centres" for the fur brigades.[93] Certainly, there was an extensive pre-contact system of lake and river trade routes in the upper Great Lakes region, which facilitated the seasonal migration of large numbers of people to these villages in the early summer.

Anthropologist Karl Schlesier and historian Richard White have argued that the world of the Anishinaabeg was shattered by the twin blows of epidemics and Iroquois attacks between the 1640s and the 1660s.[94] The large village centres identified by earlier scholars were peopled by refugees from a variety of different Anishinaabe groups, ranging from hunting bands of proto-Ojibwa, to the more socially structured Miamis, to the remnants of the once powerful Huron confederacy. While the different groups of refugees maintained their separateness to some degree, cultural forms were borrowed from other groups, and intermarriage and adoption fostered new bonds among different cultural groups.

The dissolution of some old social units and the birth of new ones made social relations extremely complicated.[95] It is important to keep in mind that most Ojibwa continued to live in small, temporary villages for most of the year. Even a semi-permanent village such as Bowating in the seventeenth century is estimated to have had no more than several hundred permanent residents, although it increased considerably in population during the summer months. While centres such as Chequamegon and Green Bay may have had mixed populations numbering in the thousands, many of these would have been migratory as well. The seasonal lifestyle, which caused the Anishinaabeg to disperse for large parts of each year, coupled with their low population density, meant that the core units of Anishinaabe society continued to be the family, clan, and band.

The role of leaders in Anishinaabe society was based on these connections. If one accepts Smith's and Roger's thesis that the early Anishinaabeg formed groups of patrilineal bands, then leadership of these bands probably centred around the senior male in the group. At some time in the past, these leaders began to be called *ogimaag* by the Anishinaabeg. When several bands came together at different times of the year, senior ogimaag performed a number of civil and ceremonial duties. At the time of contact, Euro-Americans began to apply the name "chief" to those individuals who appeared to be in charge, although the term was applied rather haphazardly.[96]

It is important to remember, however, that leadership in the Euro-American sense was absent from all Algonquian groups, with the possible exception of the small group of Miamis. Leadership among the Anishinaabeg was consensual, based largely on respect and reputation, so it appeared to be almost non-existent to the hierarchically inclined Euro-Americans. Moreover, well into the nineteenth century, the Anishinaabeg, or the portion of them now called Ojibwa, still spent the majority of their time in small groups, coming together at particular times of the year, or for specific purposes. This meant that the ratio of ogimaag compared to the population was large. Furthermore, their responsibilities were limited, since the Anishinaabeg selected other leaders to take responsibility for war expeditions and to oversee religious ceremonies.[97]

It is difficult to establish precisely when those who became known as "alliance chiefs" (because they took responsibility for dealings with outside groups) began to function, though there is considerable evidence that their role was firmly established during the "French Period."[98] Some scholars such as Felix Keesing argued that Anishinaabe/Ojibwa leaders began to emulate Euro-American models of descent in order to facilitate the transfer of property and the establishment of status in the immediate post-contact period.[99] Though Janet Chute has argued that "native values were not substantially altered during the French regime,"[100] and Schenck has maintained that they "remained 'band chiefs' in an egalitarian society" even into the nineteenth century,[101] it would seem that the growth and expansion of the Ojibwa, coupled with their growing participation in the politics of the Great Lakes region, did lead to some elaboration of band leadership structures. However, elements of the original structure did continue to exist well into the reserve period.

There is another type of "functionary" in Ojibwa society that deserves mention. The roles played by the *oshkaabewis*, or "ceremonial messenger," as they were known by the Ojibwa, included both civil and religious functions. These individuals served as attendants to the chiefs, sent out invitation sticks for both councils of war and Midewiwin ceremonies, and acted as the pipe bearer during ceremonial occasions. Euro-American observers were often confused as to the role of the oshkaabewis, and either focussed on one aspect of the role or, in some cases, confused them with band leaders.[102]

The integration of religious and political terminology and practice was a common feature of Anishinaabe life that cannot be ignored.[103] Many individuals whom Euro-American observers described as being religious leaders also were ogimaag. In many cases, they served as war chiefs in the battles with the Sioux, trade chiefs in their relations with fur traders, and alliance chiefs in their dealings with the various Euro-American government officials.[104]

Anishinaabe forms of leadership bore little resemblance to those of the Euro-Americans they encountered. Rather than being based on the direction of a single individual, Anishinaabe leadership was more consensual in approach.[105] Individuals who had received "blessings" from the manidoog, giving them specific powers, who knew the narratives of their people, and who had lived through numerous experiences in their lifetime were generally revered as "elders,"[106] whom others relied on for advice when important decisions concerning the entire band had to be made. Gatherings of all those concerned were held, the participants smoked their pipes so that their thoughts would mingle with those of the manidoog, and all present were given a chance to speak, although weight was given to the opinions of the elders. As in other aspects of Anishinaabe life, religious concepts and ceremonies played an integral role in socio-political organization and leadership.

THREE

Midewiwin Origins: Anishinaabe and Euro-American Perspectives

> The central concern of the Mide oral tradition was with origins: the creation of the world and of man, the origin of death, the introduction of the Midewiwin, and the ancestral origins of the Ojibwa people.[1]

Anishinaabe Perspectives: Midewiwin Origin Narratives

Although Midewiwin origin narratives may vary according to time, place, occasion, and the person telling the tale, they all share common assumptions concerning the nature and purpose of life. All are deeply rooted in an Anishinaabe world view, in which manidoog and visions play an important role in providing the Anishinaabeg with blessings or powers to live a long life. Midewiwin origin narratives were (and still are) recited by Mide elders during each Midewiwin ceremony.[2] The origin narratives and, indeed, the larger cycle of narratives of which they form a part, together with the rituals of the Midewiwin, provide the means by which the Ojibwa can live "the good life to the fullest."[3]

The fact that the Midewiwin was an integral part of Ojibwa cosmology signals that it played a different role from that of Jiisakiiwin or the

Waabanowiwin ceremonies with which it is often compared. All three provided their practitioners with special powers, which were widely used in Ojibwa society.[4] However, within the Midewiwin, these special powers were gained as part of a process that also taught them the meaning of life and death, their place in the universe, and the origins of the Ojibwa people. In other words, it was more than just another ceremony, for it provided an institutional setting for the teaching of the world view (religious beliefs) of the Ojibwa people.

The popular connotation of "myth," the term by which they are often known, contains the implication that such narratives have nothing to do with the real world. Euro-American scholars have long studied such narratives, or "myths," since these myths contained the deepest expressions of truth that were held by a society.[5] Many twentieth-century social scientists have begun to understand myths within the context of the local environment and local social processes, often seeing in them a legitimization of social institutions. Other scholars have used the study of myths to analyze the human mind, seeing in them examples of how humans have attempted to deal with the ambiguities of the universe and society. Literary scholar Northrop Frye has argued that myths not only shaped community identity, but also shaped the way people looked at the living and non-living world.[6] Until relatively recently, scholars virtually ignored them as sources of factual evidence. Yet such narratives, as Africanist Jan Vansina and successive authors have shown, can sometimes provide useful clues to the historical past if certain precautions are taken.[7] Nevertheless, it must be remembered that the Midewiwin narratives are not concerned with a Western linear notion of time, nor are they concerned with the date when the Midewiwin began. As Nicholas Deleary, an Ojibwa follower of the Midewiwin, has stated, "past events are remembered for their symbolic meaning rather than as mere chronological dates."[8]

It must be remembered that the Ojibwa sacred narratives, or aadizookaanag, were part of the oral tradition of the people. As such, they followed certain conventions that distinguished them from ordinary communication, and from the written word. Moreover, the oral nature of the narratives shaped how these texts were interpreted by the Ojibwa, and the role that they played in Ojibwa society.[9] Above all, the narratives were considered sacred and their transmission was considered a very special, holy act, which had tremendous significance for the life of the community. The telling of these narratives by Ojibwa elders was first and foremost a "verbal art," which took place in a social setting. The "storyteller" was both a holy man and a teacher, who transformed the story to meet his and his audience's needs, even while keeping within certain prescribed formats. Thus, a short version was considered sufficient in the training of a candidate for the first degree, but more elaborate narratives were used in the ceremonies related to higher degrees.[10] The primary function of the narratives was didactic, illustrating the process through which the Midewiwin arose and how it could benefit individuals and the Anishinaabe people as a whole, so exact wording was not essential. What was of primary importance was the process. Nevertheless, the core elements of the narratives remain relatively stable.[11]

There appear to be two, relatively distinct, traditions in the Midewiwin narratives: in the first, the agent who brings the Midewiwin to the Anishinaabeg is a manidoo or Nanabozho; in the second, the secrets of the Midewiwin are revealed to a human, who then passes on his knowledge to his/her fellow Anishinaabeg. In fact, the Ojibwa themselves would not have made such distinctions, since the gift of the Midewiwin to the Anishinaabeg was always traced back ultimately to an "other-than-human" source. Only the details differed; some versions concentrated on the reasons the Midewiwin came into being, while others concentrated more on how it was transmitted to the Anishinaabeg, and who the messenger, or oshkaabewis, was.

Many of the narratives that have been written down and published attribute the origin of the Midewiwin to Nanabozho alone, or in conjunction with Gichi-Manidoo, or with some other manidoo. The Midewiwin narratives usually occur toward the end of a cycle of narratives concerning Nanabozho, a version of which was related in the previous chapter. To recapitulate, in these narratives, the Underwater manidoog kill a wolf who is Nanabozho's brother (cousin, son, grandson), so Nanabozho seeks revenge and kills their leader.[12] The surviving Underwater manidoog then flood the world, but Nanabozho escapes by climbing a tree or building a raft, and sends down an animal (usually a muskrat) to bring back mud and re-create the world, after which he creates the Anishinaabeg.[13]

At this point in the cycle of narratives, Nanabozho usually becomes involved in founding the Midewiwin, having created the Anishinaabeg from earth and placed them on the island he had fashioned from the mud brought up to him by Muskrat. In some versions Nanabozho himself brings the Midewiwin to the Anishinaabeg; in others the manidoog meet in council and try to appease Nanabozho by offering him the Midewiwin for the Anishinaabeg.[14] In what may be the earliest extant version circa 1800, Mishibizhii (Mishibeshu), the ogimaa of the Underwater manidoog, initiates the peace-making gesture himself.[15] In some other versions, the first humans disappear after they have been created, so Nanabozho realizes he must ensure that the Anishinaabeg learn to live with other beings in the cosmos if they are to survive.[16] The Anishinaabeg must learn how to seek assistance from the manidoog, and how to make offerings to them.

Two of the most widely cited versions of the Midewiwin origin narratives include Warren's transcription dating from the 1830s or 1840s, and Hoffman's transcription from the 1890s.[17] While these two versions have come to represent Midewiwin origin narratives, there is no evidence that they were more representative than any other. It may well be that they have been preserved in print form as a matter of chance.

Warren's version is as follows:

> While our forefathers were living on the great salt water toward the rising sun, the great Megis (sea-shell),[18] showed itself above the surface of the great water, and the rays of the sun for a long period were reflected from its glossy back. It gave warmth and light to the An-ish-in-aub-ag (red race). All at once it sank into the deep, and for a time our ancestors were not blessed with its light. It rose to the surface and appeared again on the great river which drains the water of the Great Lakes, and again for a long time it gave life to our forefathers, and reflected back the rays of the sun. Again it disappeared from sight and it rose not, till it appeared to the eyes of the An-ish-in-aub-ag on the shores of the first great lake. Again it sank from sight, and death daily visited the wigwams of our forefathers, till it showed its back, and reflected the rays of the sun once more at Bow-e-ting (Sault Ste. Marie). Here it remained for a long time, but once more, and for the last time, it disappeared, and the An-ish-in-aub-ag was left in darkness and misery, till it floated and once more showed its bright back at Mo-ning-wun-a-kaun-ing (La Pointe Island), where it has since reflected back the rays of the sun, and blessed our ancestors with life, light, and wisdom. Its rays reach the remotest village of the wide spread Ojibways.[19]

This tale, as the narrator went on to explain, traces the movement of the Ojibwa people from their original homeland somewhere along the shores of the Atlantic Ocean, up the St. Lawrence, through the Great Lakes to Bowating, and then to Chequamegon (La Pointe or Madeline Island). The migration is explained in the context of the Midewiwin's having been granted to the Ojibwa in order to protect them from illness and misery.[20] Warren's source for his version was probably Flat Mouth, the Pillager chief from Leech Lake, who also provided Nicollet (and thus Schoolcraft) with much of his information on the Midewiwin.[21] Flat Mouth's family origins are not known,[22] but the Pillagers apparently originated from among the northern bands of the Boundary Waters area, who pushed south and west against the Sioux, eventually occupying the area around Red Lake and Leech Lake.[23]

Whether Flat Mouth was part of the northern or southern groups, he nevertheless was a participant in the westward migration of the Ojibwa. In fact, Flat Mouth and the Pillagers saw their village as the latest stopping point of the Midewiwin, and in later versions of the tale, the last stopping point was Leech Lake. Perhaps they felt they were approaching yet another period of "darkness and misery," since the Sioux continued to attack from the west and they were increasingly pressed from the east by the Americans. The supply of big-game animals had diminished, the fur trade no longer provided them with goods they had come to depend on, and epidemic diseases had taken a toll. Many Ojibwa, including Flat Mouth himself, temporarily abandoned the teachings of the Midewiwin and embraced the teachings of the Shawnee Prophet, and, as Tanner's narrative indicates, other minor prophets who were also active during this period.[24]

These prophets and their prophecies reflect the growing sense of powerlessness that many Ojibwa felt at the time—particularly in relation to the increasing number of Euro-Americans. For this reason, they often incorporated portions of the Christian message into the stories in the hope of obtaining some of the power associated with the Christian religious figures. Yet, they remained strongly rooted within the ancient visionary tradition, and whatever the prophets may have borrowed from Christian sources was placed within the traditional Anishinaabe world view. The Pillagers and other bands of western Ojibwa, despite growing pressures on them in the nineteenth century, were considerably more independent than most of their brethren to the east, who had borne the brunt of Euro-American advances. Thus, they continued to place their faith in the power of the Midewiwin and the Mide elders.

Warren mentioned in his book that there was another tale told by the Mide elders of Fond du Lac, in which, instead of the miigis, it was Otter who was said to preside over the Mide rites.[25] The following account from a Midewiwin origin narrative is Sikas'sige's (one of Hoffman's informants) explanation of a Mille Lacs chart,[26] but it is probably quite similar to the tale mentioned by Warren.

> When Mi'nabo'zho descended to the earth to give to the Ani'shina'beg the Mide'wiwin, he left with them this chart, Mide'wigwas'. Kit'shi Man'ido saw that his people on earth were without the means of protecting themselves against disease and death, so he sent Mi'nabo'zho to give to them the sacred gift. Mi'nabo'zho appeared over the waters and

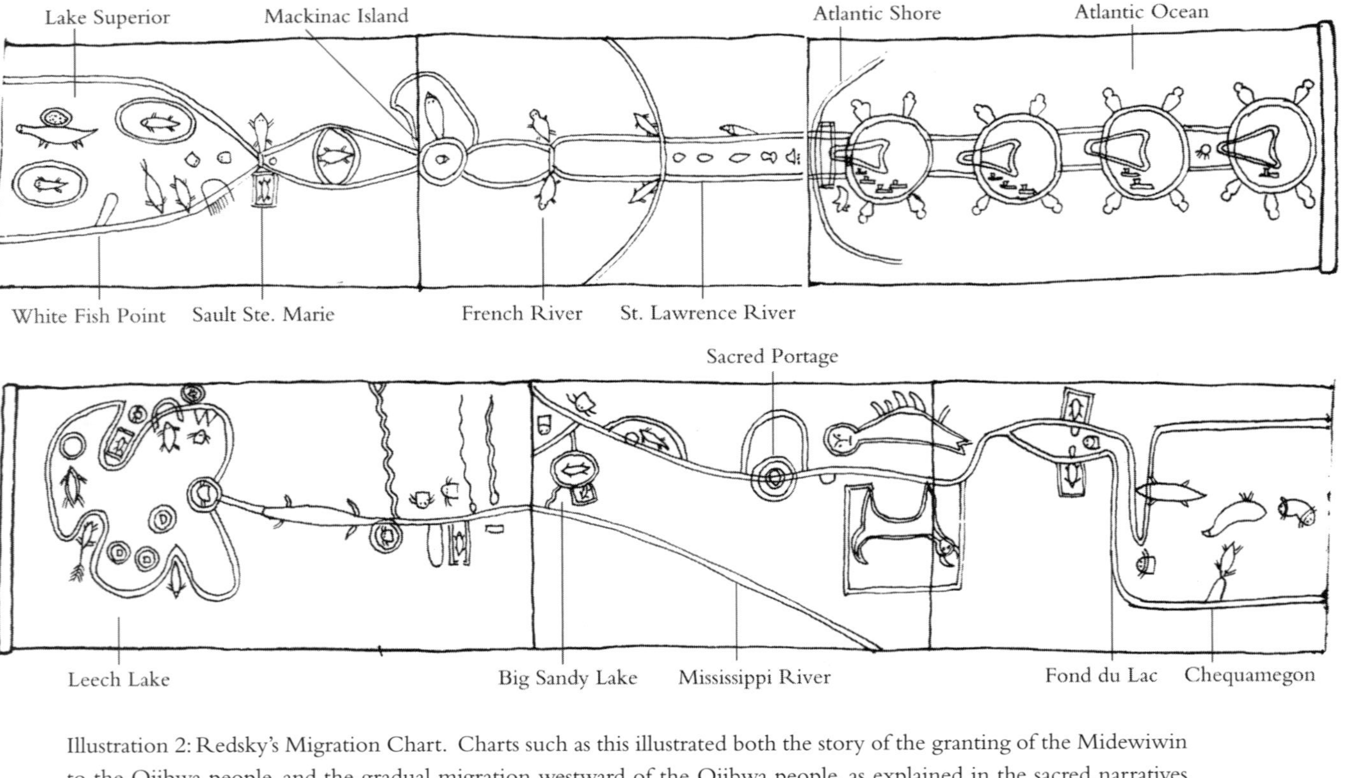

Illustration 2: Redsky's Migration Chart. Charts such as this illustrated both the story of the granting of the Midewiwin to the Ojibwa people, and the gradual migration westward of the Ojibwa people, as explained in the sacred narratives retold by William Warren in his *History of the Ojibway People*. (Redrawn from drawing by B. Nemeth. From Dewdney, *Sacred Scrolls,* 47-48. Courtesy of University of Toronto Press/Glenbow Museum.)

> while reflecting in what manner he should be able to communicate with people, he heard something laugh, just as an otter sometimes cries out. He saw something black appear upon the waters in the west which immediately disappeared beneath the surface again. Then it came up at the northern horizon, which pleased Mi'nabo'zho, as he thought he now saw someone through whom he might convey the information with which he had been charged by Ki'tshi Man'ido. When the black object disappeared beneath the waters at the north to reappear in the east, Mi'nabo'zho desired it would come to him in the middle of the waters, but it disappeared to make its reappearance in the south, where it again sank out of sight to reappear in the west when Mi'nabo'zho asked it to approach the center where there was an island, which it did.
>
> Then Ni'gik [Otter] asked Mi'nabo'zho, "Why do you come to this place?" Then the latter said, "I have pity on the An'shina'beg and wish to give them life; Ki'tshi Mani'ido gave me the power to confer the means of protecting themselves against sickness and death, and through you I will give them Mide'wiwin, and teach them the sacred rites."
>
> Then Mi'nabo'zho built a Mide'wigan in which he instructed the Otter in all the mysteries of the Mide'wiwin. The Otter sat before the door of the Mide'wigan four days, sunning himself, after which he approached the entrance where his progress was arrested by seeing two bad spirits guarding it. Through the powers possessed by Mi'nabo'zho he was enabled to pass these; when he entered the sacred lodge, the first object he beheld being the sacred stone against which those who were sick were to be seated, or laid, when undergoing the ceremonial of restoring them to health. He next saw a post painted red with a green band around the top. A sick man would also have to pray to the stone and to the post, when he is within the Mide'wigan, because within them would be the Mide spirits whose help he invoked.[27]

Sikas'sige had received a copy of the migration chart, upon which the tale is based, from the senior Mide at Mille Lacs in 1830, when, as a young boy, he had been received into the first degree of the Midewiwin.[28] Since the tale undoubtedly was originally told for instruction purposes, it provides a better context than the previous tale, of which, Warren had indicated, he had only transcribed that portion that had struck him most forcefully. The direct appearance of Gichi-Manidoo in Sikas'sige's version might at first appear to indicate a later Christian influence, since Gichi-Manidoo came to be identified with the Christian God, but this is not necessarily the case, since there are good arguments that the concept could have been either pre-contact or post-contact.[29]

Nevertheless, despite their similarities, and some possible Christian influences, there are significant internal differences in the two versions transcribed by Warren and Hoffman. Most obvious is the fact that the miigis was replaced in the second version by the otter. Since the miigis was symbolic of the Midewiwin in general, while the otter represented the first degree, it is possible that the second tale was specific to the initiation ceremony for the first degree. However, Hoffman declared that the northern bands used Otter as their guide[30] and the southern bodies believed in the miigis. Dewdney made yet another division. Taking into account some twentieth-century sources, he suggested that in the southern Mide tradition, Otter acted as the messenger of the Midewiwin, while among northerners this role was filled by the more dangerous Bear.[31]

Sikas'sige's version of the origin narrative appears to neglect the westward movement of the Midewiwin and the Ojibwa people, but the migration is spelled out in more detail in the migration chart that served as a mnemonic aid to the elders who recited the tale. This particular migration chart simply represented the resting spots of the Midewiwin as dots on a line, but Sikas'sige was able to explain to Hoffman the geographical locations of each of these "dots." While not comprehensive, Sikas'sige's commentary provides the earliest and most complete listing of place names available. His commentary has been corroborated and supplemented by migration charts found in the Mille Lacs papers interpreted by Thomas Vennum in his article on the migration songs of the Midewiwin.[32]

In his analysis of these and other migration charts, Vennum makes the point that the locations vary considerably since the Mide elder who compiled them invariably made his own village the final (western) resting point. In this way, the Mide elders "establish certain local manidoog as intercessors in the curing rites as well as endow nearby landmarks with sacred attributes."[33] The relative scarcity of names in the eastern portion of the migration no doubt reflects the fact that no migration charts exist for areas to the east of La Pointe. However, this should not lead us to believe, as Dewdney argued, that La Pointe was thus the actual site where the Midewiwin originated. Dewdney appears to have based his argument mainly on the Mide Loon Foot's chart that he had shown to Kohl.[34] As Blessing has pointed out, other charts make it even clearer that La Pointe was simply one stop (albeit an important one) where the Midewiwin was made known in the Ojibwa's westward migration.[35]

The relative scarcity of origin narratives among eastern Ojibwa may reflect how little anyone knows (Euro-American and Aboriginal alike) about the early history of the Anishinaabeg, and, specifically, about the people who were to become known historically as the Ojibwa. It also may result from the fact that many of the more eastern Ojibwa (or Mississauga, as they were often known in Upper Canada and the lower Michigan peninsula) found themselves uprooted, and in many cases were converted to Christianity much earlier than their western brethren. The leaders and many band members in these regions became adherents of one of the several Christian denominations that undertook missionary work among the people of the Great Lakes region. At a time when the Ojibwa of the southwest were beginning to identify themselves as Ojibwa in the context of Midewiwin narratives, many of the eastern Ojibwa converts, such as Peter Jones, George Copway, Peter Jacobs, and Allen Salt, were in the process of writing about the "Ojibwa nation" within a Christian context.[36] While the Midewiwin was still practised by the eastern Ojibwa during the nineteenth century, its adherents no longer played a central role in the affairs of most bands, except for those among bands in the upper Michigan peninsula and further west. Although some descriptions of the Midewiwin in the former areas exist, there are no transcriptions of any of their narratives, nor do any of their written records from the nineteenth century match those found for other areas.[37]

In another cycle of Midewiwin origin narratives, two new and seemingly unconnected elements were introduced. Most, although not all, of these narratives were collected in the Boundary Waters area of Minnesota in the twentieth century. This may account for some of their variations, since they differ in location and time. Certainly, there are implicit elements of Christianity in some of the most recent narratives. Nevertheless, the essential message continued to be that sickness and death would always be with the Anishinaabeg, but their effects could be mitigated through the Midewiwin, so that people could have a long and good life.

Whereas, in the earlier narratives, it was either the miigis or Otter who was responsible for bringing the Midewiwin to the Anishinaabeg, in many of these later narratives Gichi-Manidoo and the miigis ask Bear to be the messenger (oshkaabewis). The first portion of these narratives describes the journey of Bear westward with his Mide medicine bundle, stopping at various points to establish the Midewiwin. As with the previous versions, the last stopping point is usually the locality in which the Midewiwin is being performed. In some versions, Bear is forced to "break through" a barrier or barriers, prefiguring portions of the Midewiwin ceremony as it was enacted. Various Mide manidoog join him in order to help create new Mide ceremonials, and show how the ceremonies are to be carried out.

The second portion of this cycle of narratives involves a human intermediary in the process. Although the person is not identified in the following version given to Densmore, the narrator does explain the presence of human intermediaries in this cycle:

> So the East Manido was selected to go among these Indians and teach them. Before he left the others he told them that they must get everything ready and decide how the Mide should be taught to the Indians. Of course the East Manido could not approach the Indians in his spirit form, so he was born of an old woman who had lived with her husband all her life but had no children.[38]

In other versions of this cycle, a young boy, who is usually called Cutfoot or sometimes Odaemin, receives instructions regarding the Midewiwin.[39] In Basil Johnston's version, the boy has died from a deadly disease and has been restored to life by Nanabozho. He is then given instructions on how to make use of herbal remedies for healing. The boy grows old, and passes on his power and skills to a young man so that the Anishinaabeg will always have the gift of life. In Ojibwa elder James Redsky's (Esquekesik) version, the young man is taken across the ocean by Nanabozho. There, the teachings are imparted to him, he returns, and transmits his powers to other Anishinaabeg.

In most earlier versions, Cutfoot is given credit for having received these "blessings" in a vision, and passed them on to his fellow Anishinaabeg. One of Ruth Landes's versions focusses on this aspect:

> A certain Indian was the only one to be taught Earth midewiwin by a manito. [The manitou] was Shell, and he sent for [Cutfoot]. The Indian, then six or seven years old, was playing on the beach with his elder brother. At night the little boy did not return to the lodge, so the folks asked the elder brother.... They sought him many days.... Four years the old folks remained at the same place. One afternoon they saw someone walking down the beach.... They recognized him immediately. They fed him, of course, and asked him where he had been. He said he had been visiting, but would not say where. . . . Finally his father understood [that the boy had a mystic experience not to be divulged], quit questioning him, and told his wife to do likewise....
>
> After a time, he married and told his wife where he had been, what he had seen and heard. And he said, "I am going to do it. It is called midewiwin." No Indian had heard of it before....
>
> His elder brother became ill.... The boy said, "Oh, we'll put him through midewiwin. . . ."

> When he finished with him [the elder brother], the boy was up and around, well as ever, except for being a little thin.
>
> From then on, he [the visionary] taught the old men [the shamans] how to perform it. They claim that this is how midewiwin was started among Indians. It is a true story. The man's name was Cutfoot. He and his family lived at Yellow Hammer Beach [Madeline Island]. He had two children.[40]

Landes described another variation wherein Bear cured a woman using the Midewiwin, but there was no hint that she was the original intermediary who brought the Midewiwin to the Anishinaabeg. Landes attributed this to the "fact" that women generally were not visionaries, but it is more likely due to regional variations in the narratives. It is possible to document a number of female Midewiwin leaders, beginning with Schoolcraft's example of Catherine Wambose. More recently, a collection of narratives from the 1890s includes a tale related by Jacques LePique about a young orphan girl who was taken across the water by Gichi Ginebig (Big Snake), where she received the power of the Midewiwin from an old woman and her sons, who were the Four Winds.[41] In yet another twentieth-century version, a young man was taken by Nanabozho across the ocean to some other land, where the teachings were imparted to him. He then transmitted his power to other Anishinaabeg.[42]

Although there are numerous variations, all these narratives include a human intermediary who introduced the Midewiwin to his or her fellow Anishinaabeg. In some instances, the person had been sick, was physically impaired, or even dead and raised to life. In most, but not all, cases, the teachings and power appeared to the person in a vision. In most of the versions, there was considerable emphasis on rules and regulations for joining the Midewiwin, instructions about the ceremony itself, and rules for living a good life.

Commentators have tended to focus on the visionary aspect of these narratives. Vecsey suggests that this group of renditions of the origin narrative may represent a connection between the Midewiwin and the tradition as represented by the vision quest. In Vecsey's view, the Mide myths, as he terms them, are "stories about the gods coming to individual Indians with the promise of guardianship through the Midewiwin. Unlike traditional visionary patterns, however, in the Midewiwin myths the visionary is able to pass on the gift of the vision of the Midewiwin itself to the immediate community, and ultimately to all the Ojibwa people."[43]

Vecsey's interpretation suggests that at some time in the past, the Midewiwin began to supplant visionary experiences as a means of obtaining "blessings" or power from the manidoog—presumably when some individual received a vision empowering him or her to pass on this knowledge to other members of the community. While in normal circumstances such actions were forbidden, there are other occasions when it probably occurred. Thus, for instance, the Waabanowiwin, which is sometimes considered to be an offshoot of the Midewiwin, in some traditions is said to have been started by a young man who had a dream after his father had refused to allow him to join the Midewiwin. It is impossible to date this event, but it may have been during the eighteenth century. Similarly, the Drum Dance, which appeared in the late nineteenth century at a time when the Midewiwin was declining in influence, arose when a young Sioux girl had a vision regarding the power of the drum to revitalize the Aboriginal people. The Drum Dance was taken up in large numbers by the Ojibwa as well—even though the Sioux were still their enemies.[44] It would appear likely, therefore, that Vecsey is wrong, since visionary experiences continued to play an important role in Ojibwa society, and within the Midewiwin, for that matter.

Dewdney has argued that powerful Mide officials perverted Midewiwin rites by relying more on their visionary powers, and that the practitioners of the Midewiwin attempted to harness the power of the more dangerous spirits by absorbing them into Mide rites and ceremonies, thus giving themselves more power.[45] Dewdney envisaged a situation wherein the Midewiwin among the Ojibwa became increasingly corrupted as it moved northwards to regions where a visionary tradition persisted.

Like many other observers, Dewdney subscribed to the view that there was an "orthodox" Midewiwin. In his interpretation, this orthodoxy developed out of La Pointe/Chequamegon and spread southwestward. Deviant forms developed among other groups of Ojibwa. Orthodoxy, however, is a concept more applicable to Euro-American religions than to those of the Anishinaabeg. I would suggest that notions of orthodoxy only developed when the Midewiwin was already in decline, and practitioners had begun to adopt Christian concepts as a weapon that could be used by the Mideg in their struggle against further assimilation.

Dewdney's explanation ignores several important aspects of the role of visionaries in Ojibwa society. Visionaries who had had their power demonstrated and verified by the elders were bound to use it when asked. Since visionaries received their power to use "good and bad medicine" from a particular tutelary spirit, they had little choice in how this power was used. If they accepted the guardianship of a manidoo such as Mishibizhii, they were obliged to use "bad medicine" when asked—even if they did not want to do so. If they didn't, they risked losing all their powers. The two-edged nature of this "power" is indicated by the myth in which a man gained the power to perform marvellous cures from Mishibizhii, only to have his own wife and children die.[46] It was understood as a condition of life that power gained through visions could have both good and bad effects.

It must also be understood that candidates for the Midewiwin were initially required to have a vision. In the case of children, the sponsor would have a vision indicating that the manidoog were open to their candidacy and would ultimately confer on them the required power. Nicollet noted in his discussions with Flat Mouth in the 1830s that this system had become open to abuses.[47] Flat Mouth himself had been one of those responsible for instituting a reform that required two people to have a similar vision regarding a potential candidate before he or she could be considered. By the 1880s, when Hoffman was doing his research, the reforms appear to have been no longer in effect, since Hoffman suggested that an applicant could ask the Mide officials for permission to purchase a miigis, and if this was successful, then the procedures were the same for both types of candidates.[48] In later accounts, however, there are numerous references to visions being important for anyone who wished to gain sufficient power to function as a Mide.

Even in the 1930s, when Ruth Landes was doing much of her field research, visions were considered essential if one wished to be a "genuine" Mide official. The visionary experiences of these Mide officials no doubt help explain some of the continuing variations in both the origin narratives and ceremonial rituals. As Landes observes, "It seems reasonable to infer that the Ojibwa divergences from their older recorded forms were expedited by the people's devotion to visions [even if] the Indians always said they were transferring faithfully the teachings of past times."[49]

The foregoing examples indicate that there was an ongoing creative tension between the visionary tradition, and the formal tradition of passing on knowledge through the institution of the Midewiwin. As with all things in Anishinaabe life, the two need not, nor should not, be seen in dialectical opposition. Rather, they existed side by side, providing complementary ways of obtaining knowledge and, ultimately, power.

It could also be argued that origin narratives in which human intermediaries played a major role may also represent an adaptation of the concept of the Christian saviour. However, while there was undoubtedly a growing knowledge of Christian beliefs among the more easterly bands of Ojibwa, it must also be remembered that the role of oshkaabewis as messenger was well established in other aspects of Anishinaabe society.[50] It is more likely that Mide visions during this period occurred in the context of the vision experiences of the leaders of revitalization movements such as that of the Shawnee Prophet. So strong was the appeal of some of these movements that even some Ojibwa Mide leaders such as Flat Mouth temporarily renounced their belief in the Midewiwin and threw away their biinjigoosan (personal medicine bags) in order to follow the teachings of the Shawnee Prophet.[51]

A Mide origin story collected by Schoolcraft appears to fall into this category, since it contains elements common both to Christian beliefs and to the revitalization movements:

> About this time, a person in the shape of a human being came down from the sky; his clothing was exceedingly pure and white. . . .
>
> This divine messenger then gave to the Indians laws and rules, whereby they should be guided: first, to love and fear Kezha Monedo, and next that they must love one another. . . . He then instituted the grand medicine or metay we win dance: this ceremony was to be observed annually, and with due solemnity, and the Indians, said Nabinoi, experienced much good from it; but unfortunately the foolish young men were cheated by Mache Monedo who caused them to adopt the Wabano dance . . . and this was finally introduced into the metay we wining (ie. medicine dance) and thereby corrupted it.[52]

The above tale, Schoolcraft tells us, was originally collected from an old Ojibwa chief, Nabinoi, from the Sault Ste. Marie (Bowating) region, by Schoolcraft's brother-in-law, George Johnson, in the early part of the nineteenth century.[53] Unfortunately, no further information is given about Nabinoi. Many of Johnson's and Schoolcraft's informants were Christian converts, but in this case we are not told if this was so. We also have no way of knowing whether it was originally related in Ojibwa, although this is probable since Johnson was part Ojibwa himself, and was employed as an interpreter. Presumably Johnson translated it into English, although Schoolcraft may have altered the text. It is impossible to determine to what extent the narration was altered by Johnson and/or Schoolcraft. Although Ojibwa freely adopted Christian concepts in their narratives when such additions were seen to be useful, the allusions in this story may well have been Schoolcraft's glosses or the work of the original storytellers.[54] Schoolcraft professed to do everything possible to maintain the structure and content of the original narratives, but his versions betray his own literary aesthetics and philosophical beliefs.[55]

Schoolcraft's version of the origin of the Midewiwin, although it could be one of the earliest recorded, is interlaced with Judeo-Christian themes. Ojibwa visions usually took the form of animals, not humans, and even messengers wouldn't normally be dressed in white. However, the vision had many features similar to a vision received by Neolin, the Delaware Prophet, in 1762, particularly its emphasis on the renewal of rituals.[56] It is possible that Nabinoi had come into contact with the Delaware Prophet's message, or had heard the version from someone who had. However, since Neolin's vision was well known to Schoolcraft (he translated it for inclusion in *Algic Researches*), it is also possible that Schoolcraft altered Nabinoi's tale to make it conform more closely to that of Neolin. Certainly, the glosses about Kezha Monedo and Machi Monedo, and the excesses of the Waabano, all point to the hand of Schoolcraft, who was anxious to highlight what he considered to be the dualism of Ojibwa religion.

There is another cycle of origin narratives, collected by Jones at Garden River from an undisclosed informant around the turn of the century, which does not fall into either of the two major Midewiwin traditions.[57] The cycle begins with Nanabozho and his brother creating human beings and then manidoog to whom the Anishinaabeg could turn for help. Since the people must eventually die, it was decreed that Nanabozho's younger brother would die, so that he could look after the souls of those who had died. Thus far, the themes are relatively similar to the previous narratives. However, the main tale centres on a mythic contest of powers between Mighty One (a Potawatomi of the Eagle clan) and Black Tail of a Fish (an Ojibwa of the Bullhead clan). Mighty One, who was said to be one of the first humans, received his power from the Underwater manidoog, while Black Tail was said to be an Underwater manidoo. In the contest, Black Tail used his mystic power to kill Mighty One's wife and children, but then made peace. The manidoog of four directions, and those of above and below, hearing of the contest, came to learn about the Midewiwin and gain its medicines. Coming to Black Tail, they gave him goods and tobacco, saying:

> "Pray, do you give us of your medicine and songs, that you may impart to us knowledge of everything we desire of you."
>
> Now said Black-Tail-of-a-Fish: "Thus shall it be as long as the world lasts, from a great distance shall (the people) go to ask for medicine and songs, in just this way as you six have come."
>
> Now, therefore, was Nanabushu nearly ready to complete the various forms of the mystic rite that were to be. . . .
>
> Thereupon did Black-Tail-of-a-Fish set to work giving away the medicine; and in a while the kettle-drum and the (bear-hide) case (for

> the drum) did he give the men; when he had given them everything, it was then that he began to sing to them. And when they had learned (the songs), he then spoke to them, saying: "You shall not go back home. You (are the ones who) shall go forth to carry the mystic rite [Midewiwin] into different places. . . ."
>
> Truly went they into the four directions from whence blow the winds, and to the other side of the underworld, and yonder into the sky. It was then that thence departed Black-Tail-of-a-Fish to go to where Mighty-One was. In a while he went into where he was. Lo, he was smiled upon by him. Black-Tail-of-a-Fish was told by him: "No longer do you anger me. How could you anger me, when you really did not kill those children of mine? Simply to another land have they gone. After a while I shall go to where those children of mine are. And the same thing shall happen with you as with me when we leave this world. In after-time it shall come to pass that till the end of the world the people will sometimes strive against one another, with their children up for a wager."[58]

In another tale in this cycle, Mighty One died and, as predicted, his body became "magic paint," which provided his granddaughter with great power. She later conceived a boy child, to whom Black Tail (before he, too, died and became "magic paint") passed on the knowledge of the Midewiwin, including numerous Mide songs, which are spelled out in detail. The young boy in turn grew old as a result of singing the songs. And he spoke to the people, saying:

> "Such is the length of time that the world shall last. O ye people! I too shall soon depart hence. Off over this way from whence comes the morning shall I (go to) harken to the people. And in future time, while the babe is yet bound to the cradle-board, is when I shall be the first to be called upon by them that wish to perform the mystic rite. And by them whose child has died shall I be called upon. This is all that I have to say to you, O ye people! I am the Red-looking-One, according to the name that I have been given. It is now for you to go back home. This, no doubt, shall suffice the people as long as the world shall last. From no other place shall magic medicine ever be derived."[59]

Perhaps the most significant element in this tale is the fact that it centres on a power duel between two rival Mideg. Power struggles were an integral part of Anishinaabe life. However, they appear to have become increasingly common in ritualized form towards the end of the nineteenth century, when Ojibwa society was under stress from a number of different quarters. In one part of this tale there is even a hint that the Midewiwin itself had become engaged in a duel with the religion of the Whites. Black Tail explained "that whites will exist one day, and they will live by the manitous' directions in a way different from the Indians. If they speak ill of Mide, making fun of it, the Thunderers will be angry and destroy towns. All people should regard the mystic rite as manitou."[60]

The duel prefigures parts of the Midewiwin ritual itself—for Mighty One's wife and children die, but are revived into another life. And it is through a similar death and resurrection ritual that new initiates are welcomed into the Midewiwin, and later demonstrate their own mystic powers.[61] While it might be tempting to attribute this theme to Christian influences, it is more likely that the theme is indigenous, since it fits perfectly into the cyclical world view of the Anishinaabeg, which permeated all aspects of their existence.

It is possible to trace significant shifts over time in the Midewiwin narratives' portrayal of specific manidoog, the concepts of good and evil, and the question of the afterlife, although none of these affected the fundamental nature of the Midewiwin. Nevertheless, there are a number of ambiguities in the narratives. Some of these are easily explainable. The degree of detail and the focus of the tale could and did vary, depending upon the intended purpose of the narratives. Those connected with initiation rites for higher levels of the Midewiwin contained additional information not found at lower levels. Most significantly, individual visions of Mide officials personalized the telling of the narratives.

With the coming of the first Euro-Americans, the visions of Anishinaabeg began to change, and Midewiwin narratives also changed—sometimes in ambiguous ways. Anishinaabe Mideg received visions incorporating Christian deities and symbols into the Anishinaabe cosmology and Midewiwin narratives. However, the basic belief structure of the Midewiwin remained intact. As time went on and conditions worsened for the Anishinaabeg, prophets arose who had received visions telling them to renounce the ways of the *Wayaabishkiwed* ("White People") and return to their former lifestyle. There was no single revitalization movement among the Anishinaabeg, but many of them temporarily became followers of such leaders as the Delaware and Shawnee prophets. Other Anishinaabeg received visions that explained that the religion of the Christians was meant for the Wayaabishkiwed, while the Midewiwin was intended for the Anishinaabeg. Narratives of Aboriginal converts to Christianity who had died and been refused entry into the Christian heaven (since separate heavens existed for

Aboriginal and White men) circulated widely throughout the nineteenth century among the Anishinaabeg.[62] In the final analysis, most of the Anishinaabe people were impervious to missionary appeals that they renounce their beliefs and practices, and become Christians.

The incorporation of new figures and beliefs (from other tribes and later from Euro-Americans) into Anishinaabe cosmology was a well-established method of dealing with change.[63] However, as a result of the distinctions between Anishinaabeg and Wayaabishkiwed, Midewiwin beliefs and practices began to take on a more exclusivist form, which was alien to traditional Anishinaabe cosmology. This growing exclusivism, which was more closely akin to the revitalization movements than to traditional Anishinaabe beliefs and practices, introduced divisions into Ojibwa communities. So, too, did the acceptance of an exclusivist Christianity by other portions of the Anishinaabe community. The two tendencies ultimately helped set the stage for the development of factionalism in Ojibwa society.

Other ambiguities in the Midewiwin narratives have continued to perplex succeeding generations of Euro-Americans. Simply put, the origin narratives appear to imply that an institution that was established in order to assist the Anishinaabeg to lead the "good life" was done so with the assistance of the forces of evil. In many versions, the narratives tell how Mishibizhii (the ogimaa of the Underwater manidoog) stole the first humans, so Nanabozho decided he would create the Animikiig (Thunderers) in order to watch over them. However, as Theresa Smith explains, in some accounts, the first humans had been created by the Underwater manidoog, and in others by the Underwater manidoog in conjunction with the Thunderers.[64] In at least one tale (recounted by Johann Kohl), they were originally formed like man, but had the scales of a fish.[65] Although Kohl's tale has strong Christian overtones (including a Garden of Eden episode), there is no denying the connections between the Midewiwin and Underwater manidoog and other water creatures. In one sense, it is conceivable that the tale of the Anishinaabeg originally living along the shore of the great salt water might also refer to their mythic origins in the distant past, when they lived in the sea. Certainly, this would tie in with those narratives in which the original humans had scales. There might even be, as Smith speculates, "a rather unsettling kinship between the [Underwater] monsters and the Anishinaabeg."[66] This is certainly suggested in the tale about Mighty One and Black Tail, who is named after a creature from the water, and is sometimes termed an Underwater manidoo.

These narratives sketch a very ambiguous relationship between Mishibizhii and the Underwater manidoog on the one hand, and the institution of the Midewiwin on the other. After all, the Midewiwin came into existence in order to bring the means of life to the Anishinaabeg. Surely it would have been more "logical" (in Western terms) for the Thunderers to have been associated with the gift of the Midewiwin, since Nanabozho had created them in order to protect the Anishinaabeg from Mishibizhii. But it is precisely this ambiguity of existence that permeates all aspects of the Anishinaabe world view. Nothing is what it seems at first glance: that which may help you survive, may also result in your death, if used in the wrong way, or if used to excess. The evil Mide whom everyone fears may have the power to cure you, while the seemingly friendly stranger may bring death along with his gifts. So it is with all things in life, including the Midewiwin.

Euro-Americans often see the world in terms of dualities: us and them, good and evil, here and there, now and then. Mishibizhii and the other manidoog of the waters, such as snakes, had the potential to do evil, but they were not "evil incarnate" in the same terms as the Christian devil. Mishibizhii cannot be confused with "Matchi-Manitou," whom the Christian missionaries equated with the devil. Not only was he one of a number of manidoog who were considered to be "evil manidoog," but, as has been indicated, he also possessed the capacity for good. Nevertheless, in Smith's words, "he acted as a kind of cosmic bully," who often used his great power to disrupt things and throw creation out of balance, causing the Anishinaabeg to feel "out of control." [67] They were then left with the option of "begging for pity" and making him offerings of tobacco, or of turning to the Thunderers and begging for assistance from Mishibizhii's greatest foe. The important thing was not that one side would ever be the victor, but that everything would remain in balance—and they would feel "in control." In times such as when the pestilence visited them in the east, the time of evil practices at La Pointe described by Warren,[68] or the time when they were forced to give up their lands and settle on reservations, the world was out of balance and the Anishinaabeg felt very much out of control and at risk. Nevertheless, gradually the balance always returned, and with it, the Midewiwin in its positive aspects. Viewed from the perspective of the Anishinaabeg, Mishibizhii's role in the Midewiwin is not so anomalous as it may seem at first.

When the Midewiwin is considered from within the context of the Anishinaabe world view, it is clear that it is an integral part of this world view, rather than an appendage grafted from an alien culture. From the perspective of these narratives, contact with Euro-Americans was important, but it was not world-shattering—whatever the effects of disease, alcoholism, and the loss of their land may have been. Euro-Americans, along with some of their goods, and some of their views, were gradually incorporated into the Anishinaabe world view. It is, therefore, not surprising to find that explanations of the Midewiwin's origin and purpose began to take on accretions from the Euro-American culture. However, these accretions never altered the fundamental Anishinaabe underpinnings of the Midewiwin.

Euro-American Perspectives: The Search for Certainties

Early Euro-American observers represented a wide variety of beliefs concerning the nature of their world. Although many of them would have professed to be Christians, few, other than the missionaries, practised their beliefs with any diligence, since there were extremely few priests and ministers in the Great Lakes region until the late nineteenth century. Nevertheless, most Euro-Americans would have had a better knowledge of basic Christian beliefs than would the average nominal Christian today. While these beliefs would have varied considerably, depending upon the nature of the denomination, most Euro-Americans would have believed in a personal God who was both creator and the source of goodness, and the devil, who was the source of evil. Most believed in the natural sinfulness of humans, and the need to achieve "salvation" here on earth, so that one could reside for eternity in "heaven" after death.

Christians believed themselves to be the "People of the Book," for their beliefs were said to be contained in the writings of the Bible. And while all knowledge about how to lead a good life and achieve salvation could be found in the Bible, there were many disputes over the correct interpretation of what had been written. Members of each group believed themselves to have found the true interpretation and were anxious to convince all others of this "good news." Unlike Anishinaabe religion, which was open to a progressive revelation and was non-proselytizing, the adherents of different branches of Christianity each believed that theirs was the only true religion, and that only they would be spared the fires of eternal damnation.

Upon meeting Aboriginal people in the "new world," Euro-Americans were faced with the need to integrate them into their world view, just as the Anishinaabeg attempted to integrate the Wayaabishkiwed into theirs. Most Euro-Americans regarded these new people as "heathens," since they appeared never to have heard of the Christian gospel. Moreover, Aboriginal people were classed as "savages," since they lived in forests, which Euro-Americans found frightening, practised customs common to "wildmen," and appeared to have neither laws nor morals that conformed to Euro-American standards.[69] With the passage of time, many Euro-Americans came to believe that Aboriginal people had originally possessed a more highly developed civilization. Some, such as William Warren, suggested they were part of the lost tribes of Israel that had been banished. For Christians, Aboriginal people represented a constant reminder of the work that had yet to be accomplished in bringing God's word to the world, and of what could happen to those who repudiated the gospel. But the task of conversion was difficult. Aboriginal languages were unintelligible, so communication for most was, at best, second-hand through an interpreter. It must also be remembered that Euro-Americans encountered Aboriginal peoples on the latter's territory. While they might have outwardly held on to a belief in their inherent superiority, many Euro-Americans were no doubt frightened by the alien environment in which they found themselves. It should not be surprising, therefore, that early Euro-American descriptions of the Anishinaabeg and their religious ceremonies were strongly coloured by their own world view, and their limited understanding of Anishinaabe life. It would have been as difficult for Euro-Americans to comprehend such concepts as manidoo, miigis, bimaadiziwin, or the significance of drumming and the sweat lodge, as it was for the Anishinaabeg to grasp the meaning of "divine," "atonement," "trinity," or the significance of baptism or communion.[70]

A major problem in using Euro-American reports of the Midewiwin is that they usually referred to only a single aspect of the Midewiwin ceremonies the observer may have witnessed, or was particularly impressed with. Thus, what was described simply as a White Dog Feast, or a sweat lodge ceremony, may well have been part of the Midewiwin ceremonies—or it may have been a separate ceremony, depending upon the context in which it occurred. Since Midewiwin ceremonies usually took place over a period of several days, most observers would have had only brief glimpses of the entire event. Moreover, since observers often disapproved of "Indian" dancing and drumming, they made no effort to distinguish different types, and so often employed an arbitrary generic term for all reported occurrences. In a number of instances, for instance, what was described as loud drumming at "Waabanowiwin" ceremonies most likely took place at Midewiwin ceremonies, since the sound of the Mide water drum would have carried much further than the hand-held "tambourine" form of drum used at Waabanowiwin ceremonies. On the other hand, some ceremonies were described as Midewiwin simply because a payment of fees occurred. However, they could well have been Shaking Tent ceremonies, since Jiisakiiwininiwag were also "paid" by people who wanted their assistance in communicating with the manidoog.

Even more crucial to how we use these sources is the fact that few observers looked beyond the surface events to understand why the Ojibwa and their neighbours were performing these ceremonies.[71] Clothed in the righteousness of their own beliefs, they preferred to view such ceremonies as representing the work of primitive minds, when, in fact, the Midewiwin was more complex in structure than many of their own Christian ceremonies. Scholars, therefore, need to be as critical of Euro-American sources as they have been of Anishinaabe narratives when trying to understand the Midewiwin.

Was the Midewiwin an Indigenous Institution?

Early writers on the subject of the Midewiwin generally did not question whether it was a pre-contact or post-contact institution. The issue was only raised with the pioneering and controversial works by ethnohistorian Harold Hickerson in the 1960s, '70s, and '80s. Hickerson believed that the disruptive effects of European contact had significantly altered Aboriginal cultural expressions. Therefore, the issue of dating had special importance for him. Using an historiographic technique called "negative evidence," he concluded that the Midewiwin could not have existed prior to European contact because it had not been mentioned in any of the earliest documents.[72] Hickerson's conclusions have been accepted by many, though not all, Euro-American ethnohistorians. Many Ojibwa, however, consider his theories to be culturally arrogant as well as inaccurate.[73]

Jennifer Brown and Laura Peers have observed in the critical review attached to the revised edition of Hickerson's *The Chippewa and Their Neighbours* (1988 reprinted edition) that negative evidence does not offer a definitive and conclusive argument. This is particularly true with respect to the study of the Midewiwin if one broadens one's collection of sources to include scrolls and other artifacts. For instance, Mide artifacts collected by the Glenbow Museum strongly suggest that the Midewiwin was practised as far west as Saskatchewan during the nineteenth century, despite the fact that there are only scattered written references to this fact.

Even in the eighteenth century, when the first documents mentioned the Midewiwin by name or implication, most Euro-Americans had little comprehension of what they were trying to describe, and constantly confused or conflated the various Ojibwa ceremonies. Moreover, Hickerson was obliged to recognize that some of his nineteenth-century sources, such as the Protestant missionary William Boutwell, were biased in their statements about Ojibwa religion.[74] It is interesting to note that even though

Boutwell and his colleagues lived in what has been described as the "Midewiwin heartland," they made only a few references to it. If our history of the Midewiwin in the nineteenth century were based solely on these sources, the ceremony would have received only a passing notice! Yet Ojibwa narratives and Mide scrolls collected from this region during the nineteenth and twentieth centuries suggest that it was regularly practised and formed an integral part of Ojibwa community life.

Moreover, there is still room for further interpretation of the old sources. For instance, Hennepin, in his "A Continuation of the New Discovery," mentioned in passing that the people around the Great Lakes "believe that there is a Master of Life, as they call him, but hereof they make various applications; some of them have a lean Raven, which they carry always along with them, and which they say is the Master of their Life; others have an Owl, and some again a Bone, a Sea-Shell or some such thing."[75]

The miigis, in the form of a seashell, as has been seen, played a crucial role in both the oral traditions concerning the Midewiwin and the ceremonies themselves, and is not connected with any other Anishinaabe ceremony. It would seem likely that this chance remark indicates that some form of Midewiwin ceremonies was being practised at that time. Similarly, the remark concerning a use of a bone probably referred to a healing ceremony involving a Nenaandawiiwed (sucking bone doctor). Conversely, Hennepin's comments could well have been referring to the biinjigoosan (sacred medicine bundle) used in the Midewiwin. The skins of birds and animals were used for the different degrees, and the bundles contained several sacred objects, including bones and a miigis.

Hennepin then went on to note, "As for their Opinion concerning the Earth, they make use of a Name of a certain Genius, whom they call Micaboche, who has cover'd the whole Earth with water (as they imagine) and relate innumerable fabulous Tales, some of which have a Kind of analogy with the Universal Deluge."[76] In his work on the Midewiwin, Hoffman rightly made the connection in this quote with the Midewiwin origin myths in which Nanabozho gives the Midewiwin to the Anishinaabeg.

Hickerson chose to dwell at length on another description (from Jacques Marquette, a seventeenth-century French missionary explorer), which Hoffman had quoted: "When I arriv'd there, I was very glad to see a great Cross set up in the middle of the Village, adorn'd with several White Skins, Red Girdles, Bows and Arrows, which that good People had offer'd to the Great Manitou, to return him their Thanks for the care he had taken of them during the Winter, and that he granted them a prosperous Hunting.

Illustration 3: View of a 4th-degree Midewiwin Lodge. The roof has been removed in order to indicate the four Mide posts, including the 4th-degree cross that has been the subject of considerable controversy over whether it indicated a post-Christian influence. (From Hoffman, "Grand Medicine Society," 256.)

Manitou, is the Name they give in general to all Spirits whom they think to be above the Nature of Man."[77]

Hoffman had noted that, while Marquette appears to think that the cross was a Christian one, it really was a Midewiwin medicine pole of the fourth degree, which had been erected for entirely different reasons. This is discounted out of hand by Hickerson, who attempted to prove that the cross had, in fact, been left there by previous French missionaries.[78] Hickerson implied that the cross used as a mark of the fourth-degree Midewiwin had been appropriated from Christian sources. He did not consider that this symbol might already have meaning in Ojibwa cosmology. It is possible that the cross had been left by some French missionaries, since it was their practice to erect them in prominent places, while members of the Midewiwin who had been initiated into one of the degrees normally placed their medicine poles in secluded spots known only to them. Nevertheless, the practice of garlanding them with skins and ribbons, and painting them in different colours, is definitely related to all degrees of the Midewiwin. Moreover, there is another ancient tradition of erecting medicine poles beside houses in which the occupant had had a dream and the strength of the vision was in him or her. In the spring the owner would hold a feast, and the guests who wished a long life would bring tobacco and a garment, which they would tie to the pole.[79] The erection of decorated poles, in the form of crosses, or otherwise, was hardly new to the Anishinaabeg. Furthermore, the concept of four corners, sides, or directions was a fundamental feature of Ojibwa cosmology. Whether the cross in question was Christian does little to prove or disprove the antiquity of the Midewiwin itself.[80]

The third reason that Hickerson gave for considering the Midewiwin to be a post-contact institution was that "the payment in goods of non-Indian production as fees for instruction and initiation"[81] was an indication that the monied economy had influenced the conduct of the Midewiwin ceremony. As an economic determinist, Hickerson either ignored or made little attempt to understand the Anishinaabe world view, except in economic terms. Instead, he concentrated his analysis on the economic significance of gift-giving in the context of the fur trade. The interpretation completely ignores the fact that such gift-giving was integral to the Anishinaabe world view prior to contact with Euro-Americans, and extended beyond the Midewiwin to all aspects of Anishinaabe life that involved contact with the manidoog, including Shaking Tent ceremonies. The latter ceremonies certainly predated European contact. That such a wasteful attitude should have shocked the more materialist Euro-Americans is hardly surprising, but it should not cause us to interpret the practice in terms of "fees for service." While continued contact with growing numbers of Euro-Americans may have caused some Ojibwa gradually to adopt a more individualistic behaviour and to horde material goods, there is no concrete evidence that early Mideg (or others) kept for themselves all the presents given to them. If anything, they allowed for a sharing of goods. The question of whether the goods were Aboriginal or Euro-American in origin is seldom mentioned in either Anishinaabe or Euro-American sources. It would appear to have been of less concern to members of the Midewiwin than to followers of revitalization cult leaders such as the Delaware and Shawnee prophets.

The next reason Hickerson cited for a post-contact Midewiwin is the fact that "there were occult practices in the performance."[82] What he means precisely by this is uncertain. However, he was probably referring to the "shooting" and reviving of the candidate by the Mide officials during the initiation portion of the ceremonies, or he may have been alluding to an earlier part in the ceremonies when the Mide officials showed the candidate the contents of their medicine bundles, and explained the properties and merits of the various articles. They then employed a couple of "tests" that demonstrated the power of the Mideg, and assured everyone that the candidate was worthy. These tests usually involved a series of beads that were made to roll by themselves, as if animated, and small figurines that were made to move by themselves, as if possessed of a life of their own.[83]

Even as sympathetic an observer as Hoffman believed the latter test, in particular, to involve trickery to deceive members of the Midewiwin and visitors alike. Few Euro-American observers, no matter how sympathetic or objective, have been willing to accept the possibility that inanimate objects could be possessed of a life force, or, barring that, that the actions could be taken as symbolic. Nevertheless, it is puzzling why Hickerson should have singled out such practices in the Midewiwin as evidence of outside influences, since almost all Anishinaabe ceremonies used similar practices to demonstrate the power of the manidoog.

Hickerson's final point was that "the very existence of an organized priesthood seems improbable as an aboriginal institution."[84] He implies that "primitive" Aboriginal people could never have "developed" to such an organized stage on their own. This is consistent with his belief that the Midewiwin occurred as a result of complex forms of social organization, which, in turn, were the result of the Ojibwa's central role in the fur trade. From a materialist, evolutionary viewpoint, this explanation may sound plausible, but it shows a lack of understanding of the Ojibwa world view and the role this world view played in Anishinaabe society.[85] Suffice it to say at this point that the organizational structure of the Midewiwin, including the roles of various officials, was tightly interwoven into the fabric of Anishinaabe society and world view.

There is no evidence in any of the early Midewiwin narratives or rituals that gives any indication that the Midewiwin had developed in reaction to earlier beliefs and practices, that it was influenced by the fur trade or other aspects of Euro-American culture, or that it contained any features usually associated with an established priesthood, such as were found in more sedentary societies. On the contrary, the evidence indicates that all types of individuals, who had received power from whatever source, were incorporated into the Midewiwin. The symbolism of the rituals and beliefs continued to be consistent with beliefs of other, similar, Aboriginal cultures.[86] While individual Ojibwa could progressively gain more power in their efforts to live a "good life," and while this involved a complicated set of rituals, and considerable payment of goods, there was no organized secret society set aside from the rest of Ojibwa society. Power continued to reside in the individuals in Ojibwa society, not in the Midewiwin Society.[87]

In using nineteenth-century sources to understand pre-contact forms of Anishinaabe life and world view, as Hickerson recognized, scholars may commit the error, implicit in "upstreaming," of assuming that today's institutions have existed forever. My argument is not to suggest that changes in the Midewiwin have not occurred. Rather, it is that the changes were incorporated into the basic structure of the Ojibwa world view. The result was not a radical break with the past, but was, instead, part of a gradual adaptation process, which had been going on long before the arrival of Europeans.

The arguments of anthropologist Karl Schlesier and historian Richard White concerning the world of the Anishinaabeg and Euro-Americans in the late seventeenth and eighteenth centuries are much more convincing than those of Hickerson.[88] Looking at the same documents as did Hickerson, Schlesier and White saw in them the description of a society of refugee villages under great stress, rather than Hickerson's view of a strong, vigorous society of large, stable villages.[89] The villages that the documents describe, they argue, were composed of a diverse group of people fleeing the attacks of the Iroquois, or the ravages of epidemics. Their old world had been destroyed; most of their old hunting and fishing territories were forfeited, numerous of their kin had lost their lives, and now they were forced to seek new lives in conjunction with strangers whom they neither knew nor trusted.

While Schlesier and White may overstate their case, the world they describe is truer to the documentary evidence than the version offered by Hickerson.[90] The period following the Iroquois destruction of the Huron Confederacy in the southern Ontario peninsula in the 1650s brought French support to the Anishinaabeg, but also a new danger. The epidemics that had helped to destroy the Huron nation now threatened to wreak havoc on the refugees from the Iroquois. Moreover, the Great Lakes environment forced changes on the refugees, for not only were horticulture and large-scale fishing limited to a few locations, but the concentration of large numbers of people put severe strains on big-game resources in the surrounding area. Nevertheless, the Saulteurs (Ojibwa), along with their Ottawa (Odawa) and Huron (Wyandot) neighbours, did survive, and by the 1670s were actively engaged once more in trading furs to the French. By the next decade they had begun to act as middlemen with the Sioux.

By 1700 the tide had definitely changed, and after several disastrous defeats, the Iroquois had been forced to sue for peace. At least some of the refugees could return to their former lands. Nevertheless, historians now generally agree that the period of the diaspora contributed to the disintegration of many of these tribal groups.[91] Most severely affected were the Huron, Winnebago, and, to a lesser extent, the Menominee, Ottawa, and Potawatomi. Although most of these groups did emerge with new forms of social integration, many of their traditional cultural institutions disintegrated. The Ojibwa probably were least affected by the tremendous upheaval, since their society had been the least structured and their numbers had been widely dispersed. Nevertheless, the experiences they had faced, and would continue to face in the decades to come, placed considerable strain on their society. In some important ways, they, too, emerged from the experience a different people from before.

If one accepts that the world in which the Anishinaabeg lived during the late seventeenth and eighteenth centuries was torn asunder, it is tempting to look at the Midewiwin in terms of a "revitalization movement," as Schlesier has done,[92] or as an example of a "crisis cult," as Julia Harrison did several years earlier.[93] However, such definitions imply that the Anishinaabeg were not only reacting to new and external problems facing them, but that they drew the majority of Midewiwin beliefs and practices from outside their own tradition.

The essential elements of the Midewiwin were clearly elaborations of traditional Anishinaabe beliefs and practices. What seems likely is that the role of traditional healers and diviners took on a greater importance, and healing ceremonies became more complex, as the Anishinaabeg attempted to deal with those forces that threatened their existence. Gradually, the Midewiwin healing ceremony in response to specific illness of individuals was transformed into a communal ceremony in which all those who had been initiated demonstrated their power to overcome the increasing numbers of maladies confronting them.[94] Through this "renewal" of their powers, the Anishinaabeg were reminded of the obligations placed on them, and they were reassured that the powers received from the manidoog could and would allow them to survive any new assaults on their way of life.

Any "revitalization" that occurred was within the context of traditional Anishinaabe beliefs, unlike revitalization movements such as those of the Delaware and Shawnee prophets, whose teachings represented a major shift from traditional beliefs and often placed them in opposition to traditional religious practices such as the Midewiwin. Nevertheless, it should be noted that Mide elders also began to distinguish Anishinaabe society from that of the Euro-Americans in response to the increasingly aggressive stance of the latter.

Although the Midewiwin, as it was described by early Euro-American observers, laid stress on the knowledge of rituals in obtaining power, visions continued to be an essential element of the process. There was far less difference between the role of Jiisakiiwininiwag and Mideg in Anishinaabe society than there was between that of Catholic priests and Protestant ministers in Euro-American society. While the difference between traditional religious leaders and the leaders of revitalization movements was more pronounced, even the revitalization figures functioned within the context of traditional Anishinaabe beliefs regarding the transferral of knowledge and power from the manidoog to the Anishinaabeg. This is evident in Tanner's description of Manito-o-geezhik, a minor Ojibwa prophet who preached a newly revealed message from the "Great Spirit." Tanner explained that, while he was sceptical, such messages were received with great respect by his Ojibwa and Ottawa colleagues. The prophet called upon his brethren to give up war, thievery, defrauding, lying, and drinking alcohol, which, Tanner observed, had a salutary effect on their conduct for several years.[95] It appears that contemporary observers and later scholars have tended to emphasize the differences, and have missed the context of traditional beliefs that served as the basis of the Anishinaabe world view long after the community appeared to adopt Euro-American beliefs and institutions.

Before leaving the problem of the origin of the Midewiwin, one might consider the question of where and among whom it originated. There is almost unanimity among scholars that the Midewiwin originated among the Ojibwa or the clan-based groups that preceded them. Such beliefs are based on the fact that the earliest Euro-American records refer to the ceremony as practised among the Saulteurs (Ojibwa),[96] and on the fact that other Algonquian tribal groups that practised the Midewiwin appear to have considered that the Ojibwa gave the rites to them. Nevertheless, at the time of the Midewiwin's institutionalization, neither the Ojibwa nor most of the other Algonquian groups had strong tribal identities. Thus, it is more likely that the Midewiwin was originally an Anishinaabe healing ceremony.

It is certainly possible that the institutionalization of the ceremony may have first developed among the Saulteurs, and spread from them to other Algonquians who considered themselves Anishinaabeg. However, one should not assume that because a strong tribal component developed in the Midewiwin teachings in the late eighteenth and nineteenth centuries, the tribal component was always dominant. It is much more likely that various refugee groups that came together in large "multi-tribal" villages viewed the Midewiwin ceremonies as a reaffirmation of their ability to survive their trials.[97] While each of the disparate groups of refugees was bound together by family ties and social structures that differentiated them from other groups, most shared a common language base and world view. Most also participated in loose alliances, in which intermarriage was encouraged.[98] All had similar beliefs regarding their relationship among themselves and other creatures, including manidoog. All also believed in the culture hero and trickster figure, Nanabozho (although his name and characteristics varied somewhat), and all groups had similar earth-diver narratives regarding the creation and re-creation of the world. Since they also shared similar ideas regarding the origin and cure of disease, it should not be surprising to find reports of the Midewiwin being practised by the majority of these groups, plus several neighbouring tribes, during the late seventeenth, the eighteenth, and early nineteenth centuries.

However, since the Midewiwin died out more rapidly among many of those groups, it is the Ojibwa form of the ceremonies of the nineteenth and twentieth centuries that most of the surviving documents describe. Many of the Ojibwa materials, including Warren's published history of the Ojibwa, suggest that the Midewiwin's place of origin was Chequamegon (La Pointe). At least one modern scholar, Selwyn Dewdney, comes to the same conclusion.[99] While Chequamegon certainly became an important centre in the early growth of the Midewiwin, and in what appears to have been the gradual development of the concept of the "Ojibwa nation" during the latter part of the eighteenth and early nineteenth centuries, it cannot be singled out as the birthplace of the Midewiwin. In most of the origin and migration narratives, the origin of the Anishinaabeg and the birth of the Midewiwin began at a point far to the east. Therefore, one must look farther back in the Ojibwa past than their first settlement at Chequamegon—regardless of its pivotal role in later Ojibwa history.[100]

Indeed, it makes little sense to look for a precise place, or a single historical event that marks the origin of the Midewiwin. While most Ojibwa narratives agree that the origin took place in the east, they make no attempt to identify the precise geographical location, and note only that it occurred "in the time of our Grandfathers." In other words, the Midewiwin narratives were aadizookaanag, or sacred stories. As such, they dealt primarily in eternal truths rather than in geographic or historical truths.

FOUR

Midewiwin Ceremonies: Documentary Fragments from Euro-American Observers

Written descriptions of Midewiwin ceremonies by Euro-Americans in the eighteenth century were limited for some time to brief, enigmatic passages. Although the testimonies become more complete and more frequent in the nineteenth century, usually they continued to be no more than partial and disjointed. These fragments provide only glimpses of the ceremonies as seen and interpreted by a range of observers. Nevertheless, by viewing these fragments within their historical and social context, while at the same time using what we already know about Ojibwa religion and Ojibwa sacred narratives, it is possible to piece together the various descriptions and identify the essential components of the Midewiwin, as well as provide some tentative explanations for the variations in the ceremonies described.

An Account of the Midewiwin during the French Regime

The earliest detailed description of what commonly became known as the Midewiwin is contained in a 1710 letter by Antoine Denis Raudot, Intendant of New France.[1] Since Raudot had only second-hand knowledge of the Aboriginal peoples of the Great Lakes, it is generally believed that he relied

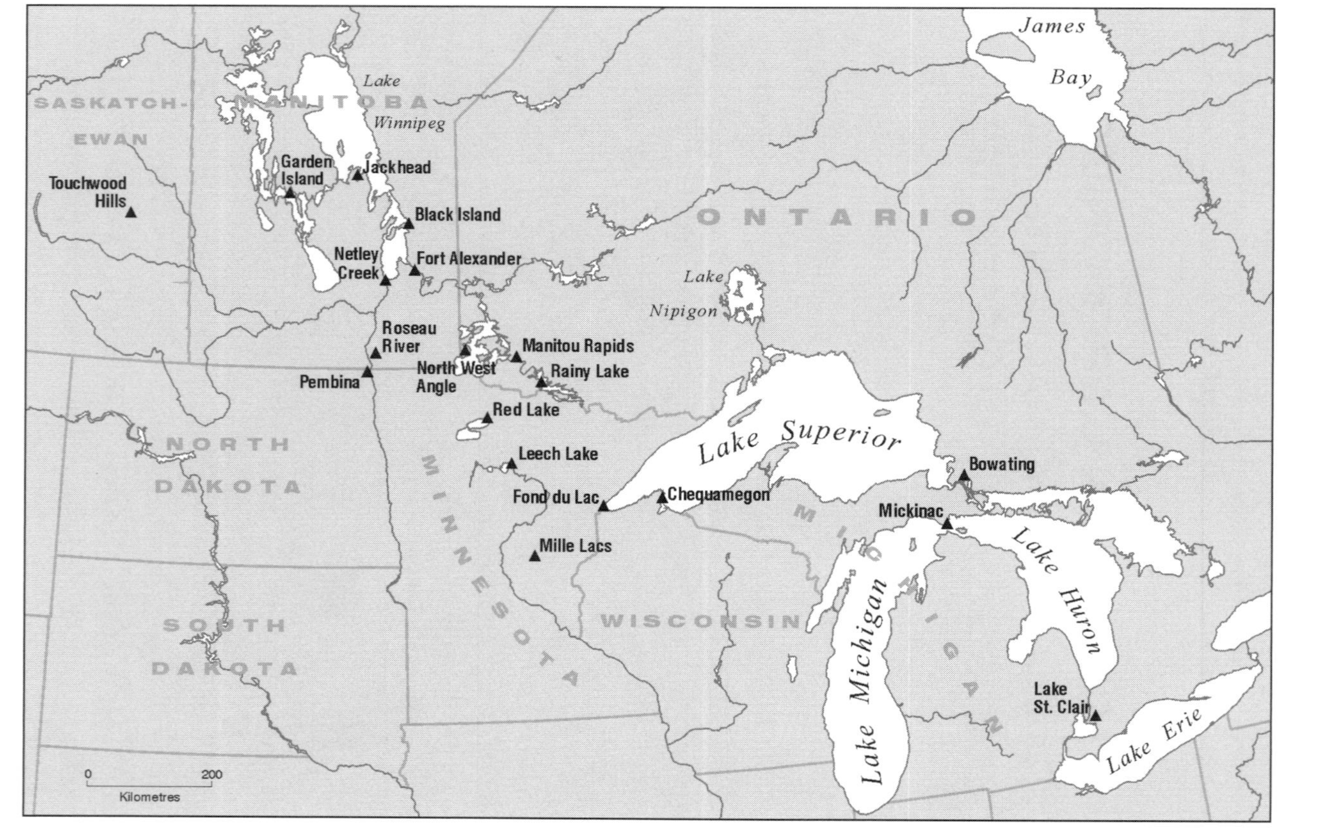

Map 2: Selected Sites of Midewiwin Ceremonies Noted during the Pre-Treaty Period.

on the memoirs of the soldier, Louis de la Porte de Louvigny, for his information. Some of his letters were published by Margry in his *Découvertes,*[2] and an English translation is in the appendix of Kinietz's *The Indians of the Western Great Lakes 1615-1760.*[3] Raudot was writing for a French audience so his descriptions were couched in terms and set in a context with which his audience would be familiar. His description is important, since both the language he used to describe the Saulteur (Ojibwa) "Jugglers," and the structure of the ceremony, prefigure most of the descriptions that follow until the present day.[4]

Raudot began by differentiating the Saulteurs from neighbouring tribes:

> Besides the dreams, dances, sacrifices, and other superstitious notions which these Saulteurs have, like the other tribes of which I have already spoken, they go further and act like our charlatans in France who travel through the towns. They distribute medicine and, so they say, they cause the people who are not friends of theirs to die by their spells; this is believed by the other Indians, for, among all these tribes, there is not a single old Indian man or woman who does not have some secret of medicine, real or pretended.
>
> The Saulteurs learn how to make people fear them by their talk, and, to convince still others more easily, they arrange with one or more persons to play the part of a dying man, a dead man, and a living man, according to what may be necessary to prove their powers.
>
> Then they make known to the public, by a harangue, that they will dance the medicine dance[5] in the hut of such and such a person and that the jugglers will show the amazing effects of their knowledge and powers. Long before the time and to the sound of the drum and with invocations to demons, they prepare the remedies or magic arts which they pretend to employ. Then, on the appointed night, they get ready their paraphernalia, consisting of a number of small bags or packets made of bark, in which there are powders and the bones of animals, and the skin of an otter, which they cause to move or jump in accordance with the movements of their bodies and their chichigoues [rattles].
>
> When all the people are assembled, one of the jugglers begins a great speech in their praise, boasting of their knowledge and their power over the life and death of men. The others applaud him; and to begin to prove what he has said, they cast some of their powder on the persons who are devoted to their interests, who immediately fall and throw themselves about like men possessed, foaming at the mouth and uttering cries. The jugglers, for their part, augment their own cries and throw more powder upon them. The dying man pretends to be dead; they carry him, they

> turn him over, but he seems unconscious and motionless. Then it is that the jugglers, triumphing in the surprise they see on the faces of everybody, shout that it is nothing; that life and death lie in their hands; that although they have taken his life, they are about to give it back to him with their remedies. During this time a dead silence is observed by all, and they watch intently. To effect this, they blow upon him with another medicine, and, invoking their Manito, they call upon the dead man, who is only dead because he is willing to be, and who, to finish the performance, gradually revives as he was before this trickery. He raises himself and then sits down and tells the assembly tales and fables about the other world, which he has seen.[6]

Raudot and his source or sources seem to have been impressed by the power that the Saulteur "jugglers" enjoyed among their own people and neighbouring tribes. The use of "medicine" to cure or kill would have been common among the other Aboriginal peoples whom the French encountered, but Raudot placed more emphasis on the Saulteur "jugglers" than he did on similar religious figures in other tribes. Yet, he gave no indication that their "medicine dance" was a new phenomenon; in fact, it can be argued that since no comment was made as to the ceremony being a recent phenomenon, Raudot believed it to have existed prior to French contact.[7]

It should also be noted that in an earlier letter (#31), Raudot had also described what came to be known as a Shaking Tent ceremony, in which he claimed "jugglers" spoke to the devil in order to be able to forecast the future—something he reluctantly agreed that they sometimes did quite well. These same "jugglers," he explained, were usually physicians who were much feared since they could also use witchcraft and spells to cause injury and death. We are left with no indication as to the connection between the descriptions of the two types of "jugglers," though it would appear that there was no competition between them, as is sometimes inferred by other observers. It is likely that they co-existed, or, in some cases, were the same individuals using different powers and performing different roles.

The "medicine dance" ceremony that Raudot described appears to have had more of the characteristics of a curing ceremony intended to help a sick or injured individual, when other forms of curing had failed, than of the complex communal ceremony for the initiation of new members, as was often described by subsequent observers.[8] As such, the rituals that Raudot described are more limited than those found in other documents. In fact, the description is limited even if the ceremony was a healing ceremony intended for a single individual. Frances Densmore's description of such a ceremony, for example, included the administration of brewed medicine to the sick person, and emphasized the significance of the medicine pole that was placed in the lodge. Such details may have been left out by Raudot's source, or by him, or they could reflect an earlier form of the ceremony.

Nevertheless, Raudot's descriptions are surprisingly complete. They include the "shooting, death, and revival" of the sick person or initiate—which was a central ritual of the Midewiwin.[9] And Raudot's descriptions also include the use of medicine bags, including an otter-skin bag, which was usually employed by first-degree Mideg. It is difficult to say whether Raudot's explanation of the actual "shooting" ritual described an earlier, less complex form, or whether this simply reflects the writer's own interpretation of the ritual, based on the explanations of his informants. Two points are worthy of note: first, the powerful ingredient in Raudot's description appears to be the medicine powder, rather than the medicine bag or the miigis shell. This seems to place Raudot's version closer to the method in which powder is applied in other Ojibwa medicine ceremonies. Secondly, Raudot appears to have combined the "shooting" ritual, which was limited to participation by the Mideg and the patient or candidate, with a later "duelling" ritual, in which all members of the Midewiwin society demonstrated the power of their medicine bags to kill and cure.

Like most Euro-American observers, Raudot believed all the participants to be charlatans who were attempting to deceive their fellow Saulteurs, so he may have simply been emphasizing those aspects that appeared to support this interpretation. While the description regarding participants is unclear, it is likely that the only observers would have been members of the sick person's family and perhaps close clan members, since the ceremony (as Raudot indicates) took place in the sick person's lodge rather than in a large, specially constructed Midewiwin lodge. The "speech" by the recovered person following the rituals would have been quite unusual. The Ojibwa had theories regarding life after death, but, unlike Christians, their beliefs and the Midewiwin ceremonies were primarily concerned with life in this world. Normally, speeches in communal Midewiwin ceremonies were made by a Mide official early in the ceremony. He would explain how Nanabozho had given the Midewiwin to the Ojibwa people so they might learn how to overcome the obstacles that faced them, and live a long and productive life. Since medicine ceremonies for individuals were often held for people who were expected to die (and thus were intended to help the survivors, and the ill person to make the transition into the next world), speeches might well be made, but they would have more closely resembled Euro-American funeral elegies, within the context of Midewiwin beliefs and practices.[10] This suggests that Raudot either confused the two ceremonies and combined portions of both into one, and/or added elements to serve his own purposes.

Certainly, by the time of Duncan Cameron's and Peter Grant's 1804 accounts,[11] the emphasis was on the communal ceremony and its various degrees of membership. In this form of the Midewiwin, both the victory over death symbolized by the "shooting" ceremony, and the passing on of knowledge of the healing properties of plants, continued to play a central part in the ceremonies as described by Euro-Americans.

This initial description of the Midewiwin (as yet unnamed) by Raudot was written during a period some writers have designated as a "golden age" for the Ojibwa. Iroquois forces had been repulsed at Bowating and the Ojibwa and their allies had signed a treaty with the Iroquois in 1703. Groups of Ojibwa and/or Ottawa began to re-occupy Manitoulin Island, as well as the Saginaw area around Detroit, and parts of southern Ontario. Previously, a number of bands had returned to the region southwest of the Great Lakes, following an alliance with the Sioux in the mid-1680s that granted them access. While the Ojibwa had lost some of their numbers to the wars, and many more to diseases and alcohol brought by the French, it must have appeared to them that the power of their spiritual leaders was indeed strong, and that bimaadiziwin, or a long life, which they sought, could still be obtained by those who followed the precepts and obtained the powers granted them through the rituals of the Midewiwin.

Challenges to the Ojibwa Way of Life

Such, of course, was not to be the case. In the following decades, the world of the Ojibwa underwent a number of dramatic changes that challenged their cosmological beliefs and practices. Within years, hostilities had broken out with their Algonquian neighbours, the Fox (Mesquakie), who were disrupting the lucrative French trade with the Sioux. The brutal war eventually ended, with French assistance, in the virtual destruction of the Fox as a separate people in 1740.[12]

In the 1730s, before the victory over the Fox, the truce with the Sioux was broken and hostilities with them resumed. Angered by the opening of the French-Cree trade in the Boundary Waters area, the Sioux murdered a son of Pierre La Vérendrye and a number of colleagues at Fort St. Charles on Lake of the Woods. In response, northern bands of Ojibwa joined the Cree and moved against northern Sioux communities such as Red Lake, from Ojibwa villages on the northern shore of Lake Superior, from Rainy

Lake, and from the Lake of the Woods region.[13] In addition, other bands of Ojibwa had begun to spread out from the Chequamegon region to the Fond du Lac region. Following the St. Louis River, they attacked the Sioux in their villages in the Mille Lacs region and began to hunt and trap in the lands drained by the St. Croix River, which the Sioux claimed as their own. Since the struggle lasted well into the nineteenth century, it serves as an important backdrop for any study of the Midewiwin. Even though there are few surviving documents related to the Midewiwin during the eighteenth century, nineteenth-century migration scrolls provide a record of how the Ojibwa remembered those years in which they had gradually pushed the numerically superior Sioux westward.

Although hostilities with the Sioux played a central role in the life of many Ojibwa who lived around Lake Superior and the Boundary Waters, they were but one of the events that affected this widely dispersed people. Other, more easterly groups of Ojibwa in the Michigan peninsula became involved in the colonial wars of the French and English in the 1750s. Charles Langlade, a Métis trader from Michilimackinac, led contingents of Ottawa, Ojibwa, Potawatomi, and Menominee into battle against English positions in regions ranging from the Ohio Valley to upper-state New York. It was in a losing cause, however, as the English triumphed in the end, and English traders and officials began to replace some of the French who had lived among and intermarried with the Ojibwa for generations. The *mekatewikwanaie* ("black robes"), or French priests, who had lived among the Aboriginal people in the region also left at this time. They had not been particularly successful in their efforts to convert many Aboriginal peoples to their world view, although some of their beliefs seem to have made an impression. In an article entitled "Blackrobe and Shaman," ethnologist Gertrude Kurath argues that the priests' fluency in Aboriginal languages contributed to their success (limited though it was), and accounts for the fact that even after their departure, many of their ideas continued to form part of the Anishinaabe world view.[14]

It was under these trying circumstances that in 1762 a Delaware man named Neolin, from the village of Tuscarawas,[15] had a vision wherein he journeyed to the spirit world and met the Master of Life, who commanded him to exhort his people to cease the use of English goods, drunkenness, wars, polygamy, and medicine songs. Word of his vision spread beyond the Delaware proper to other Algonquian groups. While few Ojibwa took up his message directly, many of them were alienated by the state of cultural disruption that existed and began actively to search for new approaches to the path of life.

Shortly after, when the Ottawa war chief named Pontiac began to rally a multitude of Algonquian and Iroquois tribes against the English, large numbers of Ojibwa joined his forces. Despite Pontiac's eventual defeat, most of the Aboriginal people in the regions of the Great Lakes, the Ohio Valley, and upper-state New York continued to resist intrusions by Euro-American colonists onto their lands.[16] During the American War of Independence, many of them fought as allies with the English against the revolutionists. In the period after the war, the influence of the Iroquois Confederacy declined, and the locus of power shifted to a western confederacy of Algonquian tribes that attempted to forestall the advance of Euro-Americans into their territories. The majority of Ojibwa were not directly involved but it was clear that their lands, too, would soon be threatened.

Once again, in the early years of the nineteenth century, the Aboriginal people around the Great Lakes rallied around religious and political leaders in an attempt to stem the tide of American expansion. On this occasion, it was two Shawnee half-brothers who provided the leadership.[17] One of them, Tecumseh, was a chief who demonstrated great skill as a political and military leader, inflicting a series of defeats upon the American forces. His half-brother, Lalawethika, had spent much of his life as an alcoholic.

However, all this changed in the fall of 1804, when Lalawethika received a number of visions in which he claimed to have been visited by the Master of Life, who allowed him a glimpse of paradise, which awaited the virtuous, and the continuous fires where evildoers were forced to dwell. Overcome, Lalawethika changed his name to Tenskwatawa (Open Door), renounced his evil ways, and set out to preach a doctrine that would renew the rituals of the Shawnees and their neighbours—thus providing them with the strength to overcome the problems that beset them. Tenskwatawa's message was not simply one of returning to the past. Although he called on all Aboriginal people to give up alcohol and many aspects of Euro-American material culture, he also told them to give up their traditional ceremonies, dances, and medicine bundles. This was not as contradictory as it might appear, since Aboriginal people knew from the sacred narratives that there had been numerous instances in the past wherein the power needed to survive in times of crisis was provided through the granting of new ceremonies. Many Ojibwa believed his message that the current crisis posed by the adoption of Euro-American customs and goods, and the misdeeds of many of the Aboriginal people (including their leaders), could only be overcome by new leaders who would receive power through new rituals.

Even if some of these rituals (such as public confessions) pointed to Christian influences, his message clearly called for the separation of Aboriginals and Americans, based on the belief that the two groups had been created separately. Where Tenskwatawa differed most significantly from traditional leaders was his claim of exclusive personal authority, coupled with his campaign to root out opponents whom he branded as "witches." At first his message was well received by many Ojibwa, including some prominent Mide leaders. However, when it became evident that he lacked the necessary power to defeat the American soldiers, Tenskwatawa's support collapsed and many of his followers returned to their traditional beliefs and rituals.[18]

Another factor had important implications for the Ojibwa. Tecumseh, along with many followers, became allies with the British in the War of 1812-1814 between Britain and the United States. The Ojibwa found themselves divided, as most of the northeastern bands supported the British, while the more westerly bands remained neutral or supported the Americans. The western bands were more concerned about their struggles with the Sioux than about the Euro-Americans, while those to the east were already facing the influx of American settlers, whom they saw as the more important enemy. When the war ended, the Aboriginal allies of the British had no reason to feel that they had "lost" the struggle, but they soon found themselves abandoned by their British allies, and powerless to stop the American juggernaut of soldiers and settlers that was slowly pushing westward. In both Upper Canada, where the British Indian Department became involved in establishing "reserves" where Aboriginal people could be "civilized," and the United States, where the movement to "remove" all Aboriginal people to lands west of the Mississippi was being implemented, colonial agencies and missionary groups made vigorous efforts to radically change the lifestyle of the Ojibwa and other Aboriginal peoples in preparation for their assimilation.

Meanwhile, the struggle between the Ojibwa and the Sioux continued unabated, despite the efforts of American authorities to broker a peace settlement. Small bands of Ojibwa engaged the numerically superior Sioux in a series of skirmishes. While the Ojibwa frequently were the victors, their life on the "frontier" was particularly precarious, since they had to be constantly on guard against a possible attack while at the same time attempting to trap furs and feed themselves during a period of diminishing resources.[19]

Nineteenth-Century Euro-American Accounts of the Midewiwin

It was, therefore, an unsettling time for the Ojibwa who lived along the shores and to the southwest of Lake Superior. They undoubtedly felt that their world was getting "out of control." They would have been most anxious to secure the protection of manidoog who would give them the power to once again attain their goal of the "good life." These concerns are clearly evident in a speech made by Flat Mouth (Eshkebugecoshe), the head chief of the Pillager band of Ojibwa, and Mide leader, to French geographer Joseph Nicollet on the occasion of the latter's visit in the 1830s. In it Flat Mouth gave vent to his feelings that his people were losing control of their lives:

> We are endlessly told to bury the war hatchet, and if we dig it up we are threatened with rods and ropes, or with being placed under the ground, *we* the *Missinabes*,[20] the Eagles, the Bears [totems], free in our own forests. . . .
>
> Thus the Americans plan to treat us as they treat their black people. . . . I am not an animal. I am not like those in the East whom they call their children and whom they treat like three or six-year-olds, rod in their hand. They purchased their lands, and now they hold them prisoner and treat them as slaves.[21]

Certainly, by the time Nicollet lived among them in the 1830s, the Pillagers and neighbouring bands of Ojibwa felt threatened. Nevertheless, they were a resourceful people who, in the past, had been able to rely on their military and negotiating skills.[22] The 1825 Treaty of Prairie du Chien, while not putting an end to hostilities with the Sioux, did recognize the Ojibwa claim to large sections of territory that had formerly been occupied by their enemy. Although many of the Ojibwa were suspicious of the American promises, they had eventually agreed to sign the treaty. The American presence was thus recognized, although the Ojibwa had not yet given up hope that the new arrivals could be resisted. Since it appeared that few human allies would come to their aid (though Flat Mouth did try to get Nicollet to serve as an intermediary to the French), their main hope would have been in obtaining "blessings" from powerful manidoog, which would give them the power to persevere against their enemies. The Midewiwin and its component parts continued to be the principal means by which such power was secured. Although the Midewiwin was primarily concerned with helping individuals achieve bimaadiziwin, the Ojibwa also used it to strengthen their collective health as a people. Nicollet, for instance, noted Flat Mouth's invitation to Mide members to a special sweat lodge ceremony before he embarked on a journey to obtain ammunition from the British trading posts for use in their ongoing struggle with the Sioux.

The prime purpose of Nicollet's American travels in the 1830s had been to search for the source of the Mississippi River, and later to carry out cartographic surveys for the American government. These brought him into the middle of the territory contested by the Ojibwa and Sioux—and gave him the opportunity to live among the Ojibwa for a number of years.

Educated by the Jesuits in mathematics, and a devout Catholic, Nicollet was at first glance an unlikely individual to take an interest in Ojibwa religious ceremonies. Nevertheless, he appears to have been able to suspend his preconceptions and enter into the life of the Ojibwa with more ease than most Euro-Americans. Martha Bray, the editor of Nicollet's works, has suggested that the Ojibwa accepted him because they recognized that he was sincere, or, perhaps, they saw in him a possible messenger to their old ally, the French king.[23] Nevertheless, Nicollet's relationships with the Ojibwa were not without problems. The local missionary William Boutwell, in a letter to the secretary of the American Board of Commissioners for Foreign Missions (ABCFM), described how Nicollet had reported some hostile remarks made by a group of Ojibwa about Major Taliafero, the Indian Agent. Taliafero confronted Flat Mouth the next time he visited and, because of his rude remarks, refused to give him ammunition. The Ojibwa were furious with the missionaries, whom they believed at first to have spread the rumour.[24] Such an incident cannot but have weakened Nicollet's relations with Flat Mouth, although he did maintain close personal relations with other Ojibwa individuals.

Nicollet stayed for a period with William Boutwell at Leech Lake, where he met Flat Mouth. He also encountered Matchi Gabow (sometimes called Stirring Man or Great Speaker), who served as Flat Mouth's oshkaabewis, calling together the Pillagers for civil and religious functions, and acting as a spokesman in their dealings with Euro-Americans.[25] During this time Nicollet began his friendship with Chagobay (Shagobai), one of the members of Flat Mouth's band. Chagobay was to serve as his main informant on the Midewiwin. It was quite unusual for Euro-Americans to be taken into such confidence regarding the Midewiwin ceremony; usually, such knowledge was available only to members and candidates awaiting initiation. The appearance of missionaries such as Boutwell was greeted by the majority of Pillagers and other bands with considerable hostility. ABCFM reports are full of incidents wherein members of the Midewiwin forced "praying Indians" to join in the Midewiwin ceremonies, trampled their crops, and

Illustration 4: Niganibines, Mide leader and hereditary chief of the Pillager band of the Leech Lake Ojibwa. Frances Densmore described the Midewiwin ceremony that was held for Niganibines at the time of his death. Niganibines's father (Eshkebugecoshe) was the powerful nineteenth-century Pillager chief and Mide who met with Joseph Nicollet and William Warren. Both men were known as Flat Mouth by the Americans. (Courtesy Minnesota Historical Society, E97.IN/r14.)

killed their cattle.[26] It is not surprising, therefore, that Nicollet noted that Chagobay had to undergo a special ceremony to be excused for his breach of trust in providing information regarding the Midewiwin to an outsider. The incident was, no doubt, much more serious than Nicollet implied, although Chagobay's punishment could have been even more severe. [27]

Nicollet's notes on the customs of the Ojibwa carry the mark of his scientific training, particularly his attention to detail and the accuracy of his terminology. He was not a trained linguist, and his work sometimes shows the effects of his idiosyncratic attempts at transliteration, but he was among the first Euro-Americans to attempt to use Ojibwa terms, rather than English or French ones, when describing Ojibwa culture and religion.[29] With the exception of a few brief accounts, such as those by the Nor'wester Peter Grant in 1804, and the brief description and songs in John Tanner's captivity narrative, which were first published in 1830, Nicollet's extended study was the first detailed description of the Midewiwin by a European since Raudot's work in the early eighteenth century.[30]

Although Nicollet had intended to publish the results of his scientific and ethnological research, he died before he was able to prepare his papers for publication. The unedited ethnological portions were later published by his American counterpart, Henry R. Schoolcraft, as part of the latter's massive work on American Aboriginal people—with no mention of the original author.[31] It was only in 1970 that Nicollet's original manuscripts were edited and published under his own name. As a result, none of the early ethnologists who wrote on the Midewiwin refer to Nicollet or his work. This is unfortunate, since the approaches of Nicollet and Schoolcraft were very different, both in their methodology and in their empathy with their subject.

The Midewiwin ceremonies described by Nicollet took place over a period of ten to fourteen days.[32] He does not make any claims to having attended all the ceremonies; Chagobay, his Ojibwa informant, was usually able to place the rituals within their proper context for him.[33] Thus, for the first time, we have a document that describes the initiation rituals new candidates underwent before becoming members of the Midewiwin. Nicollet's description allows us to identify a number of distinct elements, which can then be compared with subsequent accounts in order to determine the extent to which the ceremony changed over time and from place to place.

Before an initiation ceremony could be held, the prospective member had to be sponsored by a relative or friend who had had a dream or vision indicating that "the person was not well, that something was opposing his or her existence."[34] The proposed candidate (or his surrogate in the case of the very young or very ill) then prepared a feast and invited four Mide officials, stating his wish to become a member.[35] The following three days were taken up by sweat lodge ceremonies, which were attended by four more Mideg. If the individual was accepted by the Mideg as a candidate, a date was chosen several months hence for the ceremony proper (if the person's condition was not too serious), thus giving time for the individual to begin his or her instructions.

Nicollet was the first Euro-American observer to take account of the sweat lodge ceremony (*madoodiswan*), in relation to the Ojibwa "medicine" ceremonies. He described the construction of the lodge, the laying out of branches that serve as seats, and the bringing of hot stones, which were sprinkled with water. Nicollet was also aware of the religious significance of the ceremony, noting that the celebrants smoked, sang, and prayed each time they participated. Each sweat lodge was held in conjunction with a feast hosted by the person who had called for the madoodiswan.[36]

The second stage of the person's induction into the Midewiwin usually began in the spring when the Ojibwa were gathered in large groups to fish and make maple sugar, following their dispersal into small groups during winter to hunt for game. At this time of the year, ceremonies such as the Midewiwin, Waabanowiwin,[37] and Jiisakiiwin were held. These "religious" ceremonies were held in conjunction with other ceremonies, dances, and games. While they served quite different functions from a Euro-American perspective, all these activities were intimately connected in Ojibwa society. All had a "religious" aspect in that they were concerned with improving the chances of achieving bimaadiziwin. All had developed originally from a vision or dream, in which a powerful manidoo had promised assistance to those who followed the proper ways. Moreover, all these activities provided a social outlet through which the Ojibwa could renew old ties and forge new ones, and they offered various means of redistributing goods, so that the strong and the skilled would not have a unfair share of the goods required for survival. The major way in which the Midewiwin differed from other celebrations was that it had become a "society within a society"; some of its activities were open to anyone, but many others were open only to those Ojibwa (or other tribes) who were members of the Midewiwin.

During the next stage, the prospective candidate for the Midewiwin built a new sweat lodge and, using invitation sticks, invited eight Mide elders who would officiate at the ceremony to share in the sweat lodge rituals. Two individuals were designated to be responsible for conducting the ceremonies, but Nicollet doesn't provide us with any clue as to how they were chosen.[38] During the next three days, private ceremonies and ritual duties were performed in the individuals' lodges, while each night

Illustration 5: Midewiwin Lodge (Midewigaan), Nett Lake, 1946. Normally, when the lodge was used during the nineteenth century, the fresh saplings would have had leaves on them in order to shade participants from the sun. Sometimes, pine boughs or pieces of birchbark were also added to the structure to make it more enclosed. Euro-American observers indicated that such lodges might range in size from eighty to 200 feet in length, from thirteen to twenty feet in width, and were approximately seven feet high. (Courtesy Minnesota Historical Society, I.69.86.)

men, women, and children went from lodge to lodge, singing and dancing, and being given food to eat. On the fourth night, the candidate or candidates met with the Mideg again, in order to show the goods that were to be "paid" to the officials and to rehearse the initiation ceremonies that took place the following day.[39] Meanwhile, the *Midewigaan,* or Mide Lodge, was being constructed by *Mizhinaweg* ("stewards" responsible for ensuring the ceremonies were carried out correctly) according to prescribed requirements. Nicollet did not give a specific description of the Midewigaan, but he did indicate that it was a large rectangular structure with two entrances facing east and west. Nicollet noted that inside were two fires and a painted post called a *midewatig,* but he did not mention any stones.[40]

The next stage in the ceremonies was what is usually termed the initiation or "shooting" rituals. Nicollet described these in some detail, noting that they varied considerably "among nations," although the basic principle of the celebration was not altered. While he did not state that this part of the ceremonies was open, it appears from his description that at least other members of the Midewiwin were present, as well as the presiding Mideg. During this part of the ceremonies, the candidate brought his gifts of goods and food into the Mide Lodge suspended on a pole, entering through the east entrance and making two revolutions around the interior of the lodge. Then the candidate and the eight Mideg called out "*Kanagakana,*" and the audience answered "*Na.*"[41] Nicollet then described several songs sung by the Mideg, which spoke of the power of their medicine bags, which he termed *pinjigoosan,* made of the skin of a bear, and which contained the miigis shell that could cause or cure illness.[42] Nicollet continued:

> The candidate kneels down on a spread-out blanket. The eight [Mideg] rotate around the lodge passing south and saying "*Nikanug, nikanug*—My colleagues, my colleagues,"[43] hailing with their hands until they settle on the west side. Then they turn around and face the candidate. From this point, the eight start a series of eight revolutions around the lodge passing south, west, etc. They follow each other in line, but the revolutions are performed especially to demonstrate the power of the medicine to kill through testing it on the candidate. The leader, as he starts the first round, holds his medicine bag like a rifle, marches forward threatening the candidate with a shot he is about to fire with the bag shouting, "*Hohohoho! hohohoho—hoho! hoho! ho!*"[44] The candidate trembles, but he is only wounded by this blow. Whereupon the faculty [Mideg] move to the north end, at its appointed place, and the candidate sits down before the faculty. . . .
>
> Looking south and vis-á-vis the faculty are singers with the drum *mittigwakik*, and the *shishigwan* for accompaniment, and a little mallet for beating the drum called *pagakookwan*.[45] One of the eight delivers an oration on the power of the manitous, their power to heal or to weaken, power passed down to the *Mide* after having been transmitted from generation to generation. . . . [46]

Nicollet went on to describe how the Mideg continued to take turns in leading the rounds in which they "shot" the candidate with their medicine bags.[47] Each time he was wounded, but when the eighth and final Mide took his turn, the candidate was killed.

> The one who is to kill the candidate makes an oration before starting the eighth round: "Here is a medicine bag handed down to me from my grandfather by my father. My father said unto me that I could never miss my mark when using it. But I am old, my colleagues, help me that I may find the strength to blow, to fire upon this man over there on his knees! There is a red mark upon his heart. I shall strike there and my medicine bag shall not fail me." And he begins to threaten, "*Hohohoho! Hohohoho!*"

> He moves gradually toward the candidate, followed by the other seven members. As soon as he is within reach, he fires saying, "*Ho!*" and the candidate falls dead. . . .
>
> Now has come the time to prove by the candidate, that if the medicine has the power to weaken and kill, it can also heal and resuscitate. When the candidate collapses, a frenzy seizes the assembly and the people. The singers move over to the pole and dance around it playing the *shishigwanun* and the drum. Every assistant of the *Mide* rises to beat the rhythm, and the members of the faculty [Mideg] stand around the dead one covering his body with their medicine bags. A few moments later, they try to lift his body carefully, hoisting it on its feet, punctuating its gradual return to life with shouts, "*Ya-ha! Ya-ha!*" The candidate is now up on his feet—revived! So they give him some medicine to drink and there he stands, in perfect health. He is now initiated. He has the power of medicine, a fact the remainder of the ceremony is about to prove.[48]

Nicollet then described how the new member received his own medicine bag. After thanking the Mideg for having taken pity on him, the new member took from the bag a miigis shell, which he swallowed. He was seized by convulsions, but, using his new power and aided by the Mideg, he overcame the convulsions and restored the miigis to his bag. Then, he was ready to share in a feast with the eight Mideg, consuming eight spoonfuls of "the food of the *Mide*." Following this, the candidate distributed his presents to each of the Mideg, thanking them again for having had pity on him. Then it was time for him to demonstrate his newly acquired power by "shooting" in turn each of the Mide officials and the singers who assisted in his initiation. As he was shot, each Mide collapsed but recovered instantly, thus proving the power of the new member and their own power to recover.

When all the Mide officials had been "shot" and recovered, there was what Nicollet described as a grand finale wherein everyone became involved:

> Inside the lodge, the whole assembly is in a turmoil. The faculty members have kept the instruments and go on singing. In the course of this commotion or frenzy, the medical body is splintered into groups, each group being characterized by a certain type of medicine bag. To accomplish this, some began by going around the lodge depositing their bags in a certain place on the ground. . . . Then each member stands beside the pile containing his bag, and the sections are now formed. . . . The object of this dividing into sections in the course of the melee is to demonstrate that the various kinds of medicine all have the power. They now prove it by blowing each other out in a long-lasting and most entertaining squabble.[49]

Illustration 6: Ojibwa Drums. According to Frances Densmore, the two drums most commonly used by the early Ojibwa were the hand drum and the Mide drum.

The drum in the first illustration is a hand drum or tambourine that has a single head, although some hand drums had two heads strung over a cylindrical hoop. The figure on the drumhead is a manidoo; the wavy lines denote superior power. This particular drum was used in Waabanowiwin, but similar drums were used in other ceremonies, in some games, and as a war drum.

In the second illustration, figure "a" on the right is a Mide drum (Mitigwakik), sometimes termed a water drum by Euro-Americans. Both ends or heads of the drum, which often took the form of a hollowed-out tree partially filled with water, were covered by stretched rawhide. Leaning against it is a Mide drumstick (Baagaakokwaan). Both were considered to be gifts from Gichi-Manidoo, Mide drumsticks being considered even more sacred than the Mide drum itself. Figure "b" on the left is the type of drum commonly used at various forms of ceremonial dances. As in the case of the other two drums, it was considered both sacred and powerful. (From Hoffman, *The Midewiwin*, 223, 190.)

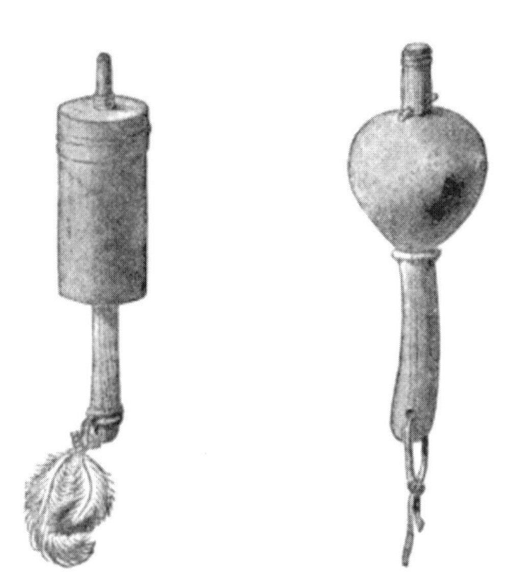

Illustration 7: Ojibwa Mide Rattles. The nineteenth-century Mide rattles were constructed either of gourds, wooden cylinders covered with hide, or metal cans filled with corn or seeds. They were also considered to be gifts from Gichi-Manidoo, and were used along with the drums during the Midewiwin ceremony, as well as during healing ceremonies. (From Hoffman, *The Midewiwin,* 191.)

This portion of the ceremony was followed, in turn, by a banquet, which brought the public portion of the ceremony to an end. The following day the new member prepared a sweat lodge and invited the eight presiding Mideg. Originally this last part of the ceremony lasted eight days, but could be reduced to four if two sweat lodge ceremonies were held daily. During this time the Mideg chose a number of medicines and explained their properties to the new member so that he could add them to his bag. "Finally, the novice offers a banquet that will mark the close of his medicine bag."[50] With this act, the Midewiwin ceremonies came to an end.

Nicollet's description is a vast improvement over any previous efforts by Euro-Americans, and over many that were to follow. It was much more informative than his American contemporary Henry Rowe Schoolcraft's writings on the subject, and much more complete than the writings of his fellow traveller from Europe, the German geographer, Johann Georg Kohl. Not only did it explain the sweat lodge ceremonies and the feast in context, but it also gave the first complete description of the "shooting ritual" and the role of the miigis shell, which, together, were central to the Midewiwin ceremonies.

It is, of course, not only possible but probable that Nicollet's document described a more fully developed ceremony than did Raudot's. If Raudot's document described what was basically an individual curing ceremony, then Nicollet's described a more communal ceremony in which individual "patients" were initiated into a society. There was also an element of an annual renewal ceremony because the ceremony was held in the spring of the year. Members of the Midewiwin gathered each spring to initiate new members and renew their own powers by which they were able to attain bimaadiziwin.[51] To what extent these changes occurred in the period following Raudot's publication is difficult to say for certain, since the accuracy of Raudot's description is questionable. Nevertheless, it seems fair to say that what was happening was a gradual development of the Midewiwin into its present form during the eighteenth and early nineteenth centuries.

Despite being a great improvement over previous descriptions of the Midewiwin, Nicollet's description is by no means without limitations. While he described all the basic ceremonies, his descriptions practically ignored the central role played in them by music and dance. Although he occasionally attempted to translate a phrase or two of songs used in the initiation rite, Nicollet appeared to have no understanding of their integral importance to the ceremonies as a whole. Similarly, while he noted the importance of tobacco to the Ojibwa, he believed it to be merely a secular habit, failing to understand its spiritual significance as a link with the manidoog. Curiously, since he devoted a fair amount of his observations to Ojibwa "picture writing," he made no mention of any type of Mide scrolls or charts, although these also played an important role in Midewiwin ceremonies. It may be that his particular informants kept this aspect from him, since the scrolls and charts were both secret and powerful medicine. However, this is unlikely. Many of these scrolls did become common knowledge to several Euro-Americans just a few years later. A similar lacuna is his total lack of reference to the content of the information that was passed on to the candidates. Nicollet made no attempt to record anything of the speeches that were made on various occasions by Mide officials. His account contains nothing regarding the origin tales, or about the larger context of how the Midewiwin fitted into Ojibwa life.

It is likely that Nicollet, in keeping with his scientific profession, was much better at describing those aspects of the Midewiwin that were subject to direct observation and precise description. Moreover, despite his often romantic characterization of Aboriginal people as "noble savages," Nicollet shared the common

Euro-American belief that Aboriginal people were incapable of complex intellectual thought. In another fragment of his notes, he makes the casual comment that "like other native nations they have no notion of a creator, no religion, no notion of immortality."[52] While Nicollet was probably referring to the fact that Ojibwa beliefs were quite different from the Christian ones to which he subscribed, it could be argued that his observation ultimately prevented him from even considering that the Ojibwa might have a totally different way of viewing the world—and that the Midewiwin ceremonies he had so laboriously described were predicated on this world view.

Nicollet's American contemporary, Henry Rowe Schoolcraft, spent much of his prodigious energy on the major area that Nicollet had neglected—attempting to discover how and what Aboriginal people thought. Born in New England in 1793, Schoolcraft obtained only a rudimentary education before apprenticing in his father's glassmaking factory, while he continued his own self-education. In 1818 he set out to achieve fame and fortune on the American frontier as a member of a number of exploring expeditions. It was while on these that he came to the attention of Governor Lewis Cass of Michigan, whose influence enabled Schoolcraft to obtain positions as Indian Agent at Sault Ste. Marie and later at Mackinac.

Although he was still mainly interested in work as a mineralogist, Schoolcraft used his position as Indian Agent to begin collecting massive amounts of data on all aspects of Aboriginal culture and life, from Aboriginal people with whom he came in contact and interviewed, and from other individuals who had lived with and written about Aboriginals. In doing this, Schoolcraft was following his scientific inclinations, and the example of his mentor, Lewis Cass, who had developed a questionnaire regarding Aboriginal people, which was distributed to everyone working among them. However, Schoolcraft went far beyond answering Cass's elaborate questionnaire.

In 1823 he had married Jane Johnson, the daughter of John Johnson, an Irish trader active in the Great Lakes fur trade, and Susan Johnson (Oshawguscoday-Wayqua), who was herself the daughter of Waubojeeg (White Fisher), an Ojibwa ogimaa (leader) from the Chequamegon region. Both Jane and her brother George were brought up speaking Ojibwe, and participated in Ojibwa ceremonies in their youth, although they were later educated in Christian Euro-American schools. Both assisted Schoolcraft extensively in his studies of Ojibwa culture and language.

Upon Cass's request, Schoolcraft took the opportunity afforded by his position and connections with the Johnson family to teach himself Ojibwe, compiling a vocabulary, declension tables of Ojibwe verbs, and the beginnings of an Ojibwe grammar. At first he thought this would be an easy task, since he considered it to be a simple language, corresponding to the Ojibwa stage of development. However, Schoolcraft lacked a solid basis in classical European languages and philology, so he found the task much more daunting than he had anticipated, even with the assistance of George and Jane Johnson. While he publicly boasted of his fluency in Ojibwe, and while many people of his day believed him to be fluent, Schoolcraft never did finish his projected works on the Ojibwa language, although he continued to believe that the study of Aboriginal languages would reveal how the "Indian mind" worked.

Gradually, his interests shifted from strictly philological studies to the study of how language affected the "mind" of the Ojibwa and other Aboriginal groups. In his introduction to *Algic Researches,* Schoolcraft explained why he had begun to collect and publish the oral narratives of various tribes: "It was found necessary to examine the mythology of the tribes as a means of acquiring an insight into their mode of thinking and reasoning, the sources of their fears and hopes, and the probable origin of their opinions and institutions. . . ."[53]

As a result of the new focus of his studies (and probably as a result of his own conversion to Presbyterianism in 1831), Schoolcraft began to stress that "the most powerful source of influence, with the Red Man, is his religion."[54] He argued that Aboriginal religion had never been comprehended by Euro-Americans, their ways and actions had long been misunderstood, while they, in turn, had never been able to understand why Euro-Americans thought and acted as they did. He believed that his position as Indian Agent and his family connections gave him a unique opportunity to provide a true picture of Aboriginal culture to the Euro-American public. Both Cass and Schoolcraft were anxious to provide an antidote to the image of "bloodthirsty savages," created by the English literary establishment of the eastern United States.

It was this romantic image that Schoolcraft set out to counteract with a "true" one, based on first-hand knowledge. Schoolcraft claimed that the two reasons why Aboriginal people had continued in their state of "barbarism" despite their interaction with Euro-Americans were due to their false religion and false ideas of government.[55] If they could be persuaded to give up these ideas, they would quickly become assimilated into American society. However, it should be noted that in some of his writings, he also argued that Aboriginal people thought and acted as they did as a result of their environment. The ideals of "savage" life were based upon the "hunt and warfare," and therefore could not be judged by civilized standards.[56] While at first glance this would seem to contradict his belief that religion was the main factor, they are closely tied together since, according to Schoolcraft, their religion had grown out of their lifestyle.

The most complete, although by no means systematic, discussion of the Midewiwin by Schoolcraft occurs in his chapter on "The Intellectual Capacity and Character of the Indian Race," in which he attempted to explain the nature of the three major religious ceremonies: the *Medawin* (Midewiwin), the *Jeesukawin* (Jiisakiiwin), and the *Wabeno* (Waabanowiwin).[57] Although he never provided a clear explanation of who his sources for this information were, it would appear that they were Catherine Wambose, Chuzco, Shawunipennais, and Shingwaukonse. Schoolcraft claimed that all four were members of the Midewiwin, but the first three were already Christian converts when they spoke to him. Shawunipennais, or Southbird, as Schoolcraft translates his name, was a Baptist convert who provided Schoolcraft with some of his information regarding pictographic writings, and words to the songs that accompanied them. Shingwaukonse, or Chingwauk, as Schoolcraft called him, was a prominent Ojibwa political and Mide leader who may have still been active in the Midewiwin when he met with Schoolcraft, since Shingwaukonse converted only shortly before his death. It was this same Shingwaukonse whose sacred scrolls Johann Kohl was later to try unsuccessfully to view—they had been destroyed at the time of Shingwaukonse's death. Janet Chute argues that Shingwaukonse was a Mide and a Waabano, as well as a war chief of a band of Ojibwa who originally lived in what is now northern Michigan near Sault Ste. Marie.[58] It is almost certain that his father was not Aboriginal, although he was brought up by his mother's people.

Since Schoolcraft was primarily concerned with mental concepts and religious rituals that supported his own preconceptions, his description of the ceremonies left much to be desired. Most of his work concerned the role of the Mideg, and their use of picture writings, rather than the ceremonies themselves. Unfortunately, with his intended audience in mind, he wrote his descriptions within a structure that would be understood by his audience, rather than one that reflected the Ojibwa world view he claimed to portray. The certainty with which he expounded his opinions, and the dramatic tenor of his writings, gave them more authenticity than they deserved.

Schoolcraft set out first to explain the distinction between the "*meda* priests who gather together in societies, [and] the '*muske-ke-win-in-ee*' [*mashkikiiwinini*] or [Ojibwa] physician." According to him, both made use of certain animals and plants to gain power, but the former were primarily interested in supplicating spirits, rather than in teaching the art of healing.

He argued that since there was no physical application of the mineral and animal matter in their medicine bags, and their power to perform happened at a distance or in secret, they were not "medicine men," as they were sometimes termed, but more properly "necromancers, or medical magii or magicians."[59] By this he implied that they relied on magic, rather than on any "natural" properties of their medicines. Furthermore, he noted, they were called upon to use magic to heal the sick only when the mashkikiiwinini had failed, indicating, he implied, that the Ojibwa who employed them had turned to supernatural means. This desire to probe the future and influence it through the use of demons (i.e. vicious spirits) is almost as old as mankind, he continued. Even during the best phases of human history, societies have been "fettered with witchcraft, sorcery and magic"; thus, Schoolcraft suggested, it is not surprising that we should find these practices among Aboriginal people.

"We must call this class of men [the Mideg] a priesthood," he insisted, since "they profess to administer holy or mysterious things—things that pass the ordinary comprehension of their listeners."[60] Their power, whether for good or evil, was not merely human, but "spiritual," in that it was the result of a spirit, or manidoo. The Aboriginals believed, Schoolcraft continued, that these priests had powers to foretell events, cure or inflict diseases, and influence life and death, and thus all other Aboriginal people lived in hope and fear of the priests. Schoolcraft appears to be the first person to apply the term "priest" to Mide officials, although he gave the term a different connotation from that of most writers. On the one hand, he appears to have wanted to give them greater status than did previous writers who had often dismissed them. However, he obviously wanted to picture them as dangerous adversaries who used the superstitions of ordinary Ojibwa in order to exercise power over them, and maintain the status quo.

Schoolcraft provided only a sketchy description of the Midewiwin ceremonies, despite the fact that he boasted he had observed them personally, and, indeed, claimed to have been initiated into the society itself in 1823.[61] Given the fact that Midewiwin members showed an extreme reluctance to allow Euro-Americans even to observe their ceremonies at this time, most commentators have totally rejected Schoolcraft's claims, although Walter J. Hoffman's similar claim later in the century has been never contested. Janet Chute discovered that Little Pine (Shingwaukonse) and several others did demonstrate a truncated form of a Midewiwin ceremony in Schoolcraft's office.[62] However, while he briefly mentioned the occasion, Schoolcraft appears to have kept no notes of what he observed during the visit. Since Schoolcraft was aware of the complicated requirements that governed the acceptance of initiates, and since he knew how reluctant members of the society were to share anything with non-members, his own statement regarding his initiation may well be a typical case of bravado to impress his readers regarding the extent to which he had been accepted by the Ojibwa.

In his description of the Midewiwin, Schoolcraft dealt with the ceremonies in a peremptory manner, since his main motive was to demonstrate the general principles of the society, in order to illustrate how the Mideg exercised their power. According to him, "the object [of the Midewiwin] is to teach the higher doctrines of spiritual existence, their nature and mode of existence, and the influence they exercise among men. It is an association of men who profess the highest knowledge known to the tribes."[63]

Schoolcraft declared that admissions to the Midewiwin Society were always made in public ceremonies, though he later qualified this by indicating that non-members could only watch (the initiatory rituals) from outside the Mide Lodge. He understood that the consideration of candidates was dependent upon their having a dream or vision, after which, if it "boded good," he was told to begin his preparations, and if these were approved, he was told to prepare a "steam-bath," where, Schoolcraft correctly claimed, the Mideg exchanged objects said to have magical or medicinal virtue. The candidate was, at this time, also initiated in the arts of healing, hunting, and the power of resisting witchcraft in others. This latter power, Schoolcraft claimed, was known as having "the power of throwing, or resisting the power to throw, bad medicine." Schoolcraft appears to have confused the purpose of the initial sweat lodge rituals with those at the end of the Midewiwin ceremony. He also appears to have confused the "public" initiation rites of the person who was applying for membership with the more private curing ceremony, which was performed for members of the society who were ill. While it is true that the two could be incorporated together, it is highly unlikely that the type of ill person mentioned by Schoolcraft would have been well enough to have undergone the lengthy initial period of instructions that he had previously outlined.

Schoolcraft described an elongated Mide Lodge specially constructed in an open space by assistants of the Midewiwin Society from newly cut poles and foliage. He noted there was no roof on the lodge so that the heavens could be seen, since, as he correctly observed, fair weather was taken as a good sign for the future. When the work was complete:

> the "master of ceremonies" . . . proceeds to it, taking his drum, rattles, and other instruments of this art. He is met by other members of the meda

> [Midewiwin] who have been invited to be present and participate in the rites. Having gone through some of the preliminary ceremonies, and chanted some of the songs, the patient is introduced. If too weak to walk, the individual is carried in on a bed or pallet, and laid down in the designated position. The exactness and order which attend every movement, is one of its peculiarities.[64]

Just when one would expect Schoolcraft to describe the initiation rituals in detail, he went off on another track and thus never did describe the "shooting" ritual that most other observers judged to be central to the Midewiwin ceremonies. This is particularly curious, since Schoolcraft had just previously explained that the Mide Lodge was built specifically "to exhibit the power of the operator, or officiating priest, in the curative art,"[65] yet he virtually ignored it. Nor did Schoolcraft mention the gifts that were given to the Mideg during the ceremony, although most other commentators have taken these to have been a sign of the Mideg's power.

Instead, Schoolcraft turned his attention to understanding the meaning of the pictography employed in what he termed the "music boards," or *kekenowin* (instructions), which were used during the Midewiwin ceremonies.[66] In fact, his discussion of the Midewiwin, Jiisakiiwin, and Waabanowiwin served mainly as background to understanding these kekenowin, for, despite his statements regarding the importance of religion, he appears to have still been mainly interested in the means by which people communicated. According to Schoolcraft, pictographic writing was divided into two types: *kekeewin,* which were pictographs that could be read and understood by everyone in the tribe; and kekenowin. The first type of pictographs were commonly used by travellers to leave messages, sometimes on grave markers to provide information about the dead person, and on rock paintings, or, as he termed them, *mussinabiks.* The other type of pictographs, kekenowin, were the teachings of the priests and prophets called Mideg. These could be read only by those who had learned them after paying the priests for the knowledge. According to Schoolcraft, kekenowin were used in the three ceremonies, plus in circumstances relating to hunting, love, and war, and when relating the history of the tribe.

Although these may seem at first to be an unlikely combination of circumstances, with the possible exception of tribal history, they all involve instances in which individuals or groups of Ojibwa would be anxious to acquire more power in order to be able to influence events, and thus gain better control of their lives. Schoolcraft might have agreed with the basics of such an explanation, since he did understand the role of manidoog in Ojibwa society, but, nevertheless, he preferred to denote the acquisition

Illustration 8: Shingwaukonse, or The Pine, as he was known to Euro-Americans, was an Ojibwa chief who worked successfully to establish a Canadian homeland at Garden River, near Sault Ste. Marie, for American Ojibwa bands threatened by removal in the nineteenth century. He was a powerful Mide leader in the 1820s and 1830s when Henry R. Schoolcraft claimed him as one of his chief sources. His exploits and powers were still legendary in the 1870s, twenty years after his death, when he was described at length by Johann G. Kohl in *Kitchi-Gami*. (Courtesy Algoma University College.)

and use of extraordinary powers as "magic or prophecy." Like most of his fellow Christians of the time, he believed that any spirits that operated outside the boundaries of Christian theology must be agents of the Christian devil who were engaged in magic—regardless of whether the end result was good or evil. The secretive nature of the contents of what Schoolcraft termed the kekenowin, and the payment of fees for the knowledge, whetted his interest in what appeared to him to be devilish rites, which he was determined to expose, not attempt to understand.

Schoolcraft had obtained what he called a "songboard" from one of the participants of the "Midewiwin ceremony," who performed for him in his office. According to him, the mnemonic symbols on it were called *Nugamoonun* (*nagamon*) by the Ojibwa, meaning "songs." Schoolcraft believed that each song had a key symbol that reminded the singer of the words and melody. The pictographs were, he argued, very close to hieroglyphic symbols. However, they did not function as symbols for sounds. He believed the unchangeable words were the key to understanding the meaning of the songs, while the melody was incidental.

Schoolcraft was probably speaking from the viewpoint of a literate Protestant for whom "the word" was the essential element of religious belief. After all, Christians had argued for centuries over the exact wording and meaning of passages from the Bible. However, for the Ojibwa, the melody was at least as important as the words. As Frances Densmore, a trained ethnomusicologist, was later to explain, Midewiwin songs were the expression of religious ideas in which the words were forced to conform to the melody.[67] Densmore further pointed out that many of the words were archaic forms whose meaning was no longer understood precisely by the singers, along with ejaculations such as *ho, ho, ho,* used at the end of a song. Mide singers could readily recognize melodies of Mide songs, and translate them onto music boards or song scrolls, which, in turn, would be clear to other Mideg, who could reproduce the melodies and words to express the same idea.

Schoolcraft provided his reader with explanations of examples of Mide songs that the mnemonic symbols on his songboard demonstrated. Unfortunately, the songboard in question is highly suspect as a Midewiwin instruction scroll, and as an example of Ojibwa pictography. Subsequent writers such as Walter Hoffman and Garrick Mallery accused Schoolcraft of adding colours to the pictographs to make them more dramatic, and of attributing metaphysical concepts to the symbols that could not be substantiated.[68] Given his overweening ambition, it is indeed possible that Schoolcraft may have added the colours to the illustration, and made the meanings of the mnemonic symbols more elaborate than they really were. It is also possible that his informants, having an idea of what he wanted, "created" one specially for the occasion, thus avoiding breaking the taboos associated with revealing the secrets of the Midewiwin. He certainly would not be the last investigator to be told by Aboriginal people what he wanted to hear.

Schoolcraft does provide a cursory explanation of each song, sometimes apparently placing them in context of the Midewiwin ceremonies, but his main object appears to have been to demonstrate how they illustrated the "strong power of necromancy" of the Mideg. Although the ceremony was called a "medicine dance" and the Mideg were often called "medicine men," Schoolcraft argued that the word *muskeke* (mashkiki) did not appear in the ceremony, and there are few allusions to it. The officials were not "*muskekewininee* or physicians, but *Meda-wininee* or *Medas*. They assemble, [he concluded] not to teach the art of healing, but the art of supplicating spirits."[69] It was these *Medas* (Mideg), plus the *Jossadeeds* (Jiisakiiwininiwag), the *Wabenos* (Waabanowag), and their counterparts in other tribes, who, Schoolcraft argued, had to be directly attacked. It was this class of people "who rise up in every tribe, with pretence of superior wisdom or skill. It is this class of impostors, who are too lazy to hunt, and too wicked to be usefully industrious, that keep the Indian mind in a turmoil . . . it is this class of men, who are mere demoniac agents of Satan. . . ."[70] Although it can be argued that Schoolcraft's feelings regarding the Ojibwa religious leaders became more pronounced following his own conversion and active participation as an evangelical Christian layman, it is possible to see the seeds of his later beliefs in his earliest writings.

Given his beliefs, it is not surprising that Schoolcraft made no effort to record any of the "speeches" of the Mideg in which they explained the gift of the Midewiwin to the Ojibwa people. Even though Schoolcraft had been among the first to collect Ojibwa narratives, he failed to place Mide origin narratives in relation to the Midewiwin ceremonies themselves. Schoolcraft's goal was simply to attack the superstitions and deceptions of the Mideg, not to attempt to understand them—no matter how much he might protest that this was his intention. Coupled with his tendency to embroider his findings (whether they were narratives, instruction scrolls, or descriptions of rituals), this has made his work highly suspect to most scholars. Nevertheless, it did not prevent his works from being read and believed by a large number of Euro-Americans during the nineteenth century.

Schoolcraft's ideas concerning Ojibwa religion and the Midewiwin were shared by many Euro-Americans, including many of the increasing number of missionaries who were attempting to convert the Ojibwa to Christianity.

Many of them, like Bishop Frederic Baraga, seldom bothered to describe Ojibwa religious ideas or practices, deeming them unworthy of their attention. Baraga was a multilingual Catholic priest from Slovenia who established missions among the Ottawa and Ojibwa at Arbre Croche in 1832 and La Pointe in 1837. Although his Ojibwe dictionary and grammar were remarkable achievements, he made few efforts to understand anything about Anishinaabe cosmology because he believed it to be the work of the devil. Others, like the Reverend William Boutwell, who lived from 1833 to 1846 at Leech Lake and the neighbouring mission at Pokegama as a representative of the American Board of Commissioners for Foreign Missions, recounted only some of the more extreme examples of "charlatanism," such as the one used by Hickerson in his discussion of the Midewiwin.[71] Still others, such as the Reverend Peter Jones, who was a driving force in the Methodist evangelization of the Ojibwa in southern Ontario, charged that the reason Mide leaders opposed Christian missionaries was because the Mideg had become wealthy as a result of receiving payment for their work as "conjurors," as he called them.[72] Jones, and other Ojibwa converts from southern Ontario, resented the amount of goods that individual Ojibwa were willing to pay in order to be initiated into the Midewiwin. They believed that the people were being fooled by imposters, and such actions conflicted dramatically with their new Methodist beliefs concerning the virtues of hard work and thrift.

Nevertheless, some missionaries were surprisingly free of the most blatant prejudices, although even their ideas often sound prejudiced to our ears. Among these was E.H. Day, who remembered his life as a Methodist missionary among the Ojibwa at Fond du Lac during the 1840s at a meeting of the Michigan Pioneer and Historical Society in 1889.[73] This places his posting at Fond du Lac just after Nicollet's stay among the Pillagers band at Leech Lake, and just before Kohl's visit to the Ojibwa at La Pointe. Unlike his Protestant predecessors at Fond du Lac, and his Catholic contemporaries who occasionally visited there, Day evidently showed an active interest in the religious character of the Ojibwa at Fond du Lac, whom he termed "a very religious people," despite the fact that most of them were heathens, having not yet accepted Christianity. And the few Catholics among them, he noted, could not be distinguished from their "heathen" brethren except for the dirty beads they occasionally counted.

These Catholics, Day might have added, were mainly kinsmen of French-Canadian traders who had married into the Ojibwa community, and, while adopting many features of Ojibwa society, continued to practise a diluted form of their father's religion. In some communities, such as Fond du Lac, they formed a fair portion of the total community. Although Euro-Americans, as yet, made up a tiny proportion of the permanent population in the Fond du Lac region, their presence was increasingly felt as steamers regularly visited the region, bringing with them Euro-American fishermen, miners, and adventurers in addition to the fur traders, government officials, and missionaries. Thus, like their kinsmen at Leech Lake, the Ojibwa at Fond du Lac found their search for the path to the good life had become increasingly difficult after the arrival of large numbers of outsiders who shared few of their values.

Day's interpreter at the time was Peter Marksman (Ma-dwa-gwun-a-yaush), a young Ojibwa convert whose uncle had been a "conjuror."[74] Marksman, who was born on the St. Croix River, appears to have been much more readily accepted into the Fond du Lac community than most missionaries, whether they were Euro-American or Anishinaabe. Certainly, he continued to demonstrate respect for his Ojibwa brethren at Fond du Lac and for their religious beliefs and practices, even though he had accepted Christian beliefs himself, and he appears to have passed on some of this respect to the Reverend Day.

In his talk to the Michigan Pioneer and Historical Society, Day gave a brief description of the manner of worship in which the "grand medicine dance," as he termed the Midewiwin, was conducted. According to him, the Midewiwin was conducted when a person became sick and the Ojibwa were not able to cure him by regular means.

> As a preliminary, all the prophets (we had four among us)[75] must fast for three days, and during that time they must not close their eyes in sleep at night. They might sleep all day, but at sundown they must commence drumming and singing, which must not stop on any account until sunrise next morning. The drum was simply a hollow log.... The drum stick (they had but one) was in the form of a cross, with which a regular tum, tum, was kept up, and could be heard all over the village. To a stranger, sleep was impossible. On the fourth morning all the village was astir. The women were all busy, bringing in long, withe-like poles, out of which a wigwam was to be made, perhaps sixty feet long and twelve feet wide. These poles were firmly set in the ground, and the tops bent over in the form of a bow and fastened together. When this was done, all but two ends were fastened with mats and blankets. Inside, in the center, near each end, a post was set firmly in the ground. These posts were painted with different colours. About four feet from the walls on the inside was a path.... Back of the path, on either side, was the place for the seating of the audience. This completed the wigwam.[76]

Day went on to explain that the next "requirement" was a feast, the most acceptable form of which was white dog, cooked in a kettle near the Mide Lodge. When this was ready, a "loud whoop," answered from all parts of the village, brought everyone together. Each person had his face and body painted, and was "naked to the loins." They came with blankets thrown over their shoulders, and a dish and pipe in their hands. Soon the entire lodge was full of smoke. Meanwhile, the sick person was brought in and put on the blankets near one of the posts,

> and around him are laid the offerings that he offers to the Great Spirit for his recovery. It may be blankets, kettles, sugar, guns, or whatever he may have: and I have known an Indian to give away the last thing he had as an offering. These things, though offered to the Great Spirit, become the property of the medicine men or conjurers. Everything being ready, the feast cooking, each one comes, bringing with him his medicine bag in which he keeps his charm. The bag may be an otter skin, or a snake skin, or anything that will hold his "mon-e-do [manidoo]." These are . . . spiral shells about an inch long. The Indians silently smoking, one of the medicine men arises . . . and commences a speech about anything or nothing, or chants a monotonous song for, perhaps two minutes, and with his medicine-bag in his hands, pointing to the sick one at the other post, starts towards him in a light trot, and with every step utters the explanation "who-ah! Who-ah!" and as he nears him, suddenly brings the bag very near the sick one, who falls over quivering, as though struck a severe blow, while the doctor trots around the patient and comes back on the other path with a satisfied grunt of "Ho-ho." Then another takes his place. . . . This continues until all of the conjurers have passed around the sick man . . . when they make the final charge. The sick man lies as though dead for some time, but finally arises and presents, or, if unable to arise, a friend presents the offering that lay around him, to the medicine men, and the patient is *supposed* to be cured.[77]

Day theorized that the spirit in the shell enters the sick person to grapple with the disease, and, with the final charge, the disease is driven away, so the person recovers. Even if the patient didn't recover, the "medicine men" kept their fees, and, he noted, their reputation did not appear to suffer.

This "shooting" ritual, as it is often designated, or "curing" ritual, as perceived by Day, was followed by the feast in which all partook. Then, he suggested, "the fun begins":

> The drum is brought in and one is seated by it to give the music. This consists of a monotonous chant, with regular strokes on the drum. Every

> Indian now brings forth his medicine bag, and a row stands on each side of the path that was made around the posts, the rows facing each other. Men, women and children . . . stand ready to begin the dance . . . each one with his medicine bag in hand. Presently one raises his medicine bag and pointing it at one opposite him utters the exclamation "Wah," and at the same time punches it at him, when the one at whom it was pointed drops as if shot and lies quivering on the ground for the space of perhaps a minute, and then gets up and joins the dance again, or takes his seat back of the dancers and takes a smoke. Meanwhile the fun waxes furious. . . . Occasionally a shout is heard, until, as day closes, wild confusion reigns, and men, women and children burst from the wigwam and the dance is done.[78]

Here we have yet another version of the Midewiwin ceremony. Given that close to fifty years had passed since Day had witnessed the ceremony and almost as many since he had worked actively among the Ojibwa, Day's description was surprisingly detailed. While he used many commonly held stereotypes to describe the proceedings and participants, the picture that he paints is still more representative than most nineteenth-century descriptions.

Much of what he described is similar to Raudot's and Nicollet's versions of events, though some new elements have been added and several others dropped. Since the location is different, and the ceremony took place one to two generations after Schoolcraft's and Nicollet's accounts, it could be argued that Day's version offers variants. It might also be argued that the Ojibwa were not concerned with ritual consistency. However, I believe that while this may be true with respect to some aspects of the ceremony, in most cases, the different versions of the ceremony are more likely the result of the differing perceptions of the observers, as filtered through their respective informants.

Day was probably most typical of his times in his reaction to the ceremonies, singling out as he did the incessant beat of the drum, the monotony of singing, and the frenzied "dancing" that followed the "shooting" ritual and the "orgy" of the dog feast. The writings of Euro-Americans during this period were full of brief references to such occurrences—and almost all showed a similar misunderstanding about the role that drumming, singing, and dancing played in the Midewiwin and other Ojibwa religious ceremonies. Men as widely apart as the American government official Thomas McKenney, in his book *Sketches of a Tour to the Lakes,*[79] and a remote Hudson's Bay Company factor at Michipicoten on the northern shores of Lake Superior[80] both commented on what they considered to be the infernal goings-on of the Ojibwa. In many cases, their knowledge of Ojibwa culture was limited, so they often confused the ceremonies they described, and even when this was not the case, they viewed the ceremonies through their own cultural filters. In the back of everyone's mind was the fear that there was some connection between these "medicine dances" and "war dances." After all, they reasoned, the Ojibwa, like other groups in both the United States and Canada, were gradually being asked to give up their lands and make significant changes to their lifestyle. Might not the "war chiefs" use their influence to incite the young men to drastic action, as some of their neighbours had done or were about to do? These fears were played upon by newspaper accounts of an increasing number of Aboriginal gatherings and all-night ceremonies accompanied by drums. Just how different the viewpoints of relatively open observers such as Day were from those of the Ojibwa can be seen in the two views regarding the role of the Mide drum. To Euro-Americans it was monotonous at best, and sinister at worst. To some members of the Midewiwin, the drumbeat represented the heartbeat of the "Creator."[81]

While Day was somewhat more moderate in his statements than Schoolcraft, he, too, believed that there was a connection between the religious beliefs and practices of the Ojibwa as exemplified in the Midewiwin, and what both considered the "savage" lifestyle of the Ojibwa people. It was this lifestyle he tended to highlight in order to contrast the practitioners of the Midewiwin with those Ojibwa who had converted to Christianity, and adopted a "civilized" lifestyle.

The differences in Day's description of the "shooting" rituals from those of Nicollet can probably best be attributed to the passage of time since Day had made his observations—with the concurrent tendency to collapse the events described. However, his interpretation of the ritual's meaning is also quite different. Nicollet had explained that when the patient/initiate was "shot" with the miigis, he was injured and died, and was then revived through the power of the medicine bags of the Mideg. According to Day, it was the power of the miigis that cured the patient. Similar explanations were given by subsequent observers who explained the power of the shell as a sort of "inoculation" that caused the patient to temporarily succumb, only to rise again more invigorated than before.

Day's version of the public duelling that followed the "shooting" or "initiation" ritual is more common than Nicollet's version, in which members of different degrees appear to form "teams" in order to demonstrate their different powers. While both men stress the "fun" aspect of this portion of the ceremony, Ruth Landes, in her detailed description of a mid-twentieth-century Midewiwin ceremony, perhaps captured the spirit of what Nicollet and Day were trying to express. She suggested that the public duelling ritual had mystic overtones similar to those of a Catholic carnival, noting that it allowed people to "let off steam" in a socially acceptable fashion.[82] Certainly, the Midewiwin was a series of rituals that had multi-faceted functions, both religious and social.

Although Day's description of the Midewiwin continued to highlight some of its more sensational aspects for the benefit of his audience, there was no demonizing of the participants. And although he made little attempt to understand what was happening, the description does give an indication that the Midewiwin was a complex series of rituals. Gradually, and however imperfectly, some of the Ojibwa's Euro-American neighbours were beginning to understand that there was much more to the Midewiwin than first impressions would have had them believe.

It remained, however, for another European visitor to dig below some of these impressions, and write more perceptively about the Midewiwin. Johann Georg Kohl was a German geographer who spent six months in the latter part of 1855 among the Ojibwa along the shores of Lake Superior in what is now northern Wisconsin and northern Michigan. Although he was there only a short time, he was a keen observer of human nature, with a fine eye for detail, and he did not let his own preconceptions cloud his efforts to understand Ojibwa stories, ceremonies, music, or picture writing. Thus, while his writings took the form of a travelogue more than that of an ethnographic report, they often provide insights that many of the other descriptions do not.

One of the three locations where Kohl spent most of his time was at the village of La Pointe on Madeleine Island in Chequamegon Bay. La Pointe had long been an important centre for the Ojibwa; however, by the 1830s the number of Ojibwa in the vicinity had dropped to approximately forty families, or 200 people. By the time that Kohl visited, the community of La Pointe had become primarily a small trading community to which the American government had attached a subagency of the Department of Indian Affairs. Reverend Sherman Hall had established a mission (church and school) there, which served both the Euro-American community and a few Ojibwa. In the mid-1830s, Bishop Baraga established a Catholic church, which primarily attracted mixed Ojibwa and French families, plus a growing number of Ojibwa. The Ojibwa community at La Pointe was considerably reduced from its peak in the late seventeenth and eighteenth centuries, but it continued to be visited by remote bands of Ojibwa who had originally come from La Pointe, and now returned there each year in order to collect their annuity payments. The agency had been closed in 1850 when the US government attempted to force the bands to move to Minnesota. Close to 400 Ojibwa had perished while attempting to collect their annuities at Sandy Lake. The next year the government rescinded the order and annuities were once again paid at La Pointe. For this reason, it still served as a natural gathering point, in much the same way that the bands had gathered together in earlier times to fish, gather berries, or make maple syrup—and it allowed Kohl to meet Ojibwa from a number of the bands who, decades earlier, had migrated southwest, taking with them the Midewiwin.

Thus, for instance, he was to meet Mongazid (Loon Foot), a chief from Fond du Lac, who had been present when Reverend Day had witnessed the Midewiwin ceremonies there, and he was to meet two Mide elders from Leech Lake. The latter two refused to provide Kohl with any information, because his "gift" of sugar had been too paltry, considering the nature of the information he wanted. Loon Foot and several other Mideg were more accommodating. Moreover, Kohl was able to witness a Midewiwin ceremony for himself at La Pointe, since the gathering of Ojibwa people following the government payments proved a good time to hold the Midewiwin ceremonies. Not only were large numbers gathered together, but candidates could use government annuities to help meet the costs of their initiation.

In the few years since Reverend Day had witnessed Midewiwin ceremonies at Fond du Lac, the position of the Ojibwa in the region had continued to deteriorate. The American government had established military supremacy in the western Great Lakes region, following the defeat of the Sauk and Mesquakie under their leader Black Hawk in the early 1830s. During the late 1830s and early 1840s, they, along with groups of Potawatomi, Menominee, and Winnebago, were forced to cede more of their lands in order to accommodate the demands of American lumbermen and farmers. This was followed by yet more treaties in the 1840s, which called for the Ojibwa along the south shore of Lake Superior, including those at La Pointe, to give up their lands. Lumbering, mining, and railway interests were increasingly interested in exploiting the resources of the area, and actively campaigned to have the Ojibwa and Ottawa removed. Almost alone among Aboriginal people in the northeastern United States, they resisted removal, without resorting to armed conflict. However, they found it difficult to adjust when they were forced to take up permanent homes on reservations set aside for them by the American government.[83] On the northern shore of Lake Superior, in Canada, treaties were longer in coming, but mining interests in particular were becoming increasingly active, and many Ojibwa leaders, such as Shingwaukonse, who had elected to take his people into Canada rather than submit to removal, were faced with similar ill-treatment there. Some Ojibwa in the Great Lakes region refused to surrender their lands, even though it meant foregoing their annuity payments, which, since the decline of the fur and fish trade, served as one of their few means of obtaining Euro-American goods, upon which they had become dependent. They preferred to eke out a living as best they could on unclaimed lands, following traditional beliefs and ways.

It is no wonder that many looked back with nostalgia to "the good times gone." More and more of the eastern Ojibwa or Mississauga, however reluctantly, and however nominally, became Christians at the same time as they searched for ways to survive—as a people, and as individuals. As Yellow Head, the Mississauga chief at Lake Simcoe, explained at a gathering in 1832, "When we embraced this religion [Methodism] it made us happy in our hearts, and we were no longer lying drunk in the streets, but lived in houses like the white men, and our women and children were comfortable and happy."[84] Granting the Methodist tenor of the quote, many of Yellow Head's fellow Mississauga did make the decision to change their way of life.

Since revitalization movements such as those of the Shawnee Prophet had become discredited, most of the Aboriginal people who wished to keep their traditional beliefs and ways followed either the ways of the Midewiwin, the Waabanowiwin, or Jiisakiiwin—or a combination of the three. While it is difficult to say precisely, it is likely that the majority of Ojibwa believed that by continuing to follow the tenets of the Midewiwin they would be able to live a good life. Some of the more northerly Ojibwa may have never practised the Midewiwin, but those in the Boundary Waters region definitely did, as the writings of Jacobs, Salt, other missionaries, and fur traders all attested. Landes's comments (based on her informants' information) that the Midewiwin was only brought to the Manitou Rapids Reserve in Ontario from Red Lake in the 1933 contradicts the reports of the Reverend Peter Jacobs, in particular, who described the Midewiwin ceremonies in the Rainy Lake area in the 1840s and 1850s.[85]

The village of La Pointe contained Protestant and Catholic churches, which included a growing number of Ojibwa members, but Kohl was still able to attend a Midewiwin ceremony a few kilometres from town, where, as he explained, "a father would present his boy for reception into the order of the Mides.... *Midewiwin*," he went on, "is the Indian term for what the Canadians call '*la grande medicine*,' that is, the great fraternity among the Indians for religious purposes. '*Midé*' (*Mide*) is a member of the fraternity, while '*gamig*' is a corruption of wigwam, always used in composition. Hence, '*Midewi-gamig*' may be translated 'temple wigwam' or, 'house of the brethren.'"[86] Kohl described the construction of the long, rectangular Mide Lodge with doors at the east and west ends, and commented on the fact that he recognized several of the Mide elders as people with whom he had become acquainted at La Pointe. Surrounding the initiate, who was a young baby still in a cradleboard, were the father and members of his family, all with faces painted a fiery red. He noted also the big drum in the centre of the lodge, which was beaten with a little wooden "hammer," and a large stone in front of the east door (which, one of his informants told him, had been placed there for the Evil Spirit). At length, he continued, they were allowed to take their place as spectators after having left an offering of tobacco. Kohl gave no indication whether he was only being allowed to witness the public element of a series of ceremonies that must have been going on for some days, or whether the ceremony he witnessed differed from the ones previously described—perhaps because the initiate was an infant. For instance, Kohl made no mention of any sweat lodge ceremonies, and his description of the "shooting" ritual, in which the candidate received the powers being sought, appears to be different from either Nicollet's or Day's versions.

Kohl disavowed any attempt to give a critical description of the ceremony he witnessed, since it was extremely complex and he was forced to rely on interpreters. However, he did provide some impressions:

> In the first place, my old prophet . . . made a speech. I noticed that he spoke very glibly, and now and then pointed to the heavens, and then fixed his eyes on the audience. He also made a movement several times over their heads, as if blessing them, just as priests do in all nations and churches. His speech was translated to me much in this way. He had addressed a prayer to the Great Spirit; then he shortly explained why they were assembled, and that a member of the tribe wished his infant to be received into the order of the Mides. He concluded by welcoming all the assembly, the high Mides and brothers, all the "aunts and uncles," the "sisters and cousins," and gave them his blessing.
>
> After this address a procession was formed of all the Mides, while the father of the child and the guests rose and leaned against the sides of the wigwam. The priests walked one after the other, with medicine-bag in the right hand.
>
> These medicine-bags, called "pindjigossan" in the Ojibbeway language, were made of the skins of the most varying animals. . . . They were all filled with valuable and sacred matters, of course not visible. The Indians imagine that a spirit or breath is exhaled from these varied contents of

> the skin-bag possessing the power to blow down and kill a person, as well as to restore him to life and strength again.[87]

Kohl went on to describe the "shooting rituals," noting that the French Canadians, who have generally best translated the Aboriginal terms, called this operation *tirer*, or *souffler*. In Kohl's description, the Mideg took turns shooting members of the public. They later used their medicine bags to revive those who were shot. At this point in the proceedings, the initiate was not involved. While Kohl noted that "it was a very comical sight, and some behaved with considerable drollery," everyone took the whole affair very seriously.[88]

After the conclusion of this part of the ceremony, the father presented his child to the Mide elders, making a short speech, which was answered by longer ones from the Mideg. This was, in turn, followed by some dancing, and then the entire audience was involved in what others have termed the "ritual duelling," in which everyone became involved using a wide variety of medicine bags. All this had taken place in the morning. That afternoon everyone gathered again in the Mide Lodge to continue the ceremonies.

Kohl noted that there was a number of branches covered with a cloth in front of the large stone. The Mideg, followed by all other members of the order, danced slowly around the cloth, looking at it; gradually, they began to stop and he noted that they began to appear to have convulsions and, after much effort, expelled some small object from their mouths. When all the shells had been produced, they appeared to recover. Later, each person took a shell from the pile and placed it in his medicine bag. The shells, he was informed, "typify the illness and wickedness which is in man, which he is enabled to expel by zealous exertions, and due attention to his religious duties."[89]

Following this, each person took a short turn at the drum, singing a song that, Kohl was told, expressed his joy in being a member of the society. Meanwhile, he noted, the men continued to smoke their pipes, part of every solemn rite. At sunset, a huge kettle full of maize broth was brought in and the Mideg received their presents. In turn, the Mideg presented the father of the child with various medicines and foods for the child, which would "guide him through life." The presiding Mide made a final speech, and the simple broth was served to all those present. It was, as Kohl observed, "an unpretending banquet" after a whole day's fatiguing ceremonies."[90]

Kohl's description of the Midewiwin ceremonies differed from those of his predecessors in a number of ways. As in Schoolcraft's and Day's descriptions, the ceremony appears to have taken place in a single day, although it is possible that the rituals concerned with the sweat lodge portion could have taken place on preceding days. While the order of some of the rituals also varied in reports from other observers, all the descriptions do contain certain common elements: the initiation or shooting ritual, coupled with a demonstration of the power that had been conferred, which involved swallowing and regurgitating the miigis; the duelling ritual; the presentation of gifts; and the final banquet. Taking into account the distinct possibility that the observers were so confused by the complexity of the ceremony that they later got the order mixed up, it is also possible that such variations were not important as long as the essential rituals were carried out.

However, as almost all observers noted, the Ojibwa made extensive use of pictographs in the ceremonies, which served both as training aids for initiates and as memory aids for Mide officials, precisely so that the ceremony would follow certain prescribed formats. Kohl made considerable efforts to obtain copies of these pictographs, along with their interpretations, since he was aware of their importance to the ceremonies. The ceremony described by Kohl contained individuals who, no doubt, had been present at the ceremonies witnessed by Schoolcraft, Day, and possibly even Nicollet, so it would seem that either the ceremonies were, in fact, closer in form and content than described, or that the observers were familiar with such variations.

Certainly, it is possible that some of the variations may have crept in following new revelations by higher degree Mideg. Selwyn Dewdney has argued that a struggle continued to exist between the Mide and vision traditions, but it is more likely that they co-existed within the Midewiwin itself.[91] Certainly the Midewiwin never replaced visions as a means of communicating with the manidoog, although, as we shall see, younger generations of Mideg in some communities no longer always received them. While the Midewiwin may not have been practised in its elaborate forms as widely among the northern bands of Ojibwa, the Jiisakiiwin and other allied ceremonies continued to be regularly practised in those areas where the Midewiwin was strongest. Observers such as Nicollet, Schoolcraft, and Kohl made as frequent references to it as they do to the Midewiwin, just as Jacobs, Evans, and others referred to the Midewiwin among northern bands of Ojibwa. The one area where it may not have been practised was among the most northerly Ojibwa who lived alongside the Cree, near the present Manitoba/Ontario border in the vicinity of the Severn River.

There may also have been more pragmatic reasons for the changes in the duration and complexity of the Midewiwin ceremonies. As the Ojibwa became more closely integrated into the rhythms of Euro-American society, the timing of multi-band ceremonies became more closely tied to the fall annuity payments—which then could be used to purchase the goods needed for entry into higher degrees, and as a means of redistributing goods among the community. Perhaps the communal aspects of the Midewiwin, during times such as these, would have become even more important, as the participants shared the increasingly meagre resources during the long winter months. At a somewhat later date towards the end of the nineteenth century, Garrick Mallery, who was an American ethnologist and a colleague of Hoffman, made an interesting observation that the spring Midewiwin ceremonies welcomed the return of the good spirits, while "those in the fall were in lamentation for the departure of the beneficent and the arrival of the maleficent spirits." [92]

Kohl mentioned in his writings that the initiation of the young baby into the society reminded him of Christian baptism, and it is quite possible that those Ojibwa who retained their traditional beliefs felt increasingly pressured to ensure that their children received protection of the manidoog at an early age. It is unclear from Kohl, or from the remarks of others, how the Midewiwin ceremony he described tied in with the long-standing Ojibwa naming ceremonies. Certainly it would have set them apart from their brethren who had their children baptised by Christian missionaries—at least from the viewpoint of the latter.

Nevertheless, while the Roman Catholic missionaries had begun to make some inroads, particularly among Ojibwa families connected by marriage to French-Canadian Catholics and their descendants, the success of Methodist and Presbyterian missionaries in making converts was still quite negligible in all areas except among the Ojibwa in southern Ontario and the Saginaw region of Michigan.[93] As long as they remained outside of treaties, the majority of the Ojibwa continued to resist the call of the missionaries to embrace their religion, and of government officials to embrace the lifestyle of their Euro-American neighbours.

FIVE

Midewiwin Ceremonies: Ethnographic Records of a Society under Siege

The situation of the Ojibwa, regardless of whether they had supported the Americans or the British in the War of 1812, remained fundamentally the same. By the mid-nineteenth century, Ojibwa everywhere felt increasingly that they were in danger of being overwhelmed by the vast numbers of Euro-Americans who were beginning to occupy their lands, and who actively strove to control every aspect of their lives. Unlike the small number of fur traders who had lived among them, often marrying into the bands, most of these newcomers saw the Ojibwa merely as obstacles to be pushed aside in the Euro-American westward expansion. Others attempted to save Ojibwa souls by having them renounce their beliefs and accept Christ as their saviour. These Christians sought to protect the Ojibwa from the worst abuses of their fellow Euro-Americans, while at the same time to instil in the Ojibwa the qualities of piety, cleanliness, temperance, and industry. American and Canadian governments claimed they could protect the Ojibwa from the abuses inflicted upon them by the recent Euro-American arrivals by reserving small blocs of land for Aboriginal settlements, and placating the new arrivals by freeing up former "Indian lands" for the exploitation of Euro-Americans. The policymakers believed that the concentration of the

Ojibwa within small areas would hasten their "civilization," since they would be forced to give up hunting and fishing and concentrate on farming or working for wages.

At the same time as the fur trade collapsed, and as big game and fish stocks began to be depleted, many of the Ojibwa succumbed to the diseases and alcohol brought by the newcomers. In some cases they agreed to surrender portions of their land in return for certain guarantees that they hoped would allow them to live in their traditional manner. In other cases, they retreated further from the waves of newcomers into areas that were unfit for farming, but Euro-Americans sought to obtain even these lands in order to exploit the lumber and mineral resources. The Ojibwa were truly a people under siege.

Those who lived in the regions now controlled by the British (Upper Canada) were the first to feel the full brunt of the massive Euro-American population increase in their territory. Almost immediately following the Royal Proclamation of 1763 (which had established British recognition of the land rights of their Great Lakes Aboriginal allies), when the British needed land to compensate Loyalists who had fought for the British during the American War of Independence, they purchased blocs of land from the local Mississauga (Ojibwa) bands.[1] Following the settlement of the War of 1812, the British government no longer felt a need for its Aboriginal allies, as Euro-American settlers now outnumbered Aboriginals. What the government did require was more land for the new settlers. After a series of land surrenders in the southern regions of Upper Canada, an ill-fated attempt was made in the 1830s by the lieutenant-governor, Sir Francis Bond Head, to move all the Aboriginal people "away from the corrupting influences of civilization" to a homeland on Manitoulin Island. Because of the opposition of the Wesleyan-Methodist missionaries, and the Aborigines' Protection Society in England, the government was compelled to stop forced surrenders of land, although the Ojibwa in the southern parts of the colony continued to relinquish lands in the Saugeen and Bruce peninsulas, and to seek new reserves throughout the 1840s and 1850s. This process continued despite the fact that they had begun to establish themselves as successful farmers.[2]

The incursions of large numbers of Euro-American settlers had devastating effects on the Ojibwa of southern Ontario, whose traditional hunting and gathering lifestyle was shattered by the agrarian practices of the newcomers. Originally the Ojibwa had accepted the land settlements with few qualifications, but, as historian Donald Smith notes, by the 1890s they recognized that the land surrenders meant just that. However, they were unable to mount an effective opposition.[3] Many Ojibwa fell victim to disease and alcoholism, while others looked for new sources of power to help them. In the 1820s and 1830s, many Ojibwa converted to Wesleyan Methodism, following the example of emerging leaders such as Peter Jones, who became both a Methodist minister and a tireless advocate of Ojibwa rights. During the next several decades, Ojibwa converts showed considerable aptitude for Western learning, and for defending the rights of their people. They formed a cadre of Aboriginal missionaries who worked among the Ojibwa throughout the Great Lakes region and westward. Although they met with varying degrees of success in winning converts, the growing presence of their followers among Ojibwa communities was a sign that the once seamless Anishinaabe society was being torn apart by increasing factionalism. The world view of members of the Christian factions differed radically from the world view of those Ojibwa who followed the teachings of the Midewiwin, even when the former consciously or unconsciously retained many of their previous beliefs.

These differences went beyond a simple transferral of allegiance from the teachings of Nanabozho to those of Jesus Christ. The Methodist version of Christianity preached a gospel in which thrift, industry, discipline, punctuality, and abstinence were as much tenets of faith as the original ten commandments. Although the Ojibwa were not overly concerned with the otherworldly message of Christianity, they were concerned with bimaadiziwin, the good life in this world. And it seemed obvious to Jacobs, Salt, and many other converts that, while Euro-American Christians were prospering, the material life of most Ojibwa was becoming substantially worse. The powers in the Ojibwa universe were definitely out of balance, and needed to be redressed. Having seen their relatives and friends succumb to alcohol, lacking the means to survive in a world in which their traditional sources of subsistence were no longer available, feeling abandoned by the spirits that had protected them in the past, and seeing the apparent ease with which their Euro-American neighbours prospered, many bright young Ojibwa such as Peter Jacobs, David Sawyer, and Peter Marksman turned to the Christian god in an attempt to ensure security and survival for themselves and their people. Even Shingwaukonse (Little Pine), who demonstrated parts of the Midewiwin ceremony for Schoolcraft, began to listen to the competing arguments of Catholic, Anglican, Methodist, and Baptist missionaries in his search for new spirit helpers. In 1833 he was received into the Anglican faith, but apparently continued to take part in Midewiwin ceremonies, and retained his religious scrolls until just before his death.[4]

While the Ojibwa were more individualistic than many of their close relations, such as the more highly structured Menominee and Potawatomi, they had always lived by an ethic of generosity, reciprocal sharing, and consensual decision making, which was closely bound up with the seasonal rounds of existence and their affinity with their natural surroundings. Many, if not all, of these values conflicted with the values promoted by the Methodists. And the contrasts provoked numerous problems between Methodist converts and traditionalists who remained faithful to the teachings of the Midewiwin. For many of the converts, the transition was too great, with the result that they reverted to their former lifestyle, although they no longer openly took part in Midewiwin ceremonies. Many other converts became nominal Christians at best, accepting the material benefits and following the outward rituals, while holding on to their traditional beliefs and values. There were other problems—when Anglican missionaries began to compete with the Methodists for Ojibwa souls, and when the agrarian experiments proved less successful than expected—thus lessening the early enthusiasm that many Ojibwa had shown for the combination of "Christianity and civilization."

To further compound the problems, many of the newly established reserves in southern Ontario began to take in very large numbers of Potawatomi and Ottawa refugees from the United States who were attempting to avoid being moved west of the Mississippi River. Among them were a fair number of Roman Catholic converts, whose arrival caused many of the Ojibwa communities in Ontario to become even further fragmented.[5] While groups of traditionalists continued to exist on many of the eastern reservations in Ontario, most, but not all, of the community leaders were at least nominally Christian. Traditional ceremonies, where they did exist, had been forced to go underground.[6]

Traditional Midewiwin beliefs remained dominant into the twentieth century among most of the Ojibwa in the Boundary Waters region from Rainy Lake, along the Rainy River, and into the Lake of the Woods region. In 1841 Wesleyan Methodist missionary Reverend William Mason, based at Fort Frances on Rainy Lake, noted, "They still practice their Media [Midewiwin], or conjuring work, in which they suppose to give and receive the power of life and death."[7] The Reverend Peter Jacobs, who took over the mission from Mason, spent the next decade in a fruitless effort to convert the local Ojibwa. An Ojibwa himself from Rama in southern Ontario, Jacobs described the opposition that he faced:

> Lac la Pluie [Rainy Lake] District is the Headquarters of Heathenism in

> the surrounding country. The other Indians come to Lac la Pluie a great distance to be initiated in the conjuring arts of the Lac la Pluie Conjurers.... They assemble their followers all along the river from Nanmakang River to Fort Alexander, distant apart from six to eight hundred miles. It is astonishing to see in their metea [Mide] lodges (heathen temples) the quantities of useful goods that are offered up as sacrifices to their heathen gods.... I am sorry to say that heathenism is now much higher than it was 8 years ago and that the Indians now only have a desire to become members of the Medea [Mide] lodge (conjuring temple) but that every one would be head conjurer because they see great gain so to be.[8]

The Midewiwin continuted to thrive in the region for years to come. Subsequent leaders of the Ojibwa in the region, such as Mawedopenais and Powassan, were powerful Mideg who carried on the struggle to maintain their own beliefs and practices, even after they had signed a treaty with the Canadian government in 1873. Although Mawedopenais (who was one of the chief spokesmen at the treaty negotiations) dressed like a "white man," lived in a good house, had begun farming on the land that he had cleared for himself, and sent his children to school to learn to read and write, he refused to have anything to do with the Christian religion, or Christian missionaries.[9] E. McColl, the Manitoba Inspector of Indian Agencies, noted in his 1883 annual report that "they object to mission schools being established on their reserves, as they did not wish their children influenced to forsake the religion of their fathers."[10] In the same report McColl provided a four-page description of Midewiwin and other ceremonies still being practised by Ojibwa bands in the Lake of the Woods region.[11] The reports also noted the very small number of Christian converts on the reserves, thus suggesting further that the Midewiwin continued to be a force in all parts of the Boundary Waters region. Both the reports of Canadian government officials and statements of missionaries in the region made it clear that there was considerable interaction between Canadian Ojibwa from Rainy Lake, Rainy River, and the Lake of the Woods with their American brethren who lived at Red Lake and other reservations in northern Minnesota. Although there are no direct references to their taking part in each other's Midewiwin ceremonies, it seems likely that they would have done so. However, unlike the Midewiwin ceremonies in Wisconsin and Minnesota, which were extensively documented, the ceremonies in Ontario and Manitoba received only passing mention, and were soon forgotten by later Euro-American commentators.

Further west at Red River, Anglican missionaries had begun to make inroads among the Cree and to a lesser extent among the Ojibwa, or

Saulteaux, as they were known there. Like their eastern brethren, the Saulteaux were being taught to read and write, to farm, and to renounce their traditional religious beliefs in favour of Christian ones. However, the early successes of such missionaries as George-Antoine Belcourt, John West, and William Cockran were not lasting, and later missionaries turned their attention further north or west.[12] As Hallowell observed, some groups of Ojibwa, such as those at Roseau River Reserve, "remained outright pagans until the beginning of the present century."[13]

In the United States, government agents' efforts to force the Ojibwa to move from their traditional lands had more tragic consequences. The Ojibwa were suspicious of the government's motives and they were determined to drive a hard bargain for themselves and their kin. At the 1842 treaty deliberations, Shingoup, the head chief from Fond du Lac (and a high-ranking Mide), answered the speech of Commissioner Stuart as follows:

> My friend we now understand the purpose you have come for, and we don't want to displease you. I am glad there are so many people to hear me. I want to know what our great Father will give us for our lands. You must not tell a lie, but tell us what our great father will give us for our lands. I want to ask you again, my father, I want to see the writing and who it is that gave our great father permission to take our minerals. . . . I want to see the Treaty which authorizes Government to take away our minerals.[14]

White Crow (Waubishgaugauge), the elderly chief of the Lac du Flambeau band (southeast of La Pointe), added, "You told us there was nothing wrong on paper. . . . It does not appear that our Father wants to buy our land except the Mineral country. I have raised the half-breeds, and I want you to provide for them, we all eat out of the same dish, we are all like one family. . . ."[15] Despite their suspicions, and their inability to have all their conditions met, most of the Ojibwa finally and reluctantly agreed to sign the treaties, seeing in them the best hope for their continued existence as a people.

The fears of leaders such as White Crow were soon realized when the American government attempted to remove all the Ojibwa to the west of the Mississippi. It was a move that would be successfully resisted, but only after considerable suffering and many deaths. The Protestant missionary at La Pointe, Sherman Hall, related the tragic story of how the Ojibwa who had ceded their lands were forced to travel great distances to Sandy Lake to collect their annuities in the late fall. Many refused, while those who made the trip had to wait for the agent to obtain the money. Sickness broke out in the camps and many died. When the payments finally arrived in December

1850, the survivors had to use most of the money to purchase provisions for the return journey. This meant walking 500 kilometres back, since their canoes were useless in the winter.[16] Although Hall had initially believed that the treaties were the only way to save the Ojibwa as a people, he later argued strongly against the forced removal of the Ojibwa in Wisconsin.

Despite the fact that most of the Protestant missionaries working with the Ojibwa opposed the government's policy of removal, and were sympathetic to the plight of the Ojibwa, their proselytization efforts were largely ineffective. Reverend Hall lamented:

> Few are desirous to learn anything of the religion of the Bible. Most seem to have the impression that the white man's religion is not made for them. His religion, mode of life, and learning are well for him; but to them they are of no use. They would not make them any more successful in hunting and fishing. Their habits are best for them. They say they are a distinct race, and the Great Spirit designed them to be different. They live different and go to a different place when they die.[17]

By the 1850s, the policy of the American government had shifted from an emphasis on removal to recognition that the Ojibwa could remain permanently on reservations in their traditional territories. In Michigan, Wisconsin, and Minnesota, many of those Ojibwa and Ottawa who had refused to move were accommodated in 1854 and 1855 with new treaties in an effort to undo some of the worst abuses of the previous era. The treaties distinguished between the Lake Superior Ojibwa, whose resources the Americans desired, and the Mississippi bands, whose lands were not immediately wanted, while the Red Lake and Pembina bands were ignored for the time being. Those Ojibwa who agreed to take up reservation life attempted to make it work, but they had few resources with which to control their own destiny. Increasingly, control was exercised by the new dispensers of resources: the government agents and missionaries. However, despite the determined efforts of local Methodist and Catholic missionaries, many of the Ojibwa (and, to a lesser extent, Ottawa) continued to hold their traditional world view, follow the teachings of the Midewiwin, and pursue their traditional seasonal rounds. Many of these traditionalists refused to accept individual allotments of land, since they viewed property as a source of resources that served the common good.[18]

On the other hand, there was a feeling among many government officials such as Alexander Ramsey, and missionaries such as Sherman Hall, that unless there was prompt action to protect them, the Ojibwa would face extinction as a people.[19] Ramsey, Hall, and others like him warned that the Ojibwa would succumb to the evils of alcohol provided by unscrupulous traders, European diseases for which they seemed to have no immunity, and starvation that ensued with the decline of their natural food resources. Only by providing them with the means to farm, by teaching them the virtues of hard work and the Christian gospel, and by destroying their traditional culture and religion, would they avoid the fate of many of the wild animals in the region.[20]

Ojibwa leaders in Minnesota were divided as to how to meet these new challenges. Like their colleagues in the British colonies, they sought assistance to restore the balance among the manidoog in order to meet the challenges that faced them. Since they knew that their survival would involve learning how to use technological skills, some of them accepted belief in a Christian deity within the context of Ojibwa cosmology. Fortuitously, they were presented with a new type of missionary in the person of John Johnson (Enmegahbowh), an Ottawa, who, as a young man, had been initiated and educated in the teachings of the Midewiwin before becoming a convert to Methodism. He had left his home in southern Ontario in the 1830s to establish a Methodist mission among the Ojibwa in the United States. Enmegahbowh married the niece of Hole-in-the-Day the Elder and his brother Strong Ground, two important Ojibwa chiefs from Sandy Lake, Minnesota. He thus established strong bonds with them and their bands, although he later opposed the confrontational policies of Hole-in-the-Day the Younger. Unlike many of the previous missionaries in the area (and unlike many of his fellow Ojibwa converts), Enmegahbowh retained his Ojibwa ethic of generosity and mutual sharing. In the 1850s, he transferred his allegiance to the Episcopalians, while retaining his influence with a large segment of the Mississippi Ojibwa who followed him to the White Earth Reservation in 1868. There, numerous other Ojibwa, who were anxious to maintain many of their traditional cultural values, became Episcopalians as a result of Enmegahbowh's influence and his program to establish subsistence farming. In this way, they believed that they might be able to reinvigorate their communities, while maintaining control of their own destiny.[21]

Among the Pillagers and neighbouring bands, many chose to live a traditional existence outside the pale of the dominant culture. The majority of this latter group continued to practise the Midewiwin, although some turned to the Drum or Dream Dance, a new ceremony introduced in the 1860s and 1870s.[22] This latter ceremony was based on the visions received by a young Sioux woman following a battle between the Sioux and the Whites. The cosmology, nevertheless, was similar to Ojibwa beliefs, in that the sacred drum and the rituals attached to it were used by members to petition the manidoog for "blessings." Membership in the society that developed was open, and the ceremonies were more frequent than the Midewiwin. Whereas the Midewiwin existed to help individuals secure a long and healthy life, the Drum religion's role was broadened to include social concerns, including peace between peoples. Some Ojibwa who practised the Drum Dance also continued to belong to the Midewiwin, but most felt that the Midewiwin had been corrupted. Many traditionalists believed that the Drum Dance rituals were a better means of providing the strength and power needed to resist the ever-increasing advances of Euro-American society.[23]

Although important chiefs such as Flat Mouth from Leech Lake and Loon Foot from Fond du Lac remained members of the Midewiwin until their deaths, even Loon Foot's sons were sent to church schools, where they became Methodists. Others, such as Great Buffalo from La Pointe, finally converted to Catholicism just before their deaths. Despite the fact that they had chosen different Christian denominations, all the chiefs followed a similar path of embracing new manidoog, whom they hoped would provide them and their people with the powers needed to adapt to the new challenges they faced.

Most of the reserves in Canada and the reservations in the United States were located on marginal land, distant from Euro-American centres of population. Even those Ojibwa who had agreed to live on the lands set aside for them made efforts to retain their old way of life. However, this was seldom possible, given the meagre natural resource base of most reservations, and the failure of the governments to live up to their obligations. Moreover, bands with different histories were brought together in large, artificially created reservations such as White Earth in the United States, while in Upper Canada, bands of Ojibwa, Ottawa, and Potawatomi, many of them refugees from the United States, were lumped together in reserves. These people brought with them a variety of backgrounds, feuds, and expectations, which, in the close quarters of their new existence, tended to flare up in factionalism. In some ways these reservations and reserves resembled the refugee centres of the late seventeenth century in that they both brought together disparate groups. However, whereas the Midewiwin had served as a cohesive force in the refugee villages, it now helped to accentuate the divisions, since it was but one of several paths to bimaadiziwin.

The Ojibwa and their Métis cousins had long coexisted and, in many cases, reservations contained families of mixed heritage.[24] When the Ojibwa signed the treaties, they had endeavoured to secure assistance for the mixed-bloods since, as White Crow argued, they were all of one family. Later, however, divisions began to develop between those who continued to follow the culture and religion of their Ojibwa ancestors, and those who followed the Christian beliefs of their French or English ancestors and made efforts to adapt to Euro-American society. Many of the Métis made their living as traders, whiskey peddlers, or Indian Affairs officials, while at the same time claiming the right to be added to the annuity rolls of the Ojibwa. Among those who formed part of this larger community was the Warren family.[25] William Warren and many of his sisters all continued to be associated with the Ojibwa people at several of the Minnesota reservations. Despite his obvious sympathy for the circumstances of the Ojibwa, and his determination to tell the story of their history and culture to the American public, Warren and his sisters were all Protestant Christians who lived in the White world, although they continued to maintain close ties to their Ojibwa relatives.[26]

Early Ethnographic Accounts of the Midewiwin among the Southwestern Ojibwa

Near the end of the nineteenth century, a new breed of professionally trained ethnographers began their mission to record for posterity the cultures and languages of the Aboriginal peoples in North America.[27] Soon, a steady stream of ethnologists visited a range of communities of the Ojibwa and their Algonquian neighbours in order to study their "traditional" beliefs and practices. Among these visitors was the American ethnologist and linguist, Dr. Walter J. Hoffman. Hoffman had begun his studies researching the folklore of Pennsylvania Germans, but later joined the staff of the US Bureau of Ethnology, where he became involved in fieldwork on the Ojibwa and Menominee.[28] Hoffman began his work on the Ojibwa as an assistant to Colonel Garrick Mallery, who had published a number of articles on the picture writing of the North American Aboriginal peoples. During 1887-88 Hoffman spent three months on the reservations at Red Lake and White Earth, concentrating primarily on the pictographic records used in the Midewiwin, while Mallery was carrying out similar research at Bad River[29] and Red Cliff reservations in the Chequamegon Bay region. The research was prompted by a desire of the Bureau of Ethnology to review the reliability of the work on Ojibwa pictographs carried out by Schoolcraft.[30]

Whereas Mallery's investigations at Bad River were inconclusive, Hoffman was fortunate in finding an active Midewiwin society functioning at White Earth and Red Lake. Moreover, he apparently took a much broader view

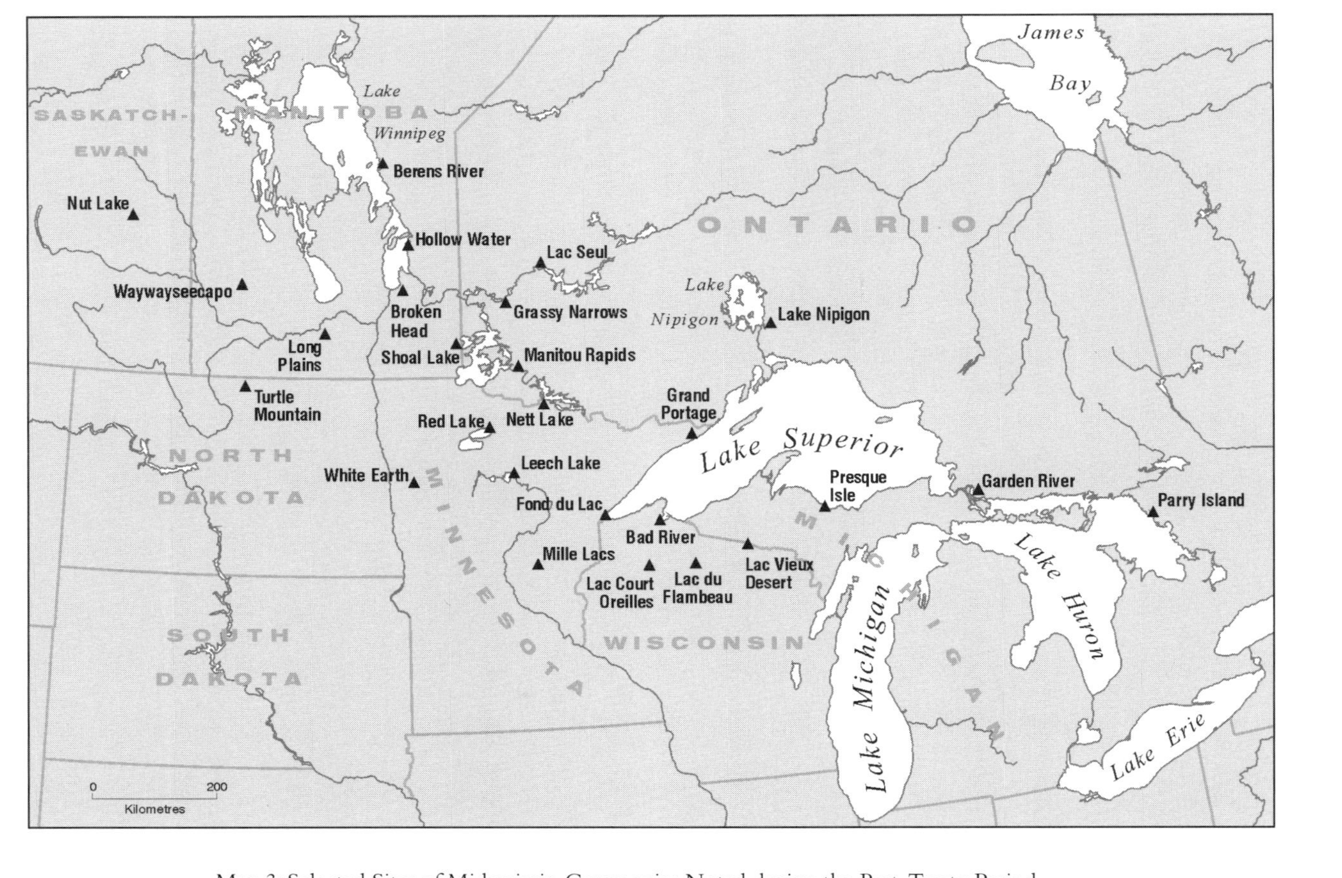

Map 3: Selected Sites of Midewiwin Ceremonies Noted during the Post-Treaty Period.

of his research activities, going far beyond collecting examples of pictographic records. This was, no doubt, due to the fact that most of these records were provided to him by Mideg—leading him to pursue this area of research more closely. Hoffman gave his readers only a cursory historical background to the Midewiwin, plus the names and background of his informants, and he devoted little attention to the social circumstances of the Ojibwa at the time he collected his information.

Although the situation of the Ojibwa at the two reservations Hoffman visited was considerably different from that at Bad River, there were also differences between Red Lake and White Earth. The reservation at White Earth, which had been created in 1867, became the home of a number of previously autonomous and culturally distinct groups of Ojibwa, who formed factions in the new reservation. In addition to the original Mississippi River bands, the reservation later accepted a band of Pillagers and some Plains Ojibwa from along the Pembina River. The majority of the Pillagers had settled on other reservations at Leech Lake, Cass Lake, and Lake Winnibigoshish. The divisions at White Earth were exacerbated by the fact that the larger group had become Episcopalians, whereas the Pillagers continued to practise the Midewiwin. Moreover, those from Pembina were mainly mixed-blood Roman Catholics.[31] The American government's practice of providing individual allotments of land rather than allowing the people to practise communal ownership further increased the fragmentation of the reservation and the alienation of many of its inhabitants.

The Red Lake reservation was much more homogeneous. The bands of Ojibwa who made up the population were more closely connected to the northern bands from Rainy Lake, Lake of the Woods, and Pembina. Unlike other reservations, Red Lake was granted permission to maintain communal land ownership. Christian missionaries had been effectively marginalized by the practitioners of the Midewiwin, who continued to be the dominant religious group until the twentieth century.[32] Among other things, the missionaries were accused of being responsible for acting as "evil shamans" or "witches" who used their "evil powers" to cause the pulmonary disease that had resulted in a great number of deaths at Red Lake. The efforts of both Protestant and Catholic missionaries to establish schools among them were thwarted by the Mide leaders, who opposed the teaching of Christian doctrines. The Red Lake Ojibwa also steadfastly refused to take up agricultural pursuits as long as they were able to hunt buffalo—to the dismay of the missionaries. These factors, and the relatively isolated location of the reservation, meant that there was far less cultural upheaval than at

White Earth, and far less assimilation of individuals than on most other reservations located in Wisconsin and Michigan.

Despite their limited successes, the Ojibwa who wished to maintain the old ways generally feared for the future. Everywhere, it seemed, the old ways were under attack. Their lands were being lost and, with them, the ability to provide for themselves. The rights of hereditary chiefs were being usurped by government officials or government-appointed leaders, while teachers and ministers were beginning to take over many of the teaching roles and ritual functions of the Mide elders. Government officials and missionaries were taking steps to prohibit the celebration of Aboriginal ceremonies and the practices of Aboriginal "medicine men."

In 1889 President Harrison of the United States promulgated a new Indian policy, which demanded that Aboriginal peoples accept absorption into national life as American citizens, give up their tribal relationships, and conform to the norms of the dominant society. Traditional religious rituals and secular amusements were strongly discouraged by the Office of Indian Affairs. The principle of severalty resulted in most of the lands that had been retained for the Ojibwa being sold off, since speculators were able to convince individual landholders to sell. By the early twentieth century, only twenty percent of the lands that they had been ceded remained in Aboriginal hands. When the Sioux protested the loss of their lands and continued to dance the Ghost Dance, the US Army was called in, and massacred over 100 people, including women and children, in December 1890 at Wounded Knee. It was in this context of uncertainty for the future that Hoffman was able to gain the confidence of some Ojibwa. As he explained:

> [The Ojibwa] tribal ties will be broken and their primitive customs and rites be abandoned.
>
> The chief Mide priests, being aware of the momentous consequences of such a change in their habits, and foreseeing the impracticability of much longer continuing the ceremonies of so-called 'pagan rites,' became willing to impart them to me, in order that a complete description might be made and preserved for the future information of their descendants.[33]

The resulting 300-page document, entitled "The Midewiwin or 'Grand Medicine Society' of the Ojibwa," is the most comprehensive account ever produced on the Midewiwin.[34] The major part of the document provided detailed information on the preparation and initiation of candidates for the four degrees, as well as information on the Ghost Midewiwin. Other sections provided background information on the Midewiwin in general, on the role of "shamans," a description of the Mide Lodge, plus supplementary notes on pictographs, music, dress, and ornaments.

As one would expect of a trained ethnologist and linguist, Hoffman's study was at once comprehensive and detailed. Despite the fact that his information had been gleaned from a number of sources and informants, he provided, for the first time, a general overview of the ceremonies, the officials who conducted them, the religious objects that were employed, and something of the teachings that were imparted. Surprisingly, although he provided meticulous translations of Mide songs from the original Ojibwa, in which he noted the archaic nature of many of the words, Hoffman did not record Ojibwa terms for the Mide officials, or for many of the artifacts that were used in the ceremonies. Although he gave both an Ojibwa name and a scientific name for the miigis or cowrie shell used in the Midewiwin ceremony, he created the impression that only this particular shell had a vital significance, although other types of shells were also used by the Ojibwa. Similarly, he failed to explain that such objects were used by a wide variety of Aboriginal groups in both North and South America as a powerful means of either causing or curing illness.

While his work was relatively free of Christian bias, Hoffman continued to view the Ojibwa as "primitives" and the Mideg as "charlatans." Indeed, despite his claim to have been initiated into the society himself,[35] Hoffman stated in the introduction to his report that the purpose of the Midewiwin was twofold: "first, to preserve the traditions [which he had just mentioned], and second, to give a certain class of ambitious men and women sufficient influence through their acknowledged power of exorcism and necromancy to lead a comfortable life at the expense of the credulous."[36] Thus, for all his academic credentials, and his participation in both the Midewiwin of the Ojibwa and the *Mitawit* of the Menominee, Hoffman's work exhibited a strong Euro-American bias.

Like many nineteenth-century social scientists, Hoffman sought to classify everything he studied, using a combination of Euro-American concepts and categories, and information from his informants. For instance, he followed Schoolcraft's depiction of three classes of "shamans," one of which was the Mide. Unlike Schoolcraft, who saw all classes of shamans as evil, Hoffman depicted the role of the "Jes'sakkids" (Jiisakiiwininiwag) as one of "invoking and causing evil, while that of the Mide is to avert it."[37] However, despite the best efforts of Euro-Americans such as Schoolcraft and Hoffman, the Ojibwa world can not be divided up into mutually exclusive, discrete classes and categories.

In a later portion of the work, Hoffman explained that in his experience, there was considerable variation in "the dramatization of the ritual."[38] He implied that some of the differences he encountered could be attributed to the separation of the Ojibwa nation at Sault Ste. Marie into northern and southern divisions, between which groups there was limited intercourse. In addition, he explained, individual Mideg operated independently, with the result that pictographic inscriptions on Mide charts could not always be interpreted by other Mideg. While Hoffman was no doubt correct in his explanations of some of the variations he encountered, he failed to adequately address such fundamental problems as the relationship of Jiiskiiwininiwag and Waabanowag to the Midewiwin, or the relationship of "good" manidoog or Mideg to "evil" manidoog or Mideg.

However, these limitations are quibbles about a work that has provided successive generations with a comprehensive insight into a world view that might otherwise have been lost. Hoffman's work has been invaluable in its meticulous transcription of the words, music, and pictographs used in the Midewiwin ceremonies. So accurate are his transcriptions of some of the instructions, along with origin and song charts, that present-day Ojibwa have turned to his work in their attempts to revive the Midewiwin.

Hoffman was the first observer to provide a comprehensive explanation of the four levels or degrees of the Midewiwin, along with their corresponding initiation ceremonies and subsequent powers.[39] This hierarchical aspect of the society caused many Euro-Americans to speculate that the Midewiwin had been influenced by Freemasonry, since they assumed that Aboriginal hunters and gatherers could never have conceived of such a complex structure on their own. Hoffman's account illustrates just how complex the Midewiwin was, but there are no connections with Freemasonry ideas or rituals, other than that both are based on the progressive acquisition of knowledge and power, which was symbolized by different levels or degrees.

The complexity of his subject matter appears to have proved bewildering even for Hoffman, since, despite his best attempts at being systematic, his coverage of the four degrees is quite confusing. His goal was to begin with an overall explanation of what he took to be the first-degree ceremonies, and then explain more briefly the differences that existed as candidates were initiated into progressively higher degrees. However, he is not always consistent in his explanations. This may be partly due to the fact that his main informants were from different locations. At other times, it appears that Hoffman simply neglected to explain specific differences that occurred at the various levels, since he interspersed many of his descriptions with extended explanations of musical instruments used, descriptions of songs, and tables of plants and their properties.

It is possible, nevertheless, to outline a number of areas in which Hoffman did describe the differences among the degrees. Thus, for instance, he both described and illustrated the changes in the Mide Lodge (Midewigaan) for each of the four degrees. The major changes involved the placement of additional Mide posts (midewatig) in the lodges, and the fact that the fourth-degree lodge had openings on all four sides, rather than at just the east and west ends. Hoffman also described and illustrated the different designs and colours of face painting used by Mideg. His description constitutes one of the few records of this practice, which appears to have died out in the late nineteenth century. Hoffman mentioned the sacred medicine bags (*midewayaan* or *biinjigoosan*) and the fact that each degree had a distinct midewayaan. However, he spent little time describing them or explaining their difference, leaving that to later observers such as Frances Densmore and Fred Blessing.

Along with several other observers, Hoffman noted that prospective candidates for the first degree had to satisfy Mide officials that they had received a vision that was legitimate and appropriate. Hoffman does, however, seem to suggest that individuals who had not received a vision could instead "purchase a Miigis."[40] This would tie in with other observers' statements that visions were becoming less common, and Mallery's statement that some individuals tried to stimulate visions through the use of alcohol. It might also explain why those individuals who did have visions (such as Jiisakiiwininiwag) were more respected and more feared than some others.

Hoffman went on to explain that in the year preceding the ceremony, the candidate underwent instruction from senior Mide officials. Approximately two weeks before the ceremony, a senior Mide (oshkaabewis) sent out invitation sticks to all those who would attend. About five days before, the candidate underwent purification in a series of sweat lodge rituals that prepared him or her for the ceremonies to come. Then, after providing tobacco to his instructors, he or she was taught to make effigies, and the officials demonstrated their supernatural powers to candidates by causing strings of beads to roll and effigy figures to move unaided. This was no doubt one of the rituals that led Euro-American observers to label the Mideg as "conjurors," but for those involved, it demonstrated that Gichi-Manidoo looked favourably on the ceremony to come.

Hoffman's description of the initiation of the candidate is similar to those of previous observers such as Nicollet, although Hoffman's descriptions are far more complete, based as they are on the pictorial instructions of the sacred scrolls or charts used by his informants. Unlike most other observers, Hoffman placed emphasis on what he termed the "Mide sermon," which took place in the sweat lodge just before the main ceremony. In it, the head Mide official told the candidate to listen carefully, for Gichi-Manidoo would be made known to him, and the spirit would give him life, which would never fail. Hoffman described in considerable detail the procession from the sweat lodge to the Midewigaan, the tour around the interior of the Midewigaan, and the ceremonial presentation of the gifts and tobacco to the manidoog. He goes into similar detail about the so-called "shooting ceremony," in which the Mide officials "shot" the candidate with the midewayaan (which contained a miigis shell) while uttering the ejaculation "ho, ho, ho, ho, ho," and then revived him by placing their midewayaan on his prostrate body. Hoffman explained that the candidate slowly revived, and, after taking a miigis from his mouth, sang a song thanking his fellow Mideg for giving him life.

Hoffman noted that at the conclusion of this ceremony, the new Mide tested his new powers by using his midewayaan to "shoot" those present until everyone had been subjected to the power of his miigis. Each of them fell down as though dead, and then gradually recovered. Then, Hoffman explained, all those present took their midewayaan and, uttering "ho, ho, ho, ho, ho," "shot" each other, fell down, and then recovered. However, while other commentators paid considerable attention to this part of what some termed the "public duelling" ritual, Hoffman passed over it and the feast that followed with scarcely any comments. He did, however, note that following the feast, the senior Mide recounted the oral traditions of the Anishinaabeg and the origin of the Midewiwin, together with the benefits that were derived from it. Then the new Mide sang some new songs to all those present, accompanying himself on a drum. The ceremony slowly drew to a close.

Whereas previous observers had merely noted that candidates were required to pay the Mideg a large quantity of presents in order to move from one degree to the next, Hoffman explained that the presents were ultimately being offered to the Mide manidoog:

> This practice is not entirely based on mercenary motives, but it is firmly believed that when a secret or remedy has been paid for it cannot be imparted for nothing, as then its virtue would be impaired, if not entirely destroyed by the manido or guardian spirit under whose special protection it may be supposed to be held or controlled.[41]

Nevertheless, as Hoffman noted, the value of goods required as payment doubled for each degree attained. When one takes into account that

Illustration 9: Interior view of a Midewiwin Lodge from the eastern entrance showing the sacred stone, blanket, cedar degree post, and some gifts in the form of blankets suspended from the ceiling. (From Hoffman, *The Midewiwin,* 188.)

candidates were also required to provide tobacco and presents for the training sessions, plus food for the banquets, it is easy to see why few people could afford the "cost," however defined.

According to Hoffman's account, the second-, third-, and fourth-degree ceremonies were mainly repetitions of the first. He implied that the main addition was the power of the tutelary manidoo for the particular degree. Unfortunately, Hoffman was not clear about what these were for each degree, since they seem to have varied. He was, however, somewhat more informative as to the types of powers or blessings acquired by candidates who were accepted into each degree. Members of the first degree mainly gained the power of preparing what was termed "hunters' medicine" (such as described by Tanner in Chapter Two), and learned songs to the manidoog who acted as keepers of the different animal species. They were also taught an elemental knowledge of the powers of particular plants that could be used for healing and other purposes. These powers helped ensure the survival of themselves and their families, particularly in times of scarcity or danger.

Members of the second degree received similar but stronger powers related to curing and protection, as well as the power to use bad medicine against enemies. Hoffman particularly noted their power to cause facial paralyses or "twisted mouths." There were numerous victims of this malady, which Hoffman and many other Euro-Americans speculated was caused by the use of small amounts of strychnia or some other poison.[42] Mideg of the second degree also acquired additional powers that allowed them to see into the future and to hear what was happening at great distances, as well as to leave their physical bodies and assume other shapes. Hoffman implied that *"Mi'tsha Mides,"* or "Bad Mideg," who employed these powers for evil purposes, often assumed the form of a bear, in which guise the Mide might kill his victim. Such persons, he suggested, were called "witches."[43] In another context, he implied that such perversion of the Midewiwin was the result of "Bad Mideg" who were connected with Waabanowag.[44] Hoffman also stated that second-degree Mideg acquired the powers to act as "sucking bone" doctors (called *nenaandawiiwejig* by the Ojibwa). These powers allowed them to cure illnesses that were caused by the intrusion of a foreign object—often at the hand of an enemy.

Few members of the Midewiwin, in Hoffman's experience, ever proceeded beyond the second degree, partly due to the high cost of initiation. However, those who received the required instruction, made the offerings, and were initiated, acquired even greater supernatural powers, under the tutelage of the bear manidoo.[45] Their powers of exorcism were greater, their knowledge of medicines expanded, and their powers of prophecy (divination) were much increased. It was at this point, Hoffman seems to suggest, that their powers became equivalent to those of Jiisakiiwininiwag, who received their powers directly from a manidoo in a vision. Hoffman suggested elsewhere that Jiisakiiwininiwag could and sometimes did become members of the Midewiwin, but he provided no indication of whether they were required to go through the three degrees or simply began at the third level.

Those few who attained the fourth degree were believed to have powers that were beyond belief. Hoffman's informants suggested that their powers came close to those of Nanabozho, and such individuals alone were able to communicate directly with Gitchi-Manidoo. However, these powers were two-edged, for there were great temptations to use them for evil purposes or personal aggrandizement. Waabanowag of this degree were especially feared because of their power to inflict injury, and their astounding performances with fire.[46] Hoffman mentioned that malevolent spirits, including *Mishibishi* (Mishibizhii), the panther, and Makwa, the bear, and *Meshike* (Mikinaak), the turtle, guarded the Mide Lodge and attempted to resist the candidate's entrance during the rites for the higher degrees. They had to be driven away by good manidoog. The power of these evil spirits would appear to add to the sense that the power gained by people who entered these degrees could be used for evil as well as good purposes. The fact that the manidoog served both as tutelary spirits and malevolent spirits added to the sense of ambiguity.

Hoffman included a special section in his work on variations of the Midewiwin, including something he termed the "Dzhibai Mide'wigan" or "Ghost Lodge." Hoffman noted that the Ghost Lodge differed from the regular Mide Lodge in that the openings were on the north and south axis, rather than the east and west. Since the fourth-degree lodge also had north and south entrances (in addition to east and west ones), this may have added to its sinister reputation, because the Ojibwa feared the afterlife and the spirits of the Ghost Lodge. This is among the earliest recorded use of the term Ghost Lodge by Euro-Americans, but variations of the rituals described had been present among the Ojibwa for some time. It might be tempting to connect this variation of the Midewiwin with the Ghost Dance revitalization movement that swept across the Midwest in the 1890s, but this would be a mistake. Despite the similarity of the name, the relative proximity of the Lakota (western) Sioux to the Minnesota Ojibwa, and the mutual acceptance of other ceremonies, there is no evidence that Ghost Lodge and Ghost Dance ceremonies had anything in common, other than some shared concerns.

The Ghost Lodge Midewiwin, according to Hoffman, was conducted for those children who had died before reaching the age of puberty and thus were unable to be initiated into the Midewiwin. Such children, Hoffman explained, had been "dedicated" to the Midewiwin at their naming ceremony shortly after their birth. At this ceremony, a Mide elder had been chosen to name the child from a vision he or she had received. If the elder's vision indicated that the child would become a Mide, instructions would begin as the child grew older, but the initiation ceremony only occurred following puberty. If the child died before then, the father would announce his intention of acting as a substitute for the child and become a member of the society. Such membership would ensure that the deceased child was freed from the "Ghost Gambler" who held his victims under his power in a world of shadows. The deceased child would then be guided on the journey to a new abode in the afterlife, which was peopled by members of the Midewiwin.[47]

Several aspects of Hoffman's account provide insights into what he believed to be the gradual evolution of the Midewiwin. Most notable is his statement that its members were not admitted until puberty, although two and possibly all three of the previous observers described ceremonies in which young children, even infants, were admitted, with their parents serving as proxies during the initiation ceremonies. It is uncertain whether the young girl described in Nicollet's account was pre-pubertal, but the children in both Kohl's and Day's accounts definitely were.

It is possible that Hoffman's account indicates a developmental change. However, it is more likely that Hoffman was generalizing from a single incident, or misunderstood his informant, since this is the only record of such a prohibition. Regardless, the development of the Ghost Midewiwin, and special funeral ceremonies for members of the Midewiwin, do indicate a further development away from a simple curing ceremony into a ceremony that gave members strength to cope in both this life and the next. Anishinaabe beliefs included a belief in the soul—in fact, in two souls, one of which wandered around burial grounds and old haunts, while the other pursued a path that led to its final resting place. However, the Anishinaabeg were more interested in the life of this world than in the afterlife. Belief in an afterworld that was reserved for members of the Midewiwin Society added an exclusivist element, which was not present in the earlier Anishinaabe world view. As such, it would appear to be a reaction to Christian concepts of a heaven reserved for those who believed in Christian salvation.[48]

Hoffman also mentioned that special Mide ceremonies were carried out for sick persons who presumably had not been cured by other means.[49] In cases where the patient could not be successfully treated by a Mide in the patient's own lodge, and his family could afford the fees for initiation into the first degree, the patient was carried into the specially constructed Mide Lodge. It was believed that the evil manidoo could be expelled in this sacred structure, "at which place alone the presence of Ki'tshi Man'ido may be felt," if the ceremonies were performed and the patient promised to devote his life to the teachings and services of the society.[50] If the patient showed improvement, the songs took on a more boastful character and the rituals for the first-degree ceremony were carried out. If the patient continued to worsen, singing and the use of the rattle continued until the patient died.

Unlike previous Euro-American observers who picked out several aspects that appeared important to them, Hoffman's account of the Midewiwin is an exhaustive, integrated study. His explanation of the structure of the Mide Lodge, including the sacred posts, the sacred stone, the pole upon which the presents are hung, plus the Mide drum, drumstick, and rattle used by the Mide officials, is far more complete than all previous accounts. He even described and illustrated the facial decoration of the participants, and the decoration of the sacred poles used in each of the four degrees, noting the variations in colour.[51] Such details, along with the examples of birchbark scrolls, give a remarkably vivid picture of a complex ceremony.

Hoffman was the first observer to take the "sermons" of the Mide officials seriously. He noted how the Mideg used these sermons to explain the origin of the Midewiwin and how it had aided the Ojibwa in their migration westward. What Hoffman termed "sermons" were oral narratives that Mideg passed on to new members of the Midewiwin. Storyboards, in the form of origin and migration charts, which had been copied on birchbark scrolls, served as mnemonic aids and teaching devices for the Mideg. As Dewdney and Thomas Vennum later showed in more detail, it was these migration charts that detailed the various migrations of different bands of Ojibwa westward over a period of approximately two centuries.[52] As such, they recorded not only the westward progress of the Midewiwin, but also noted the various Ojibwa settlements that had been established during this period, and thus helped establish the Ojibwa claim to the land.

The charts also provided insights into the development of the concept of the Ojibwa as a people who were part of, but separate from, other members of the Anishinaabeg. In the eighteenth century, when large refugee villages existed, the Midewiwin had served as a trans-tribal connecting force, which helped to bring different groups of the Anishinaabeg together. In the nineteenth century, during the period of the Ojibwa westward migration, the Midewiwin appears to be more closely identified with the new tribal groups such as the Ojibwa who were beginning to emerge as distinct groupings of the Anishinaabeg. Although the Ojibwa continued to speak of themselves in terms of local groupings, and there was no central political figure to whom they owed allegiance, the existing narratives and migration charts of the tribal historians, or *kanawencikewinini*,[53] describe a people with a common heritage and a sense of a common homeland won on the field of battle. It must be remembered, nevertheless, that these records refer to only one of several groups of Ojibwa who lived during this period. What documentary sources we have, though, suggest that a similar sense of self-awareness did exist among other groups as well as those studied by Hoffman.[54] For instance, although the Ojibwa who continued to live in Wisconsin sometimes participated in joint Midewiwin ceremonies with other groups such as the Menominee, the rituals of the different groups had begun to diverge, although the underlying concepts remained similar.

As he had done with the migration charts, Hoffman carefully copied many of the Mide songs that formed part of the ceremonies, and explained the meaning of the symbols that acted as memory aids for the Mideg.[55] He pointed out that the mnemonic symbols employed by the Mideg did not always mean the same thing, as Schoolcraft had maintained. A bear, for instance, might represent the guardian manidoo of the society, a singer impersonating a bear manidoo, the exorcism of a malevolent bear spirit, or the desired capture of a bear. The only way to know the correct interpretation was to be told by the person who owned the chart. Moreover, he explained, Mideg prepared their own songs and often did not sing them twice in the same manner. Although he did attempt to notate several songs, he felt that the words were the important element, believing that the melody would be unrecognizable without the words. Hoffman's interpretation was later challenged by Frances Densmore in her work on Ojibwa music, published from 1910 to 1913.

So comprehensive is Hoffman's work that it is easy to forget he was describing the Midewiwin as it existed at a particular moment (the 1880s) on two Minnesota reservations. While several of the charts presumably went back at least to the early nineteenth century, and the narratives he recorded traced their origin to a more distant past, the Midewiwin was not a static institution. In documenting the Midewiwin ceremonies at Red Lake and White Earth reservations so thoroughly, Hoffman inadvertently created an orthodox canon against which all other examples have since been judged.

Yet, it is arguable to what extent Hoffman's informants were representatives of a "pure" form of the Midewiwin, or if, indeed, such a concept is valid. Like Nicollet's informant Chagobay, two of the informants mentioned by Hoffman, Sikas'sige and Skweko'mik, were lower-level Mideg who had limited socio-political status in their communities. As such, they were considerably less influential than Flat Mouth, Loon Foot, or Shingwaukonse had been during the previous generation, and lacked their knowledge and power. Although this does not necessarily mean that their information was less reliable (since both relied on birchbark records that were several generations old, and Sikas'sige was able to rely on his fourth-degree wife for back-up information), it may indicate that the more powerful members of the Midewiwin were not in favour of providing the information to Hoffman. It must also be remembered that what Hoffman recorded was not the flowering of the strong, vibrant religion that was observed by Nicollet, Schoolcraft, Day, and Kohl. Particularly at White Earth, but also at Red Lake, Hoffman encountered a beleaguered religion whose dwindling adherents looked back to a better past, even though they continued to seek blessings to help them to deal with an increasingly uncertain future.

Nevertheless, the Midewiwin, as it was practised at Red Lake, White Earth, and surrounding reservations, was more vigorous than it was in more acculturated Ojibwa communities.[56] Dewdney and Fred Blessing have both argued that the most "orthodox" forms of the Midewiwin could be found among the Minnesota Ojibwa.[57] At the time Hoffman recorded his material, these groups were on the outer fringes of Ojibwa society. They continued to consider Chequamegon as their spiritual centre, and Bowating as their ancestral homeland, even though the Midewiwin beliefs and practices had declined considerably in the latter communities.

The relative isolation of White Earth and Red Lake from Euro-Americans placed them in a more favourable position to maintain a separate world view. Nevertheless, if contemporary scholars use the views and practices of Hoffman's informants as the norm, they risk judging future descriptions by standards that would have been antithetical to the Anishinaabe world view in which the Mideg sought to interpret the Midewiwin to its members in terms of the local situation.[58] Hoffman himself noted that there was considerable variation between the rituals, pictography, and narratives that he compiled, and those at other reservations. Frances Densmore, the ethnologist whose work both complemented and to some extent corrected Hoffman's, also made this point when she observed that ritual exactness was not obligatory in the Midewiwin. She explained that while the ceremony had a general outline, which was universally followed, the details varied in different localities. The problem remains as to which elements of the Midewiwin were fundamental and which details might vary. Densmore stated that the chief aim of the Midewiwin was to "secure health and long life to its adherents." She added that "music forms an essential means to that end." A long life, she argued, was coincident with goodness, and evil inevitably reacted on the offender. There was, she went on, no reference to war or enemies in the ceremonies, and propitiation was absent from its teaching and practice.[59]

Although Densmore's description of the main aim of the Midewiwin agreed with Hoffman's and that of most other observers, her understanding of the society differed in several significant ways. Not only was she the first to understand the fundamental role of music in the ceremony, and in Ojibwa society in general, but she was the first to paint a positive picture of the society and its adherents. According to her, the "good life" that its members sought was one free from evil and, she suggested, from war and revenge. It is significant, therefore, that Densmore played down any aspects of the Midewiwin that dealt with the temptation by high-degree Mideg to use their power for evil purposes. She made a conscious decision not to include any examples of "bad medicine" in her descriptions. Her denial that the Midewiwin ceremonies were attempts to appease the manidoog marked a complete turnaround from the once-popular views of Schoolcraft. Since Densmore was the first woman to write extensively on the Midewiwin, and since she made use of many female informants, it is tempting to attribute her perspective to her gender. However, the only other study of the Midewiwin by a woman, Ruth Landes's *Ojibwa Religion and the Midewiwin*, concentrated almost exclusively on all the aspects that Densmore avoided, and presented a picture of a society in which evil predominated. Densmore's views may be attributed, rather, to the liberal beliefs of her parents, who had raised her to accept that the neighbouring Aboriginal people had customs different from their own.[60]

Densmore's observations, even though they were not focussed on the Midewiwin itself, represented a new level of understanding on the part of Euro-Americans. Born in Red Wing, Minnesota, in 1867, Densmore received a traditional musical education with emphasis on piano, but became interested in the music of North American Aboriginal people through her close contact with the neighbouring Sioux and Ojibwa, and through reading the work of Alice C. Fletcher, a pioneer in the field of ethnomusicology. Although she later departed from Fletcher's ideas about the structure of Aboriginal music, she followed Fletcher's idea that "music envelopes like an atmosphere, every religious, tribal, and social ceremony as well as every personal experience."[61] Early in her life, Densmore decided she wanted to devote her life to the study of Aboriginal society and particularly Aboriginal music. She set about educating herself by reading everything that had been written on the subject. Following a 1905 visit to Grand Portage, on the north shore of Lake Superior in Minnesota, where she witnessed a Midewiwin ceremony,[62] she became determined to describe Aboriginal music on its own terms, rather than arranging it to suit Euro-American sensibilities. Shortly afterwards she began her work in earnest with the financial assistance of the Bureau of American Ethnology in the Smithsonian Institution.

Twenty years had passed since Hoffman had spent time with a number of informants at Red Lake and White Earth reservations, during which period the traditional lifestyle of the Ojibwa, including the Midewiwin, was constantly under attack. Densmore's sources for songs were men and women singers from the White Earth, Leech Lake, Red Lake, and Bois Fort reservations. Despite the fact that Red Lake continued to be a stronghold of traditionalism (or perhaps because it was), she did not obtain any Midewiwin songs from there. Her informants on other aspects of the Midewiwin came from the Otter Tail, Mille Lacs, and Fond du Lac bands, although most of the explanations were given by two elderly men and one woman from White Earth: Main'ans (Little Wolf), Gage'win, and Na'waji'bigo'kwe. All three were high-degree members of the Midewiwin, though Densmore does not make clear their role in reservation society.

Given her background and training, Densmore's analysis of the Midewiwin was, to a large extent, from a musical perspective. Songs, she believed, represented the musical expression of religious ideas. However, unlike those before her, for whom Ojibwa melody and harmonics were exotic but boring, Densmore argued that rhythm and melody were the essential elements of Ojibwa music, since they expressed the idea of the song; words were forced to conform to the melody.[63] Like Hoffman before her, she noted that many of these words were archaic forms, which were difficult for contemporary Ojibwa to translate exactly, or meaningless syllables that filled out the measures of melody. She had been informed, she explained, that the words might change slightly as long as the idea remained the same. Densmore tested out her theories concerning melody by playing a Mide song and having members of the Midewiwin from a different reserve draw a series of mnemonic pictures to represent the song. She then asked the original Mideg from whom she had collected the song to reproduce it from the mnemonics.[64] Densmore made a number of such comparisons and was able to conclude that the mnemonics represented the melody of the song.

Densmore believed that music was of such importance that the Mideg exerted their power through a combination of music and medicine. For a cure to work, it was necessary to use both the proper medicine and the proper song. She noted that in some of the Mide songs, the medicine bags (or, more properly, the manidoo) were sometimes represented as speaking. It was the song that made the charm effective. Densmore noted that rhythm was most peculiar in songs intended to produce "magic," including those that gave success in hunting and healing.[65]

Densmore explained that the Midewiwin was a multi-level society, open to both men and women. According to her, it had eight levels or degrees, which could be attained after the appropriate instruction had been received and the required gifts were bestowed. She observed that meetings were held each spring, and could also be held in the fall. Since fair weather was symbolic of health and happiness, efforts were made to begin the ceremony on a sunny day. Members were required to attend one meeting a year so as to restore their "spirit power." Smaller gatherings could also be held in order to treat the sick. Mide officials were members holding high degrees, and were chosen for the office at each meeting.

Densmore did not go into the same detail regarding the eight degrees as Hoffman had done for the four he described, but she did provide explanations for some aspects Hoffman had neglected. Thus, she noted that when a candidate had chosen a Mide to lead the ceremony at which he or she was to be initiated, they together then chose four others (who were normally not as high-degree as the leader) to assist them. Although Densmore did not provide a name for the leader, Ruth Landes later described him as *Gitchi Webid*, or "chief person," while the remaining officials were called *webids,* or "assistant chiefs." The first of those chosen was the oshkaabewis, whose duty it was to announce the ceremony and invite members to attend. He carried tobacco for them to smoke and announced the names of the officers to the people. Throughout the remainder of the ceremony, the oshkaabewis acted as the general director of the events. Following the completion of the sweat lodge ceremonies, the remaining officers were chosen. These included the *ne'mita'maun* (*naagaanid*, whom Landes later termed the *naganid,* or "Bowsman") and the *we'daked'* (*weedaakeed*, whom Landes termed the *wedaged,* or "Steersman"), both of whom played important roles in the initiation or shooting ritual.[66] Densmore also distinguished a small group of specially appointed singers whom she termed the *zagimag*. While many Mide songs were sung by the candidate or other officials as part of individual rituals, the zagimag were responsible for singing the *nimiwug* (*niimi'idi-nagamon*) or dancing songs, which distinguished those points in the ceremony when anyone could dance.

Densmore compared this form of the Midewiwin ceremony, in which members were initiated into various degrees, with another form more specifically devoted to curing and used when traditional curing methods failed. This was a final attempt to prolong life, and if even it failed, the ceremony made the patient's last hours more comfortable. Densmore thus clarified the reason for the different versions of the Midewiwin described by previous Euro-American observers. Rather than a single Midewiwin ceremony with fixed rituals, there were several ceremonies in which the rituals varied, depending upon the occasion. Densmore was fortunate in being present at a curing ceremony for Niganibines, the hereditary chief of the Pillager band, and son of Flat Mouth.[67] In this case the leader, oshkaabewis, and eight other Mideg were selected to carry out the ceremony. A special Mide Lodge was constructed, along with a medicine pole. The patient was carried to the lodge where Mide officials, relatives, and friends gathered. Medicine songs were sung, the patient was given a medicinal brew to drink, and the Mideg "shot" their medicine bags at him. If, as in the case of Niganibines, the patient died, a form of "funeral ceremony" was held at which the

Midewiwin beliefs were reviewed for the benefit of the family, and the spirit of the deceased was given instructions to help him on his journey to the land of the spirits.

This Midewiwin curing ceremony was contrasted with what Densmore termed the *Djasakid* (Jiisakiiwin) curing ceremony. The latter name, she explained, was applied to both "jugglers" and doctors. The Jiisakiiwininiwag were distinguished from Mideg in that the latter obtained their supernatural power and songs from a vision received through fasting. Densmore described how the person she termed a Djasakid treated the patient by swallowing and then regurgitating bones.[68]

Densmore's description of the main Midewiwin ceremony resembled Hoffman's, except for her emphasis on the significance of music and songs in the rituals. Her training as a musician enabled her to offer new insights into the melodic structure and function of Mide songs, although her interpretation of the songs was lacking in some instances. Thomas Vennum, a trained musicologist and linguist, attributed some of Densmore's difficulties to her incorrect translation of some of the Ojibwa words. Moreover, while he agreed with her that the melody was important, and that words were not fixed, Vennum supported Hoffman's view that the melodies of the same Mide song text could vary with individuals. What was important was the *idea* expressed by the words (even though these, too, might vary slightly).

Both Densmore and Hoffman grasped part, but not all, of the significance of the symbolism of the tree pictograph in Midewiwin ceremonies. Taking as his example some of Hoffman's explanations of song pictographs made by Little Frenchman, and Densmore's explanations of several songs in which the pictograph incorporates a tree, Thomas Vennum takes issue with parts of their interpretations. He suggests that although they were aware that the tree pictograph represented the tree climbed by Nanabozho during the deluge, Densmore and Hoffman appear not to have been aware of other meanings. Decades earlier, Johann Kohl had noted that the Ojibwa Mideg also saw the tree as the "path of life" and made a connection with the *baagaakokwaan*, or drumstick. In the Mide Lodge the tree was represented as a degree post. The tree/degree post stood for the restorative power of the Midewiwin; planting the tree represented establishing the Mide religion as a way of life, the trunk symbolizing the proper path and the branches as dead ends. At other times, Vennum said, it was used to symbolize the spread of the Ojibwa people from their place of origin.[69] Vennum might have added that a tree, the white pine in particular, because of its height and straightness, had a special significance as a name that could give power

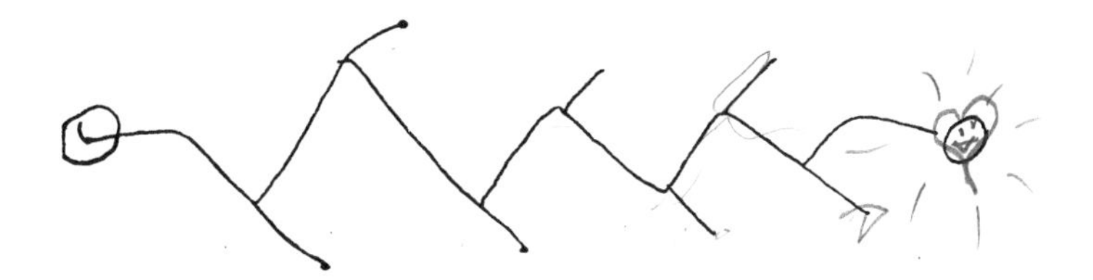

Illustration 10: The Path of Life. Drawing of a pictograph used as an instructional aid in Midewiwin ceremonies, as explained to Frances Densmore by Main'ans (Albert Little Wolf), an informant from White Earth. The diagram represents the path of life from youth to old age, each tangent representing a temptation that must be overcome if one is to live to old age. (Bureau of Ethnology Bulletin 45, p. 24. Reproduced in Densmore, *Chippewa Customs*, 88-89.)

to its holder. Shingwaukonse, the noted leader and Mide, was named Pine or Little Pine.

Thus, the tree pictograph, which is found throughout Ojibwa sacred scrolls in various forms, and which Densmore used to illustrate several of the songs that she had collected, has a number of different meanings, depending upon the context.[70] It is important to keep in mind this variability of meaning in Ojibwa symbols, songs, and narratives. Too often, observers have seized on one interpretation and tried to apply it to all instances. The efforts of several generations of scholars to unlock the meaning of the origin and migration song charts (and words) are not just a case of scholarly detective work. From the Ojibwa viewpoint, the process of achieving understanding can be seen as a case of removing the various layers of meaning so that the kernel or seed of the story finally becomes apparent. As the layers are removed, our understanding of the Midewiwin (and the Anishinaabe world view) becomes clearer, so that formerly meaningless acts gradually can be put into context. As this happens, one's own biases and preconceptions break down and one can approach the beliefs and ceremonies with a more positive attitude.

Densmore devoted extensive notes to the context in which the Mide song was sung. In reviewing these notes, Vennum has argued that her interpretation of the meaning of the accompanying pictographs (song pictures) failed to capture the idea that she correctly judged to be so important. Although Vennum may be correct that Densmore's explanations of the song pictures are flawed, it might be recalled that she noted that the Mideg themselves would often gather to debate the meanings of the song pictures and other sacred pictographs. Meanings were not precise, even for the initiated.

If Hoffman and, to a lesser extent, Densmore believed they were describing a dying tradition, they underestimated the Midewiwin's strength and resilience. Almost forty years later, in the 1930s and 1940s in northern Michigan, at Lac Vieux Desert (Katikitegan) near the Wisconsin border, anthropologist Vernon Kinietz observed that the Midewiwin was unopposed. In fact, he noted, some of the villagers who had been Christians had recently joined the Midewiwin.[71] Kinietz and his fellow anthropologists, Victor Barnouw, who studied Ojibwa culture at Lac du Flambeau, and Robert Ritzenthaler, who carried out fieldwork at Lac Court Oreilles, together give us yet another glimpse of the ceremony itself and the role that it played during the first half of the twentieth century. Their combined work provides evidence for the persistence of Euro-American views of the Midewiwin, despite the increasing willingness of the participants to allow outsiders to observe the ceremonies.

The Ojibwa in these three communities formed part of the Lake Superior Chippewa (Ojibwa) who had signed the 1854 Treaty with the American government. The Lac du Flambeau and Lac Court Oreilles bands had been allotted small tracts of land in regions where the practice of traditional subsistence patterns and the adaptation to the money economy proved equally difficult. A combination of government- and church-run schools attempted to teach the English language as well as American values and vocational skills. Most Ojibwa began to take on the outward characteristics of their Euro-American neighbours, although reservation life brought with it a general deterioration of living conditions as the inhabitants struggled unsuccessfully to make a living. A combination of poor housing, alcoholism, and disease led to a health crisis, which continued to grow worse with the passing years.

"Traditionalists" attempted to separate into autonomous villages in which they continued to speak Ojibwa, and to practise the Midewiwin, while attempting to eke out a subsistence living. At the time of the 1854 treaty, a large number of Ojibwa at L'Anse (near Keewenaw Bay) elected to leave that relatively acculturated community and establish a new village (Katikitegan) at Lac Vieux Desert, where they could continue to live their lives as their ancestors had done. A smaller number of Ojibwa at Lac Court Oreilles established a separate village (Old Village), where they lived according to the old ways.

The three anthropologists, along with A. Irving Hallowell (who spent some time among the Lac du Flambeau Ojibwa in order to compare them with the people at Berens River, Manitoba), were representative of a new group of scholars interested in studying the acculturation of Aboriginal people. While each approached the task from a different perspective, all were interested in the implications of acculturation for the Ojibwa world view. They investigated not only areas of Ojibwa life in which there had been change, but also those in which there had been stability. As a result, they exhibited a special interest in those communities that showed elements of persistence in values and practices. For this reason, Kinietz and Barnouw concentrated their efforts on the geographically and socially isolated communities of Katikitegan and Old Village. Their research provided concrete evidence that despite the dire predictions of an earlier generation of Euro-Americans, the Midewiwin had not completely died out.

Ritzenthaler entitled his study of the Ojibwa "Chippewa Preoccupation with Health." He began by asserting that the Ojibwa were approximately eighty percent acculturated at the time of his study, and that Catholicism had made substantial inroads into the community at Lac du Flambeau, but that the Ojibwa continued to demonstrate an inordinate interest in health and healing. His study concluded that this preoccupation was demonstrated in their ceremonies, such as the Midewiwin, their traditional concepts of disease, the curative and preventative techniques employed by healers, and the prestige these healers were accorded by other band members.[72] Unfortunately, Ritzenthaler was vague as to the extent these views were shared by the acculturated members of the community. However, given the nature of his thesis, it must be assumed that many of the otherwise acculturated Ojibwa continued to maintain traditional views regarding health and disease. Ritzenthaler found there were many concrete reasons for their health concerns at the time of his studies, but argued that these concerns had been present among the Ojibwa for some time. In fact, he maintained that the Ojibwa preoccupation with health had its origins in the pre-contact period, although the concerns had intensified in the post-contact period, due to serious health problems as a result of early contacts and the later establishment of reservations.[73] Ritzenthaler implied that the preoccupation with health concerns was at least in part a result of what Hallowell termed a personality structure that made them feel responsible for their own situation.[74]

Ritzenthaler argued that the Midewiwin, as it existed among the Ojibwa at Lac du Flambeau, was dominated by its curative functions, and sickness had become the main prerequisite for membership. He contrasted this with the situation at Hoffman's time when, he argued, the entrance into the Midewiwin was "a natural, routine part of a person's life, and candidates spent a considerable amount of time and paid huge amounts in goods in order to gain medicinal knowledge."[75] According to Ritzenthaler, the twentieth-century Ojibwa had retained only the most essential or useful parts of the ceremony—that is, those parts that helped them deal with medical problems.

Kinietz also believed the Midewiwin had undergone many changes since earlier times. However, his interpretation of what had happened differed somewhat from Ritzenthaler's. According to Kinietz, many of the changes in the ceremony took place as a result of borrowing from Christianity, and by now the "native ceremony [Midewiwin] may well be called a church denomination."[76] Kinietz went on to explain that, at Lac Vieux Desert, Ojibwa called the ceremony "our church," and, indeed, a number of former Catholics had become members of the Midewiwin. Whereas in previous times, the Midewiwin had many characteristics of a secret society, at Lac Vieux Desert almost all the village belonged, and only White visitors were barred. Nevertheless, according to both Kinietz's informant, John Pete, and Barnouw's informant, Tom Badger, the main purpose of the Midewiwin was to help its adherents to regain health or to ensure its continuance. The miigis continued to play a central role in both scholars' accounts of the Midewiwin ceremony, but a new element had been added to the ceremonies at Lac Vieux Desert and Lac Court Oreilles. When other remedies failed to heal a sick person, the Mide fastened a miigis on the patient (called "borrowing life"), indicating that a Midewiwin ceremony would have to be held before a cure could "clear up the account."[77] This aspect of the ceremony led Ritzenthaler to conclude that at Lac du Flambeau the "old ritual, meaning, and accoutrements of the Midewiwin had been sloughed off within the last fifty years, and in this condensation process the religion has withdrawn into and seized upon the curative aspect as the important one...."[78] He reported that "in the 1940s even babies who were, or had been, ill could be inducted into the Society, and that seems to have been another distinct departure from the old tradition."[79] The more detailed accounts of the Midewiwin at the neighbouring communities of Lac Court Oreilles and Lac Vieux Desert suggest that the functions of the ceremonies remained broader than Ritzenthaler (or Barnouw and Kinietz) would have us believe. Many of the rituals varied more in form than in substance.

The main ceremony itself, particularly those parts that involved the miigis, was much closer to the ceremonies described by earlier observers than Ritzenthaler believed. However, Kinietz and Barnouw (through their informants) do provide examples of how some of the rituals in the ceremony were evolving. As Kinietz observed, "Formerly, people were able to swallow and disgorge them [miigis], but now they only hold them in their mouths—during four circuits of the lodge. Then each puts his miigis away in his medicine skin."[80] In fairness, one should acknowledge that the swallowing and regurgitation of the miigis may have been replaced by the simple placing of the miigis in the participant's mouth, but the belief in the power attributed to the miigis remained unchanged.

The "shooting ceremony," in which the officials threw their "medicine skins" at a point (shoulder, elbow, knee) in order to strengthen it, also remained fundamentally the same, although there were some minor variations. In Barnouw's account, any part of the body might be marked with coloured pigment and shot with medicine bundles, rather than the specified areas that other accounts mentioned. Whereas earlier accounts had employed the image (and vocabulary) of shooting arrows, the officials now "loaded their guns" with miigis shells.[81] Both observers related how, at another point in the ceremony, when the miigis was placed in the candidate's mouth, he fell over as if dead, until he was revived by the power of the Mide's medicine bundle. Tom Badger explained, when describing the public duelling, "If you had a hide pointed at you, you would get sick and die. The only way you could get well then would be to join the Midewiwin. It's dangerous, when they're pointing their hides."[82] Thus, we can conclude that while the Midewiwin may have taken on the outward appearance of just another religious denomination, its members were well aware that Mide officials continued to possess powers that made them both respected and feared.

Other essential aspects of the Midewiwin also remained unchanged. Kinietz recorded the use of the sacred phrases "Ho! Ho! Ho!" on several occasions during the ceremony, but principally in connection with the shooting rituals.[83] The staging of a Midewiwin continued to require a considerable accumulation of goods, including food and alcoholic drink for several feasts, in addition to payment to the Mide officials and the assistants responsible for erecting the lodge. Kinietz implied that the introduction of alcohol in the ceremonies was new, but Mallery, Hoffman, and Alexander Henry the Younger had all noted this in their accounts in the nineteenth century.[84] Both Barnouw and Kinietz also described the teaching that occurred during the ceremony. Candidates were given instructions regarding the ceremony itself as well as the origins of the Midewiwin. The medium of instruction appeared to have changed from pictographs drawn on birchbark scrolls and boards to pictographs drawn in sand or dirt, but in every instance, the intention was to provide memory aids for the participants.

Barnouw explained that "the naganit explains the meaning of the marks in a heap of earth to the wamidewit [candidate]. He tells him that if he doesn't listen, he will go off on the top road . . . if he goes off on that road, he won't live long. But he says that if the wamidewit listens carefully, he will go along the path to the point where your hair starts to turn white."[85]

In this brief speech by the *naagaanid* (leader), the functions of the Midewiwin were clearly broader than that of a simple curing ceremony for a specific illness. What is being expounded upon is the necessity of keeping to the path of life set out by the Midewiwin in order to live to old age. Once again, it would appear that Euro-American observers focussed almost entirely on a single aspect of the rituals, to the exclusion of the broader teachings of the Midewiwin.

Nevertheless, despite the many similarities of the anthropological reports and older accounts of the Midewiwin, it is equally clear that entry into the Midewiwin had lost much of its early rigour. Candidates were no longer required to have a vision before applying for admission, nor were they (and Mide officials) required to undergo cleansing in a sweat lodge at the beginning of the ceremony.[86] Tom Badger, Barnouw's main informant, explained that he had never been visited by a guardian spirit during his vision quest—a fact he attributed to his mother's giving him food to eat during his fast. This, he claimed, accounted for his limited powers as a Mide.[87]

A number of aspects of the ceremonies themselves also changed. Kinietz singled out the lack of secrecy as one of the most important changes, but it would appear that the practice at Katikitegan was the exception rather than the rule.[88] The medicine stone and the *midewatig,* or posts in the lodge, appear to have passed out of use, although they were referred to in the ceremonies. However, the water drum (*mitigwakik*) and rattle continued to be used. Another innovation at Katikitegan was that medicine bundles were inherited or sold, rather than being buried at the death of a Mide.[89] Sweat lodge rituals were no longer part of the ceremony. This, coupled with the fact that visions were no longer required, are further evidence that entry into the Midewiwin had become much easier. The number of Mide officials was smaller than formerly, since the pool of trained people was limited, and, as might be expected, arguments regarding the accurate details of different rituals were intense. However, from Barnouw's description, it appears that the functions of the officials were more specialized than previously recorded.[90] Although instructions continued to be given during the ceremony, the series of teaching sessions before the ceremony was no longer carried out, and the description of the origin myth within the ceremony had been considerably shortened. However, Barnouw's collection of myths does indicate that the cycle of myths continued to exist in the same basic format. Whereas instruction in medicines had previously been a vital part of a candidate's initiation, the informants indicated that this knowledge was no longer passed on to the same extent within the context of the Midewiwin. They maintained that even at the higher degrees, medicines were used only to cure minor ailments, and were never used to cause illnesses. According to Kinietz, people continued to believe that physical ailments were mainly the result of supernatural causes, which required the aid of traditional healers who possessed supernatural gifts that allowed them to effect cures.

Both Kinietz's and Barnouw's informants appear to have been anxious to minimize the role of the Midewiwin as a place for individuals to gain knowledge, power, and prestige. Except for Tom Badger's brief remarks regarding the power of the medicine bags to actually kill, there was little indication that such power carried with it the potential to do both good and evil. If the powers of the Mide officials were more limited than in previous times, one would expect the prestige of the Mideg in their communities to be diminished. This certainly appears to have been the case, for even in the traditional villages, the Mideg do not appear to have played leading roles in the life of the community. However, it may also be that these groups of Ojibwa had learned to be more cautious in revealing the true nature of their ceremonies to outsiders, given the increased efforts of church and government officials to suppress the practice of Aboriginal religions. Finally, the descriptions may indicate the particular perspective of the observers themselves, since they were specifically interested in the curing aspects of the Midewiwin.

The preceding accounts vary considerably from those of Ruth Landes, who carried out anthropological research among the Ojibwa of the Cass Lake reservation in Minnesota and the Manitou Reserve near Elmo, Ontario, during the early 1930s. The first results of this fieldwork appeared in *Ojibwa Sociology* (1937) and *The Ojibwa Woman* (1938), in which Landes dealt with what she termed the highly individualistic nature of Ojibwa hunting and gathering society. Years later, Landes put together much of her earlier field studies into what has become the modern classic, *Ojibwa Religion and the Midewiwin*. Like Schoolcraft before her, Landes believed that the Ojibwa were shaped by their environment. She painted a bleak picture of a lonely hunter who "felt himself a soul at bay, against cosmic forces personalized as cynical or terrorizing . . . life is a battle with the manidoo for meat and blanket; and a battle one must fight all alone, desperately, for mere survival."[91] Landes's vision of Ojibwa society was one in which suspicion, fear, and conflict predominated. Quarrels, duels, blood feuds, various forms of sexual aggression, and psychic disorders were, according to her, part of the Ojibwa character. Landes approached the study of the Midewiwin within this context. Predictably, her explanation focussed on the "sorcery" practised by "shamans" who used their powers primarily for evil purposes. Will Rogers (Hole-in-the-Sky), from the Cass Lake Pillager band, who served as her primary informant, apparently had an alarming reputation as an "evil shaman" but was finally bested in combat and ended his days in a mental hospital. Landes painted a picture of a boastful man who both threatened and charmed those around him. Her other informant, Maggie Wilson, from Manitou Rapids, though part Cree and a nominal Christian, was a well-known visionary who appears to have served as a counterpoise to Rogers. Yet, even Wilson could hardly be considered to have been a "good shaman" if Landes's description is to be taken at face value.[92]

Given her understanding of Ojibwa society as individualistic or "atomistic," it is not surprising that Landes posed the question as to why the Midewiwin society flourished among them. She answered her own question by explaining that "rampant individualism also operated here too."[93] This, she explained, was the reason Will Rogers had agreed to teach her without first consulting his Mide colleagues. According to her, each Mide's public status rested on private visionary accomplishments, but was given public acknowledgement in the "mutual challenges and covert duels" in which they engaged. The excitement in every Midewiwin ceremony was generated as much by the Mide's performance as by the cure itself.[94]

Landes acknowledged that the Mide origin tales spoke of the Midewiwin bringing "life" for the Ojibwa. However, she interpreted this as a blessing that resolved the conflict between good and evil among the manidoog. She argued that while public Mide teachings might stress positive virtues and inspire hope, the Mideg were traditionally the enemies of the people. They used tactics of fear and aggression to indoctrinate the people, and used sorcery to keep them terrorized by causing illness or even death among their victims. However, according to Landes, the Ojibwa notion of "terrorize" could best be described as inspiring respect. She believed that evil manidoog and evil Mideg were considered "evil" because they were "unscrupulous" or "highly skilled" (in manipulation). In Landes's view, power and evil were seen to be related, rather than evil being a misuse of power.[95]

The main events of the Midewiwin ceremony, as described by Landes, outwardly resemble the nineteenth-century ceremonies far more than they resemble the ceremonies described by Kinietz and Barnouw. To begin with, they lasted seven to eight days and were closed to non-members except for the final day, which the public could attend. Personal visions, though not required of all applicants for membership, played an important part in the Midewiwin observed by Landes. Sweat lodges were also an essential part of the Midewiwin, and sweat rituals were used at several points during the ceremony. Landes classed members into three groups: cured patients, ritual officers, and curing "shamans" or Mide doctors.[96] This differed from Hoffman, who made no distinctions among Midewiwin members.[97] The curing "shamans" or Mide doctors, Landes suggested, were set apart since they "merged with the Supernaturals and addressed one another as 'manito.'"[98]

According to Landes, patient members could not automatically become either ritual officers, or curing "shamans, "regardless of the degree they might hold. Special instruction was required, and normally visions were required of them in order that they might demonstrate their superior power. These offices generally ran in bilateral family lines (and included both sexes), since family members were able to receive instruction at reduced rates and shared in the fees paid by candidates. This, at times, caused tensions between family and non-family members, regarding what Landes termed "nepotism."

The Midewiwin described by Landes was structured as four Earth grades followed by four Sky grades, although she noted that few people ever proceeded beyond the third grade, because the fees increased markedly with each grade. Landes noted, as Hoffman had observed earlier, that those who went through the highest grades inevitably found that the power they acquired was "increasingly open to abuse," with the result that these Mideg were both respected and feared. In Landes's understanding, "good shamans" ranked below "evil" ones, and were much less respected.[99]

Perhaps because she had paid for a lengthy series of instructions from Will Rogers, Landes's account of the actual ceremonies was, if anything, more detailed than Hoffman's had been. Landes described the different rituals that were conducted on each succeeding day, and provided names and explanations of the duties of the presiding Mide ceremonial officials. Although her explanation was at times confusing or confused, it was much more focussed than Hoffman's, which was interspersed with side explanations from a variety of Ojibwa and non-Ojibwa sources. Nevertheless, Landes's work described a generic ceremony, while Hoffman provided details of the ceremonies for each of the first four grades or degrees.

In contrast to Hoffman's description of the Midewiwin, Landes's work provides a personal flavour. Not only were Will Rogers's (Hole) and

Everwind's (another Mide) activities described in such a way that the men became individual human beings, but Landes inserted herself into the process, so there is less of a feeling of subject and object in her work. Thus, for instance, she described the weeks she spent transcribing Mide narratives and pictographs from Hole's scroll in order to understand them. Her description of the discussions of the Mideg also revealed a very different side to them: "There was no firm limit to the number of elaborations about the midé tale. Hole and others, like Everwind's circle revealed that imaginative men like to speculate on ethical, philosophic, therapeutic, and even novelistic implications hidden in the tale. . . . Hole would walk miles to talk midéwiwin with his colleague, Everwind."[100] It is hard to believe that these are the same men whom she claimed regularly engaged in quarrels, blood feuds, various forms of sexual aggression, and who suffered from psychic disorders, although it is not impossible that she was describing two sides of the same individuals.

Landes herself made few comments about these apparent contradictions, but she did find significant differences between the Midewiwin that Hoffman had observed and the ones presided over by Hole and Everwind. If anything, she believed that the ceremonies she observed were closer to the Menominee form of the Midewiwin described by Hoffman, particularly with regard to the origin narratives.[101]

Ethnographic Accounts of the Midewiwin among the Western Ojibwa

The majority of the accounts of the Midewiwin described thus far have concentrated on those Ojibwa who have often been categorized as the Southwestern Ojibwa by Euro-American scholars. It would be wrong, however, to suggest, as some scholars have done, that the Midewiwin was confined essentially to this group of Ojibwa.[102] Usually such statements are based on the early documents, and are contrasted with later documents that indicate the Midewiwin had been drastically altered, or was in a state of irreversible decline. Often the different forms of the Midewiwin are attributed to cultural differences among the different groups of Ojibwa. However, while there are some cultural differences between the Southwestern Ojibwa and other groups of Ojibwa, these differences were not significant with respect to the practice of the Midewiwin. Indeed, as will be seen, with few exceptions, the variations within one group were often greater than among the Southwestern Ojibwa, the Western Ojibwa, and the Northern Ojibwa.[103] Determining how one distinguishes the Ojibwa of western Canada, North Dakota, and Montana is difficult since various terms, such as Saulteaux, Bungi, and Plains Ojibwa, have been and continue to be used by scholars and the people themselves. I have elected to use the term "Western Ojibwa" primarily as a geographical marker.

The first major ethnological report that dealt with the Midewiwin among the Western Ojibwa was by Alanson Skinner in his study of the groups who lived mainly in southern Manitoba and North Dakota.[104] Noting that the separation of the Western Ojibwa from the Ojibwa proper had taken place in relatively recent times, he contended that by their own account they had intermarried to some extent with the Cree, Ojibwa, Assiniboine, and Ottawa, and, more recently, had associated with local bands of Sioux who had fled north to Canada from Minnesota in the late nineteenth century. He might have also noted that Ojibwa also frequently intermarried with French and Métis in the area. Skinner's brief explanation was amplified and expanded, first by James Howard in his follow-up study of the Plains Ojibwa in 1977, and more recently by Laura Peers's more comprehensive history *The Ojibwa of Western Canada* in 1994.[105]

As Peers and John Milloy have pointed out, the adaptations of Cree and Ojibwa migrants to Plains culture can not be seen simply in terms of environmental determinism.[106] The changes that took place were the result of complex forces, including inter-tribal connections, which were partly a response to the advent of the European fur trade, and were connected to both the spread of European diseases and the decline of the vast herds of buffalo. In this new and rapidly changing world, the Ojibwa were numerically small and, it can be argued, played a relatively secondary role. Certainly, the *lingua franca* of trade was Cree or Cree-based, and Plains Cree believed Plains Ojibwa to be their inferiors.[107] And yet, the early statements of traders throughout the prairie region during this period often made reference to how members of other tribal groups feared and respected the superior power of Ojibwa spiritual leaders.[108] Some writers, such as Hugh Dempsey in his biography of Big Bear, suggest that this reputation led to the ready acceptance of the Ojibwa by other tribal groups on the plains.[109] Big Bear, who was to figure prominently as a powerful "Cree" leader in the 1885 Rebellion, had been raised as Cree, but his father, at least, was an Ojibwa member of a mixed Cree and Ojibwa band. It was natural for members to participate in each other's ceremonies, and to adopt some aspects of each other's value systems.[110] At the same time, both the Cree and Ojibwa were in the process of adapting to life in the parklands and on the plains, and adopting some of the practices and values of other Plains groups who had preceded them there. Peers has further speculated that the Ojibwa reputation may have been directly related to the

Midewiwin ceremonies and the powers gained during these ceremonies.[111] This led some Cree to become followers of the Midewiwin and adopt the Midewiwin rituals of their Ojibwa neighbours.[112] Nevertheless, given the fact that among many Western Ojibwa, the Sun Dance ceremonies replaced the Midewiwin, it is probable that the Ojibwa were more influenced by the Cree and Assiniboine than the reverse.

Although the religious beliefs of tribal groups may have differed, they were similar in a number of fundamental ways, including their understanding of the concept of power. Thus, neighbouring Cree or Assiniboine understood the concept of Ojibwa traditional healers receiving power from manidoog. They would have appreciated the capacity of Ojibwa traditional healers to use this power to heal, and feared their ability to use this power to maim or kill. Not only were these Ojibwa spiritual leaders sought out because of their power, but members of other tribal groups welcomed the chance to share in these powers by participating in Ojibwa ceremonies such as the Midewiwin.

Despite the relative paucity of detailed early reports concerning the practice of the Midewiwin in these parts, there is no reason to doubt it was as well established there as among the Ojibwa of Minnesota. Alexander Henry the Younger, David Thompson, George Nelson, and John Tanner all made brief references to Midewiwin and Waabanowiwin ceremonies in the early 1800s.[113] A. Irving Hallowell provided a good historical overview of some of these observations in what he termed a "post-mortem record of a ceremony which once was of major importance in the native culture of the Saulteaux Indians of the Lake Winnipeg Country."[114] While adding his voice to a long line of ethnologists who announced the demise of the Midewiwin, Hallowell correlated a considerable amount of otherwise unavailable information regarding its practice. Although his own focus of interest was Berens River and bands residing on the east shore of Lake Winnipeg, much of his research dealt with the practice of the Midewiwin among groups to the south, including many who were considered Plains Ojibwa.

According to Hallowell's data, the Midewiwin had been celebrated in a number of locations before treaties were signed and the Ojibwa confined to reserves. He mentioned Tanner's reference to such a ceremony at a location south of Riding Mountain and west of Lake Manitoba in the early 1800s. Hallowell was told that the Midewiwin had been held on Garden Island at the northern end of Lake Manitoba, during the nineteenth century, and this would appear to be corroborated by George Nelson's reference to a Midewiwin ceremony at Jack Head in 1819.[115] Various observers, beginning with Henry in the early 1800s, have commented on the Midewiwin held near the confluence of the Roseau River and the Red River. Hallowell also mentioned J.J. Hargrave's reference to "dog feasts" near Lower Fort Garry, which may have been Midewiwin ceremonies, and to Rev. Cockran's 1832 reference to what also could have been a Midewiwin ceremony at Netley Creek. Coupled with Peter Jacob's reference to a Midewiwin ceremony near Fort Alexander in 1852, and the previous reference to Midewiwin ceremonies on the Brokenhead River, one can safely conclude that the ceremony was of major importance to the Ojibwa of western Canada throughout the nineteenth century.

However, by the time Skinner arrived to do his field research in the early twentieth century, the Midewiwin was no longer a dominant force in the lives of most of these Ojibwa. Several factors appear to have been involved in its gradual decline. Among those Ojibwa who elected to maintain their traditional religion, many had turned to the Sun Dance ceremonies, which they adopted from their Plains neighbours. Others, including members of the St. Peter's band, elected to become Christians. Later, Canadian government officials joined forces with Christian missionaries in an effort to "vigorously suppress" all forms of Aboriginal religious ceremonies. The principal tool by which this was accomplished was Section 114 of the Revised Indian Act (1895). While the regulations did not specifically forbid ceremonies such as the Sun Dance and Midewiwin, the Department of Indian Affairs adopted tactics such as requiring that individuals present travel passes, in order to prevent them from attending gatherings at other reserves, withholding agency food rations required to feed those present at gatherings, and impeding the sale of trade goods for use in the ceremonies. As Katherine Pettipas has commented in her book on the government repression of indigenous religious ceremonies on the prairies, "the Indian Department regarded conservative traditional ritual leaders as major impediments to the assimilation process. Consequently, officials were committed to using every possible means to divest them of their spiritual and secular power."[116] Under these circumstances, it is not surprising that members of the Long Plains band were extremely reluctant to discuss the practice of the Midewiwin with visiting ethnologists.

Skinner did present some "meagre data" on the Midewiwin, as it was practised by the Western Ojibwa, in his 1920 comparative study of what he termed the "Medicine Ceremony." From what he was able to learn, the ceremony "differs little from that of the Ojibwa proper, with whom they sometimes come in contact."[117] Individuals who became sick during the winter brought blankets, calicos, and other gifts in the spring in order to purchase information regarding cures. They were instructed and given a medicine bag, which contained miigis shells and certain paints and medicines. Four degrees were recognized, though very few people attained the rank of fourth degree. Skinner was able to obtain two birchbark charts, one of which gave instructions concerning the "Jipai" or Ghost Midewiwin. When the birchbark roll was transferred to Skinner, "[the informant] claimed that it was the oldest and greatest of rolls, and 'descended,' through copying, from the original roll which first was made to contain the directions and ritual of the four degrees."[118]

Skinner's chief informant regarding the Midewiwin was Ogimauwinini (Chief of Men), an elderly man who had become a third-degree Mide. As a youth he had participated in the *Okitcita*, a formal council of "strong-hearted men" who maintained order in camp, regulated the buffalo hunts, and took part in forays against enemy forces before they had been confined to the Long Plains Reservation. Ogimauwinini had received his training in the Midewiwin from Naigis (Someone Shaking) from Brokenhead Reserve. Hallowell mentioned that the inhabitants of Brokenhead River (Reserve) had remained pagan for years, and that their head man, Nenagis, was the most widely known Mide south of Lake Winnipeg.[119]

Ogimauwinini provided Skinner with a brief overview of the Midewiwin ceremony but was unwilling to give him detailed explanations of the scrolls, or the names of the manidoog involved, since these things were too sacred to share even with fellow Mideg. From the explanation, however, it is clear that the celebrants asked the manidoog for help in their quest for long life. However, nothing was included in Skinner's description regarding the "initiation rite," nor the public duelling—no doubt since these rituals not only contained the essence of the ceremony, but also because these were the practices most likely to bring on further government repression.

During the 1950s, James Howard carried out fieldwork among the Western Ojibwa, so it is possible to determine the changes that had taken place since the 1920s and 1930s when Skinner and Hallowell produced their brief reports. What is immediately apparent is that despite earlier predictions that the Midewiwin would die out, ceremonies were still being conducted, though the number of adherents had declined and the ceremonies took place on only a few reserves.[120] The decline in active members may confirm that attempts by government and Christian churches to ban ceremonies such as the Midewiwin and Sun Dance were successful. However, even individuals who no longer practised the Midewiwin or the Sun Dance continued to understand the world in terms of manidoog, who conferred blessings or caused evil to happen. The basic structure of the Ojibwa world view does not appear to have been significantly affected, despite the banning of their ceremonies. An interesting sidelight to Howard's research was the Western Ojibwa's continued incorporation of many concepts and manidoog of more northerly Ojibwa. Thus, for instance, the *Wihtigokanak* (*wiindigoo*), or cannibalistic ice monsters, continued to play an important role in their beliefs. And even more telling was Howard's discovery that the culture hero was known both as *Nanapus* (Nanabozho), in the case of other southern Ojibwa, and also as *Wisakedzak,* as he was known to the more northerly Ojibwa and Cree.

According to Howard's interpretation, the Ojibwa world was a dualistic one in which the "good" Thunderbirds and the "evil" Underwater Panthers were constantly at war. Since humans had both qualities within them, it was necessary to keep the forces in balance. Yet, as we have seen, the situation was more complicated than Howard suggested. Even he realized that the Underwater Panthers imparted some of their knowledge of medicines (which were mainly obtained from plants) to humans as part of the Midewiwin. These medicines were still common on most Ojibwa reservations, and members of the Midewiwin were renowned for their knowledge of them.[121]

Howard, like Ritzenthaler before him, believed that for the Ojibwa (including the Western Ojibwa), the Midewiwin was primarily a response to their concerns about health and the threats to health represented by individual traditional healers. According to Howard, "by incorporating the tribal shamans into an organized group, where their medicinal and supernatural knowledge conferred great prestige, and even wealth, and at the same time making membership in this group open to non-shamans, the threat to the community from evil magic was minimized and the positive aspect of shamanistic lore turned to best account."[122] Certainly *Tsisakids* (Jiisakiiwininiwag) remained few in number and often were members of the Midewiwin, so it could perhaps be argued that the Midewiwin was successful. Most accounts, such as those by Hoffman, Densmore, Kinietz, and Barnouw, appear to confirm this. However, if Landes and Blessing are to be believed, then the problem of evil Mideg (who caused illness and even death) continued to exist within the Midewiwin itself. The underlying problem was that with increased power came the temptation to use it in ways that caused harm to others.

It is interesting to note that although Joseph Greatwalker, Howard's informant, who was a Midewiwin member from Waywayseecappo Reserve, informed Howard that the sole purpose of the Midewiwin was "the promotion of health and longevity," Greatwalker's first action on entering the encampment was to purchase some "swamp root medicine" in order to ward off the purposeful machinations of "bad medicine men" who might "shoot" them while they were there.[123] What Howard witnessed was an example of the ongoing tension between those aspects of the Midewiwin that stressed positive teachings and practices leading to health and longevity, and the ever-present possibility that Mideg would use their power to cause illness and premature death.

Though Howard joined those predicting the death of the Midewiwin, his description of the ceremony he attended has none of the characteristics of a society in decline. Much of Howard's description bears an uncanny resemblance to the first complete description rendered by Joseph Nicollet in the 1830s. Like Nicollet before him, Howard began by explaining how the rites were conducted by an official called the *skabewis* (oshkaabewis). He proceeded through the presentation of the gifts to the leading of the songs by the oshkaabewis. Howard reported that on the third day of the ceremony, the "shooting" of the candidates took place. The ritual described by Howard is basically the same as reported by other observers. Although Howard was unable to stay for the remainder of the ceremonies, his informants had explained to him that another part of it involved a ritual vomiting (in which the shell was regurgitated) induced by herbal medicines, and a "shooting" (duelling) rite and dance in which new candidates and observers alike were indiscriminately "shot."

Howard explained that the shells in the medicine bags were believed to be the scales of the Underwater Panther, who had taught the rites to Nanabozho as related in the origin myth. In the shooting, the shells left the bag and entered the body of the person being shot. This belief, Howard explained, was an ancient and widespread custom in the northern part of the hemisphere, widely associated with "witches" and "shamans," which had been ritualized and regulated in the Midewiwin ceremony in order to protect its members from attack by "shamans" outside the order.[124] The belief that the intrusion of a foreign object may be a cause of pain, illness, or even death is an integral part of the world view of many Aboriginal groups throughout the Americas and, in turn, may explain their willingness to incorporate the Midewiwin into their belief system.

Accounts of the Midewiwin among the Northern Ojibwa

I use the term "Northern Ojibwa" to apply to those groups who lived primarily to the east of Lake Winnipeg and the watershed that drained into it, and those who lived north of Lake Superior along the Severn River and

Albany River watersheds, which drain into Hudson Bay. The names and composition of the groups that lived in these regions have been subject to vigorous debate. Generally, it now appears that groups of Ojibwa gradually moved west and north into portions of the Hudson Bay lowlands throughout the eighteenth century or even earlier.[125] The Lowland (Swampy) Cree they encountered were distantly related, and shared many beliefs and customs. By the beginning of the nineteenth century, there was considerable overlap in the two groups' territories, and many of them spoke a mixed dialect, thus indicating that here, too, a composite culture was beginning to develop. Scholars tended to minimize the amount of fur-trade activity that actually took place in this region, since it was cut off from the territory to the north and west of Lake Winnipeg, where most activity took place. Historical geographer Victor Lytwyn, however, demonstrated that the region was the scene of intensive fur-trade activity, beginning in the latter half of the seventeenth century.[126] Nevertheless, other Euro-American influences, particularly the influence of missionaries and government officials, were much slower in coming, and had less impact here, than among the Ojibwa in other places.

The first extended study of the Northern Ojibwa, or Northern Saulteaux, as he called them, was carried out by Alanson Skinner in 1909 for the American Museum of Natural History in conjunction with a related study of a group he termed the Eastern Cree.[127] Skinner explained in his work that since the main purpose of the study was to look at the material culture of the people, "very little attempt was made to secure information in regard to shamanism and the midewiwin, or medicine lodge society."[128] Nevertheless, he did collect basic information, although he tended to mix up descriptions of the ceremonial practices among the more southerly Ojibwa with his observations concerning the Northern Ojibwa—thus throwing into question the validity of his findings.

Skinner based his scanty information on the Midewiwin among the Northern Ojibwa on a report by Jabez Williams, the Hudson's Bay Company (HBC) factor at Osnaburgh House, who had attended a Midewiwin ceremony at the northwest angle of Lake of the Woods.[129] Although Osnaburgh House falls within the northern region, the Ojibwa in the Lake of the Woods region are generally considered today to have been more closely related to the Lake Winnipeg Saulteaux, the Ojibwa of Red Lake, or even to the Plains Ojibwa of Pembina. Skinner stated that at the time he did his fieldwork, the Midewiwin was not practised north of Lac Seul, although in former times it had been practised as far north as Fort Hope among the Northern Ojibwa. However, he provided little evidence to support this latter claim, other than the testimony of a "conjuror" at Fort Hope, who appears to have been a Jiisakiiwinini, rather than a Mide.[130]

Skinner's account regarding the Northern Ojibwa and Cree is supplemented, and, to a certain extent, contradicted by anthropologist John M. Cooper and by A.I. Hallowell.[131] Cooper's most extended study, which included both fieldwork and original source materials, dealt with the concept of the "supreme being" among the northern Algonquians. His study concentrated on a very limited concept and was concerned primarily with the Cree, but he did consider possible Ojibwa influences on Cree religious beliefs and practices. He acknowledged the close association of the Cree and inland Ojibwa, particularly along the upper Albany. He also acknowledged that the Cree traditional healer was termed a *miteo*, but stated that the term referred to a practitioner of the Shaking Tent. This led Cooper to believe that Skinner's informants were either Ojibwa descendants living among the Cree, or visiting Woodland Cree.[132]

Hallowell's article, "The Passing of the Midewiwin," provided considerable information regarding the practice of the Midewiwin in the region east of Lake Winnipeg. He identified a number of locations and Mide leaders, beginning with Black Island, where the Mide leader was Sekanakwégabau (The One Who Reaches the Sky). Following the signing of the treaty, the Hollow Water Reserve (I.R.10) was organized on the adjoining mainland near the mouth of the river by that name. Kagiwébit, who died in 1919, and Wabanang, who died in 1932, were said to have been the last leaders of the Midewiwin there.[133] Further north, at the narrows, the Midewiwin was practised on both sides of Lake Winnipeg for many years. The earliest Midewiwin ceremonies in this region, according to Hallowell's informants, were held at Dog Head on the western side of the lake, and Jack Head on the eastern side. Yellow Legs, the paternal great-grandfather of Chief William Berens of Berens River, was apparently the first Mide leader in this region before he took up residence at Berens River. Later, a Mide leader called Sagatcíweas (Peter Stoney), who had come originally from St. Peter's Reserve on the Red River, assumed the role.[134] On Stoney's death, Wawasan (Lightning) of Jack Head was the only person to hold Midewiwin ceremonies.

According to Hallowell, Berens River marked the northernmost point that the Midewiwin was held on the eastern side of Lake Winnipeg, for he was unable to find any evidence of it ever having been practised at Island Lake, Deer Lake, or Sandy Lake, although Ojibwa people lived in these communities. The Midewiwin, however, was practised occasionally at Little Grand Rapids and at Poplar Narrows, where Tetabaiyabin (Daylight All around the Sky) was a very influential leader.[135] However, it was not practised after his death in 1922. Further up the river at Pekangikum (Pikangikum), it was practised until 1920 when the Mide leader Pindandakwan moved to Lac Seul. Hallowell pointed out that there was an informal connection among the various Mide leaders in the region, since all of them belonged to the Sturgeon clan and were related.

Hallowell ended his article with a note regarding the connections between the Mideg on the eastern shore of Lake Winnipeg and Lac Seul, where some of them obtained their medicines. He suggested that the Midewiwin may well have been "disseminated all the way from the Lac Seul Ojibwa to the Ojibwa on the western shore of Lake Winnipeg and perhaps beyond."[136] This is a plausible explanation, particularly since connections have been demonstrated in the genealogies of the regions. However, a valid argument could be made for influences disseminating from the Ojibwa communities near Red River, which, in turn, could well have been influenced by the bands of Ojibwa and Ottawa who had emigrated from Minnesota and Wisconsin to the woodlands and plains of southern Manitoba.

Both Skinner and Hallowell referred to another description of the Midewiwin as it was practised at Berens River. James Stewart, an HBC employee, provided what Hallowell believed to have been a description of the last Midewiwin performed at Berens River in the 1850s.[137] As such, it would *appear* to be one of the earliest extended descriptions of the Midewiwin—anywhere. Stewart explained that:

> The name of the feast is "Metawin" or "feast of long life." The head-centre lodge, or tent, was established in the east by some of the divinities.... The centre lodge remains in the east ... but on account of the migrations of the Indians, they received power and instructions to establish subordinate lodges....
>
> Each lodge had its Grand Master of Medicine, a Master of Ceremonies, and other minor officers. Each member of the lodge had in his possession the bag of life. This bag consisted of the skin of a certain bird or animal ... and contained medicine of the most select kind.[138]

Stewart explained that through the intercession of a Mr. Cummings, and "a liberal quantity of tobacco, tea and sugar from myself," he was permitted to enter the Mide Lodge where the ceremonies took place. Having been told to deposit his offerings in front of some wooden images of deities, he was invited to partake in a feast of boiled sturgeon. Stewart's account included a relatively detailed explanation of the origin of the Midewiwin, which was given by a Mide whom Stewart called Bear.[139]

Unless one knew otherwise, this document could be taken as a more or less accurate description of the Midewiwin at Berens River in the 1850s. Seeming anomalies could be accounted for by the fact that James Stewart was recounting events that had taken place almost fifty years earlier. The reference to an identifiable person (Bear) lends credibility to the account. Nevertheless, the account was not what it seemed. Instead, it was actually a composite of personal experience and a series of articles written by James Settee, Jr., a Christian Cree whose father had been an Anglican missionary. Stewart had spent two years with the Hudson's Bay Company in Norway House and Berens River in the early 1850s, but subsequently moved to Red River, where he spent some time as a newspaperman in the 1880s. While he was the editor of the *Selkirk Record*, he published a series of articles by Settee.[140] The references to Bear, and terms such as "Grand Master" (Stewart was an active member of the Masons and a Presbyterian), were undoubtedly his, and it is possible that Stewart could have witnessed part of a Midewiwin ceremony at Berens River in the 1850s. However, the fact that other passages were copied from Settee's article raises doubts about the validity of the entire account.

There are, for instance, what appear to be anomalies in his account of the origin narrative. The first paragraph reads like a Christian creation account of the Great Spirit (God) creating the first man and woman. The second paragraph digresses to tell the story of two snakes: a rattlesnake and a *natawa*. A chief, whose son had been killed by the natawa, was visited by an enormous snake at the gravesite, where the snake addressed him as "Old man of the plain." Later, after the snake had turned into an old, white-haired man, he taught the chief the pipe ceremony, before teaching him the ceremonies and rites of "the tent of long life."[141] Selwyn Dewdney appears not to have been aware of Stewart's account, but one of the snake scrolls that he analyzed was from Berens River. Dewdney speculated that these scrolls reflected an alternative tradition, which originated in the Leech Lake area.[142]

Following his explanation of the origin tale, Stewart began his description of the Midewiwin ceremonies. He explained that the feast was announced by sending out a portion of tobacco to all members of the lodge. After the Mide Lodge had been erected, all the members, led by the "Grand Master" and "Master of Ceremonies," marched around it three times, and then the "Grand Master" addressed the company:

> The Great Spirit, who dwelleth in the heavens, bless you all and send you long life. The white haired man brings with him life and has given me life

> which I give to all my brothers and sisters. Our forefathers left us this tent to teach our children, and your life depends upon the secrets of your own breast. Prepare your magic beads and medicine skins of the tent of life, to cast your beads on the sick and dying men who may be placed before you to restore life. Your magic beads shall pierce the rocks, the spirits who preside over our secret councils shall bless your efforts to restore health and long life. The path of our ancestors teaching us the use of countless herbs and roots growing in this our world will sing the song of enchantment, when each member will offer with gratitude to his teacher, the offerings he may have brought with him to speak and receive long life.[143]

The above passage, aside from the Masonic-like terms to describe the Mide officials, appears to be taken from Settee's original article. This would explain the "Biblical" language and concepts.

Stewart went on to explain the by-now-familiar "initiation ritual" in which the Mide officials took turns "shooting" the candidate, who thereupon collapsed. The candidate was then revived by the officials blowing upon him and placing their medicine bags upon him. Following this, the Mide officials demonstrated their power by swallowing a miigis shell, which "magically" appeared in their medicine bags. This was followed in turn by the distribution of the trade goods, which each candidate had brought as payment, to the officials. After the initiation rite was completed, the "public duelling ritual" commenced. Stewart noted that throughout this time, a number of the women were gathering fish for the ongoing feast, and any dog that entered the lodge was killed and added to the pot.

It is difficult to make a judgement as to where or when Stewart or Settee obtained their information regarding the Midewiwin they described. It is a curious amalgam of Masonic and Christian accretions to a Mide account. And yet, the picture it presents is surprisingly sympathetic. This is particularly true when it is compared to the negative accounts by missionaries such as James Evans and Peter Jacobs. Ironically, it showed fewer Christian influences than the accounts of twentieth-century Ojibwa such as James Redsky and Norval Morriseau.

The final two accounts of the Midewiwin among the Northern Ojibwa represent a departure from their predecessors in that they are the work of Ojibwa rather than Euro-Americans.[144] James Redsky (Esquekesik, Last Man in the Sky), was born at Rice Bay, on Lake of the Woods, in 1899, and was educated at mission schools at Shoal Lake and Kenora. However, he initially ignored the Christian religion, and followed the Midewiwin teachings of his uncle, eventually becoming the leading Mide in the Lake of the Woods region. Much later, at the age of sixty-five, he was made an elder of

Illustration 11: James Redsky Senior, a twentieth-century Canadian Ojibwa Mide from Shoal Lake who maintained his Mide beliefs in the mid-twentieth century when many of his fellow Ojibwa abandoned them. In 1960, at the age of 65, he was ordained an elder in the Presbyterian Church but did not renounce his Mide beliefs. Instead, he convinced the Christians that there was no contradiction in the two faiths and that the Midewiwin deserved respect, not condemnation. (From Dewdney, *Sacred Scrolls,* 179. Courtesy of Glenbow Museum, University of Toronto Press.)

the Presbyterian Church, but he never renounced his Mide beliefs. Although he lived at the very edge of the Shield where it merged into the plains, Redsky's narratives are concerned with the Ojibwa of Lac Seul, Lake Nipigon, Wabigoon, and Lake of the Woods, and their efforts to fend off the marauding Sioux. In a book edited by James Stevens, he recounts the exploits of a local Ojibwa named Mis-quona-queb. Among the narratives are some concerning Mis-quona-queb's initiation into the Midewiwin. Other narratives recount the creation of the world, mankind, and the Midewiwin, and the way of life according to the Midewiwin. The collection also includes a migration story of the Ojibwa and the Midewiwin. In a sense, Redsky's narratives function as a means of teaching the truths of the Midewiwin as he understood them. The following extracts provide an indication of how Christianity had affected the articulation of traditional Anishinaabe religion:

> The Ojibways who belong to the Mide-wi-win believe that God made the world and that we, his children, might live the everlasting life. . . .
>
> When God created the world, in the beginning He set aside a path of life. . . .
>
> There are a lot of tasks to perform to follow the way of life of the Mide-wi-win. As the important saying goes: "Love thy neighbour as thyself."[145]

Redsky explained that after an Ojibwa had dreamed about the Midewiwin, it was necessary for him to have a sweat bath before he could enter the Mide Lodge. The next day, after the sweat bath, the *Mide-winini* was ready to enter the Mide Lodge and proceed with the initiation. During the initiation ceremony, the miigis were placed on the initiate's body according to the degree into which the person was being initiated. Birchbark scrolls were used in order to ensure that all the procedures were carried out correctly.[146] Selwyn Dewdney spent a substantial portion of his book *The Sacred Scrolls of the Southern Ojibway* analyzing Redsky's origin, migration, and master scrolls. Dewdney attempted to provide interpretations of Redsky's and other scrolls, and also to use the scrolls to help understand more about the Midewiwin itself. Although he did come up with a number of very creative interpretations, which have some general applications, he became too enmeshed in trying to explain the fine points of individual charts, which were meant to be specifically used as mnenomic records of local Midewiwin ceremonies.

Dewdney and Fred Blessing, on whose work Dewdney based some of his ideas, both believed there were orthodox and deviant traditions in the

Midewiwin. Their interpretation developed from talking to Mideg in the Minnesota triangle, which Blessing considered the bastion of orthodoxy. However, the very concept of orthodoxy is foreign to the traditional Anishinaabe world view. Although debates took place between rival Mideg, notions regarding orthodoxy and deviancy depended, to a large extent, upon the perception of the individuals involved in the dispute. There is considerable evidence of power struggles between Mideg, but nothing suggests that the battles were fought over issues of doctrinal or ritual purity.

Redsky's versions of Midewiwin narratives were heavily overlaid with Christian terminology and some Christian concepts, although the underlying structure and functions of the Midewiwin ceremonies remained fundamentally unchanged. Candidates continued to seek the means to obtain a long life and the ability to protect themselves from evil forces. However, Gichi-Manidoo and Maji-Manidoo had begun to share a role with the Thunderbirds and Mishibizhii in being the forces behind good and evil. As a result, Redsky's narrative emphasized the duality of good and evil. Moreover, the Christian concept of sin, which manifested itself in the doing of evil, was evident in his stories.

These concepts became even more pronounced in the writings of Norval Morriseau (Copper Thunderbird), an Ojibwa from the Lake Nipigon region in northwestern Ontario, who was born in 1931. Located just fifty kilometres north of Lake Superior, Lake Nipigon had served as the point of departure for the fur brigades heading into the Little North since the eighteenth century, so that Aboriginal people were positioned on a well-travelled route, despite their seemingly isolated location.[147] Although Morriseau became far better known as one of the first Ojibwa artists to gain an international reputation, his artistic works derived their inspiration from Mide scrolls and the sacred narratives of his people. With the assistance of Selwyn Dewdney, he set down many of these narratives in print, along with some of his personal observations.

Morriseau's narratives reflect his dual heritage from his grandfather, who had been a Mide, and his grandmother, who was a devout Roman Catholic. While he considered himself to be a Christian, he believed that "we must never forget our great legends, traditions, and folklore."[148] Nevertheless, by the time Morriseau came to write down his thoughts, it seems the practice of the Midewiwin was a distant reality, for his description of it is considerably less detailed than his description of the Shaking Tent and Sweat Lodge ceremonies. Morriseau's descriptions are also illustrative of how Midewiwin ceremonies and other traditional ceremonies were viewed in light of Christian beliefs—not merely among Euro-Americans, but particularly among members of the Aboriginal community.

According to Morriseau, a *Midawin (*Midewiwin*)* society had existed in the Lake Nipigon area. New members had to pay a great amount of goods and pass tests in order to become members of the society and be given a medicine bag containing great powers. He explained that in the Mide Lodge, there were two tables of food, one containing good food, and another containing partly cooked dog meat and broth. Candidates were made to eat the latter in order to pass the tests, and were also made to swallow live snakes whose tails had been cut off. During the Midewiwin ceremony, the medicine bags, which were made of different kinds of hide, seemed to come alive: "the bear skin began to growl, and the fox skins began to bark. . . ." New members were asked to point their bags at other new members, and out of the bag would shoot forth magic powers so that the person would fall to the ground, spitting blood and dying. However, he would be revived again as if nothing had happened.[149]

Morriseau went on to explain that his grandfather had dreamed of a bear, who became his guardian and provided him with the power to do good. One time, however, his grandfather had got into a fight with a couple of conjurers and gave them a good "licking." As a result, they used bad medicine to make him sick, and although he had gone to another Mide in order to have him suck out the bad medicine, he recovered for a while, but died about a year later.

Morriseau's description of the Midewiwin included a number of details that were no doubt the result of his Christian upbringing. However, this had served only to strengthen his belief in the power of "conjurors," as he termed them. Further on in his material, he made this connection explicit when he stated that "a lot of Ojibwa who turned devoted Christians of the Catholic faith believe it is the devil himself who gives power to all conjurors. . . . If the devil came to you in a dream and told you that you will be powerful in return for your soul you would not accept that offer. But, if the devil appears in a medicine dream in the shape of an angel or in a different way like a thunderbird or some demi-god he will tell the same thing and you would accept because you would not know he is the devil himself." However, he went on, "all the conjurers who use their powers for evil no matter what good intentions, one has to pay later."[150]

Morriseau was hardly alone in his experience in combining beliefs from both the Midewiwin and Christian traditions. Edward Rogers and Garth Taylor both assert that by the 1930s most Ojibwa and Cree were at least nominal Christians, although they continued to retain some aspects of their traditional belief system, particularly the concept of "power." While Shaking Tent ceremonies and Waabanowiwin ceremonies continued to be practised in a few places, Midewiwin ceremonies appear to have died out almost completely, although a few Mide leaders continue to be mentioned in reports.[151]

The paucity of written accounts of the Midewiwin should not, however, cause us to believe that the Midewiwin was entirely dead, for it was during the late 1950s and 1960s that Selwyn Dewdney's obsession with pictographs and Midewiwin sacred scrolls began. Although Selwyn Dewdney was neither an Ojibwa himself, nor a trained ethnologist, he devoted the latter part of his life to preserving and understanding the rock art and sacred birchbark scrolls of the Ojibwa. Dewdney had moved to Kenora, Ontario, in 1926 as the son of the Anglican Bishop of Keewatin. As a child, and later as an adult, he developed a love for canoeing the waters of northwestern Ontario, and a deep respect for the Ojibwa people who had lived in the Lake of the Woods and surrounding regions.[152] Even after he left to pursue his education as an artist at the Ontario College of Art, and later when he worked as an art teacher in southern Ontario, Dewdney maintained an ongoing interest in the Ojibwa pictographs he had discovered as a child.

In the 1950s he teamed up with Dr. Kenneth E. Kidd, the Curator of Ethnology at the Royal Ontario Museum, in a project that involved recording and helping to preserve hundreds of pictographs found mainly along the rivers and lakes of the Canadian Shield in Ontario and Minnesota.[153] Dewdney combed the region by canoe, carefully photographing the pictographs, painstakingly making scale copies of some, and tracing others directly on Chinese rice paper. He later recorded the painting media used, and attempted to categorize the pictographs by form, content, and style. At the same time, Kidd drew upon his anthropological background in order to date the pictographs and place them within the context of Ojibwa culture as it was then known.

Kidd followed in the footsteps of Garrick Mallery, an early American ethnologist who was the first person to study Aboriginal pictographs. Both men believed it was possible to interpret pictographs if the researcher relied on the existing knowledge of contemporary Aboriginal society. Since there were a decreasing number of Ojibwa who were still familiar with traditional ways, Dewdney and Kidd turned to the collections of Ojibwa sacred narratives and the sacred birchbark scrolls of the Midewiwin for clues as to the meaning of the rock pictographs. Although Kidd and Dewdney were aware of the work of Schoolcraft, Hoffman, and others in collecting and describing such materials, they did not fully realize how much more Midewiwin material continued to exist in Ojibwa communities.

Fortuitously, Dewdney was given access to several collections of Midewiwin birchbark scrolls from the regions around Lac Seul, Rainy River, and Shoal Lake during his work on the pictographs project. The fact that such materials continued to be used by Ojibwa Mideg helped pique his interest in the sacred scrolls, and gradually he gained a broader interest in all aspects of the Midewiwin. Eventually this interest was to lead him on a search for birchbark scrolls in North American and European museums and archives, which mirrored his earlier search for pictographs by the rivers and lakes of the Canadian Shield. Although few of these sacred scrolls had accompanying explanations, Dewdney hoped he would be able to find patterns in scrolls that had been collected from diverse geographical communities during the nineteenth and early twentieth centuries.

In the course of his research Dewdney came into contact with another non-academic named Fred Blessing, who was also involved in the collecting and interpreting of Midewiwin and other religious objects. However, while most of Dewdney's early work had been carried out among the Northern and Western Ojibwa, Blessing's research was concentrated on the Southwestern Ojibwa. Blessing had made it his mission to preserve, document, and interpret the materials he collected from Ojibwa elders who lacked students willing or able to become initiates in the Midewiwin, or from converts who had not yet destroyed the vestiges of their past. Although Dewdney and Blessing approached their work from different perspectives, and possessed different talents, they both shared an empathy with their Ojibwa counterparts that is evident even in their written work. Perhaps it was this empathy that prompted many Ojibwa Mide elders to trust Dewdney and Blessing with ensuring the safe storage of their most treasured possessions.[154]

While I do not concur with Dewdney's and Blessing's belief that orthodox forms of the Midewiwin existed only among the Southwestern Ojibwa, I have no doubt that at various times and in various places the Midewiwin (like many other religious movements) has gone through periods of intense turmoil when evil leaders sometimes threatened the very communities they should have helped protect. At the very least, Dewdney's collection of sacred Midewiwin scrolls is evidence that considerable variation did occur in Midewiwin teachings and practices. However one might disagree with some of his interpretations, Dewdney's work on understanding the Mide sacred scrolls stands, in many ways, as the artistic equivalent to Densmore's work on the role of music in the Midewiwin, in that it provides us with a more contextualized view of the Midewiwin. Both works serve not only as complements to Hoffman's mammoth study, but are in themselves valuable repositories of original source material.

Even as the imminent demise of the Midewiwin was once again being predicted by many Euro-Americans, new generations of Ojibwa began to seek out Mide elders who could teach them the old ways and help them to rediscover their heritage and their unique world view. About the same time, in the 1970s and 1980s, a new generation of Euro-Americans began to exhibit a more open attitude to learning about Aboriginal culture. The republishing of nineteenth-century authors such as George Copway and William Warren helped to rekindle an interest in Ojibwa heritage. More importantly, for the first time in a century, Ojibwa authors began to publish new accounts of their people. Basil Johnston, an Ojibwa scholar who worked in the Department of Ethnology at the Royal Ontario Museum, published two works on Ojibwa heritage and ceremonies (including the Midewiwin) in 1976 and 1982, and followed these studies up with a book on Ojibwa spirituality in 1995. Written for Ojibwa and Euro-American audiences, Johnston's books presented the Midewiwin from an Ojibwa perspective, using stories and figures of speech that attempt to capture the oral style used by Mide elders. Likewise, in 1988, Edward Benton-Banai, the Director of the Red School House in St. Paul, Minnesota, published a popular account of Ojibwa history, culture, and religion, which was based on the oral traditions of Ojibwa elders.

New generations of Ojibwa who had lost their language and much of their heritage were thus able to use written records in order to begin to regain part of their lost oral traditions. With the growth of both informal and formal Ojibwa educational opportunities, this process of cultural and religious regeneration has accelerated. An important part of the process has been the revival of Midewiwin ceremonies, which once again draw participants from distant points in Canada and the United States. Today's participants are as often urban dwellers as they are reserve- or reservation-based. Many are part of a growing number of middle-class professionals who believe that the teachings of the Midewiwin provide them with the best means to survive in the modern world. Unlike many of their nineteenth-century counterparts, who felt compelled to abandon their traditional ways, or to create separate traditional communities, these Ojibwa find no contradictions between their traditional beliefs and contemporary lifestyles. Rather, they argue that contemporary North American society would do well to listen to some of the traditional teachings of the Midewiwin regarding personal relations with our neighbours and the environment.

An increasing number of Euro-Americans have likewise been ready to move beyond the scientific belief structures that have dominated nineteenth- and much of twentieth-century society. As holistic medical approaches, which combine physical, spiritual, and ethical elements, become more accepted, the holistic healing practices of Mideg appear less esoteric—especially when viewed within the context of the Anishinaabe world view. While fundamentalist Christian missionaries and some members of the mainstream churches continue to identify Mideg with the false prophets and sorcerers of the Bible, a growing number of Christians have come to recognize that the two religions hold many truths in common. In some communities Mide elders and Christian clergy have even begun to cooperate in ministering to the community. Nevertheless, the scars of the past have cut deep, and divisions between those Ojibwa who follow the teachings of the Midewiwin, and those who follow the teachings of the Christian Bible, are far from being healed.

Traditional Mide narratives speak of a recurring series of circumstances in which the Midewiwin Lodge was erected, and the people prospered. Each time, however, the teachings were gradually forgotten or misused by evil people. When that happened, Ojibwa society suffered greatly. Each time, though, the teachings were revived, the Midewiwin Lodge was erected again, and, once more, the people were able to live a long and productive life. It would appear that we are again entering such a period. While this contemporary revival of the Midewiwin would be a fascinating topic in itself, an in-depth analysis is outside the scope of this historical study.

SIX

Toward a New Understanding of the Midewiwin

Throughout the centuries of contact, Euro-Americans have been both fascinated and repelled by the religious beliefs and practices of various Aboriginal groups. Nowhere has this been more evident than in the number and variety of Euro-American narratives that describe, explain, attack, and defame the Midewiwin, as practised by the Ojibwa. Over the past two centuries, successive commentators representing various ethnic groups, religious persuasions, and academic disciplines have written newspaper and journal articles, popular books, and academic treatises on the mysteries of the Midewiwin. If there is one theme common to all these narratives, it is the Midewiwin as the "other." Whether Mideg were described as charlatans, agents of the Devil, deranged individuals, or social misfits makes little difference—Euro-American images have been almost universally negative. However much commentators might have disagreed among themselves, they were, for the most part, united in their criticisms of the Midewiwin. Little wonder, then, that adherents of the Midewiwin have been loath to share their beliefs or their sacred rituals with Euro-Americans who, in the past, have misrepresented their beliefs, destroyed or profaned their sacred relics, and forbidden them to take part in Midewiwin ceremonies.

By their very nature, Euro-American explanations have been the work of "outside observers" who have relied primarily on Ojibwa informants and occasional attendance at some ceremonies open to the community. Writers have sought to explain the Midewiwin to their fellow Euro-Americans, to engage in polemics with its teachings, and to preserve the teachings and rituals for posterity. Only a few have been proficient in the language, and, despite the fact that several have claimed to have been initiated into the ceremony, none have been practitioners. Euro-American scholars have employed a number of different methodologies in an effort to better understand the Midewiwin. Writers of the earliest accounts concentrated on the external characteristics of the ceremonies they witnessed or that were reported to them. Subsequent writers have sought to explain the philosophical or religious conceptions upon which the ceremony was based, using an analysis of specific texts and the structure of the language. Still others have attempted to place it within the context of broader religious, psychological, socio-economical, or historical patterns.

Early French and later English writers on the subject of Ojibwa religion were usually educated individuals, well versed in Biblical studies and the Christian tradition, writing for literate audiences with a similar world view. There were a few unvarnished accounts written by ordinary people, mainly the passing observations of fur traders. John Tanner's account, although heavily edited, stands alone as one of the few accounts written by an "insider." Most of the more extensive narratives attempted, with limited success, to fit the Ojibwa belief system into Western structures of thought. However, in doing so, they had great difficulty in comprehending a cosmology in which their own separate categories of the transcendent (God) and the immanent (indwelling sense of the holy) were subsumed into the single word "manidoo." They had an equally difficult time in comprehending a transcendent figure who could be both singular and multiple in form and nature. It was perhaps for this reason that many accounts concentrated on externals and rituals, which were easier for their audiences to comprehend, since this kind of information was more straightforward, and since they probably had a greater emotional effect on their attended audiences.

With the writings of Henry R. Schoolcraft and his contemporaries, there was a perceptible shift in emphasis. Schoolcraft's purpose was explicitly ideological. He set out to counter the eighteenth-century myths of the "Noble Savage" and to expose what he considered to be the falsehoods of the traditional Aboriginal religious healers such as powerful Mideg, whom he believed were preventing assimilation of the Ojibwa into American society. Nevertheless, Schoolcraft, Nicollet, and Kohl were the first Euro-Americans to examine seriously the beliefs of Aboriginal people in an effort to understand their world view. Their writings mark the beginning of an attempt to systematically describe the Midewiwin, even though they failed in their efforts, and even if Schoolcraft, in particular, further perpetuated distorted images of the Midewiwin and the Ojibwa who followed its tenets.

At approximately the same time, a number of acculturated Ojibwa and mixed-blood individuals, including Peter Jones, George Copway, and William Warren, published works on the Ojibwa in an effort to bring their history, culture, and impending doom to the notice of Euro-Americans. They were able to provide an "insider's" perspective, but their general acceptance of Euro-American beliefs and values distorted their vision. It is questionable to what extent even Warren's work truly represents the traditional Ojibwa perspective he was attempting to portray. Nevertheless, their works are important, for they represent the first attempts by Ojibwa individuals to translate their oral traditions into the printed word. Assimilated as they may have been, their works provided readers with an alternative image of Ojibwa culture.

The works of Hoffman and Densmore and their successors mark another important shift in emphasis from the recorded observations of dedicated amateurs, to the detailed writings of professional ethnographers, which were based on extended fieldwork using Aboriginal informants. Their efforts to preserve the vanishing cultural records of America's Aboriginal peoples coincided with a similar desire on the part of some traditional Ojibwa Mide leaders. As a result, these practitioners were willing to pass on unusually detailed descriptions, songs, and pictographs that, in the past, had been considered highly secret.

The detailed account of Hoffman, and the insights offered by Densmore, added significantly to an understanding of the Midewiwin, even though many of Hoffman's comments and observations are somewhat dismissive. Despite this, his work on the Midewiwin has taken on a canonical status, and has become the measure by which other descriptions are judged to be orthodox or deviant. Unfortunately, since no other detailed descriptions exist from the nineteenth century, it is impossible to say if all Ojibwa Midewiwin ceremonies were similar to the one he described. From the fragments that do exist, this would not seem to be the case.

During the twentieth century, a number of relatively detailed accounts have been transcribed by both amateur and trained ethnographers. In addition, Mide narratives and scrolls have been collected from an even wider number of communities. It is possible, therefore, to form a better idea of the geographical and historical variations in the Midewiwin, taking into account the problems in translating and transcribing materials, and the world views of the individuals providing the descriptions. And it is possible, I believe, to use the information previously collected by Euro-Americans, regardless of how flawed or biased it may be, along with the few works by Ojibwa individuals on the Midewiwin that do exist, to provide a composite picture of the Midewiwin as it may have existed in the past.

Past accounts have primarily focussed on the ceremonial aspects of the Midewiwin, including the elaborate rituals such as the cleansing ceremonies in sweat lodges; the construction of the Mide Lodge; the instruction sessions for the initiates; the ceremonial feasts, processions, drumming, dancing, and singing; the "shooting" ritual of the initiation rite; and the public duelling ritual, carried out over a period of from one to fourteen days as a regular part of spring and fall celebrations. The appearance of the Midewiwin as part of the yearly rounds indicates it was a well-established cultic practice, rather than a new "crisis cult" that had sprung up in reaction to Euro-American intrusions and disease. The fact that shorter, less elaborate Mide rituals were held for certain "crisis" situations, such as curing ceremonies when regular cures had failed to work, and after the death of individuals, may indicate that it evolved at some time in the past from earlier curing rituals, or from the Feast of the Dead, but the evidence is too scanty to make any firm statements.

The practitioners of the Midewiwin have been described as a secret society, in contrast to other types of traditional healers such as the Jiisakiiwininiwag, who operated independently. However, too much should not be made of this distinction. Although scholars such as Hickerson have maintained that this indicated a greater sense of collectivity among the Ojibwa, this may not be entirely borne out in practice. It must be remembered that the Midewiwin did not function as a strong collective force among the Ojibwa. Medicine bundles and sacred songs were a personal possession, rather than a clan or band possession, as was common among some neighbouring groups. While there is evidence that Mideg began to pass on and share sacred songs in the later nineteenth century, the power continued to reside with the individual, not the collective. It is difficult to determine the exact organizational structure of the Midewiwin before Hoffman's account in the late nineteenth century, but other accounts suggest that there was no permanent set of officials. Rather, they were chosen from a pool of powerful Mideg for each ceremony—probably this was done mainly on the basis of the kinship connections of the person being initiated. Certainly by the second half of the nineteenth century, and into the twentieth century, the picture that emerges is of Mideg who came together briefly during Midewiwin ceremonies, but who functioned independently, sometimes in opposition to one another.

Midewiwin documents and some Euro-American accounts suggest that the twin objectives of the Midewiwin were to promote a long life through the teaching of the art of right living and the proper use of herbs; and secondly, to provide access to the manidoog in order to seek help in accomplishing this goal. These two aspects have often been separated by observers, who have concentrated on the initiation and public duelling rituals, the curing ritual, or the sacred scrolls, in contrast to the broader ethical and social concerns with which the Midewiwin was concerned.

However, I believe the two objectives were intimately connected. Mideg were blessed by the Mide manidoog with the power of the miigis, as well as with the power of specific plants and herbs, both of which became part of their medicine bags. In both cases Mide officials helped the new candidates, but the manidoog, not the officials, were responsible for the transfer of power. To be blessed with these powers meant that the odds of surviving to old age would be improved, since the recipients would be better able to locate game, cure illnesses, and deal with enemies.

Mide officials also taught members how to deal properly with their brothers and sisters, human and non-human. The ceremony offered the opportunity for members to experience their beliefs through drama and ritual. Thus, for instance, the Mide officials, as they entered the Mide Lodge, became Bear breaking through the barriers in order to bring the Midewiwin to the Anishinaabeg, while the dance procession taught the initiate the road of life that was to be followed. The gift of goods to the Mide officials was a public acknowledgement of the power's worth, and the respect that was accorded it. Even the combination of danger and entertainment in the public duelling ritual reminded the people of the ambiguity of life in much the same way as did the stories of Nanabozho.

A third, related objective of the Midewiwin, although it was not explicitly stated, was to help foster self-knowledge and a sense of identity for members. The origin and other narratives recounted during the training sessions, and the rituals of the ceremony itself, helped the members place themselves (both personally and also as members of the Anishinaabeg) within a familiar cosmos where everyone was personally connected. Midewiwin migration scrolls documented the stopping places of the Midewiwin during the westward migration of the Ojibwa. They were clearly used to help inculcate a sense of a common heritage and a common homeland among the scattered groups of Ojibwa.

Many commentators on the Midewiwin have emphasized the distinction between the two means of obtaining power among the Anishinaabeg: through visions, and through teaching the learned knowledge. The normal interpretation is that the process was an evolutionary one in which visionary tradition was replaced by the more complex Midewiwin tradition, in which the knowledge to increase one's power was passed on as the initiate moved up through the various levels or degrees of the Midewiwin. There is no doubt that the Midewiwin did provide another way of obtaining power for those who lacked a visionary experience. However, nineteenth-century accounts do not indicate that this process replaced the visionary experience, or that a conflict between these two ways of acquiring power existed, although some observers such as Selwyn Dewdney believed this to be the case in the twentieth century. In fact, most sources indicate that the methods coexisted. All but a few twentieth-century accounts indicate that candidates for the Midewiwin (or their sponsors) were still required to have a visionary experience before being considered for admission to the Midewiwin, because Mideg were concerned that the ceremonies would be compromised otherwise.

An aspect of the Midewiwin that is paradoxical and needs to be addressed is the question of how the Anishinaabeg dealt with the problem of evil in connection with the Midewiwin. Warren's graphic description of the evil times at Chequamegon illustrates what might be called the systemic version of evil, in which whole segments of the community were believed to have succumbed to a form of behaviour that has been described as being everything from merely antisocial, to an indication of bearwalkers or witchcraft, to a result of some type of cosmic imbalance.[1]

Bearwalkers, though not specifically connected to the Midewiwin in the accounts that I consulted, are mentioned by a variety of nineteenth- and twentieth-century writers on the subject of the Midewiwin. Many Ojibwa believed them to be evil Mideg who had transformed themselves in order to cause havoc at night. They continue to be part of the world view of both followers of the Midewiwin, and Catholics in some Ojibwa communities such as those on Manitoulin Island.[2]

At other times, suffering or evil was described in terms of duels between "good" and "bad" shamans. In much of the literature, this takes the form of "good" Mideg and "bad" Waabanowag or Jiisakiiwininiwag, but sometimes the situation is reversed. Such was the case, for instance, at Parry Island.[3] Some commentators have considered these duels as expressions of kin- and clan-feuds, or as examples of factionalism between Midewiwin followers and Christians. Certainly there is evidence that the "badness" of a particular Mide may have depended on the perspective of the informant. However, the literature and oral tradition include many examples of individuals whose actions were evil by anybody's standard.

Part of this confusion regarding good and bad Mideg can perhaps be explained by the fact that Mishibizhii, who is usually considered to be the tutelary manidoo who gives powers to heal to members of the Midewiwin, is also feared for his evil powers. Receiving power from Mishibizhii is not like signing a pact with the devil (as in the Western tradition of Mephistopheles), but there is the danger that power can be used for evil purposes if things get out of balance and, therefore, out of control. For this reason, powerful Mideg were and are both respected and feared.

There can be little doubt that the Midewiwin is deeply rooted in Ojibwa culture. In fact, I would argue that it forms an integral part of their world view, and, as such, did not arise as some form of crisis or revitalization cult in response to Euro-American contact. Rather than being an esoteric ceremony performed by a limited number of Ojibwa individuals, the Midewiwin functioned as the religion of the Anishinaabeg, celebrated in a variety of ceremonies, led by individuals who had been given power by manidoog.

There have been changes in these ceremonies since the time of earliest recorded contact, but this should not imply that the changes have been evolutionary. The visionary tradition has always been an important part of the Midewiwin, since it confirmed that the manidoog had spoken to the candidates who hoped to have their power increased. And since visions were unique, their messages varied according to the manidoo, the time, and the place. Although different versions of the origin and migration narratives developed, these continuing revelations did not change the essential nature of the underlying message of the Midewiwin, nor did they alter the essential rituals in which the candidates received power in the form of blessings. From time to time, radically new visions may have resulted in new religious leaders and new religious rituals such the Waabanowiwin. Although the Waabanowiwin remained a separate ceremony, Waabanowag were recognized as individuals with power and were incorporated into the Midewiwin, like the Jiisakiiwininiwag before them. While there is evidence that Mideg began to pass on and share sacred songs in the nineteenth century, at other times, some candidates attempted to induce visions using alcohol, or to purchase the right to be initiated, but such instances are considered to be aberrations.

Some members of the Ojibwa, including some prominent Mide leaders, did, however, become followers of the Shawnee Prophet for a short period of time, and other, lesser known prophets also attracted a few followers. Although they briefly disrupted the Ojibwa religious scene, such inter-tribal crisis or revitalization movements had little or no ongoing effect on the practice of the Midewiwin. More important was the interaction of the Western Ojibwa with the Cree, Assiniboine, and Sioux during the nineteenth century. Members of the Minnesota and Wisconsin Ojibwa were presented with a sacred drum and taught the rituals of the Drum or Dream Dance in the late nineteenth century. Although it was often practised in conjunction with the Midewiwin, in some regions it replaced the latter as the main religious practice. Many Western Ojibwa also joined in the performance of the Sun Dance of their Plains neighbours, while some of the Cree participated in Midewiwin ceremonies.

Ojibwa interactions with Euro-Americans also had an influence on their religious life. It has been argued that Christian beliefs had some impact on some Midewiwin concepts. This, in itself, is hardly surprising since Aninshinaabe cosmology was all-encompassing, and while the Mideg might not agree with Christians, the latter had become part of the Ojibwa world and had to be taken into account. However, any incorporation that may have occurred was carried out in terms of the Ojibwa world view, not the Christian Euro-American one.

Many changes to the Midewiwin occurred during the late nineteenth and early twentieth centuries at a time when the Midewiwin was under siege by Christian missionaries and government officials. Thus, for instance, the introduction of the wage economy and the six-day work-week, and bans on inter-tribal and even inter-community gatherings temporarily forced communities to hold smaller, local gatherings, and to simplify the ceremonies, since they were limited to one or two days. Sweat lodge rituals were dropped in some communities when young men no longer wanted to make the effort, and the time devoted to teaching the narratives and medical lore was reduced as old leaders died and fewer new leaders were chosen. Young people educated in residential schools returned with no knowledge of the teachings or workings of the Midewiwin, and often with a bias against it, as a result of the indoctrination by their teachers.

As the Ojibwa became part of the larger North American society, the Midewiwin lost its central role in Ojibwa communities, and became separated from the community at large. In some ways it functioned much like a church denomination that affected only its members. Some Ojibwa who wished to follow the traditional ways attempted to form separate communities, but they had limited degrees of success in stemming the tide, as government and church officials used all possible means to ensure Ojibwa compliance with Euro-American norms of belief and practice.

Some Ojibwa, including prominent Mide leaders such as Shingwaukonse at Garden Lake, Ontario, decided that the only hope of survival lay in becoming Christians. Since few Christian churches at that time were willing to make any accommodations to the Anishinaabe world view or culture, the new converts felt obliged to deny their past and censure their brethren who continued to practise the Midewiwin. Only in a few cases, such as among the Episcopalian followers of Enmegahbowh at White Earth, Minnesota, were Christian Ojibwa able to integrate their new Christian beliefs with traditional Ojibwa ethics and practices.

Some of the Ojibwa, such as James Redsky of Shoal Lake, Ontario, adopted a syncretic approach. While he remained a traditional Mide elder until his death, he also was ordained an elder in the local Presbyterian Church. He saw no opposition between his two beliefs, and was successful in convincing the local church officials that the two institutions could work together for the betterment of the community. Many others outwardly became Christians while continuing to adhere to the Ojibwa world view in the privacy of their own lives, so strongly was it engrained in their being.

What is remarkable is that despite all the upheavals and changes the Ojibwa experienced, a few individuals, such as Dan Raincloud, from Red Lake, Minnesota, were able to learn the old ways of the Midewiwin, and continued to function as traditional Mide healers.[4] Often this was done in the face of scepticism from their own community and the derision of the non-Aboriginal community. Gradually, however, it appears that many Ojibwa have begun to rediscover these ways for themselves.

In retrospect, it is this combination of flexibility and tenacity that is, in my view, one of the main characteristics of the Midewiwin Society. Given the vast area in which the Ojibwa lived, the different historical circumstances in which they have found themselves, and the nature of Ojibwa society, this characteristic is not surprising. However, such diversity needs to be understood within the general context of the basic elements of the Midewiwin, which Warren delineated in the opening passage of this book. There may have been many different visions, even different rituals, but the underlying world view of its members has remained the same.

Endnotes

Chapter One

1. William W. Warren, *History of the Ojibway People* (St. Paul: Minnesota Historical Society Press, 1984), 79-80.

2. William Warren was the son of an American fur trader, Lyman Warren, who came to the Lake Superior region from New England in 1818, and Mary Cadotte, the daughter of a French trader and granddaughter of White Crane, the hereditary chief of La Pointe village. Warren was born in 1825, learned Ojibwe in early childhood, attended the missionary schools at La Pointe and Mackinaw, and later was sent to New England to attend the Oneida Institute, where he received the beginnings of a classical education. He served as interpreter at La Pointe and later at Crow Wing and Gull Lake in Minnesota. He died in 1853 following a prolonged illness, and just shortly after completing his book. See Warren, *History of the Ojibway,* 9-20. See also the Densmore Papers (Minnesota Historical Society Research Center), which contain an historical account of the Warren family by Mary Warren English, William's sister; and Theresa M. Schenck, "The Cadottes: Five Generations of Fur Traders on Lake Superior," in *The Fur Trade Revisited: Selected Papers of the Sixth North American Fur Trade Conference, Mackinac Island, Michigan, 1991* (East Lansing: Michigan State University Press, 1994), 189-198.

3. Charles E. Cleland, *Rites of Conquest: The History and Culture of Michigan's Native Americans* (Ann Arbor: University of Michigan Press, 1992), 32-34.

4. Nanabozho is the name of the Ojibwa culture hero and trickster. It is transcribed in various ways: Wenabozho, Wenaposo, Man-ab-o-sho, Minabozho, Manabus, Nanabush, Nanab'oozoo, Nenabozho, etc., and is related to other northeastern Algonquian figures such as Gloscap (Gluskabe) among the Micmac, and Penobscot, or Wee-suck-a-jock (Wisakedzak), among the Cree. I have adopted what seems to me the most commonly used form.

5. I have opted to use the Ojibwe spelling, "manidoo," rather than the English term "manitou."

6. "Mide" refers to a member of the Midewiwin.

7. Warren, *History of the Ojibway*, 80-83.

8. The spelling of these two terms varies considerably in written accounts, but the concept is relatively constant. Nevertheless, following contact with Euro-Americans, aadizookaanag among some groups blended with European fairy tales told to the Ojibwa. See, for instance, Frances Densmore, *Chippewa Customs* (St. Paul: Minnesota Historical Society, 1979), 104-106. Jennifer Brown has a good, concise explanation of the mythic and anecdotal concepts of history in her article, "Northern Algonquians from Lake Superior and Hudson Bay to Manitoba in the Historical Period," in *Native Peoples: The Canadian Experience*, ed. R. Bruce Morrison and C. Roderick Wilson (Toronto: McClelland and Stewart, 1986), 225-227.

9. Cleland, *Rites of Conquest*, 4,10. In her study of the Ojibwa leader, Shingwaukonse, Janet Chute relates that current elders make reference to him in their telling of adisokan (aadizookaanag)—thus indicating how the historical and mythic past can come together. See Chute, *The Legacy of Shingwaukonse: A Century of Native Leadership* (Toronto: University of Toronto Press, 1998).

10. Basil Johnston is an Ojibwa from Cape Croker, Ontario, and a former employee of the Royal Ontario Museum, who has done much to describe Ojibwa society from an insider's perspective. See especially his works entitled *Ojibwa Ceremonies* (Toronto: McClelland and Stewart, 1982), *Ojibwa Heritage* (New York: Columbia University Press,1976), and *The Manitous: The Spiritual World of the Ojibway* (Toronto: Key Porter Books,1995). Edward Benton-Banai, an American Ojibwa who resides in Minneapolis and is the author of *The Mishomis Book: Voice of the Ojibway* (Hayward, WI: Indian Country Communications, 1988), is a leading figure in the recent revival of the Midewiwin among Ojibwa in both the United States and Canada. Nicholas Deleary is an Ojibwa scholar at Carleton University. His MA thesis, "Midewiwin: An Aboriginal Spiritual Institution. Symbols of Continuity: A Native Studies Culture-based Perspective" (Carleton University, 1990), is about the Midewiwin from a believer's perspective.

11. The ideas of Harold Hickerson, an ethnohistorian specializing in Ojibwa society and history, have influenced a wide range of Euro-American scholars writing about the Midewiwin.

12. Johnston, *The Manitous,* 243.

13. Early French Jesuits such as Allouez, fur traders such as Perrot, and clerical explorers such as Hennepin all provided descriptions of Aboriginal "jugglers," "sorcerers," and "wizards," as did their English counterparts, such as Alexander Henry, William Keating, and others. It was only in the nineteenth century, with the "scientific" attempt to understand the Aboriginal mind, that efforts were made to name and describe Mide traditional healers using indigenous terms.

14. I am indebted to Charles Cleland for his excellent presentation of Ojibwa and Euro-American versions of history and culture in *Rites of Conquest*. While my interpretation differs in many respects from his, he demonstrated how it could be done.

15. For instance, the Iroquois were termed Naudoways or "Adders," and the Dakota (Sioux) were termed either Naudowasewug, which again refers to adders, or as Aboinug, "roasters" (Warren, *History of the Ojibway*, 83, 36).

16. Cleland, *Rites of Conquest*, 39-41.

17. Warren, *History of the Ojibway,* 39.

18. Ibid., 81. Warren's rendition of oral history was echoed by various literate Ojibwa (see, for example, Andrew Blackbird, *History of the Ottawa and Chippewa Indians of Michigan* [Ypsilanti, Michigan, 1887]; George Copway, *The Traditional History and Characteristic Sketches of the Ojibway Nation* [Toronto: Coles, 1972]; and Peter Jones, *History of the Ojebway Indians; with especial reference to their conversion to Christianity* [London: A.W. Bennett, 1861]), but has generally been discounted by Euro-American scholars. Donald Fixico has attempted to demonstrate that the three groups continued to maintain an alliance of Three Fires into the nineteenth century. His argument implies that Anishinaabe tribal identities existed in the early seventeenth century. See his "The Alliance of the Three Fires in Trade and War, 1630-1812," *Michigan Historical Review* 20, 2 (1994): 2-23.

19. Warren estimates that there were 9000 Ojibwa in the United States in 1850 (*History of the Ojibway*, 38). Peter Schmalz cites a figure from an 1846 Gazetteer of approximately 2400 in southern Ontario south of the Georgian Bay area, where close to 2000 more dwelt. See Schmalz, *The Ojibwa of Southern Ontario* (Toronto: University of Toronto Press, 1991), 176-178. While no similar figures exist for the numerous bands in northwestern Ontario, Manitoba, and Saskatchewan, they must have numbered at least several thousand more.

20. The most straightforward exploration of this plethora of names is given by Laura Peers in her *The Ojibwa of Western Canada 1780 to 1870* (Winnipeg: University of Manitoba Press, 1994), xv-xvii. Other synonyms are provided in volumes 6 (*Subarctic,* 1981) and 15 (*Northeast,* 1978) of *The Handbook of North American Indians* (Washington: Smithsonian Institution Press).

21. Harold Hickerson, "The Sociohistorical Significance of Two Chippewa Ceremonials," *American Anthropologist* 68 (1963): 67-85. Hickerson's article on the post-contact Midewiwin origins appears to have convinced the majority of scholars who have written on the subject in the past few decades. While Hoffman (1891) and Kinietz (1947) argued that it predated Christianity, and Densmore (1979) accepted Warren's account without comment, others, such as Landes (1968), Dewdney (1975), Blessing (1977), Vecsey (1983), and Harrison (1984), generally accepted Hickerson's arguments, although Harrison and Vecsey (1984) did qualify them somewhat.

    At least one scholar, James Howard (*The Plains-Ojibwa or Bungi* [Lincoln, NB: J&L Reprint Co., 1977], 133), continued to maintain that the Midewiwin was rooted in the Aboriginal past. While acknowledging that Hickerson's argument might be valid for the eighteenth and nineteenth centuries, Howard accused Hickerson of "throwing out the baby with the bath water" for failing to consider how the Midewiwin fit into the Ojibwa world view.

22. Karl Schlesier, "Rethinking the Midewiwin and the Plains ceremonial called the Sun Dance," *Plains Anthropologist* 35, 127 (1990): 1-27.

23. Julia D. Harrison, in her MA thesis "The Midewiwin: The Retention of an Ideology" (University of Calgary, 1982), views the Midewiwin in the context of "crisis cults" that developed in response to European pressures. Thus, she also accepts that it was a post-contact phenomenon during a period of upheaval for the Ojibwa.

24. In their revised and expanded edition of Hickerson's *The Chippewa and their Neighbours*, which includes a chapter on the origin of the Midewiwin, Jennifer Brown and Laura Peers question a number of Hickerson's arguments, and suggest alternate

interpretations. See Harold Hickerson, *The Chippewa and Their Neighbours: A Study in Ethnohistory* (Prospect Heights, Ill: Waveland Press, 1988), 142-143.

25. Ake Hultkrantz, *The Religions of the American Indians,* trans. Monica Setterwall (Berkeley: University of California Press, 1979), 116-128. John A. Grim, *The Shaman: Patterns of Siberian and Ojibway Healing* (Norman: University of Oklahoma Press, 1983).

26. Although Hickerson would no doubt have agreed with Hultkrantz's general observations regarding a shift in the Ojibwa world view, his emphasis was different. From an anthropological perspective, the most significant fact was that the change took place because of a more sedentary lifestyle. For proof, Hickerson and others argue that the Midewiwin was most active in the larger centres among the southwestern Ojibwa. While Hultkrantz agreed that the change from a hunting and gathering society to an agricultural society was a factor, he argued that most of the symbolism and rituals continued to be based on their former lifestyle.

27. The literature surrounding the concepts of orality and literacy is far beyond the scope of this work. However, Ong (*Orality and Literacy*, 1982) remains a standard work on the subject. Harold Coward provides a good introduction to the spiritual power of both oral and written scripture, while indicating their differences (see his "The Spiritual Power of Oral and Written Scripture," in *Silence, the Word and the Sacred,* ed. E.D. Blodgett and H.G. Coward [Waterloo: Wilfrid Laurier Press, 1989]). Ivan Illich and Barry Sanders, while writing about "the alphabetization" of the popular (Western) mind, present a more traditional evolutionary view of the differences between orality and literacy. See Ivan Illich and Barry Sanders, *The Alphabetization of the Popular Mind* (New York: Vintage Books, 1988).

28. Jan Vansina, *Oral Tradition as History* (Madison: University of Wisconsin Press, 1985). While most of the recent analytical work relating to Ojibwa sacred narratives (aadizookaanag), such as that by Overholt and Callicott (*Clothed-in-fur and Other Tales*, 1982), Vecsey ("Midewiwin Myths of Origin," 1984), and Smith (*The Island of the Anishinaabeg*, 1995), has been concerned with world view and religion, Vecsey, in particular, demonstrates that narratives can also play a role in helping us to understand how the Midewiwin evolved. See Christopher Vecsey, "Midewiwin Myths of Origin," in *Papers of the Fifteenth Algonquian Conference*, ed. William Cowan (Ottawa: Carleton University Press, 1984).

29. Henry Rowe Schoolcraft, *Algic Researches, comprising inquiries respecting the mental characteristics of the North American Indians* (New York: Harper & Bros., 1839), 31-43.

30. Warren, *History of the Ojibway.*

31. Frances Densmore, *Chippewa Music,* 2 vols., Bureau of American Ethnology Bulletins 45 and 53 (Washington: Smithsonian Institution Press, 1910-1913).

32. Selwyn Dewdney, *The Sacred Scrolls of the Southern Ojibway* (Toronto: Glenbow-Alberta Institute/University of Toronto Press, 1975). Fred K. Blessing, *The Ojibway Indians Observed, Papers of Fred. K. Blessing Jr., on the Ojibway Indians,* from *The Minnesota Archeologist* (St. Paul: Minnesota Archeological Society, 1977). Although Schoolcraft set out to provide more in-depth descriptions of Midewiwin ceremonies as part of his multi-volume work on American Aboriginal peoples (see his *Information Respecting the History, Condition and Prospects of the Indian Tribes of the United States*, 6 vols. [Philadelphia: Lippincott, Grambo & Co., 1851-1857]), the first professional

studies were completed by Walter James Hoffman for the Bureau of American Ethnology. See his "The Midewiwin or 'Grand Medicine Society' of the Ojibwa," in *Seventh Annual Report to the Smithsonian Institution, 1885-1886* (Washington: Smithsonian Institution Press, 1891), and "The Menomini Indians," in *Fourteenth Annual Report to the Smithsonian Institution, 1892-1893* (Washington: Smithsonian Institution Press, 1896). Subsequently, a series of ethnologists such as Densmore (1910-1913, 1929), Skinner (1911, 1915, 1920), Cooper (1928), Coleman (1929), Reagan (1933), Jenness (1935), Kinietz (1947), Ritzenthaler (1953), Kurath (1959), Barnouw (1960), and Howard (1977) completed in-depth, first-person reports that focussed on the Midewiwin among a wide range of Ojibwa, as well as Ottawa, Menominee, and other neighbouring tribes. Their work was augmented by that of Blessing and Dewdney, two non-ethnologists who also provided detailed information about aspects of the Midewiwin.

33. Thomas Vennum Jr., "Ojibwa Origin-Migration Songs of the *mitewiwin*," *Journal of American Folklore* 91 (1978): 753-791.

34. Ronald Wright, *Stolen Continents: The "New World" through Indian Eyes* (Toronto: Penguin Books, 1992), 5.

35. Mary Black-Rogers's article on Ojibwa ontology and world view regarding the Ojibwa concept of "power" will be discussed in more detail in Chapter Two. See Mary Black, "Ojibwa Power Belief System," in *The Anthropology of Power,* ed. R.R. Fogelson and R.N. Adams (New York: Academic Press, 1977).

36. There are a number of first-person reports of such conflicts, such as that related by John Tanner in his autobiography, *A Narrative of the Captivity and Adventures of John Tanner during Thirty Years Residence Among the Indians in the Interior of North America* (Minneapolis: Ross & Haines Reprint Edition, 1956).

37. They included Walter J. Hoffman, Frances Densmore, Vernon W. Kinietz, M. Bernard Coleman, Robert E. Ritzenthaler, Ruth Landes, Victor Barnouw, A. Irving Hallowell, James H. Howard, Diamond Jenness, Fred Blessing, and Selwyn Dewdney.

38. Harold Coward describes some of the reasons for the transition to the written. See Coward, "The Spiritual Power," 122-123.

39. It is a hope that is being realized. Increasing numbers of Ojibwa from all walks of life have begun to return to the teachings of the Midewiwin during the last decade, following its nadir in the 1940s and 1950s when only a few elderly Mide practitioners remained.

40. An example is the ceremony held for Niganibines (Flat Mouth Jr.), the nineteenth-century hereditary chief of the Pillager band of Leech Lake Ojibwa. See Densmore, *Chippewa Music*, 51-55. At least one early twentieth-century observer, who spent ten months working with the Ojibwa, was led to suggest that there were "two general forms of the Midewiwin...." One was individual, without public ceremony, and the other was social, since it involved a society of men and women who practised common rituals in a public ceremony. See the Fox anthropologist William Jones in *Ontario Archaeological Report #12*, Toronto, 1905, pp. 145-146.

41. Ruth Landes, in her book *Ojibwa Religion and the Midewiwin* (Madison: University of Wisconsin Press, 1968), pp. 189-206, gives the most thorough exposition of this variation, although there are many references to it among later sources.

42. Adolph M. Greenberg and James Morrison, "Group Identities in the Boreal Forest: The Origin of the Northern Ojibwa," *Ethnohistory* 29, 2 (1982): 91.

43. A. Irving Hallowell, "The Passing of the Midewiwin in the Lake Winnipeg Region," *American Anthropologist* New Series 38 (1937): 32-51.

44. This can be substantiated by brief references in accounts of early Euro-American observers, as well as from Midewiwin artifacts that date from the nineteenth and twentieth centuries. See also Peers's (*Ojibwa of Western Canada*, 148-153) comments regarding the reputation of the Ojibwa throughout the west for their strong "medicine" powers.

45. Johnston, *Ojibwa Heritage*; *Ojibwa Ceremonies*; *The Manitous*.

46. Benton-Banai, *The Mishomis Book*.

47. Richard White, *The Middle Ground: Indians, Empires and Republics in the Great Lakes Region, 1650-1815* (New York: Cambridge University Press, 1991), 51. Bruce Greenfield, "The Oral in the Written: The Irony of Representation in Louis Hennepin's *Description de la Louisiane*," *Historial Reflections/Reflexions Historiques* 21, 2 (1995): 252.

Chapter Two

1. I apply this term to those Algonquian people who had not as yet begun to conceive of themselves as groups with a corporate identity of "Ojibwa," "Odawa" (Ottawa), or "Potawatomi," but who did consider themselves as Anishinaabeg. I believe it is more meaningful than the more technical and more restrictive term "proto-Ojibwa," given the continuing debate as to precisely which groups should be included in the latter term. The singular and adjectival forms are written as *Anishinaabe*, while the plural form is written *Anishinaabeg*.

2. This process of a gradual unfolding has been well told from a personal perspective by Fred McTaggart, a young folklorist working among the Fox or Mesquakie, in a book entitled *Wolf that I Am: In Search of the Red Earth People* (Boston: Houghton Mifflin, 1976). When he had gone searching for beautiful Aboriginal stories, he was rebuffed because, as he was told (in a very indirect way), "Our stories have a definite purpose; they are teaching stories."

3. Frances Densmore, *Chippewa Customs* (St. Paul: Minnesota Historical Society, 1979), 98.

4. Stan Cuthand (in Jennifer S.H. Brown and Robert Brightman, eds., *The Orders of the Dreamed: George Nelson on Cree and Northern Ojibwa Religion and Myth, 1823* [Winnipeg: University of Manitoba Press, 1988],190) provides one of the best explanations in ordinary English of how the concepts of the original people and the trickster figures are connected.

   Similarly, Janet Chute, in her book, *The Legacy of Shingwaukonse* (Toronto: University of Toronto Press, 1998), relates how the information she was seeking was given to her in piecemeal fashion. It was, as one elder explained, like a seed that had to go through a process of testing (like a pine cone goes through fire) before its "power" was released, and growth could occur.

5. Chibiabos also figures prominently in Potawatomi tales as the messenger to the Land of the Dead (see Robert Ritzenthaler and Pat Ritzenthaler, *The Woodland Indians of the Western Great Lakes* [Prospect Heights: Waveland Press, 1983], 130). Among contemporary Ojibwa, he is associated with ghosts (his name is closely linked to *jibay/cheebi*, the soul that leaves the body after death and seeks the land of the dead/souls). According to Ojibwa historian Basil Johnston, in *The Manitous: The Spiritual World of the Ojibway* (Toronto: Key Porter Books, 1995), 49, Chibiabos taught the Ojibwa about dream quests, music, and communicating in general with the manidoog. Usually he is considered to be Nanabozho's younger brother, but in this tale, he is called his grandson.
6. Henry Rowe Schoolcraft, *Indian Legends*, ed. Mentor L. Williams (East Lansing: Michigan State University Press, 1991), 77. Neither Schoolcraft nor Mentor Williams provide any indication as to the origin of this particular version, although Schoolcraft does provide a lengthy introduction to his original collection of *Algic Researches, comprising inquiries respecting the mental characteristics of the North American Indians* (New York: Harper & Bros., 1839), and a more specific introduction to the "Nanabozho cycle." Victor Barnouw, in his 1940s collection *Wisconsin Chippewa Myths and Tales and their Relation to Chippewa Life* (Madison: University of Wisconsin Press, 1977), included a series of "Wenebojo" tales, part of which contains a passage remarkably similar to Schoolcraft's tale collected in the previous century. The most scholarly version can be found in William Jones, *Ojibwa Texts,* part I, ed. Truman Michelson (Leyden, New York: Publications of the American Ethnological Society, 1917).
7. William M. Clements, "Schoolcraft as Textmaker," *Journal of the American Foklklore Society* 103 (1990): 177-192.
8. A. Irving Hallowell, "Ojibwa Ontology, Behaviour and World View," in *Culture and History*, ed. Stanley Diamond (London: Oxford University Press, 1960).
9. Mary Black, "Ojibwa Power Belief System," in *The Anthropology of Power*, ed. R.R Fogelson and R.N. Adams (New York: Academic Press, 1977).
10. Dewdney makes this observation in his introduction to Norval Morriseau's *Legends of My People the Great Ojibway*, ed. Selwyn Dewdney (Toronto: Ryerson Press, 1965), xx-xxi.
11. I am defining the term "world view" as a way of looking at reality, using basic assumptions that provide a way of thinking about the world/universe. The term "cosmology" is increasingly connected to scientific theories of the universe, but it has long been used to describe religious theories of the universe, so I use these terms synonymously.
12. Irving Hallowell, "Some Emperical Aspects of Northern Saulteaux Religion," *American Anthropologist*, New Series 36 (1934): 389-404.
13. Densmore (*Chippewa Customs*, 14) gives *o'djitcag'* as the Ojibwa word meaning "soul" or "spirit" of a person; *djibe* as "spirit"; and *odjib'* as meaning "ghost or shadow." Bishop Frederic Baraga translated "my soul" as *nin tchitchag* (see *A Dictionary of the Ojibway Language*) and John Nichols translates "my spirit" as *injichaag* (see *A Concise Dictionary of Minnesota Ojibwe*). The Ojibwa believed that people had two souls. The djibe (jeebi/cheebi) left the body at death, undertaking a four-day journey to the Land of Souls. Jeebis were sometimes seen near the graves of the dead, particularly if the proper rituals had not been performed and the jeebi was unable to reach the other world.

The "odjitcag" remained with a person's body while the person was alive, although it was free to separate from the body for short periods, allowing powerful individuals to take on different forms to make journeys to distant places to gather information.

14. William Jones, "The Algonkin Manitou," *Journal of American Folklore* 18 (1905): 183-190.

15. Christopher Vecsey, *Traditional Ojibwa Religion and its Historical Changes* (Philadelphia: American Philosophical Society, 1983). Black, "Power Belief System."

16. Johnston, *The Manitous,* xxi.

17. Catherine Albanese, *Nature Religion in America: From the Algonkian Indians to the New Age* (Chicago: University of Chicago, 1990). Albanese, in turn, refers to Neal Salisbury's work, *Manitou and Providence: Indians, Europeans, and the Making of New England, 1500-1643* (New York: Oxford University Press, 1982), which describes the earliest encounters between groups of the Algonquian people and early Euro-Americans.

18. William W. Warren, *History of the Ojibway People* (St. Paul: Minnesota Historical Society Press, 1994), 27.

19. William Jones, *Ojibway Texts*, part II, ed. Trueman Michelson (Leyden, NY: Publications of the American Ethnological Society, 1919), 322-323.

20. Victor Barnouw, *Wisconsin Chippewa Myths and Tales and Their Relation to Chippewa Life* (Madison: University of Wisconsin Press, 1977), 41.

21. Theresa Smith, *The Island of the Anishnaabeg: Thunderers and Water Monsters in the Traditional Ojibwe Life-World* (Moscow, ID: University of Idaho Press, 1995), 44-47.

22. See Brown and Brightman, *Orders of the Dreamed*, 108-110, for a good explanation of the various forms that these figures take.

23. Although the popular spelling for these terms is *Gitchi Manitou* and *Matchi Manitou,* I have used Nichols's and Nyholm's orthography. See John D. Nichols and Earl Nyholm, *A Concise Dictionary of Minnesota Ojibwe* (Minneapolis: University of Minnesota Press, 1995).

24. The earliest Euro-American references to Nanabozho sometimes referred to him as the "Great Hare" or "Great Rabbit," believing that he was associated with the form of a rabbit, and some groups of Ojibwa have continued until recently to make similar associations. However, most contemporary stories about Nanabozho portray him in his human form. Among some groups of Northern Ojibwa/Saulteaux, and, to some extent, among the Bungi or Plains Ojibwa, Nanabozho is known as *Wisakedjak,* or both characters appear in stories as trickster/transformer figures. It has been commonly believed that Wisakedjak refers to the figure of whisky-jack or the Canada (grey) jay, but Brown and Brightman argue that the name goes back to the Proto-Algonquian parent language and is unanalyzable (see Brown and Brightman, *Orders of the Dreamed*, 125-126).

25. John Cooper, *The North Algonquian Supreme Being* (New York: AMS Reprint Edition, 1978).

26. Vernon Kinietz, "Chippewa Village: The Story of Katikitegan," *Cranbrook Institute of Science Bulletin*, 25 (1947).

27. See Louis Masson, *Les Bourgeois de la Compagnie du Nord-Ouest*, 2 vols, 1889-1890 (New York: Antiquarian Press, 1960).

28. There is still considerable scholarly controversy as to whether a supreme being was part of original Anishinaabe cosmology, or was an adaptation from Christian beliefs. In his collection of "legends," Schoolcraft includes a Saginaw tale about the spirit of evil and the spirit of good. In his notes, he states it is impossible to tell "how much is due to ideas communicated to the Indian mind, since the discovery of America" (see Schoolcraft, *Indian Legends,* 204). Skinner, for instance, was convinced that all such beliefs were post-contact. My own belief is that such a figure did exist, but has become intertwined with the concept of the Christian God.

29. Frank Speck, *Myths and Folk-lore of the Timis-Kaming Algonquin and Timagami Ojibwa,* Anthropological Series, no. 9 (Ottawa: Memoirs of the Canadian Geological Survey of Canada, No. 71, 1915), 28.

30. Sam Gill, *Mother Earth: An American Story* (Chicago: University of Chicago Press, 1987).

31. John Tanner, *A Narrative of the Captivity and Adventures of John Tanner during Thirty Years Residence Among the Indians in the Interior of North America*, ed. Edwin James (Minneapolis: Ross & Haines Reprint Edition, 1956), 184.

32. Black, "Power Belief System," 143.

33. Hallowell, "Ojibwa Ontology," 226-227.

34. Mary Black, "Ojibwa Taxonomy and Percept Ambiguity," *Ethos* 5, 1 (1977): 93.

35. There are few areas in which the clash of world views becomes as obvious as the question of the terms "natural" and "supernatural," "sacred" and "profane," or "transcendent" and "immanent" in describing concepts of reality. Anthropologists and scholars of religion often take opposing sides, since their own world views differ. In this conflict of interpretations, my own opinion is that, rather than there being an absence of the supernatural in the Ojibwa world view, or a distinction between the natural and supernatural, there is a continuity, with the sacred conceived of as manifest in the natural world as well as transcendently. As Theresa Smith has remarked in *The Island of the Anishnaabeg* (pp. 22-24), such characterizations need not be seen as disparaging, "for the failure to discover the sacred in one's environment is less a product of sophistication than of alienation." She notes that the Ojibwa with whom she has worked on Manitoulin Island gave the impression that White people were the simple ones. Smith concludes, and I agree, that if we are to understand the Aboriginal (Ojibwa) experience of religion, we must begin by using an heuristic approach to religion, which does more than describe the role of religion in society, and steers free of judgements regarding the content of the religious experience.

36. Black, "Ojibwa Taxonomy," 99-100.

37. Christopher Vecsey, "Midewiwin Myths of Origin," in *Papers of the Fifteenth Algonquian Conference,* ed. William Cowan (Ottawa: Carleton University, 1984), 458.

38. Warren, *History of the Ojibway*, 110-111; Hoffman, "The Midewiwin," 236; Tanner, *A Narrative of the Captivity*, 343.

39. Ake Hultkrantz, *Native Religions of North America: The Power of Visions and Fertility* (San Francisco: Harper and Row, 1987), 17. John A. Grim, *The Shaman: Patterns of Siberian and Ojibway Healing* (Norman, Oklahoma: University of Oklahoma Press, 1983).

40. See James H. Howard, *The Plains-Ojibwa or Bungi* (Lincoln, Nebraska: J&L Reprint Co., 1977), 121-122. Howard believed that the Métis had assimilated this belief from the French part of their dual heritage.

41. Densmore, *Chippewa Customs*, 98.

42. Hallowell has a good description and a chart illustrating the role of dreams in Ojibwa life, based on his work at Berens River. See A. Irving Hallowell, *The Ojibwa of Berens River, Manitoba*, ed. Jennifer S.H. Brown (Fort Worth, Texas: Harcourt Brace Jovanovich, 1992), 84-92.

43. Ruth Landes noted that the Ojibwa distinguished between ordinary dreams and dreams in which power was conveyed. (See her *Ojibwa Religion and the Midewiwin* [Madison: University of Wisconsin Press, 1968], 30-31.) According to Schoolcraft, the term *apowa* was used to specify dreams of power. However, Baraga defined *apowa* as an ominous, unlucky dream, and Densmore defined it as an important personal warning received in a dream. This may indicate that the term really applied to an evil vision, which might be unsolicited and in which a person was "blessed" with powers that could bring harm to others.

44. Densmore, *Chippewa Customs*, 78-79. The Ojibwe for "I dream," *nin bawadjige*, is also the term used for "medicine," as is the term *inabandumowin*, "the vision seen." However, it appears that the Ojibwa did make a distinction between ordinary dreams that had value as a communication link with the manidoog, and those received during the vision quest.

45. Michael Angel, "The Ojibwa-Missionary Encounter at Rainy Lake Mission, 1839-1857," MA thesis, University of Manitoba, 1986.

46. Landes, *Ojibwa Religion*, 31. Black-Rogers's article, "Power Belief System," summarizes her findings regarding contemporary Ojibwa ideas related to power and control. According to her, they began by speaking of the classes of *bimaasdiziwad*, or "living things," then of the "manitou" or "powers" possessed by each of the different classes. I have reservations as to whether her complex taxonomy is not a Western-inspired version of Ojibwa thought processes, and, if it is accurate, whether it can be generalized to other groups of Ojibwa and particularly to those living hundreds of years earlier.

47. Peter Jones, *History of the Ojebway Indians; with especial reference to their conversion to Christianity* (London: A.W. Bennett, 1861), 145-147.

48. Henry Rowe Schoolcraft, *Information Respecting the History, Condition and Prospects of the Indian Tribes of the United States*, 6 vols. (Philadelphia: Lippincott, Grambo & Co., 1851-1857), vol. 1, 114.

49. Henry Rowe Schoolcraft, *The Indian in His Wigwam, or Characteristics of the Red Race in American* (Buffalo: Derby and Hudson, 1848), 169.

50. Schoolcraft, *Information Respecting*, 391-396.

51. Schoolcraft made attempts to categorize all Ojibwa/Anishinaabe religious practitioners/traditional healers into three groups—Mideg, Jiisakiiwininiwag, and Waabanowag—and this categorization has been followed by many others down to the present day. Swedish scholar Ake Hultkrantz, in his study of American Aboriginal religions, developed an alternate framework consisting of shamans, medicine men, and priests, when writing about Aboriginal American religious groups. Among the Ojibwa, he considered Jiisakiiwininiwag as shamans, and Mideg as medicine men,

since the former received their power through trance-induced visions, while the latter used a combination of visions and teaching to pass on knowledge and power. Contemporary American scholar John Grim has used the designation "shaman" to encompass all forms of Ojibwa religious figures/traditional healers. Increasingly, scholars have begun to study these figures in terms of the Ojibwa world view, rather than using Euro-American forms of categorization.

52. This term has numerous spellings in Ojibwe, depending upon the orthography used and how the noun is formed. Others include: Baraga: *Tchissakiwin*; Nicollet: *Jisakan*; Schoolcraft: *Jessakid*, *Jossekeed* (person); Hoffman: *Jessakkid* (person); Densmore: *Dja'sakid* (person). *Jaasakid* is the gerund form of the *Jissakiiwinini*, and is the form most commonly used, although the spelling varies considerably.

52. While almost all commentators have described versions of the Shaking Tent ceremony, the most comprehensive study is by Hallowell in *The Role of Conjuring in Saulteaux Society* (Philadelphia: University of Pennsylvania Press, 1942), who provides an historiographic review of early works in addition to describing the Berens River ceremonies in some detail. More recently, Brown and Brightman (*The Orders of the Dreamed,* 146-158) have discussed the Shaking Tent ceremony in the context of descriptions by fur trader George Nelson. Ake Hultkrantz looks at the ceremony from an hermeneutical perspective among a number of North American Aboriginal groups in *The Religions of the American Indians* (Berkeley: University of California Press, 1979), 84-102, while John Grim compares the belief systems of Ojibwa Jiisakiiwininiwag (whom he terms "shamans") with Siberian shamans in *The Shaman.*

54. Alexander Henry the Elder, *Travels and Adventures in Canada and the Indian Territories between the Years 1760 and 1766*, ed. James Bain (Edmonton: Hurtig, 1965), 158.

55. Ibid., 159.

56. Ibid., 162.

57. Masson, *Les Bourgeois*, 264.

58. Joseph N. Nicollet, *The Journals of Joseph N. Nicollet: A Scientist on the Mississippi Headwater with Notes on Indian Life, 1836-37*, trans. André Fertey, ed. Martha Coleman Bray (St. Paul: Minnesota Historical Society, 1970), 216-218. Schoolcraft's description is lifted almost verbatim from Nicollet's earlier unpublished papers without any indication as to its source. The main contribution Schoolcraft adds is the time and location of Nicollet's observation.

59. Brown & Brightman, *Orders of the Dreamed*, 39-44;102-107.

60. Many Ojibwa who became Christians continued to believe in the powers of Jiisakiiwininiwag but, like Euro-Americans, believed that the source of the manidoo power was, in fact, the devil. The ceremony thus became the epitome of evil. See, for example, the papers of Norval Morriseau, pp.11-12.

61. Walter James Hoffman, "The Midewiwin or 'Grand Medicine Society' of the Ojibwa," in *Seventh Annual Report to the Smithsonian Institution, 1885-1886*, Bureau of American Ethnology (Washington: Smithsonian Institution Press, 1891).

62. Norval Morriseau, a twentieth-century Ojibwa from the Lake Nipigon region, explained that if the Jiisakiiwinini was asked to use the ceremony for evil purposes, and given gifts, he had no choice but to comply or he would lose his powers (Morriseau Papers:11-12, Glenbow Museum Archive, Calgary).

63. To further complicate the issue, Nichols and Nyholm, in their contemporary dictionary of Ojibwe, *A Concise Dictionary of Minnesota Ojibwe*, consider the former a doctor and the latter a traditional healer.

64. Hoffman, "The Midwiwin," 159.

65. Ibid., 254-255. Densmore (*Chippewa Customs*, 45-46) relates a similar incident in which a person she calls a Jaasakiid uses sucking bones to cure a patient.

66. Tanner, *A Narrative of the Captivity*, 376-378.

67. Ibid., 164. As Tanner explains: "A drawing, or a little image, is made to represent the man, woman, or animal, on which the power of the medicine is to be tried; then the part representing the heart is punctured with a sharp instrument, if the design is to cause death, and a little medicine is applied. The drawing or image ... is called *imuzzi-ne-neen*." Tanner declined, in this case, since the medicine included *onaman*, which was associated with "bad medicine."

68. Hoffman reported the case of a neighbouring Scandinavian who, possessed of strange desires concerning a young Ojibwa woman, discovered some objects under his bed that he believed had influenced his affections.

69. In his description of the third-degree Midewiwin, Hoffman had a number of descriptive notes on the Jiisakiiwinini, including a curious description of the ceremony used by the Nenaandawiiwed, or "sucking bone" doctor, which he attributes to the Jiisakiiwinini. Whether he confused the two, or whether the people at White Earth at that time had integrated the two ceremonies, is impossible to determine (Hoffman, "The Midewiwin," 254-255).

70. The Ojibwe verb *waaban* means "to be dawn" or "to be tomorrow." This has led Basil Johnston to suggest that the ceremony might have been borrowed from an eastern tribe of the Algonquian, or that it might refer to the practice of conducting ceremonies during the night and concluding them at dawn. See Basil Johnston, *Ojibway Ceremonies* (Toronto: McClelland & Stewart, 1982), 115.

71. Frances Densmore, *Chippewa Music*, 2 vols., Bureau of American Ethnology Bulletins 45 and 53 (Washington: Smithsonian Institution, 1910-1913), 66.

72. David Thompson, *Travels in Western North America, 1784-1812*, ed. Victor G. Hopwood (Toronto: Macmillan, 1971), 178.

73. Thomas L. McKenney, *Sketches of a Tour to the Lakes* (Minneapolis: Ross & Haines, 1972), 170-171.

74. Ibid., 265.

75. Tanner, *Narrative of the Captivity*, 122. It is possible that the moralizing reflects the influence of Tanner's editor, or Tanner's own retrospective judgement on his past life.

76. Warren, *History of the Ojibway*, 109. In Warren's history, Chequamegon was the central Ojibwa village, and an important Midewiwin site. Warren suggested that the sudden outbreak of evil practices, including cannibalism, may have been the result of a combination of a failure of crops and the inability to hunt because of being hemmed in by enemies. Various writers have speculated that the evil "shamans" were renegade Mideg or Waabanowag. Regardless of the cause, groups of Ojibwa did begin to move further west, and gradually Midewiwin ceremonies began to be held at sites such as Leech Lake and Red Lake.

77. Alanson Skinner, "Associations and Ceremonies of the Menomini Indians," *Anthropological Papers of the American Museum of Natural History* 13, 2 (1915).

78. William Jones, *Ojibwa Texts*, part 2, ed. Truman Michelson (Leyden, NY: Publications of the American Ethnological Society, 1919), 317-318.

79. Johnston (*Ojibway Ceremonies*, 115-116) contends that they formed a society entirely separate from the Midewiwin, but this view is at variance with other accounts.

80. Diamond Jenness, *The Ojibwa Indians of Parry Island,* Department of Mines Bulletin 78 (Ottawa: National Museum of Canada, 1935).

81. This term was usually used to describe a blend of European tobaccos and the dried bark of red willows, although in at least one narrative that recounts the origin of tobacco, there was a distinction between *bakwécpakuzìgunen* (which his informant termed wild kinnikinnick), *gekádugnugèkwukin* (a sweet kinnikinnick, which was difficult to find around Lac du Flambeau), and *memiskwákwakin miskwabímizin* (a kinnikinnick made from red bushes). See Barnouw, *Wisconsin Chippewa Myths*, 29-30.

82. Densmore, *Chippewa Music*, 2.

83. While Catholics were often equally at a loss in this regard, perhaps the Catholic use of external signs such as incense and crosses, the understanding of the Catholic mass as a reenactment of a meal, and even the Catholic concept of paying for indulgences, facilitated some sort of understanding, which was impossible with Protestants, whose religious beliefs and practices focussed on the Word.

84. This is not to say that the Anishinaabeg must not have been equally confused by the ideas and actions of their Euro-American neighbours, particularly since the religious ideas of those Euro-Americans who were Christian were exclusionist, and represented a multitude of different versions of what was perceived as being the truth. The Ojibwa initially had no exclusivist tendencies, accepting whatsoever was proven to have power.

85. Black-Rogers's informants ("Power Belief Systems," 149-150) thus "classed" love medicine, hunting medicine, and gambling medicine as bad medicine, since they caused others to lose their autonomy. Morriseau (Papers, 12) uses the word "conjuring" to describe bad medicine, though by this, he means only those types that were used to harm people

86. Warren, *History of the Ojibway*, 109-111.

87. A vivid example of these "witch hunts" occurred in the post-contact period in connection with the rise of the Handsome Lake revitalization movement, in which Handsome Lake carried out a "witch-hunt" against rivals such as Red Jacket, as well as a number of neighbouring Delaware Christians, several of whom were killed (see Anthony Wallace, "Revitalization Movements," *American Anthropologist* 58 [1956]: 264-281). In her studies of the Midewiwin (1965) and the Prairie Potawatomi (1970), Ruth Landes described similar situations, though the final outcome was not as dramatic. It is interesting that the Rev. Peter Jones, who spent some of his early years living among the Iroquois, devoted a section to witchcraft in his book on the Ojibwa (see Jones, *History of the Ojebway Indians).* Jones's account described what others have termed "shamanistic duels." He attributed the power used by the "conjurors," as he termed them, to the evil spirit.

88. Wallace, "Revitalization Movements"; also Wallace, *Religion: An Anthropological View* (New York: Random House, 1966), 177-187.

89. Wallace, *Religion*, 180-181.

90. In his paper "The Question of Ojibwa Clans" (in *Actes du vingtième congrès des algonquinistes*, ed. William Cowan [Ottawa:Carleton University, 1989]), Charles Bishop gives a good overview of the controversy regarding the geographical location of the proto-Ojibwa, as do Theresa Schenck in her 1997 book on the Lake Superior Ojibwa, and Janet Chute in her 1998 book on Shingwaukonse.

91. James G.E. Smith, "Leadership Among the Indians of the Northern Woodlands," in *Currents in Anthropology: Essays in Honor of Sol Tax*, ed. Robert Hinshaw (The Hague: Mouton, 1979). Edward S. Rogers, "Band Organization Among the Indians of Eastern Subarctic Canada," in *Contributions to Anthropology: Band Societies*, ed. David Damas, Anthropological Series 84, Bulletin 228 (Ottawa: National Museum of Canada, 1969); also E. Rogers, "Cultural Adaptations: The Northern Ojibwa of the Boreal Forest, 1670-1980," in *Boreal Forest Adaptations: The Northern Algonkians*, ed. A. Theodore Steegmann (New York: Plenum Press, 1983). Charles Callender, *Social Organization of the Central Algonkian Indians* (Milwaukee: Milwaukee Public Museum, 1962).

92. Theresa Schenck, *"The Voice of the Crane Echoes Afar": The Sociopolitical Organization of the Lake Superior Ojibwa, 1640-1855* (New York: Garland Publishing, 1997), 19-23, 37, 52-57. Schenck believes these were the same people as the Sauteurs mentioned by some of the early Jesuits. Warren relates the story of a debate between the heads of the Loon and the Crane clans as to which was the premier clan—a debate the Crane leader won (Warren, *History of the Ojibway*, 87-89). Warren explains that the crane is known in Ojibwe as *Uj-e-jauk*. Baraga's dictionary gives the Ojibwa word as *Adjidjad*, but includes *Otchitchak* in brackets.

93. Leo G. Waisberg, "An Ethnological and Historical Outline of the Rainy Lake Ojibwa," in *An Historical Synthesis of the Manitou Mounds Site on the Rainy River, Ontario*, vol. 1 (Cornwall: Parks Canada Office, National Historic Sites Branch, 1978), 162-168.

94. Karl Schlesier, "Rethinking the Midewiwin and the Plains ceremonial called the Sun Dance," *Plains Anthropologist* 35, 127 (1990). Richard White, *The Middle Ground: Indians, Empires, and Republics in The Great Lakes Region, 1650-1815* (New York: Cambridge University Press, 1991).

95. To make matters even more difficult for the historian, the early writings of ethnologists who studied these tribes and codified them are full of internal contradictions, since they sought to freeze and codify what was, in effect, a world in flux. See White, *The Middle Ground,* 16.

96. Baraga gives *ogima* as the name for "chief," indicating that assistant or second chiefs were called *anikeogimia* (the prefix *anike* signifying futurality). A war chief or captain was called a *maiaossewinini*, from the word *Maiaosse,* "to march forward at the head of a band." "Ogimaa" is still used today to denote a chief, boss, or leader (see Nichols and Nyholm, *A Dictionary of Minnesota Ojibwe,* 105).

97. This may have led Schoolcraft, Warren, and later writers to make a distinction between "civil chiefs" and "war chiefs." It is also probable that other individuals took responsibility for leading large hunting parties, and even for overseeing the harvesting

of wild rice (see Thomas Vennum Jr., *Wild Rice and the Ojibwa People* [St. Paul: Minnesota Historical Society Press, 1988], 183-194).

98. Bishop, "The Question of Ojibwa Clans." The dates for the "French period" are 1720 to 1761, according to Helen Hornbeck Tanner, *Atlas of Great Lakes Indian History* (Norman: Newberry Library/University of Oklahoma Press, 1986).

99. Felix M. Keesing, *The Menomini Indians of Wisconsin* (New York: Johnson Reprint Corporation, 1971), 774.

100. Janet Elizabeth Chute, *The Legacy of Shingwaukonse: A Century of Native Leadership* (Toronto: University of Toronto Press, 1998).

101. Schenck, *The Voice of the Crane.*

102. Baraga defined the *oshkaabewiss* as "the waiter or attendant of an Indian Chief," but made no mention of any religious functions; Nicollet used the term to refer to the person who sent out invitation sticks for both councils of war and the Midewiwin; and Grant termed the agent of *Kitchi Manitou*, and the person who served food at a feast preceeding a war party, *Michinawois*. Kinietz termed the person who carried the invitations for the Midewiwin an *ouskadawis*, while Howard noted that among the Plains Ojibwa the person who conducted the Midewiwin was termed a *skabewis*. Skinner, in his studies of the Plains Ojibwa, discovered that the term *skaupewis* was used to denote the servant of the *Okitchita* who maintained order in camp. Kohl referred to a person whose duty it was to fill the bowls of pipes as a *skabewis* or *dresseur.* Densmore, as has been seen, used the term "messenger" as a gloss for *ockabewis* in her rendition of Odinigun's origin narrative, but she also used it to describe the Mide official who sent out invitations for the Midewiwin ceremony.

It is interesting to note that when the Ojibwa signed Treaty 3 with the Canadian government, chiefs, soldiers (war chiefs), messengers (oshkaabewis), and councillors (speakers) were identified on the pay lists.

103. In his discussion of the early Ojibwa occupation of Chequamegon, Warren made this very point. While his intention, here, was to stress the role of the Midewiwin in the development of nascent Ojibwa nationalism, the obverse is equally true—that the leading Mide priests were also important political leaders. See Warren, *History of the Ojibway People,* 99-100.

104. Shingwaukonse, in his previously quoted explanation of how "prophets" obtained powers through visions, concluded with the statement: "Such . . . was the ancient custom, and the celebrated old war-captains rose to their power in this manner" (see Schoolcraft, *Information Respecting the History*, vol. 1, p. 111).

105. Perhaps this was a means of group regulation of those who possessed special powers from the manidoog. Unfortunately, Anishinaabe tales that speak of this period do not go into details regarding their organizational structure.

106. I have used the English word here as it has become so widely used by contemporary Aboriginal people. Baraga (1992) gives no translation for "elder" as such, but does indicate that *kitchi aiaans* refers to "grown folks" or "great noble folks."

Chapter Three

1. Selwyn Dewdney, *The Sacred Scrolls of the Southern Ojibway* (Toronto: University of Toronto for the Glenbow-Alberta Institute, 1975), 23.

2. Thomas Vennum Jr., "Ojibwa Origin-Migration songs of the *mitewiwin*," *Journal of American Folklore* 91 (1978): 753-791.

3. The Ojibwa scholar and practitioner Nicholas Deleary maintains that the main characteristic of the Midewiwin is that it is life-giving and extends life. He ties this in with the Ojibwa concept of *pimadaziwin* (or bimaadiziwin), which he understands as meaning "living the good life to the fullest." See Nicholas Deleary, "Midewiwin: An Aboriginal Spiritual Institution. Symbols of Continuity: A Native Studies Culture-based Perspective," Master's thesis, Carleton University, 1990, pp.19-20.

4. Jiisakiiwininiwag, Waabanowag, and Mideg were all able to amaze and confound Euro-Americans with visionary and healing powers for which the latter had no explanation, and all of them operated within the context of the Ojibwa world view. However, only within the Midewiwin was a teaching function an integral part of the ceremonial process—even if this was most often either missed or ignored by Euro-American observers. When this institutionalization took place is open to question.

5. William Doty and Christopher Vecsey have presented extensive historiographical studies of the various schools of thought by which a long train of scholars has approached the study of myths, and, in particular, the assumption that myths do not reflect reality. See William Doty, *Mythology: The Study of Myths and Rituals* (Birmingham: University of Alabama Press, 1986); Christopher Vecsey, *Imagine Ourselves Richly: Mythic Narratives of North American Indians* (New York: Crossroad, 1988). Paul Ricoeur's article "MYTH: Myth and History," pp. 273-282 in the *Encyclopedia of Religion,* vol.10 (ed. Mircea Eliade, London: Simon & Schuster and Prentice Hall International, 1995) provides an excellent examination of myth and history, particularly with reference to linear and cyclical concepts of time.

6. Northrop Frye, *Words with Power: Being a Second Study of the Bible and Literature* (Toronto: Penguin, 1990)

7. Jan Vansina, *Oral Tradition as History* (Madison: University of Wisconsin, 1985). In a recent article, Moodie, Catchpole, and Abel have demonstrated that Northern Athapaskan oral traditions can be transmitted for many hundreds of years, and still be of historical value (see D. Wayne Moodie, A.J.W. Catchpole, and Kerry Abel, "Northern Athapaskan Oral Tradition and the White River Volcano," *Ethnohistory* 39, 2 [1992]: 148-171).

8. Deleary, "Midewiwin," 35. Historians of religion generally try to distinguish between the truths expressed by myths and historical facts. It may be possible to verify some events as historical facts, but the significance of the myths lies in the truths they express. Both believers and scholars need to be careful not to read sacred narratives as one would read books of science. Karen Armstrong, in her recent book *The Battle for God* (New York: Knopf, 2000), argues that it is precisely this confusion of mythos with logos that has contributed to the rise of religious fundamentalism. People in the pre-modern world were not as concerned with what actually happened as with the meaning of the event.

9. In a recent article on the writings of Louis Hennepin, Bruce Greenfield explores some of these different ways of knowing, and their implications for understanding the interaction between Aboriginals and Euro-Americans. See his "The Oral in the Written: The Irony of Representation in Louis Hennepin's *Description de la Louisiane,*" *Historical Reflections/Reflexions Historiques* 21, 2 (1995): 243-259.

10. Dewdney, *The Sacred Scrolls*, 23; Vennum, "Ojibwa Origin-Migration songs," 754.

11. Vecsey, *Imagine Ourselves Richly*, 21.

12. This tale is widespread among all the divisions of the Ojibwa, including the northern bands and their Cree neighbours, where the figure of Nanabozho has been replaced by Wisakedzak. See the version of this tale collected by Alanson Skinner in "Notes on the Eastern Cree and Northern Saulteaux," *Anthropological Papers of the American Museum of Natural History* 9 (1911): 173ff. Robert Brightman provides a good explanation and comparison of the Cree and Ojibwa narratives involving Nanabozho and Wisakedzak (see Jennifer S.H. Brown and Robert Brightman, eds., *The Orders of the Dreamed: George Nelson on Cree and Northern Ojibwa Religion and Myth, 1823* [Winnipeg: University of Manitoba Press, 1988]).

13. Scholars have interpreted these tales in a variety of ways. For instance, Vecsey provides a structuralist, and Theresa Smith provides an hermeneutical, analysis of the tales. See Vecsey, *Imagine Ourselves Richly*; and Theresa S. Smith, *The Island of the Anishnaabeg: Thunderers and Water Monsters in the Traditional Ojibwe Life-World* (Moscow, Idaho: University of Idaho Press, 1995).

14. William Jones, *Ojibwa Texts*, part II, ed. Truman Michelson (Leyden, New York: Publications of the American Ethnological Society, 1919), 547-559. Victor Barnouw, *Wisconsin Chippewa Myths and Tales and their Relation to Chippewa Life* (Madison: University of Wisconsin Press, 1977), 41-43.

15. John Tanner, *A Narrative of the Captivity and Adventures of John Tanner during Thirty Years Residence Among the Indians in the Interior of North American*, ed. Edwin James (Minneapolis: Ross & Haines Reprint Edition, 1956), 185. The difficulty of making any definitive statements with regard to dating is illustrated by the fact that the other version of an origin tale that features Mishibizhii is related by Norval Morriseau in the 1960s from around Lake Nipigon (see his *Legends of My People the Great Ojibway*, ed. Selwyn Dewdney [Toronto: Ryerson Press, 1965], 55). It appears to be similar to Tanner's circa-1800 version from around the Pembina Valley, despite the differences in time and geographic location—and despite the fact that most of Morriseau's other tales show strong Christian influences.

16. William Jones, *Ojibwa Texts*, part I, ed. Truman Michelson (Leyden, NY: Publications of the American Ethnological Society, 1917).

17. However, Hoffman's informant dates from the 1830s so the works are probably more contemporaneous than would appear at first.

18. The *miigis,* or "cowrie shell," as it has been termed by Hoffman (see Walter James Hoffman, "The Midewiwin or 'Grand Medicine Society' of the Ojibwa," in *Seventh Annual Report to the Smithsonian Institution, 1885-1886,* Bureau of American Ethnology [Washington: Smithsonian Institution Press, 1891], 145-300) and others, was one of the central symbols of the Midewiwin. While many Euro-American observers made great efforts to provide a precise scientific description of it, its

importance lies in the power it possessed, not in its biological classification. Twentieth-century versions of the Midewiwin provide a much wider variety of descriptions of shells.

19. William Warren, *History of the Ojibway People* (St. Paul: Minnesota Historical Society Press, 1984), 78-79.

20. A full explanation of this tale is given in the quote at the beginning of Chapter One. This is the most common explanation, but there is at least one alternate explanation given in Jones's collection of Ojibwe texts. According to the editor, Truman Michelson, the Midewiwin is equated with life itself, and the otter's path is the path of life: each time a lodge is put up, he leaves the gift of life to all who become members (see Jones, *Ojibwa Texts*, part II, pp. 570-571).

21. J. Fletcher Williams, in his memoir of William W. Warren, in the 1885 edition of Warren's work, speaks of the elderly Flat Mouth coming to talk with Warren, whom he called "his grandson" (see Warren, *History of the Ojibway*, 17). It is also possible that Warren's source was Pizhiki (Great Buffalo), the senior chief at La Pointe, with whom Warren also had many dealings.

22. Flat Mouth's father was Yellow Head, which might lead one to speculate that either he or his grandfather was Euro-American or of mixed ancestry. Regardless of his precise background, culturally Flat Mouth was definitely Ojibwa.

23. Although Warren and Hickerson disagree regarding the specifics, both place the Pillagers among what Warren calls the "Northern Ojibwa," although in his description of the major clans, Warren lists the Bear clan as being southern. It is likely there was intermarriage between the two groups. At the same time, other bands under such leaders as Biauswah and his son, Catawbedai (Flat Mouth's contemporary), had moved south and west from La Pointe to the regions around Fond du Lac and Sandy Lake.

24. Tanner, *A Narrative of the Captivity*, 168-169. The Shawnee Prophet (Tenskwatawa) was a member of the Shawnee Tribe, and a brother of Tecumseh. Following a vision, he spread a message renouncing White customs and goods, as well as witchcraft. The latter put him in conflict with many traditional leaders. However, for a time he attracted followers from many tribes in the Great Lakes and Ohio Valley regions, including many Ojibwa.

25. Warren, *History of the Ojibway*, 81.

26. Hoffman, "The Midewiwin," 155.

27. Ibid., 175-176.

28. Hoffman relates that while Sikas'sige never advanced beyond the second degree, he later became a Mide official at White Earth Reservation, where Hoffman met him. Since his charts originated in Mille Lacs, he would have been part of the more southerly tradition. An explanation of Midewiwin degrees is given in Chapter Five of this book.

29. This is not to say that some origin narratives do not adapt some aspects of Christian theology. In Loon Foot's account to Kohl in the 1850s (see Johann Georg Kohl, *Kitchi Gami: Life Among the Lake Superior Ojibway*, trans. Lascelles Wraxall [St. Paul: Minnesota Historical Society Press, 1985], 195-199), Gichi-Manidoo creates a garden in which the first man and woman eat the forbidden fruit, albeit in a uniquely

Midewiwin context. Many later versions, such as James Redsky's (Esquekesik), intermingle Midewiwin and Christian beliefs to a considerable degree. See James Redsky (Esquekesik), *Great Leader of the Ojibway: Mis-quona-queb*, ed. James R. Stevens (Toronto: McClelland and Stewart, 1972).

30. Hoffman, "The Midewiwin," 184.

31. See Dewdney, *The Sacred Scrolls*, 158. The twentieth-century narratives such as those related by Redsky (from the Boundary Waters region) intermingled the miigis and Otter (Nigig) and added in Bear (Makwa) as important figures in bringing the Midewiwin to the Anishinaabeg (Redsky, *Great Leader*, 100-106). It appears that the different accounts are variations on the same theme, rather than indicate significantly different traditions.

32. Thomas Vennum, Jr., *Wild Rice and the Ojibwa People* (St. Paul: Minnesota Historical Society, 1988), 752-774.

33. Ibid., 762.

34. Dewdney, *The Sacred Scrolls.*

35. Fred K. Blessing, *The Ojibway Indians Observed, Papers of Fred K. Blessing Jr., on the Ojibway Indians,* in *The Minnesota Archeologist* (St. Paul: Minnesota Archeological Society, 1977), 107. Ojibwa migration charts provide a supplement to the narrative quoted from Warren at the beginning of Chapter One. Such narratives and migration charts plot the westward movement of the Ojibwa over the past couple of centuries. The migration charts are distinguished from other sacred scrolls in that they contain pictographs that are mnemonics for the place-names of the real or legendary stopping places where the messenger in the form of the cowrie, Otter, or Bear stopped and erected the Midewiwin Lodge on the Ojibwa's westward migration.

36. Salt never published his work, but the manuscript for the beginnings of his "Ojibwa History" is located in the National Archives of Canada.

37. The description of the large Midewiwin ceremony at Walpole Island in the 1840s by Methodist missionary James Evans appears to be an exception. The American Methodist missionary, E.H. Day (see his "Sketches of the Northwest," *Collections and Researches made by the Michigan Pioneer and Historical Society* 14 [1890]), and other missionaries also mention Midewiwin ceremonies among the Saginaw Ojibwa in lower Michigan during the nineteenth century.

38. Frances Densmore, *Chippewa Music*, vol. 1, Bureau of American Ethnology Bulletins 45 and 53 (Washington: Smithsonian Institution, 1910-1913), 21.

39. The name Cutfoot is used in versions by A.B. Reagan ("Some notes on the Grand Medicine Society of the Bois Fort Ojibway," *America Illustrated* 27 [1933]: 516-517); Ruth Landes (*Ojibwa Religion and the Midewiwin* [Madison: University of Wisconsin Press, 1968], 95-113); and Redsky (*Great Leader*, 80-81). Basil Johnston's version uses the name Heartberry or Strawberry (*Ojibway Heritage* [New York: Columbia University Press, 1976], 81-84).

40. Landes, *Ojibwa Religion*, 110-111. All inserts are Landes's except the last, which is mine.

41. Homer H. Kidder, *Ojibwa myths and halfbreed tales, of Charlotte Kobawgam and Jacques la Pique, 1893-1895*, recorded with notes by Homer H. Kidder, ed. Arthur P. Bourgeois (Detroit: Wayne State University, 1994), 52-54.

42. Dewdney, *The Sacred Scrolls*, 34-45.

43. Christopher Vecsey, "Midewiwin Myths of Origin," in *Papers of the Fifteenth Algonquian Conference*, ed. William Cowan (Ottawa: Carleton University, 1984), 461-462.

44. Thomas Vennum, Jr., *The Ojibwa Dance Drum: Its History and Construction* (Washington: Smithsonian Institution Press, 1982), 44-47).

45. Dewdney, *The Sacred Scrolls*, 157-158.

46. This myth was related to Johann Kohl (*Kitchi Gami*, 423-425) and quoted by Theresa Smith (*The Island of the Anishnaabeg*, 109-110).

47. Joseph Nicollet, *The Journals of Joseph N. Nicollet: A Scientist on the Mississippi Headwater with Notes on Indian Life, 1836-37*, trans. André Fertey, ed. Martha Coleman Bray (St. Paul: Minnestota Historical Society, 1970), 199.

48. Hoffman, "The Midewiwin," 163-164.

49. Landes, *Ojibwa Religion*, 112.

50. The term "oshkaabewis," in the sense of either an attendant or of a messenger with religious, social, or military functions, is found in a variety of sources, such as Joseph Nicollet (*The Journals*); James H. Howard (*The Plains-Ojibwa or Bungi* [Lincoln, NB: J&L Reprint Co., 1977]); Alanson Skinner "Plains Ojibwa Tales," *Journal of American Folk-lore* 32 (1920): 280-305; and others.

51. Tanner reported an incident in which Esh-ke-bak-ke-koo-sha called upon Tanner's party to throw away their medicine bags, except for the ones used for war and hunting, and showed them new remedies. See Tanner, *A Narrative of the Captivity*, 179-180. See also Warren, *History of the Ojibway People,* 324-325.

52. Schoolcraft, the tale of Mash-kwa-sha-kwong, from *The Indian in His Wigwam*, 114-115.

53. John Johnson, George's father, was an Irishman who became active in the fur trade, spending time at Mackinac Island and La Pointe on Chequamegon Bay. His mother was Ojibwa. George accompanied Schoolcraft on several of his expeditions as an interpreter, and was similarly employed at La Pointe and Sault Ste. Marie agencies. George's sister Jane became Schoolcraft's wife.

54. The same story, edited by Mentor L. Williams, appears in a new collection: Schoolcraft's *Indian Legends* (East Lansing: Michigan State University Press, 1991), 272. Williams, too, believes that in some instances, Schoolcraft or one of the Johnsons may have tampered with the original story.

55. William M. Clements, "Schoolcraft as Textmaker," *Journal of the American Folklore Society* 103 (1990).

56. In his study of Neolin and several other prophetic leaders, Gregory Dowd makes the argument that this call for ritual renewal was because Aboriginal people believed their sufferings were the result of their spiritual failures. Ritual was of importance precisely because, along with visions, it made possible the assistance of the manidoog. See Gregory Evans Dowd, *A Spirited Resistance: The North American Indian Struggle for Unity, 1745-1815* (Baltimore: Johns Hopkins Press, 1992), 33-34, 128.

57. Jones, *Ojibwa Texts*, part II, 547-609. Basil Johnston has another printed version of this tale. See his *Ojibway Ceremonies* (Toronto: McClelland and Stewart, 1982), 95-100.

58. Jones, *Ojibwa Texts*, part I, 569-573.

59. Ibid., 608-609.

60. Jones, *Ojibwa Texts*, part II, 571.

61. This theme of birth, death, and resurrection occurs in another form in the tale of the old man who is replaced by the young boy who then grows old, and in the end of the final tale, which reminds the listeners that he (the old man) will return when he is called upon to perform the "mystic rite" for their newly born or recently deceased children.

62. Robert Berkhofer describes this phenomenon in some detail and gives examples from a wide range of tribal groups. See his *Salvation and the Savage* (Lexington: University of Kentucky Press, 1965), 107.

63. See James Axtell, *The Invasion Within: The Contest of Cultures in Colonial North America* (New York: Oxford University Press, 1985), 282; and Dowd (*A Spirited Resistance*, 18), who both argue that traditional Aboriginal societies had a flexibility that allowed them to adopt new ceremonies and practices that had been borrowed in a traditionally sanctioned way.

64. Smith, *The Island of the Anishnaabeg*, 184-185.

65. Kohl, *Kitchi Gami*, 195.

66. Smith, *The Island of the Anishnaabeg*, 184.

67. Ibid., 104-106.

68. Warren, *History of the Ojibway People*, 109-110.

69. James Axtell and Cornelius Jaenen provide good overviews of the early attempts of English and French cultures to come to terms with their Aboriginal neighbours, and the new land in which they lived. See Axtell, *The Invasion Within;* and Cornelius Jaenen, *Friend and Foe: Aspects of French-Amerindian Cultural Contact in the Sixteenth and Seventeenth Centuries* (New York: Columbia University Press, 1976). Roderick Nash's *Wilderness and the American Mind* (New Haven: Yale University Press, 1973) is a classic exposition of the intellectual history of American attitudes towards nature and, by extension, the original inhabitants of North America.

70. Wilber B. Hinsdale, "Religion at the Algonquian Level," *Papers of the Michigan Academy of Science, Arts and Letters* 5 (1926): 21. I admit to having turned Hinsdale's quote on its head, but the implications are the same for both groups.

71. Even E.H. Day, who spent several pages describing the Midewiwin, makes only passing reference to one of the "medicine men" who makes a speech "about something or nothing," or "chants a monotonous song" (Day, "Sketches of the Northwest," 213). Yet, Day had a very capable Ojibwa interpreter in Peter Marksman, who was Ojibwa himself, and who undoubtedly could have put the ceremonies into context for the Christian clergyman.

72. Hickerson, *The Chippewa and Their Neighbours*, 51.

73. A few contemporary Euro-American scholars such as Howard (*The Plains-Ojibwa*, 133-134) have taken issue with Hickerson's arguments. Deleary (in his thesis "Midewiwin") is, as far as I am aware, the only Ojibwa scholar to use both Anishinaabe oral tradition and Euro-American documents to critique Hickerson's arguments.

74. Hickerson, *The Chippewa and Their Neighbours*, 55.

75. Louis Hennepin, "A Continuation of the New Discovery," in *Hennepin's Narrative from La Louisiane*, Illinois Historical Collections, 1, quoted in Hoffman, "The Midewiwin," 152.

76. Ibid., 154.

77. Ibid., 155.

78. Hickerson, *The Chippewa and Their Neighbours*, 60-62.

79. Densmore, *Chippewa Music*, 248.

80. In his critique of the post-contact origin of the Midewiwin hypothesis, Deleary, in this case, agrees with Hickerson that the cross probably was Christian.

81. Hickerson, *The Chippewa and Their Neighbours*, 54.

82. Ibid.

83. Hoffman, "The Midewiwin," 204-205.

84. Hickerson, *The Chippewa and Their Neighbours*, 54.

85. In *The Chippewa and Their Neighbours*, Hickerson provides a good, brief overview of the methodologies used by different schools of historians, and later he provides a survey of historical approaches in social anthropology, for ethnohistorians. He does not state the theoretical basis of his own particular approach, but his own concentration was clearly on the material aspects of an evolving culture. While much of his work was groundbreaking at the time he was writing, his vision of Ojibwa society was skewed by his too narrow concentration on environmental and economic factors.

86. The symbolism in the "shooting ritual" is found in other Aboriginal groups in both North and South America. The initiate is "shot" and then brought back to life with the touch of the Mide's sacred medicine bag. In the case of the Ojibwa, the word used for "shoot" refers to using a bow and arrow, not a gun, suggesting an earlier origin than the fur-trade period.

87. There was no permanent organizational structure in the Midewiwin, other than that individuals possessed differing degrees of supernatural power, which were symbolized by the type of sacred medicine bag they had. This distinguished the Midewiwin from many of their neighbours, for whom sacred medicine bundles were usually a clan possession. Officials for each Midewiwin ceremony were chosen by the participating Mideg, and could vary from one ceremony to the next. Moreover, participation in Midewiwin ceremonies in no way prevented Mideg from using powers obtained from other sources, or from acting as Jiisakiiwininiwag or Waabanowag.

88. Karl Schlesier, "Rethinking the Midewiwin and the Plains Ceremonial called the Sun Dance," *Plains Anthropologist* 35, 127 (1990): 1-27. Richard White, *The Middle Ground: Indians, Empires, and Republics in the Great Lakes Region, 1650-1815* (New York: Cambridge University Press, 1991).

89. Harold Hickerson, "The Sociohistorical Significance of Two Chippewa Ceremonials," *American Anthropologist* 68 (1963): 72-75.

90. All historians are forced to rely mainly on a limited number of documents, such as the multi-volume *Jesuit Relations* (1899), plus the documents collected in the works of Margry (1879), Blair (1911-12), Thwaites (1896-1901), and Kellogg (1925).

91. While neither would appear to fully subscribe to Schlesier's and White's thesis, both Charles Cleland and Robert Bieder, in their respective historical studies of Aboriginal American communities in Michigan and Wisconsin, describe the period as one of social disintegration for the groups involved. See Charles E. Cleland, *Rites of Conquest: The History and Culture of Michigan's Native Americans* (Ann Arbor: University of Michigan Press, 1992); and Robert E. Bieder, *Native American Communities in Wisconsin, 1600-1960* (Madison: University of Wisconsin Press, 1995).

92. Schlesier, "Rethinking the Midewiwin."

93. Julia Harrison, "The Midewiwin: The Retention of an Ideology," Master's thesis, University of Calgary, 1982.

94. John Grim argues that the Midewiwin grew out of traditional Ojibwa healing rituals in response to the crises of the late seventeenth century. See his *The Shaman: Patterns of Siberian and Ojibway Healing* (Norman: University of Oklahoma Press, 1983), 71-73.

95. Tanner, *A Narrative of the Captivity*, 169.

96. *Saulteurs* was the French term for Anishinaabe bands who lived around Bowating. Later, a variation of the name (Saulteaux) was applied to the Ojibwa bands who resided in the region surrounding the Red River Settlement along with bands of Cree and Assiniboine.

97. Karl Schlesier makes a similar statement regarding the communal binding function of the Midewiwin among the disparate groups in the multi-tribal villages, although he implies far greater differences among the different groups than probably existed. See his "Rethinking the Midewiwin," 10.

98. The most common of these was the Alliance of the Three Fires, which existed between the Ojibwas, Ottawas, and Potawatomies from the mid-1700s (see Donald Fixico, "The Alliance of the Three Fires in Trade and War, 1630-1812," *Michigan Historical Review* 20, 2 [1994]:1-25). However, there were others, such as the alliance formed by the above three tribes plus the Wyandots (Huron-Petuns) against the Sioux in the 1720s, and the Confederacy, which the British formed in conjunction with Shawnee, Delawares, Wyandots, Miamis, Ojibwas, Ottawas, Potawatomies, and others in the late 1790s. See Thomas Forsyth in *The Indian Tribes of the Upper Mississippi Valley and Region of the Great Lakes*, ed. and trans. Emma Blair (Cleveland: Arthur H. Clarke, 1911-1912), vol. 2, 188-192.

99. Dewdney, *The Sacred Scrolls*, 172-174.

100. Deleary argues that the "Dawnlanders" mentioned in Midewiwin narratives refers to the Delaware (Leni Lenape), whom other Algonquians considered as "Grandfathers." He backs up his claim with quotes from the eighteenth-century American Moravian missionary David Zeisberger that suggest that the Delaware had an initiation ceremony in which initiates became "physicians, great hunters, rich men, mantewits," and that the Munsee (a linguistic sub-group of the Delaware) called these individuals *Mede'u*, which signified "conjuror," or men of superior knowledge and supernatural powers (Deleary, "Mediwiwn," 72).

Chapter Four

1. There were other, though briefer, accounts of the Midewiwin among other Anishinaabe groups, such as Jacques de Sabrevois's account of the "medelinne" among the Potawatomi, and there were scattered references to Midewiwin-like ceremonies by the Jesuit missionaries.

2. Pierre Margry, *Découvertes et establissements des Francais dans l'Ouest et dans le Sud de l'Amérique*, 6 vols. (Paris: Maisonneuve, 1879-1888). Similar short references to the Midewiwin and the Waabanowiwin can be found in Nor'Wester Alexander Henry the Younger's *Journal* during the years from 1800 to 1804, while he traded along the Pembina River. Fellow fur trader David Thompson, who had been in the same general region a couple of years earlier, confined his comments to describing in his *Narrative* a Waabanowiwin ceremony, which he believed had replaced the older ceremonies. See Alexander Henry the Younger, *The Journals of Alexander Henry the Younger, 1799-1814* (Toronto: Champlain Society, 1988), 73, 118, 130, 157-158; and David Thompson, *David Thompson's Narrative, 1784-1812* (Toronto: Champlain Society, 1962), 191-193.

3. Vernon Kinietz, *The Indians of the Western Great Lakes, 1615-1760* (Ann Arbor: University of Michigan Press, 1972). Raudot's compilation, though second-hand, provides one of the earliest and most complete descriptions of Ojibwa life. His series of letters describes everything from the homes, dress, the food they ate and how it was obtained, to their form of government, marriage and mortuary practices, as well as their religious ideas and practices. While he displayed most of the prejudices of his time towards Aboriginal people, his sources appear to have been keen observers.

4. The words "juggler" (*jongleur*) and "conjuror" have long implied that the person described was a trickster or imposter. They are used in this sense in many documents to describe various types of Anishinaabe religious figures and traditional healers. Euro-American sceptics, who prided themselves on their rationality, focussed on the elements of duplicity in the feats of manipulation that Mideg allegedly used to deceive their fellow Ojibwa about their powers. For many Christians, the words carried an additional connotation of someone who tampered with forbidden powers, used magic potions and charms, and often sold their souls to the devil. Steeped in a tradition in which such false prophets were very real, many Christians viewed the Mideg as both charlatans and evil figures capable of wreaking havoc. By contrast, American Spiritualists saw in the Midewiwin ceremonies a manifestation of their belief in spirits, charms, and communication with the other world.

5. Although only a portion of the Midewiwin ceremonies was devoted to dancing, Euro-American observers seemed to be particularly disturbed by the appearance of dancing in what was supposed to be a religious ceremony—perhaps because dance was considered to be a profane activity among Christians.

6. Kinietz, *The Indians of the Western Great Lakes*, 372-374 - Letter #47.

7. In an earlier letter (323), Raudot said that he would explain for his readers the dress, customs, and religion of the "savages," and "of the way of things before the arrival of the French in this country" (see Kinietz, *The Indians of the Western Great Lakes*, 341). It is also worthy of note that in another letter (#40), Raudot remarked that "Feasts of the Dead" were held every three years by various nations, thus indicating that the Midewiwin had not replaced the Feast of the Dead, as Hickerson has suggested.

8. Subsequent accounts, such as those by Hoffman and Densmore, do make a distinction between public Midewiwin ceremonies, which were generally held during spring and/or fall gatherings when individuals or their surrogates would be initiated into one of the degrees of the Midewiwin, and private healing ceremonies, which were held for very ill individuals who normally were already members of the Midewiwin. See Walter James Hoffman, "The Menomini Indians," in *Fourteenth Annual Report to the Smithsonian Institution*, Bureau of American Ethnology (Washington: Smithsonian Institution Press, 1896), Pt. 1, 3-328; and Frances Densmore, "An Ojibwa Prayer Ceremony," *American Anthropologist*, new series 9 (1907): 443-444.

9. I use the word "ceremony" to describe the Midewiwin, although in some senses it is closer to what might be defined as a religion, since it is in many ways all-encompassing. However, "ceremony" is the term most commonly used when speaking of the Midewiwin, or when comparing it to the Wabaanowiwin, Shaking Tent, etc. I use the term "ritual" when referring to parts of the larger ceremony (such as the sweat lodge rituals, the "shooting" ritual, etc.), which appear to form discrete parts of the larger whole.

10. The best description of such a ceremony is by Frances Densmore in her book *Chippewa Customs* (St. Paul: Minnesota Historical Society, 1979), 74-75, in which she describes the Midewiwin ceremony held at the time of the impending death of a Mide elder and chief of the Pillager band of Ojibwa. This individual was the son of another famous chief and Mide leader of the same name.

11. Louis F.R. Masson, *Les Bourgeois de la Compagnie du Nord-Ouest*, 2 vols. (New York: Antiquarian Press, 1960), 261-262; 361.

12. There are fleeting references in written documents to the fact that the Fox and their immediate allies, the Mascouten, along with the Sauk and Miami, two other allied Algonquian groups, also practised the Midewiwin.

13. While there is still disagreement among academics, it seems likely that the groups known as the Moosoni and Muskego were, in fact, Ojibwa groups allied with the Cree.

14. Gertrude P. Kurath, "Blackrobe and Shaman: The Christianization of Michigan Algonquians," *Papers of the Michigan Academy of Science, Arts and Letters* 44 (1959): 209-215.

15. Tuscarawas (not to be confused with the Iroquois site) was located just south of Lake Erie in the Ohio Valley. The Delaware were an Algonquian people who were known as the "Grandfather of all Tribes," due to their supposed antiquity. They had suffered much from wars and continuing encroachments on their lands, which had caused them to move several times.

16. Gregory Dowd provides a good overview of this struggle, including its spiritual underpinnings in the series of revitalization movements that developed in the latter half of the eighteenth and early nineteenth centuries. See Gregory Evans Dowd, *A Spirited Resistance: The North American Indian Struggle for Unity, 1745-1815* (Baltimore: Johns Hopkins Press, 1992).

17. The Shawnee were a southerly group of Algonquian speakers who had been harried by American settlers for some time. Faced with frequent moves and battles, their society had slowly begun to disintegrate.

18. Tenskwatawa was one of many so-called "prophets" who arose during this period among both the Anishinaabeg and their Iroquoian neighbours, but his message, linked as it was to his brother Tecumseh's call for unified military resistance to American encroachments, was especially potent. Gregory Dowd, in his book *A Spirited Resistance*, provides one of the best explanations of the messages and activities of these prophets, including some such as the Ottawa "The Trout," who had an influence on some Ojibwa. Several other prophets are mentioned in the journals of Euro-Americans such as Alexander Henry the Younger and David Thompson, plus in John Tanner's captivity narrative. All these prophets had limited success in convincing their colleagues of the validity of their visions—no doubt since they were unable to demonstrate their newly acquired power. However, their very existence is indicative of the unsettled nature of the Ojibwa world view during this period in their history.

19. The documents of the American Board of Commissioners for Foreign Missions (ABCFM) contain letters from missionaries Ely, Boutwell, and others, describing raids of the Sioux on Ojibwa villages.

20. The italics are Nicollet's. "Missinabes" in this context probably refers to "Anishinaabeg," which Nicollet mis-transcribes. Flat Mouth made it clear that he believed that the land was theirs and that he would not give it up at any price, since his people would then lose their autonomy, which was especially important to the Anishinaabeg.

21. Joseph N. Nicollet, *The Journals of Joseph N. Nicollet: A Scientist on the Mississippi Headwater with Notes on Indian Life, 1836-37*, trans. André Fertey, ed. Martha Coleman Bray (St. Paul: Minnesota Historical Society, 1970), 114.

22. Flat Mouth, in particular, proved to be very adept at manoeuvring among the various competing Euro-American factions. He neither rejected nor embraced Euro-American society outright.

23. Nicollet, *The Journals*, 21.

24. Letter of W.T. Boutwell to David Greene, Dec 21, 1836, ABCFM mss. 74, no.91.

25. Matchi Gabow (various spellings) is mentioned by such diverse sources as Schoolcraft, Boutwell, and Kohl as being threatening and antagonistic—an evil person who personified Euro-American images of a Mide. He was a huge man, had five wives, and was reputed by some sources to have killed Governor Semple during the Battle of Seven Oaks.

26. See letters from Boutwell, Ayer, and Ely in the ABCFM mss.

27. Nicollet, *The Journals*, 19. Mideg could and did use a number of means to discipline those who had strayed from the path of the Mide. Christian missionaries often related how their converts were being "harassed" in different ways by Mideg. Reputedly, medicines were used in order to cause the victim to develop a facial distortion, or to cause death.

29. Since Nicollet used French phonetics to transliterate Ojibwe, I have chosen the more common spelling by which they are known.

30. Grant's description was published in Masson's compilation of original documents in 1889-1890. Although John Tanner, who was a white man raised by Ottawa and Ojibwa families, had the opportunity to provide an insider's view, his account contains only a brief description of the Midewiwin ceremonies as such, and these show the

editorial influence of Edwin James, who helped prepare the manuscript for publication. Tanner is useful in his compilation of a number of Mide songs. There were numerous other brief references to the Midewiwin during this period by a variety of fur traders, missionaries, and government officials. Whether this indicates that the Midewiwin was becoming more active, or, as is more likely, that the number of Euro-Americans in the area had increased substantially, is difficult to say.

31. Schoolcraft's massive multi-volume compilation of "knowledge" regarding North American Aboriginal people is filled with unedited fragments from the writings of many people, including an article by William Warren on the Ojibwa, but Nicollet's appears to be the only instance in which Schoolcraft fails to give credit to the author. It is unclear whether Nicollet intended that his account be published by Schoolcraft, or whether he sent a copy as information and intended to publish it later himself.

32. Nicollet notes that the ceremonies he attended were for the initiation of Obiygouaden's (Chief of the Land) daughter. Obiygouaden was another Pillager chief. See Nicollet, *The Journals*, 80, 200.

33. In this he was quite unlike his Euro-American counterpart, Henry Rowe Schoolcraft, who claimed on a number of occasions to have been inducted into the Midewiwin himself.

34. Nicollet, *The Journals*, 199. Nicollet indicated that because of abuses, Flat Mouth had reformed the system and required that at least two people have such a vision before the candidate would be considered.

35. It is noteworthy that most of the Euro-American descriptions during the nineteenth century describe ceremonies in which children are initiated into the first degree of the Midewiwin. Later, when they were old enough to make choices of their own, they might decide to advance further in their knowledge and acquire more powers.

36. Nicollet outlined a number of circumstances for which the madoodiswan (sweat lodge) ceremony was carried out, first among which was initiation into the Midewiwin. In each case, the desired object was to communicate with the manidoog in order to derive power to be able to carry out some action, be it a desire by an individual to be cured, or the desire of a chief to win the approval of his people for a foray against an enemy.

37. The Waabanowiwin, which was also quite prevalent during this period, was considered by many to be a deviant offshoot of the Midewiwin, but it was also concerned with acquiring "blessings" from powerful manidoog for its adherents.

38. Elsewhere, he uses the term *Oshkabewis* to refer to the Mide elders he had encountered among the Sioux. See Nicollet, *The Journals*, 211.

39. Nicollet indicates that the goods were comprised of blankets, fabric, kettles, rifles, traps, etc., in quantities large enough to make a package for each of the eight Mide elders.

40. Most observers have described the Mide Lodge as a rectangular structure with openings facing east and west. The fires mentioned by Nicollet and later by Densmore were probably kept burning for the Mideg to use them to light their sacred pipes, so that invocations could be made to the manidoog at various times during the ceremonies. The smoke from the kinnikinnick (tobacco) acted as an offering as invocations were made to the east, west, north, and south, plus upward and downward.

The post or posts (mitewatig) in the lodge represented the tree or path of life. The number, colouring, shape, and placement varied with the degree. A sacred stone was placed near the eastern entrance where the initiation of candidates took place, while two other sacred stones were later placed at the foot of the candidate's degree pole. Such stones were considered to be alive and possessed of great power.

41. Nicollet does not give a translation of this term, which he quoted as being used in other Ojibwa ceremonies, and it is not found in any of the accounts of Ojibwa ceremonies by other observers. "*Na*," according to Baraga, is a particle denoting interrogation—"is it so?" "will it be so?"

42. *Pinjigoosan* is the same term used by Baraga and Kohl for medicine bags in general, but most other observers have used the more specific term *midewayaan* to refer to the medicine bags used by Mideg. Similar bags or bundles were considered sacred sources of power by many other Aboriginal groups, although most were owned communally (by clans) rather than individually. The use of a bear pinjigoosan was usually a sign that the Mide was of the fourth degree and thus was possessed of considerable power to do good and evil. As later commentators were to note, each degree was distinguished by the bag of a different animal or animals.

43. *Nikanug* or *Niikaanag* (Nichols) was a ritual term, which was usually translated as "brothers." It was used specifically to designate other members of the Midewiwin, and is still used as such today.

44. This ejaculation, which most Euro-American observers found merely amusing, was, in fact, according to Nicholas Deleary, an essential part of the Midewiwin ceremony. The word does not have any "meaning" as such, but the words were believed to convey power from the person who uttered them. See Deleary, "Midewiwin: An Aboriginal Spiritual Institution," Master's thesis, Carleton University, 1990. See also the article by Klaus Klostermaier, "The Creative Function of the Word" (in *Language in Indian Philosophy and Religion*, ed. Harold Coward [Waterloo: Wilfrid Laurier University Press, 1978]), regarding similar traditions among the peoples of the Indian subcontinent.

45. Nicollet's spelling is idiosyncratic according to today's standards, but the Ojibwa words he uses are the ones commonly given in most accounts. The Mide or water drum was termed a *mittigwakik* (*Mitiwakik*—Nichols) by Nicollet. It was usually a hollowed-out portion of a tree trunk with deerskin at both ends, and was partially filled with water so that the pitch could be changed. The *pagaakookwan* (*baaga'akokwaan*—Nichols) was a carved mallet used to beat the drum and was considered more sacred than the drum itself. The *shishiigwan* (*zhilshiigwan*—Nichols) was a rattle, originally made out of a gourd or hollow piece of wood, and filled with pebbles, seeds, or shot to create different pitches. Later ones were made from tin cans.

46. Nicollet, *The Journals*, 203-204.

47. As Nicollet (*The Journals*, 206) explains, the Ojibwe verb that described the act of "blowing" or "shooting" with the medicine bag was the same one (*bimojige*) used to describe shooting with a bow and arrow. (The verb "to shoot with a gun" was *pashkisige/baashkizige*.) Fred Blessing is the only person to provide an Ojibwe word for the ceremony, which he gives as *ah-pah-gee-TAH-ah-GAY,* which may be *aabaakawizi* (Nichols—"revive," "to come to"). See Fred K. Blessing, *The Ojibway*

Indians Observed, Papers of Fred. K. Blessing Jr., in *The Minnesota Archeologist* (St. Paul: Minnesota Archeological Society, 1977), 114.

48. Nicollet, *The Journals*, 204-205.

49. Ibid., 207.

50. Ibid., 208.

51. Annual renewal ceremonies were practised by other Algonquian tribes such as the Delaware, whose Big House ceremonies were carried out each fall. See, for example, Ives Goddard's chapter on the Delaware in *Handbook of North American Indians*, vol. 15, *Northeast* (Washington: Smithsonian Institution, 1978), 231-232.

52. Nicollet, *The Journals*, 255.

53. Henry Rowe Schoolcraft, *Algic Researches, comprising inquiries respecting the mental characteristics of the North American Indians* (New York: Harper & Bros., 1839), 585.

54. Henry Rowe Schoolcraft, *The Indian in His Wigwam, or Characteristics of the Red Race in America* (Buffalo: Derby and Hudson, 1848), 66.

55. Schoolcraft, *The Indian in His Wigwam*, 67-68; Henry Rowe Schoolcraft, *Information Respecting the History, Condition and Prospects of the Indian Tribes of the United States*, vol. 1 (Philadelphia: Lippincott, Grambo & Co., 1851-1857), 412.

56. Schoolcraft, *Information Respecting*, vol. 1, xiv.

57. Ibid., 259. Schoolcraft used different spellings for these three ceremonies, but since his spelling varied within his own writings, I have chosen to maintain my standard spelling even when writing about his ideas.

58. Janet Elizabeth Chute, *The Legacy of Shingwaukonse: A Century of Native Leadership* (Toronto: University of Toronto Press, 1998).

59. Schoolcraft, *Information Respecting*, vol. 6, 366.

60. Ibid., vol. 4, 640.

61. Ibid., vol. 1, 861; vol. 5, 71.

62. Chute, *Legacy of Shingwaukonse*, 110, 248.

63. Schoolcraft, *Information Respecting*, vol. 5, 420.

64. Ibid., vol.1, 360.

65. Ibid.

66. Baraga listed *kikendamiiwen* as the verb "to publish," "make known," "to announce," and *kikendassowin* as the noun indicating "knowledge" or "science." He gave the word *kikinawadakwaigan* as indicating the mark on a tree used by travellers, and *kikinawadjitchigan* as any sign or mark. Given Baraga's and Schoolcraft's relative knowledge of Ojibwe, it is probable that the latter was doing a bit of creative wordsmithing when he claimed the Ojibwa had specific terms for the two types of pictographs. I have used Schoolcraft's spelling, since his use of the term is unique.

67. Densmore, *Chippewa Music*, vol. 1, 14-15.

68. Walter James Hoffman, "The Midewiwin or 'Grand Medicine Society' of the Ojibwa," Bureau of American Ethnology, in *Seventh Annual Report to the Smithsonian Institution, 1885-1886* (Washington: Smithsonian Institution Press, 1891), 287-288. Garrick

Mallery, *Picture-Writing of the American Indians*, 2 vols. (New York: Dover Reprint, 1972).

69. Schoolcraft, *Information Respecting*, vol.1, 366.

70. Ibid., vol.4, 637, 640.

71. Harold Hickerson, *The Chippewa and Their Neighbours: A Study in Ethnohistory* (Prospect Heights: Waveland Press, 1988), 55.

72. Peter Jones, *History of the Ojebway Indians; with especial reference to their conversion to Christianity* (London: A.W. Bennett, 1861), 143-145.

73. E.H. Day, "Sketches of the Northwest," *Collections and Researches Made by the Michigan Pioneer and Historical Society* 14 (1890): 205-232.

74. Day, "Sketches," 219. In John Pitezel's biography of Marksman (1901), he related that Marksman had told him that his father was a "medicine man" (Mide) and one of the hereditary chiefs at Mackinac before he moved west, while his mother was a "half-breed" and also a "professor of medicine." He was trained in the rites of the Midewiwin until the age of fifteen, but later converted to Christianity. See John Pitezal, *Life of Peter Marksman* (Cincinnati: Western Book Concern, 1901).

75. Almost certainly these included the head chief Shingoup, and Mongazid (Loon Foot), a secondary chief, both of whom Day mentions later on in his address. The latter individual became a main source of information on the Midewiwin for Kohl in the 1850s. They were both contemporaries of Flat Mouth and Matchi Gabow in Leech Lake, of Shingwaukonse from the area around Sault Ste. Marie, of Pizhiki (Great Buffalo) at La Pointe, and Gogubunuga, a Rainy Lake chief—all of whom were prominent Mide elders.

76. Day, "Sketches," 212.

77. Ibid., 213.

78. Ibid., 214.

79. Thomas L. McKenney, *Sketches of a Tour to the Lakes* (Minneapolis: Ross & Haines, 1972), 170-173. McKenney was appointed a treaty commissioner for the United States government, and was present at Fond du Lac in 1826 for the reaffirmation of the Treaty of Prairie du Chien. He had actively supported the cause of Aboriginal people, but this was his first trip west and his daily journal provides a first-hand example of how they appeared to eastern officials. He did not witness a Midewiwin ceremony as such, but he did witness and describe two Waabanowiwin ceremonies.

80. HBC Archives, Michipicoten Journal, June 11, 1830.

81. Fred Blessing and Basil Johnston both suggested that the origin of the name *Midewiwin*, in fact, may be linked to the sound of the heart and/or drum. See Blessing, *The Ojibway Indians Observed*, 76; and Basil Johnston, *Ojibway Ceremonies* (Toronto: McClelland & Stewart, 1982), 95.

82. Ruth Landes, *Ojibwa Religion and the Midewiwin* (Madison: University of Wisconsin Press, 1968), 163.

83. Robert E. Bieder, *Native American Communities in Wisconsin, 1600-1960* (Madison: University of Wisconsin Press, 1995), 166-167. The papers of Sherman Hall, the Protestant missionary at La Pointe and later at Bad River Reservation, provide details

of many of the sufferings of the Lake Superior Ojibwa during this period (see Sherman Hall Papers, Minnesota Historical Society Research Center).

84. Pitezel, *Life of Peter Marksman*, 198.

85. Landes, *Ojibwa Religion*, 177-178. Michael R. Angel, "The Ojibwa-Missionary Encounter at Rainy Lake Mission, 1839-1857," Master's thesis, University of Manitoba, 1986, pp. 136-140. Wesleyan Methodist Missionary Society, Foreign Missions, *Correspondence, 1840-1850, Jacobs to Adler, July 21, 1858.* Jacobs was an Ojibwa convert from southern Ontario, who served as a Methodist missionary at Fort Frances for approximately ten years, and provided copious reports to his missionary superiors in London, England.

86. Johann Georg Kohl, *Kitchi Gami: Life Among the Lake Superior Ojibway*, trans. Lascelles Wraxall (St. Paul: Minnesota Historical Society Press, 1985), 40-41.

87. Ibid., 43-44.

88. Ibid., 45.

89. Ibid., 49.

90. Ibid., 52.

91. Selwyn Dewdney, *The Sacred Scrolls of the Southern Ojibway* (Toronto: Glenbow-Alberta Institute/University of Toronto, 1975), 158-160; 172-174.

92. Mallery, *Picture-Writing*, 508.

93. The ABCFM and Methodist Society missionaries were quite frank in their reports, often detailing how both they and potential converts were harassed by Midewiwin members in order to discourage people from becoming Christians. While the Catholic missionaries were more glowing in their reports about their success, there were large traditionalist factions even in such long-standing Catholic communities as Arbre Croche.

Chapter Five

1. Not all the land settlements were for Euro-American Loyalists; major land grants were provided to the Iroquois allies of the British.

2. Peter S. Schmalz, *The Ojibwa of Southern Ontario* (Toronto: University of Toronto Press, 1991), 130-146.

3. Donald B. Smith, "The Dispossession of the Mississauga Indians," *Ontario History* 73 (1981): 67-87.

4. Janet Chute has an excellent account of Little Pine's conversion. She delves into the complex spiritual, material, and political factors that undoubtedly contributed to the decisions of Aboriginal leaders such as Little Pine to accept Christianity. See Janet Chute, *The Legacy of Shingwaukonse: A Century of Native Leadership* (Toronto: University of Toronto Press, 1998).

5. Schmalz, *Ojibwa of Southern Ontario*, 200-204.

6. Edward S. Rogers and Donald B. Smith, eds., *Aboriginal Ontario: Historical Perspectives on the First Nations* (Toronto: Dundurn Press, 1994), 368-370.

7. William Mason to James Evans, 9 June 1841, Wesleyan Methodist Missionary Society (WMMS), Foreign Missions, Correspondence, 1840-1850.

8. Peter Jacobs, 21 July 1848, WMMS, *op.cit.*

9. Leo G. Waisberg and Marie-Ange Beaudry, *Manitou Mounds: Historical Evaluation of the Mission Lot* (Parks Canada, Ontario Regional Office, 1984), 49-54. Waisberg and Beaudry draw upon comments taken from the reports of the Reverend Robert Phair, an Anglican missionary who had been given instructions to establish a mission at Long Sault Indian Reserve.

10. E. McColl, *Annual Report for the Year Ended 31 December, 1882*, Sessional Papers No. 5 (Ottawa: Canada, Department of Indian Affairs, 1883), 131.

11. While McColl did not state he actually witnessed the Midewiwin ceremonies at Lake of the Woods (see the 1882 *Annual Report*, pp. 134-135), he stated that he witnessed the ceremony at Rainy Lake the previous year. See *Annual Report, op. cit.*, p. 91.

12. John Webster Grant, *Moon of Wintertime: Missionaries and the Indians of Canada in Encounter since 1538* (Toronto: University of Toronto Press, 1984), 102-107.

13. A. Irving Hallowell, "The Passing of the Midewiwin in the Lake Winnipeg Region," *American Anthropologist* New Series 38 (1937):40.

14. L.H. Wheeler to David Green, May 3, 1843. Box 3. ABCFM. Minnesota Historical Society Research Center, St. Paul, Minnesota.

15. Ibid.

16. Hall to Treat, December 30, 1850. ABCFM.

17. Hall to Green, October 24, 1838. ABCFM mss 141, no. 122.

18. Charles E. Cleland, *Rites of Conquest: The History and Culture of Michigan's Native Americans* (Ann Arbor: University of Michigan Press, 1992), 242.

19. Ramsey served for some time as the Superintendent of Indian Affairs for what was then termed the "Northwest" country, and was governor of the new state of Minnesota. Hall was in charge of the American Board of Foreign Commissioners' mission from 1831 to 1853, first at La Pointe and later at Bad River when most of the band moved there. Although his skills in Ojibwa were far less than those of Bishop Baraga, he was equally committed to the well-being of those whom he considered to be his flock, and fought vigorously for their rights.

20. *Annual Report* (Washington: US Office of the Commissioner of Indian Affairs, 1850).

21. See Melissa Meyer, *The White Earth Tragedy: Ethnicity and Dispossession at a Minnesota Anishinaabe Reservation, 1889-1920* (Lincoln: University of Nebraska Press, 1994). Meyer provides a good, in-depth analysis of the religious patterns at White Earth, including Enmegahbowh's successful synthesis of Christian beliefs and Ojibwa cultural values.

22. In addition to Hoffman's and Densmore's writings on the subject, S.A. Barrett has written a book entitled *The Dream Dance of the Chippewa and Menominee Indians of Northern Wisconsin*, and George and Louise Spindler devoted considerable attention to it in their book on the Menominee (*Dreamers without Power: The Menomini Indians*). Barrett also compares the Dream Dance and Ghost Dance movements, and, while admitting there are some similarities, argues that they were separate developments.

23. Walter Hoffman provided a brief sketch of "the Dreamers" among the Menominee in which his informant explained that *Kitche Manito* had become angry at the corruption of the *Mitawat* (Midewiwin), and thus gave them the Drum Dance (see his "The Menomini Indians," in *Fourteenth Annual Report to the Smithsonian Institution, 1892-93*, Bureau of American Ethnology, Pt. 1 [Washington: Smithsonian Institution Press, 1896], 157-161). While he never mentioned its appearance among the Minnesota Ojibwa, Robert Bieder notes that the dance was practised by traditionalists in the Lac du Flambeau region of Wisconsin, where it had been introduced by the Menominee or the Potawatomi. See Bieder's *Native American Communities in Wisconsin, 1600-1960* (Madison: University of Wisconsin Press, 1995), 170.

24. Treaty # 3, which was signed by the Boundary Waters Ojibwa, was one of the few treaties in Canada that allowed Métis to take treaty along with the Aboriginal people, although they were not allowed to establish a separate Métis reserve as they had requested. Nevertheless, Métis formed a significant proportion of the population of Couchiching Reserve, and individual Métis played significant roles in several other Ojibwa reserves. While Métis families usually were Catholic, and while there were some divisions, for the most part, the tensions were not as serious as on American reservations such as White Earth.

25. The Warren family cannot, of course, be classed along with the normal run of "mixed-blood" traders. Nevertheless, Lyman Warren, William Warren's father, had been the American Fur Trade Company's agent at La Pointe until he was replaced in 1838 for alleged mismanagement (see Crooks to Halsey, Sept. 20, 1838, American Fur Company Papers, MHSRC, St. Paul). Following this, he engaged in many attempts to clear his name and gain compensation. He was one of the "mixed-blood" traders who claimed and received compensation for Aboriginal debts at the very treaty for which his son William acted as interpreter (see Crooks to Halsey, Sept. 6, 1839; Report from Borup, Lapointe, Sept. 15, 1839 [AFC, MHSRC]). William Warren's *History of the Ojibway People* was part of his attempt to bring the past glory and present plight of the Ojibwa to the attention of the Euro-Americans. He died before he was able to complete a projected work on the Midewiwin religion.

26. One of his sisters provides a glimpse of this life in some notes she gave to Frances Densmore. (Densmore Papers, Notes on the life of Mrs. Julia Warren Spears, MHSRC.)

27. Since Hinsley and Bieder have covered the early work of American ethnologists and the Smithsonian Institution thoroughly, I have not attempted to give anything more than a brief overview of the significance of this work. See Curtis M. Hinsley, *Savages and Scientists: The Smithsonian Institution and the Development of American Anthropology, 1846-1910* (Washington: Smithsonian Institution Press, 1981); and Robert Bieder, *Science Encounters the Indian: The Early Years of American Ethnology* (Norman: University of Oklahoma Press, 1986).

28. Hoffman died at the age of fifty-three in 1899, following a two-year period as the American Consul in Mannheim, Germany, during which time he studied European collections and records of American Aboriginal peoples.

29. The Bad River Reservation was made up of Ojibwa from their community at La Pointe on Madeline Island who had moved to the mainland near the present town of

Ashland, since the local Protestant missionary, Rev. Leonard Wheeler, believed the soil on Madeline Island was unsuitable for extensive agriculture.

30. Mallery attributed his limited results to the "stronger influence of civilization" in the latter two communities. By the late 1880s, the remaining members of the La Pointe band had moved to the Bad River Reservation located near Odanah, Wisconsin, at the south end of Chequamegon Bay, where some attempted to farm under the tutelage of the Presbyterian missionary while others worked in various small industries. Mallery was able to find only a few elderly Ojibwa there who were still familiar with the Midewiwin ceremonies and had Mide charts that they were willing to show him. Since he was primarily interested in a comparative study of pictographs, it was this aspect that dominated his writings. He devoted only a few comments to the Midewiwin itself, which are a combination of commonly known facts and equally common misconceptions. It would appear that Mallery himself never observed a Midewiwin ceremony.

31. Meyer, *White Earth Tragedy*, 118-125.

32. Even the missionaries were forced to tone down their usual enthusiasm regarding their efforts and to speak of the "gradual" changes that had taken place. In a series of letters that were later published in the 1849 *Oberlin Evangelist*, J.P. Bardwell spoke mainly of farming successes, but noted that the Aboriginal people seldom adopted English modes of dress, and were indifferent to having their children attend school. The church had only nine or ten converts after several decades of efforts, although the Ojibwa continued to observe the *Mitewe* (Midewiwin) quite frequently (see J. P. Bardwell to Henry Cowles, July 30, 1849, Grace Lee Nute Papers, Box 14, MHSRC).

33. Walter J. Hoffman, "The Midewiwin or 'Grand Medicine Society' of the Ojibwa," in *Seventh Annual Report to the Smithsonian Institution, 1885-1886*, Bureau of American Ethnology (Washington: Smithsonian Institution Press, 1891), 299-300. Hoffman had indicated earlier that the Mideg he had spoken to admitted that much of the information regarding the Midewiwin had been lost as a result of the death of the Mide leaders, and the lack of younger candidates to whom they could pass on their knowledge, since most of the latter had adopted Christian beliefs (see "The Midewiwin," 167).

34. Hoffman later published another extensive work on the Menominee, which included a significant portion on the *Mitawit* Society, as Hoffman termed the Menominee form of the Midewiwin. "Mitawit" was the spelling adopted by Hoffman, although subsequent scholars such as Skinner believed that the correct term was *Mitawin*. Both Hoffman and Alanson Skinner, who also published a detailed account of the *Metawin* (Mitawit) Society, comment on the similarities of the two ceremonies, although they noted that the Mitawit was a pale reflection of the Midewiwin, since the Mitawit ceremonies had lost most of the ancient rituals (see Hoffman, "The Menomini Indians"; and Alanson Skinner, *Medicine Ceremony of the Menomini, Iowa and Whapeton Dakota,* Indian Notes and Monographs, 4 [New York: Museum of the American Indian, Heye Foundtion, 1930]). Members of the Ojibwa, Potawatomi, and Menominee continued to share each other's ceremonies. The language and ritual differences do not appear to have posed any difficulties, since they shared a common Anishinaabe cosmology and the underlying functions of the ceremonies remained the same. However, the influence of the Mitawit had begun to decline in the 1880s with

the introduction of Drum or Dream Dance ceremonies, which had a relatively open membership and thus provided easier access to sacred knowledge and power. By the time that the Spindlers were doing research in the 1950s and 1960s, there were few elders who still knew the rituals (see Spindler and Spindler, *Dreamers without Power,* 54).

35. According to the 1889-90 *Annual Report* of the Bureau of Ethnology (p. xxvii), Dr. Hoffman "had been initiated into the mysteries of the four degrees of the society, by which he was able to record its ceremonials," and Hoffman alluded to this himself in the 1892-93 report, which included his study of the Menominee (Hoffman, "The Menomini Indians," 70).

36. Hoffman, "The Midewiwin," 151.

37. Ibid., 157-158. Unfortunately, the example he used of someone averting evil was that of a person who was usually termed a "sucking bone" doctor, but whom both Hoffman (in another section of the work [p. 254]) and Frances Densmore (*Chippewa Customs* [St. Paul: Minnesota Historical Society, 1979], 44-45) equate with a Jiisakiiwinini. Such examples of confusion (which occur several times throughout the work) are indicative of the difficulty that Euro-Americans experienced in attempting to make sense of the Ojibwa world view.

38. Hoffman, "The Midewiwin," 164, 184ff.

39. Why Hoffman's informants limited their explanations to four degrees is not known, since Warren, writing in the 1850s, had noted that the Midewiwin, as it had existed in the golden days of Chequamegon, had eight degrees; David Spencer, a missionary at Red Lake in 1848, quotes an origin story that also suggests eight degrees. Similarly, one of Kohl's pictographs shows a representation of a Mide Lodge with eight steps running through it. Frances Densmore, writing in 1910, also noted that the Midewiwin had eight degrees, though she gave no details regarding the last four degrees.

It remained for Ruth Landes (*Ojibwa Religion and the Midewiwin* [Madison: University of Wisconsin Press, 1968], 114ff) to provide a more detailed description of the four "earth grades," and the four "sky grades," which were used when the fourth-degree initiation failed to achieve a cure. In the latter degrees, the Great Spirit replaced the miigis manidoo, and the Eagle replaced the Bear manidoo.

Selwyn Dewdney (in *The Sacred Scrolls of the Southern Ojibway* [Toronto: Glenbow-Alberta Institute/University of Toronto, 1975], 111-114) also addressed the problem. He noted that Redsky's scrolls, which have a Plains influence, were the only ones that provided instruction for the last four degrees. According to him, those who qualified for the sky degrees had perverted ambitions, for the Mide master of the fourth degree was supposed to have reached the apex of manidoo power. While the instructions and rituals of the last four degrees were relatively simple (mainly repetitions of the first four degrees), the fees were exorbitant.

40. Hoffman, "The Midewiwin," 164.

41. Ibid., 221.

42. Ibid., 226-227. Hoffman and successive commentators were unable to provide a satisfactory explanation for the paralysis he described. The belief in the power of witches or bad Mideg is still common among many Ojibwa, regardless of their religious beliefs.

43. Ibid., 168-169. At first glance, both the concept and term "witch" might be considered to be Euro-American. However, the concept was also present among Algonquian societies, where witches were believed to be indicative of the work of evil spirits who were intent on destroying the society. Thus, for instance, Tenskwatawa (the Shawnee Prophet) carried on a campaign against "Christian witches" among the Shawnee and the Wyandots, who, he felt, were trying to destroy traditional society. Warren's description of the evil spirit at Chequamegon prior to the Ojibway dispersal is another example of this phenomenon (see William Warren, *History of the Ojibway People* [St. Paul: Minnesota Historical Society, 1984], 109-110). It could be argued that similar situations existed in some communities during the twentieth century, following the breakdown of Ojibwa society in the post-reservation period.

44. Hoffman, "The Midewiwin," 236-237.

45. Normally the bear was associated with the fourth degree in other descriptions of the Midewiwin. The manidoo associated with the third degree was usually the snowy owl.

46. Waabanowag were generally considered to be a deviant offshoot of the Midewiwin society, but could also become members of it.

47. Hoffman, "The Midewiwin," 278-281.

48. Another aspect of the Ghost Lodge ceremony, which had practical applications for this world, was touched upon by a Protestant missionary at Red Lake in the 1840s. David Spencer, in a short description of the "Medicine Dance" at Red Lake, explained that when an individual died, the nearest relative made up an image of the departed to which were added various valuables, along with a dish, spoon, and food, so that the deceased would have sustenance on his journey. Thus far, Spencer's account is standard; however, his next statements are very revealing: "thereafter, other valuables were added as they became available." After a year or so, the relative would hold a Midewiwin for the purpose of redistributing these valuables to the most distant relatives of the deceased. Spencer was writing an article on the Midewiwin for the *American Missionary* (vol. 3 [1848]: 23-24, Grace Lee Nute Papers, Box 14). While he might have been somewhat confused in that the "relatives" were probably Mide "ritual brothers" (who might well be relatives), the quote is a good example of the redistributive functions of the Midewiwin.

49. Hoffman's description of this Mide healing ceremony is reminiscent of Raudot's early eighteenth-century account, which appears to provide further evidence that individual and communal versions of the Midewiwin continued to co-exist.

50. Hoffman, "The Midewiwin," 281.

51. Hoffman's description is based on the statement of a man named Ojibwa, his informant from Sandy Lake (see Hoffman, "The Midewiwin," 181).

52. See Dewdney, *The Sacred Scrolls*; and Thomas Vennum Jr., "Ojibwa Origin-Migration Songs of the *mitewiwin*," *Journal of American Folklore* 91 (1978): 753-791.

53. Vennum, "Origin-Migration Songs," 753.

54. Although the Midewiwin continued to serve as an important part of the identity of many Ojibwa, the writings of Christian Ojibwa, such as William Warren, George Copway, and Peter Jones, are also indicative of a growing sense that the Ojibwa were a

distinct people, and illustrate the ways that individual Ojibwa were defining themselves and their communities.

55. Little Frenchman and Leading Feather, two Mideg from Red Lake, were Hoffman's main sources for this information (see Hoffman, "The Midewiwin," 191, 290). Although he didn't give any indication as to their status in the Midewiwin, he did note that the song charts were "imperfectly interpreted" by them, and implied that this was because the songs were not their own, so that they were not certain of the true meaning of the pictographs.

56. Among other Algonquian tribal groups, this deterioration of Midewiwin practices was more severe, if one compares Hoffman's study of the *Mitawit* ceremony among the Menominee. Even though the time period of the two studies was almost identical, and the two tribes were closely related and situated, the descriptions show two quite different developments.

57. Dewdney, *The Sacred Scrolls*; Fred K. Blessing, *The Ojibway Indians Observed, Papers of Fred K. Blessing, Jr. on the Ojibway Indians,* from *The Minnesota Archeologist* (St. Paul: Minnesota Archeological Society, 1977).

58. If, for instance, Hoffman had included the Ojibwa at Manitou Rapids and Fort Frances (Rainy Lake) as part of his study, he might have expanded the range of documents on the Midewiwin. The Midewiwin had been a powerful force there at least until the 1860s (see Michael Angel, "The Ojibwa-Missionary Encounter at Rainy Lake Mission, 1839-1857," Master's thesis, University of Manitoba, 1985), and while acculturation gradually occurred, the Midewiwin continued to be practised well into the twentieth century. Similarly, Shingwaukonse and his relatives embraced Christianity, but the Midewiwin he had been involved with continued to be practised at Garden River in the early twentieth century when the American ethnologist William Jones collected his Midewiwin narratives there. Since the Midewiwin developed somewhat differently in locations such as these, the tendency has been to term them "deviant" forms, which have developed outside the region from which most of the Euro-American materials were collected.

59. Densmore, *Chippewa Music*, 13. While Densmore's published work falls in the twentieth century, I believe that it is closer to Hoffman's than to those who followed her. Certainly, the changes in Ojibwa society separating Hoffman's and Densmore's descriptions were relatively minor. By the time that succeeding ethnologists such as Kinietz, Landes, and Howard carried out their work, Ojibwa society had changed considerably and the Midewiwin with it.

60. Densmore, *Chippewa Customs*, from Introduction by Nina M. Archabal.

61. As quoted in Nina M. Archabal's introduction to Densmore, *Chippewa Customs*, n.p.

62. Densmore published an article on her experience in the *American Anthropologist*, New Series 9 (April-June, 1907): 443.

63. Densmore, *Chippewa Music*, 2; *Chippewa Customs*, 95.

64. Densmore, *Chippewa Music*, 14-16.

65. Densmore, *Chippewa Customs*, 20. However, in another section of the book Densmore emphasized the importance of charms in Ojibwa culture, but never mentioned music with respect to them. See pp. 107-114.

66. Baraga defined the *wedaked* as a "steersman" or "pilot," and the *naganisid* as "he that is foremost," overseer, boss.

67. Densmore, *Chippewa Music*, 51-55.

68. Many Euro-American observers have treated this type of curer as a distinct class from the Jiisakiiwinini, although both used different methods than the Mide. The fact that almost every observer comes away with a slightly different interpretation of the categories and the names of the different healers is indicative of the difficulty in arriving at an "authentic" version. It is next to impossible to determine whether these differences indicate misunderstandings on the part of the observers, or were simply variations on a theme.

69. Vennum, "Origin-Migration Songs."

70. Ibid., 769-774.

71. Vernon W. Kinietz, "Chippewa Village: The Story of Katikitegan," *Cranbrook Institute of Science Bulletin*, 25 (1947): 175.

72. Robert E. Ritzenthaler, "Chippewa Preoccupation with Health," *Bulletin of the Public Museum of the City of Milwaukee* 19 (1953): 228-229.

73. Ibid., 229.

74. Hallowell argued that the Lac du Flambeau Ojibwa were still Ojibwa in personality, even though they had looked and outwardly lived like their White neighbours. For Hallowell, as for Barnouw, this meant that Ojibwa society continued to be "atomistic" since "it functioned in terms of internalized controls; the individual felt the full brunt of responsibility for his own acts" (as quoted in Edmund J. Danziger, *The Chippewas of Lake Superior* [Norman: University of Oklahoma Press, 1979], 151).

75. Ritzenthaler, "Chippewa Preoccupation," 185.

76. Kinietz, "Chippewa Village," 175.

77. This element of the sick person wearing a miigis shell around the neck appears to have been common to the Midewiwin, as it was practised in all three Wisconsin communities.

78. Ritzenthaler, "Chippewa Preoccupation," 185.

79. Robert E. Ritzenthaler and Pat Ritzenthaler, *The Woodland Indians of the Western Great Lakes* (Prospect Heights: Waveland Press, 1983), 87. Ritzenthaler was mistaken in this assertion since, as been demonstrated, earlier writers such as Nicollet and Kohl report children being inducted into the Midewiwin in the nineteenth century.

80. Kinietz, "Chippewa Village," 196.

81. Victor Barnouw, "Reminiscences of a Chippewa Mide Priest," *Wisconsin Archeologist* 35, 4 (1960): 92.

82. Ibid., 97.

83. Barnouw described the phrase as "he' he' he'!" This may be just his rendition of the phrase, although he does also record a number of other phrases that do not appear in other documents concerning the Midewiwin.

84. Kinietz, "Chippewa Village," 173; Mallery, *Picture-Writing*, 203; Hoffman, "The Midewiwin, 164; Henry the Younger, *Journal*.

85. Barnouw, "Reminiscences," 87. Barnouw explained that *naganit* was the Ojibwa term for the "leader" of the Midewiwin ceremony. He indicated that the leader did not have to be a Mide "priest," although the duties would have demanded someone with a considerable degree of knowledge. The candidate was called the *wamidewit*, while the *wedunikagmaget* ("one who speaks for another") took the place of *gichi manido* (Kitchi Manitou) in the ceremonies ("Reminiscences," 78-82). The *skawbewis* (oshkaabewis) invited people to the ceremony, and filled their pipe bowls with tobacco and their food bowls with food.

86. John Pete, the chief Mide at Lac Vieux Desert, never specifically noted that visions were required in order to join the Midewiwin, but in his description of a curing ceremony, he did allude to them as though they were still commonly sought and received (Kinietz, "Chippewa Village," 169). However, Kinietz indicated that the only things required to join the society were "the desire and the price" ("Chippewa Village," 206).

87. Barnouw, "Reminiscences," 84, 87, 106.

88. Kinietz, "Chippewa Village," 18.

89. Ibid., 208-209.

90. Barnouw, "Reminiscences," 78-82.

91. Landes, *Ojibwa Religion*, 7-8.

92. Ibid., 16-20.

93. Ibid., 71.

94. Ibid., 72.

95. Ibid., 95.

96. Ibid., 76-77.

97. Hoffman, "The Midewiwin," 151-152.

98. Landes, *Ojibwa Religion*, 44.

99. Ibid., 9.

100. Ibid., 109.

101. Ibid., 112.

102. See, for example, Hickerson's argument that the growth of the Midewiwin was a function of the development of large, sedentary villages in this region, which contrasted with the small hunting and gathering clans that lived further north. See Harold Hickerson, "The Sociohistorical Significance of Two Chippewa Ceremonials," *American Anthropologist* 68 (1963); and *The Chippewa and Their Neighbors: A Study in Ethnohistory* (Prospect Heights: Waveland Press, 1988).

103. Differences did occur among those Ojibwa who lived in close contact with other Aboriginal groups such as the Cree and the Assiniboine, as well as among those Ojibwa who were most influenced by Euro-American culture and religion.

104. Skinner's informants came mainly from the Long Plains Reserve near Portage la Prairie and Turtle Mountain Reservation in North Dakota, with a few references to Cowesses and Sakimay reserves in Saskatchewan. James Howard's follow-up study concentrated mainly on the Turtle Mountain band, although his description of a

Midewiwin ceremony is from Waywayseecappo Reserve in Manitoba. Neither report mentions the band at Roseau River, where Alexander Henry the Younger noted the Midewiwin was held annually in the early 1800s. Hallowell mentions that the Roseau River band remained "pagan until well into the twentieth century." See his article "The Passing of the Midewiwin," 40. The article provides an excellent summary of Midewiwin ceremonies among Western Ojibwa throughout the region in the late eighteenth and nineteenth centuries.

105. Skinner himself wrote a comparative study of the Midewiwin among a number of Algonquian and Siouan groups in 1920, among which were the Western Ojibwa. In it he acknowledged that he had used information collected in 1913 for his information on the Western Ojibwa.

106. John S. Milloy, *The Plains Cree: Trade, Diplomacy and War, 1790 to 1870* (Winnipeg: University of Manitoba Press, 1988); Laura Peers, *The Ojibwa of Western Canada 1780 to 1870* (Winnipeg: University of Manitoa Press, 1994).

107. This statement is according to Peter Erasmus, a Métis interpreter during the 1870 treaty negotiations, as described by Peers, *The Ojibwa of Western Canada*, 120.

108. See, for example, Elliott Coues, ed., *New Light on the Early History of the Greater Northwest: The Manuscript Journals of Alexander Henry [the younger] ... and of David Thompson* (Minneapolis: Ross & Haines, 1965); David Thompson, *Travels in Western North America, 1784-1812*, ed. Victor Hopwood (Toronto: Macmillan, 1971); and The Manuscript Papers of John McLoughlin in the Public Archives of Manitoba.

109. Hugh Dempsey, *Big Bear: The End of Freedom* (Vancouver: Douglas and McIntyre, 1984), 17.

110. The Glenbow Museum collection includes Mide medicine bags, birchbark song scrolls, and Mide drums, from Nut Lake, Kinistino, and Poor Man's reserves in Saskatchewan. Most are Ojibwa, but a number are also Cree. Some of the artifacts date back to the nineteenth century, but the most recent was used in a Midewiwin ceremony in Nut Lake in 1973. Tapes from the Cree Oral History Project further substantiate that some Cree did practise the Midewiwin.

111. Peers, *The Ojibwa of Western Canada*, 45.

112. Midewiwin artifacts collected in western Canada have been identified as Cree. We also know that at least some Cree leaders such as Starblanket were not only members but Mide officials (Letter of E. Ahenakew to Dr. Paul Wallace, Paul Wallace Papers, American Philosophical Society Library, Philadelphia).

113. Their descriptions contradict the statements of Skinner's informants that the Waabanowiwin had never been practised among the Plains Ojibwa.

114. A. Irving Hallowell, "Passing of the Midewiwin in the Lake Winnipeg Region," *American Anthropologist*, New Series 38 (1937): 32.

115. As quoted in Peers, *The Ojibwa of Western Canada*, 81.

116. Katherine Pettipas, *Severing the Ties that Bind: Government Repression of Indigenous Religious Ceremonies on the Prairies* (Winnipeg: University of Manitoba Press, 1994), 115.

117. Alanson Skinner, "Plains Ojibwa Tales," *Journal of American Folk-lore* 32(1920): 311.

118. Ibid., 318.

119. Hallowell, "The Passing of the Midewiwin" 42-43.

120. Howard also briefly mentioned the Waabanowiwin, which, he explained, no longer existed among the Plains Ojibwa, though its bad reputation remained. He also mentioned that the *Tsisakawin* (Jiisakiiwin) was practically extinct, but a few people continued to practise traditional healing as *Nanandoiwewid* (Nenaandawiiwejig). Howard contrasted the decline of the Midewiwin to the flourishing of the Sun Dance, which continued to be performed on all Plains Ojibwa reserves with the exception of Peguis and Roseau River.

121. James H. Howard, *The Plains-Ojibwa or Bungi* (Lincoln: J&L Reprint Co., 1977), 113-115; 120-121.

122. Ibid., 133-134.

123. Ibid., 135-136.

124. Ibid., 141.

125. Victor P. Lytwyn, *Muskekowuck Athinuwick: Original People of the Great Swampy Land* (Winnipeg: University of Manitoba Press, 2002), 41-42.

126. Victor P. Lytwyn, *The Fur Trade of the Little North: Indians, Pedlars, and Englishmen East of Lake Winnipeg, 1760-1821* (Winnipeg: Rupert's Land Research Centre, 1986), 29.

127. At the time, Skinner was twenty-three years of age, and this was his first extended piece of fieldwork. In his study he briefly described a religious ceremony among the Cree, which he believed resembled the Midewiwin of the Southern Ojibwa. He also quoted an earlier nineteenth-century work of the French missionary Emile Petitot, that described a "*Mitwei*" ceremony, which Skinner believed was a Woodland Cree version of the Midewiwin.

128. Alanson Skinner, "Notes on the Eastern Cree and Northern Saulteaux," *Anthropological Papers of the American Museum of Natural History* 13, 2 (1911): 152.

129. Charles Bishop suggested that the practice of the Midewiwin at Osnaburgh House disappeared around the 1870s when missionary activities were intensified (see his *The Northern Ojibwa and the Fur Trade: A Historical and Ecological Study* [Toronto: Holt, Rinehart & Winston, 1974], 89).

130. See Edward S. Rogers, "Cultural Adaptations: The Northern Ojibwa of the Boreal Forest, 1670-1980," in *Boreal Forest Adaptations: The Northern Algonkians*, ed. A. Theodore Steegmann (New York: Plenum Press, 1983), 90. Rogers believes that a line can be drawn between those groups of Ojibwa who live at Deer Lake and those of Pikangikum. The northern group at Deer Lake lack clan names, and the Midewiwin, and do not have "sucking bone" doctors, although they practised Shaking Tent ceremonies.

131. John M. Cooper, *The North Algonquian Supreme Being* (AMS Reprint Edition, 1978); Cooper, *Notes on the Ethnology of the Otchipwe of Lake of the Woods and Rainy River*, Anthropological Series, 3 (Washington: Catholic University of America, 1936); Hallowell, "The Passing of the Midewiwin."

132. Cooper, *Supreme Being*, 76-77.

133. Hallowell, "The Passing of the Midewiwin," 44-45.

134. Hallowell elaborated on this in subsequent works, providing Sagatcíweas's full English name, and explaining that he was a leader of the Midewiwin from the

Bloodvein River region who never became a Christian convert. Stoney opposed William Berens "for the chieftainship in 1875," and although Stoney was considered very powerful, Berens won, epitomizing "the acculturative influence that anticipated future developments." See Irving Hallowell, *The Ojibwa of Berens River, Manitoba,* ed. Jennifer S.H. Brown, Case Studies in Cultural Anthropology (Fort Worth: Harcourt Brace Jovanovich, 1992), 36.

135. Hallowell, "The Passing of the Midewiwin," 50.

136. Ibid., 51.

137. Although Stewart provided no dates as to when he observed the ceremony, Hallowell was able to draw his conclusions from the fact that the HBC official, whom Stewart identified as his interpreter, was in charge at Berens River in the 1850s (Hallowell, "The Passing of the Midewiwin," 49).

138. James Stewart, "Rupert's Land Indians in the Olden Time," *Archaeological Report* (Toronto: Ontario Ministry of Education, 1904), 94.

139. Hallowell learned from descendants that this was "Masque (*Makwa* or Bear in English)," the son of Yellow Legs, who had succeeded his father at Berens River as the chief Mide (Hallowell, "The Passing of the Midewiwin," 49).

140. *Selkirk Record,* June 3, 10, 17, 1887. I would to thank Jennifer Brown for bringing this case to my attention. The information was uncovered by Hugh Dempsey in the course of doing research for an edited version of Stewart's personal memoir, "Life in Rupertsland."

141. Stewart, "Rupert's Land Indians," 95-97.

142. Dewdney, *The Sacred Scrolls*, 142-144. Warren stated that the names *Naud-o-wa-se-wug,* which was sometimes applied to the Dakotas (Sioux), and *Naud-o-waig,* to the Iroquois, meant "adders" (*History of the Ojibwa*, 93). The catalogue of plants and animals at the end of John Tanner's work translated *nau-to-way* (*natawa*) as a type of rattler (John Tanner, *A Narrative of the Captivity and Adventures of John Tanner during Thirty Years Residence Among the Indians in the Interior of North America* [Minneapolis: Ross & Haines Reprint Edition, 1956], 303). Baraga's dictionary lists "*Newe*" as Hisser, a kind of serpent. Both snakes are native to the plains rather than to the Shield, which may suggest some sort of connection between the ceremony at Berens River and those of the Plains Ojibwa.

143. Stewart, "Rupert's Land Indians," 98.

144. Both books were edited by Euro-Americans, and both writers were nominally Christians, although Redsky continued to be a practitioner of the Midewiwin. Redsky and Morriseau reflect the first attempts to describe the ceremonies from the Ojibwa perspective since the nineteenth-century efforts of such Ojibwa writers as Peter Jones, George Copway, and Peter Jacobs.

145. James (Esquekesik) Redsky, *Great Leader of the Ojibway: Mis-quona-queb*, ed. James R. Stevens (Toronto: McClelland and Stewart, 1972), 90-91.

146. Ibid., 107-108.

147. Lytwyn, *The Fur Trade*, 24.

148. Morriseau Mss. P. 22, Glenbow Museum Archive (GMA), Calgary.

149. Ibid.

150. Ibid., 21.

151. As quoted in Rogers's and Smith's *Aboriginal Ontario*. Rogers also mentioned the persistence of the Wabaanowiwin among Ojibwa in southern Ontario. While he acknowledged that the Midewiwin had existed there, he indicated that there was little written about it. See also Paul Radin's article, "An Introductive Inquiry in the Study of Ojibway Religion, *Ontario Historical Society Papers and Records* (n.d.): 210-218; and Diamond Jenness's mention of both the Wabaanowiwin and Midewiwin in his work on *The Ojibwa Indians of Parry Island* (Ottawa: National Museum of Canada, 1935), 103-106.

152. Dewdney provides a vivid account of his love for the Canadian north, his passion for art and canoeing, and his profound respect for Aboriginal culture in his autobiography entitled *Daylight in the Swamp. Memoirs of Selywn Dewdney,* ed. A.K. Dewdney (Toronto: Dundurn Press, 1997).

153. Dewdney and Kidd describe the background to their research, and attempt some interpretations of the pictographs in *Indian Rock Paintings of the Great Lakes* (Toronto: University of Toronto Press, 1962).

154. Dewdney's main writings on the Midewiwin can be found in *The Sacred Scrolls of the Southern Ojibway.* In it, his emphasis is on documenting and analyzing the scrolls, but he does so within the context of the Midewiwin. Fred Blessing's major contributions to understanding the Midewiwin can be found in a collection of his articles entitled *The Ojibway Indians Observed.*

Chapter Six

1. William Warren, *History of the Ojibway People* (St. Paul: Minnesota Historical Society Press, 1984), 108-112.
2. Theresa Smith, *The Island of the Anishnaabeg: Thunderers and Water Monsters in the Traditional Ojibwe Life-World* (Moscow: University of Idaho Press, 1995), 36-37.
3. Diamond Jenness, *The Ojibwa Indians of Parry Island,* Department of Mines Bulletin 78 (Ottawa: National Museum of Canada, 1935).
4. Mary Black-Rogers, "Dan Raincloud: 'Keeping Our Indian Way,'" in *Being and Becoming Indian: Biographical Studies of North American Frontiers,* ed. James A. Clifton (Chicago: The Dorsey Press, 1989).

Glossary

The orthography used follows, in most instances, the system adopted by John D. Nichols and Earl Nyholm in *A Concise Dictionary of Minnesota Ojibwe,* and is intended as a guide for readers of this book. Definitions reflect both historical and contemporary usage of the terms.

Aadizookaan, Aadizookaanag (pl). 1. Sacred narratives or traditional stories of the Anishinaabeg (often called stories, myths, legends, or tales by Euro-American compilers). **2.** Original people, characters of a sacred narrative, sometimes termed "our grandfathers."

Animikii, Animikiig (pl). Thunderer or Thunderbird, the main sky manidoo.

Anishinaabe, Anishinaabeg (pl). 1. Person or human being. **2.** Aboriginal person. **3.** Name by which Ojibwa, Odawa (Ottawa), and Potawatomi know themselves.

Baagaakokwaan. Drumming stick used with the Mide drum (Densmore).

Bawaagan, bawaaganag (pl). Guardian or dream spirit.

Bawaajigewin. Dream.

Biinjigoosan. Sacred medicine bag or bundle.

Bimaadiziwin. Life. The term is used to signify a long, productive, and healthy life—the goal of all Anishinaabeg.

Dewe'igan. Hand drum such as those used in Jiisakiiwin and Wabanowiwin ceremonies.

Dibaajimowin. Story or narrative involving human beings in the recent past, in distinction to **Aadizookaan** (sacred narratives).

Ganawenjigewinini. Preservation man, keeper of tribal records and Mide records.

Gichi-Manidoo. Great Manidoo or Great Spirit, now often equated with the Christian idea of God.

Inaabandamowin. Vision seen or dream used in "medicine" (Densmore).

Inaapawe. An ominous, unlucky dream, or personal warning received in a dream, according to early commentators (Densmore).

Injichaag. "My soul," "spirit." This soul remained with the person's body while he or she was alive, although it could free itself for short periods. The ghost soul or **jiibay** left the person's body at death and travelled to the land of souls, and was often seen near graves.

Jiibay Midewigaan. Ghost Lodge. A variation of the Midewiwin conducted for young children who had died before reaching the age when they could be initiated into the regular Midewiwin.

Jiisakaan. Shaking tent or lodge.

Jiisakiiwin. The "Shaking Tent" or "Conjuring Lodge" ceremony, as it was usually described by Euro-Americans, which allowed the Anishinaabeg to communicate directly with "other-than-human" spirits or manidoog in order to predict the future or see at a distance.

Jiisakiiwinini, Jiisakiiwininiwag (pl). Anishinaabeg who had been given special powers, and who used the Shaking Tent to communicate with the manidoog. Often termed a **Jaasakiid** (various spellings) by Euro-American observers.

Madoodiswan. Sweat lodge used both for healing purposes, and for purification purposes as part of the larger Midewiwin ceremonies.

Maji-Manidoo. Evil manidoo, an underworld figure who is often identified with Mishibizhii or the Christian devil by Euro-American commentators.

Manidoo, Manidoog (pl). Spirit, deity, god, manitou.

Manidookaazowin. Ceremony in which an individual gained (supernatural) power.

Mashkiki. Medicine. The Anishinabeg distinguished between curing medicines, protection medicines, and bad medicines. Euro-Americans used the concept to create a class of persons they termed "Medicine men" (mashkikiiwinini), who used various forms of mashkiki to cure and cause illness, locate game or enemy warriors, or secure the affections of the opposite sex.

Mashkikiiwinini, Mashkikiiwininiwag (pl). Doctor or physician in modern Ojibwe. Some nineteenth-century Euro-Americans used the term to distinguish this type of traditional healer, who used herbs, from Mide healers, whom they believed used sorcery. A woman healer was termed a **Mashkiiiwininiikwe.**

Mazinaakizon. Picture; used sometimes to refer to the pictographs used as memory aids in Mide ceremonies.

Mide, Mideg (pl). A practitioner of the Midewiwin religion. Female practitioners were called **Midekwe** from the Ojibwe word **ikwe** for woman. A candidate or initiate was termed a **medewid** (Baraga).

Midewayaan. General term for a Mide medicine bag or sacred bundle, which contained a miigis along with various herbs and charms. It was referred to as a **biinjigoosan** (various spellings) by some observers. More specific names were used to describe bags associated with different degrees and the animal skins used to construct the bag.

Midewiwin. Great Medicine Society, Medicine Dance. An institutionalized society, which worked to maintain bimaadiziwin among the Anishinaabeg, through a complex number of rituals and teachings involving a series of different levels or degrees. The name is thought by some to refer to the sound of the drum.

Midewigaan. Mide Lodge where many of the ceremonies and the teaching took place. Generally with east and west entrances. Lake Superior is often used as a metaphor of the Midewigaan with Bowating as the eastern entrance.

Midewiigwaas. Birchbark scroll used as mnemonic aid in the Midewiwin ceremony.

Midewatig. Mide post placed at the entrance of the midewigaan. Perhaps related to the Ojibwe word for "tree," **mitig**, since it represented the restorative powers of the tree of life. In turn, "planting" the post symbolized establishing the Midewiwin as the way for life.

Miigis. Sacred cowrie shell, which is featured prominently in Mide narratives and which Mideg carry in their midewayaan and ritually shoot initiates with in order to bring the latter life and power.

Mikinaak. The Turtle, the person who acted as the messenger between manidoog and Jiisakiiwinini in the Shaking Tent ceremony.

Mishibizhii. The Underwater Panther, the name of the principal Underwater manidoo.

Mitigwakik. Mide water drum, made from a hollowed log and partially filled with water, causing the sound to travel long distances.

Mizhinawe, Mizhinaweg (pl). "Managers" or "stewards" who, according to Nicollet, were chosen to be responsible for constructing the Midewigaan and ensuring that the Midewiwin ceremonies were carried out correctly.

Nagamon. Ojibwe word for song; a Mide spiritual song is called a manidoo-nagamon.

Nanabozho. Name of the chief character in traditional Ojibwe narratives, who had both human and non-human characteristics, and who acted as a messenger, bringing the Midewiwin to the Anishinaabeg. He had both great powers and human limitations. Sometimes termed a trickster or transformer figure. The spelling of this name varies considerably from document to document.

Naagaanid. "He who leads"; described as the "Bowsman" in several sources. One of the Mide officials who conducted the Midewiwin ceremony.

Nenaandawiiwed, Nenaandawiiwejig (pl). The term currently applied to traditional healers. In the nineteenth century the term was often used as a synonym for what was termed a "sucking bone doctor," who drew out the illness or evil from his patients.

Niikaan, Niikaanag (pl). Mide brother, used in a ritual sense.

Niimi'idi-nagamon. Refers to dancing songs where anyone could dance. Densmore uses the term "nimiwug" in her works.

Nookomis. "My grandmother," the traditional keeper of knowledge in Anishinaabe narratives.

Ogimaa, Ogimaag (pl). Chief, leader, boss.

Opwaagan. Pipe for smoking.

Oshkaabewis. 1. Ceremonial messenger. **2.** Mide official who sent out invitations, and during the ceremony filled the participants' pipes with tobacco and their bowls with food, and, according to some sources, fulfilled other duties as well. **3.** Civil official who sent out invitations for meetings, pipe bearer.

Wayaabishkiwed. White person, as distinguished from an Anishinaabe.

Waabano, Waabanowag (pl). A member of the Waabanowiwin Society.

Waabanowiwin. Society of the Dawn, a healing society in which members traditionally used rituals involving fire, which took place at night and finished at dawn. Viewed by many Euro-Americans as a rival society to the Midewiwin.

Weedaakeed. "He who steers"; known as the "steersman" or "pilot" in English. A main Mide official in the Midewiwin ceremony.

Wiindigoo. Winter cannibal or ice monster, which craved human flesh.

Zhiishiigwan, Zhiishiigwanag (pl). Rattles used in the Midewiwin ceremonies.

Bibliography

Archival Sources

American Philosophical Society Library

Paul Wallace Papers (B/W15p)

Ahenakew, E.

Minnesota Historical Society Research Center

American Fur Company. 1831-1849 Calendar of Papers. 3 vols.

American Board of Commissioners for Foreign Missions Papers.

Box 1- 7: Correspondence 1827-1860.

Densmore, Frances. Papers

Box 1

Edmund F. Ely. Papers

Box 1-2: Diary and some Correspondence

Sherman Hall. Papers

Box 1-2: Diary and Correspondence

Jedediah Stevens. Papers

Mission Journal

Grace Lee Nute. Papers.

Box 1-14: Miscellaneous

U.S. Office of Indian Affairs.

Letters received (1818-1830)

Glenbow-Alberta Institute

Selwyn Dewdney Ojibway Scrolls Project

Box 1-2 Mss.

Norval Morriseau Fragment
Box 1 Mss.
Cree Oral History Project (1970-71)
29 Sound tape reels (ncludes interviews that discuss the Midewiwin)

University of Michigan Library
Henry Rowe Schoolcraft. Papers. (1788-1906) Microfilm.
Reel Nos. 1-48, 60.

Hudson's Bay Archives, Winnipeg

Public Archives of Manitoba
Michipicoten (1797-1877)
Post Journals M79-M80
Sault Ste. Marie (1818-1864)
Journals M131
Correspondence M224-M225
McLoughlin Papers

University of Manitoba Library, Winnipeg
James Evans Letters and Papers (Microfilm)

Public Archives of Canada, Ottawa
Allan Salt Papers. MG 29 D 53
Journal (1854-55)

In Possession of Dr. Jennifer Brown, Winnipeg.
James Stewart unpublished manuscript
"Life in Rupertsland, 1851-52," edited with an introduction by Hugh A. Dempsey, n.d.

Published Sources

Albanese, Catherine L.
1990 *Nature Religion in America: From the Algonkian Indians to the New Age.* Chicago: University of Chicago.

Angel, Michael R.
1986 "The Ojibwa-Missionary Encounter at Rainy Lake Mission, 1839-1857." Master's Thesis. University of Manitoba.

Armour, David A.

1983 "From Drummond Island: an Indian view of Michigan history." *Michigan History* 67, no. 3:17-22.

Axtell, James

1981 *The European and the Indian: Essays in the Ethnohistory of Colonial America*. New York: Oxford University Press.

1985 *The Invasion Within: The Contest of Cultures in Colonial North America*. New York: Oxford University Press.

Balikci, Asen

1956 "Note sur le Midewiwin." *Anthropologica* II: 165-217.

Baraga, Frederic

1847 *Answers to the Inquiries respecting the History, Present Conditions and Future Prospects of the Indian Tribes*. L'Ance, Lake Superior.

1990 *The Diary of Bishop Frederic Baraga, First Bishop of Marquette, Michigan*, edited and annotated by Regis M. Walling and Rev. N. Daniel Rupp. Detroit: Wayne State University Press.

1992 *A Dictionary of the Ojibway Language*. With a new foreword by John D. Nichols. St. Paul: Minnesota Historical Press. First published as *A Dictionary of the Otchipwe Language* by Beauchemin & Valois, Montreal, 1878, 1880.

Barnouw, Victor

1950 "The Southern Ojibwa Wisconsin Chippewa." American Anthropological Association *Memoirs* 72:

1960 "Reminiscences of a Chippewa Mide Priest." Recorded by Victor Barnouw. *Wisconsin Archeologist* 35, no. 4: 83-112.

1977 *Wisconsin Chippewa Myths and Tales and their Relation to Chippewa Life*. Madison: University of Wisconsin.

Barrett, S.A.

1979 *The Dream Dance of the Chippewa and Menominee Indians of Northern Wisconsin*. 1911. Reprint edition, New York: AMS.

Benson, Maxine

1970 "Schoolcraft, James, and the 'White Indian.'" *Michigan History* 54: 311-328.

Benton-Banai, Edward

1988 *The Mishomis Book: Voice of the Ojibway*. Hayward, WI: Indian Country Communications.

Berkhofer, Robert F.

1965 *Salvation and the Savage*. Lexington: University of Kentucky Press.

1978 *The White Man's Indian.* New York: Knopf.

Bieder, Robert E.

1986 *Science Encounters the Indian, 1820-1880: The Early Years of American Ethnology.* Norman: University of Oklahoma Press.

1995 *Native American Communities in Wisconsin, 1600-1960.* Madison: University of Wisconsin Press.

Bishop, Charles A.

1974 *The Northern Ojibwa and the Fur Trade: A Historical and Ecological Study.* Toronto: Holt, Rinehart & Winston.

1982 "The Indian Inhabitants of Northern Ontario at the Time of Contact: Socio-Territorial Considerations. In *Approaches to Algonquian Archaeology*, edited by M.G. Hanna and B. Kooyman, pp. 253-73. Calgary: University of Calgary.

1989 "The Question of Ojibwa Clans." In *Actes du vingtième congrès des algonquinistes*, edited by William Cowan, pp. 43-61. Ottawa: Carleton University.

Black, Mary B.

1977a "Ojibwa Power Belief System." In *The Anthropology of Power,* edited by R. R. Fogelson and R. N. Adams, pp. 141-151. New York: Academic Press.

1977b "Ojibwa Taxonomy and Percept Ambiguity." *Ethos* 5, no.1: 90-118.

Black-Rogers, Mary B.

1989 "Dan Raincloud: 'Keeping Our Indian Way.'" In *Being and Becoming Indian: Biographical Studies of North American Frontiers*, edited by James A. Clifton, pp. 226-248. Chicago: The Dorsey Press.

Blackbird, Andrew J.

1887 *History of the Ottawa and Chippewa Indians of Michigan.* Ypsilanti, Michigan.

Blackburn, George M.

1970 "George Johnston: Indian Agent and Copper Hunter." *Michigan History* 14, no. 1: 108-121.

Blair, Emma, ed.

1911-12 *The Indian Tribes of the Upper Mississippi Valley and Region of the Great Lakes*, edited and translated by Emma Blair. Two volumes in one. Cleveland: Arthur H. Clarke.

Blakeslee, Allen D.

1890 *The Religious Customs of the Ojibwa Indians.* Haywood, Wisconsin: no publisher.

Blessing, Fred K.

1956 "An Exhibition of Mide Magic." *The Minnesota Archeologist* 20, no. 4: 9-13.

1956 "Miscellany." *The Minnesota Archeologist* 20, no. 4: 14-17.

1977 *The Ojibway Indians Observed. Papers of Fred K. Blessing, Jr., on the Ojibway Indians.* In *The Minnesota Archeologist.* St. Paul: Minnesota Archeological Society.

Brown, Jennifer S.H.

1985 "Central Manitoba Saulteaux in the 19th Century." In *Papers of the Sixteenth Algonquian Conference*, edited by William Cowan, pp. 1-8. Ottawa: Carleton University.

1986 "Northern Algonquians from Lake Superior and Hudson Bay to Manitoba in the Historical Period," In *Native Peoples: The Canadian Experience,* edited by R. Bruce Morrison and C. Roderick Wilson. Toronto: McClelland & Stewart.

1989 "A Place in Your Mind for Them All: Chief William Berens." In *Being and Becoming Indian: Biographical Studies of North American Frontiers*, edited by James A. Clinton, pp. 204-225. Chicago: Dorsey Press.

Brown, Jennifer S.H., and Robert Brightman

1988 *The Orders of the Dreamed: George Nelson on Cree and Northern Ojibwa Religion and Myth, 1823.* Winnipeg: University of Manitoba Press.

Brown, Jennifer S.H., and Maureen Matthews

1993 "Fair Wind, Medicine and Consolation on the Berens River." *Journal of the Canadian Historical Association* New Series 4: 55-74.

Bruchac, Joseph

1993 *The Native American Sweat Lodge: History and Legends.* Freedom, California: Crossing Press.

Burton, Frederick R.

1909 *American Primitive Music, with Especial Attention to the Ojibwas.* New York: Moffat, Yard.

Bushnell, D. I.

1905 "An Ojibway Ceremony." *American Anthropologist* n.s., no. 7: 69-73.

Cadieux, Lorenzo

1957-58 "Missionaires jesuites au Nipigon." SCHEC *Rapport*: 91-102.

Cadzow, D.A.

1926 "Bark Records of the Bungi Midewin Society." *Indian Notes* 3, no. 2: 123-134.

Callender, Charles

1962 *Social Organization of the Central Algonkian Indians.* Milwaukee: Milwaukee Public Museum.

Campbell, Joseph

1988 *The Power of Myth.* New York: Doubleday.

Carrière, Gaston.

1953 *Missionnaire sans toit. Le P. Jean-Nicolas Laverlochère, O.M.I. 1811-1884.* Montreal: Rayonnement.

Carver, James

1974 *Travels through North America in the Years 1766, 1767 and 1768.* 1778. Facsimile edition, Toronto: Coles.

Chamberlain, Alexander F.

1993 "New Religions among the North American Indians." *Journal of Religious Psychology* 6: 1-49.

Chamberlin, J.E.

1975 *The Harrowing of Eden: White Attitudes towards Native Americans.* New York: Seabury Press.

Champagne, Duane

1983 "Social Structure, Revitalization Movements and State Building: Social Change in Four Native American Communities." *American Sociological Review* 48: 754-763.

Churchill, Ward

1988 "Sam Gill's Mother Earth: Colonialism, Genocide and the Expropriation of Indigenous Spiritual Tradition in Contemporary Academia." *American Indian Culture and Research Journal* 12, no.3: 49-67.

Chute, Janet Elizabeth

1998 *The Legacy of Shingwaukonse: A Century of Native Leadership.* Toronto: University of Toronto Press.

Cleland, Charles E.

1982 "The Inland Shore Fishery of the Northern Great Lakes: Its Development and Importance in Prehistory." *American Antiquity* 47, no. 4: 761-784.

1992 *Rites of Conquest: The History and Culture of Michigan's Native Americans.* Ann Arbor: University of Michigan Press.

Clements, William M.

1990 "Schoolcraft as Textmaker." *Journal of the American Folklore Society* 103: 177-192.

Clifford, James

1986 *Writing Culture: the poetics and politics of ethnography: a School of American Research Seminar.* Berkeley: University of California Press.

Clifton, James A.

1977 *The Prairie People: Continuity and Change in Potawatomi Indian Culture, 1665-1965.* Lawrence, Kansas: Regents Press.

Coatsworth, Emerson S.

1957 *The Indians of Quetico*. From field notes and research by Robert C. Dailey. Toronto: Published for the Quetico Foundation by University of Toronto Press.

Coleman, Dr. A.P.

1897 *Sixth Report of the Ontario Bureau of Mines, 1896*. Toronto: Queen's Printer, Government of Ontario.

Coleman, M. Bernard

1929 "Religion and Magic among the Cass Lake Ojibwa." *Primitive Man* 2: 52-55.

1937 "The Religion of the Ojibwe of Northern Minnesota." *Primitive Man* 10: 33-57.

1962 *Ojibwa Myths and Legends*. Sr. Bernard Coleman, Ellen Frogner, and Estelle Eich. Minneapolis: Ross & Haines.

Conway, Thor

1990 *Spirits on Stone: the Agawa Pictographs*. Written and illustrated by Thor and Julie Conway. Echo Bay, Ont.: Heritage Discoveries.

Cooper, John M.

1928 "Field Notes on Northern Algonkian Magic." *Proceedings of the International Congress of Americanists* 23: 513-518.

1929 "Field notes on the Ojibway of Northern Ontario." *Journal of the Washington Academy of Science* 19: 128.

1936 *Notes on the Ethnology of the Otchipwe of Lake of the Woods and Rainy Lake*. Anthropological Series, 3. Washington, D.C.: Catholic University of America.

1978 *The North Algonquian Supreme Being*. 1934. AMS Reprint Edition.

Copway, George

1972 *The Traditional History and Characteristic Sketches of the Ojibway Nation*. 1850. Facsimile edition, Toronto: Coles.

Coues, Elliott, ed.

1965 *New Light on the Early History of the Greater Northwest: The Manuscript Journals of Alexander Henry [the younger] . . . and of David Thompson*. 1897. Reprint edition, Minneapolis: Ross & Haines.

Coward, Harold G.

1989 "The Spiritual Power of Oral and Written Scripture." In *Silence, the Word and the Sacred*, edited by E.D. Blodgett and H.G. Coward. Waterloo: Wilfrid Laurier Press.

Dailey, Robert C.

1958 "The Midewiwin, Ontario's First Medical Society." *Ontario History* 50, no. 3: 133-138.

Danziger, Edmund Jefferson

1979 *The Chippewas of Lake Superior*. Norman, Oklahoma: University of Oklahoma Press.

Davidson, John F.

1945 "Ojibwa Songs." *Journal of American Folklore* 58, no. 230: 303-305.

Davidson, John Nelson

1892 *Missions on Chequamegon Bay.* Reprinted from Vol. 12, Wisconsin Historical Collections. Madison: State Historical Society of Wisconsin.

Day, E.H.

1890 "Sketches of the Northwest." *Collections and Researches made by the Michigan Pioneer and Historical Society* 14: 205-232.

Deleary, Nicholas

1990 "Midewiwin: an Aboriginal Spiritual Institution. Symbols of Continuity: A Native Studies Culture-based Perspective." Master's Thesis. Carleton University.

Dempsey, Hugh

1984 *Big Bear: The End of Freedom.* Vancouver: Douglas and McIntyre.

Densmore, Frances

1907 "An Ojibwa Prayer Ceremony." *American Anthropologist.* New Series 9: 443-444.

1910-13 *Chippewa Music.* Two volumes. Bureau of American Ethnology Bulletins 45 and 53. Washington: Smithsonian Institution Press.

1932 "An Explanation of a Trick Performed by Indian Jugglers." *American Anthropologist.* New Series 34: 310-314.

1953 "The Belief of the Indian in a Connection between Song and the Supernatural." Bureau of American Ethnology Bulletin 151. In *Anthropological Papers,* No. 37, pp. 217-223.

1979 *Chippewa Customs.* With an introduction by Nina Marchetti Archabal, 1929. Reprint edition, St. Paul, Minnesota: Minnesota Historical Society.

Dewdney, Selwyn

1970 "Ecological Notes on the Ojibway Shaman-Artist." *Arts/Canada* 27: 17-28.

1975 *The Sacred Scrolls of the Southern Ojibway.* Toronto: Published for the Glenbow-Alberta Institute by the University of Toronto.

1997. *Daylight in the Swamp. Memoirs of Selwyn Dewdney,* edited by A.K. Dewdney. Toronto: Dundurn Press.

Dewdney, Selwyn, and K.E. Kidd

1962 *Indian Rock Paintings of the Great Lakes.* Toronto: University of Toronto Press.

Dorsey, James Owen

1889-90 "A Study of Siouan Cults." Bureau of Ethnology. *Annual Report to the Smithsonian Institution.* Washington: Smithsonian Society Press.

Dorson, Richard

1952 *Bloodstoppers & Bearwalkers: Folk Tradition of the Upper Peninsula.* Cambridge: Harvard University Press.

Doty, William

1986 *Mythology: The Study of Myths and Rituals.* Birmingham: University of Alabama Press.

Dowd, Gregory Evans

1992 *A Spirited Resistance: The North American Indian Struggle for Unity, 1745-1815.* Baltimore: Johns Hopkins Press.

Duerr, Hans Peter

1985 *Dreamtime: Concerning the Boundary between Wilderness and Civilization*, translated by Felicitas Goodman. 1978. London: Basil Blackwell.

Edmunds, R. David

1985 "Main Poc: Potawatomi Wabeno." *American Indian Quarterly* (Summer): 250-272.

Eliade, Mircea

1972 *Shamanism: Archaic Techniques of Ecstasy.* Princeton: Princeton University Press.

En-me-gah-bowh's Story.

1904 Minneapolis: Women's Auxiliary, St. Barnabas Hospital.

Fiddler, Chief Thomas, and James R. Stevens

1985 *Killing the Shamen.* Moonbeam, Ontario: Penumbra Press.

Firth, Raymond

1973 *Symbols, Public and Private.* Ithaca, N.Y.: Cornell University Press.

Fixico, Donald L.

1994 "The Alliance of the Three Fires in Trade and War, 1630-1812." *Michigan Historical Review* 20, no. 2: 2-23.

Flannery, Regina

1940 "The Cultural Position of the Spanish River Indians." *Primitive Man* 13, no. 1: 1-25.

Forsyth, Thomas

1911-12 *The Indian Tribes of the Upper Mississippi Valley and Region of the Great Lakes,* edited and translated by Emma Blair. Volume 2. Cleveland: Arthur H. Clarke.

Fox, John Sharpless, ed.

1909-10 "Narrative of the travels and adventures of a merchant voyageur in the savage territories of northern America leaving Montreal the 28th of May 1783 (to 1820), by Jean Bêtiste Perrault." *Michigan Pioneer and Historical Collections* 37: 506-619.

Frost, Rev. R.

1904 *Sketches of Indian Life by Frost, for Thirty Years a Missionary to the Indians.* Toronto: Wm. Briggs.

Frye, Northrop

1990. *Words with Power: Being a Second Study of The Bible and Literature.* Toronto: Penguin.

Geertz, Clifford

1974 "'From the Native's Point of View': On the Nature of Anthropological Understanding." In *Meaning in Anthropology*, edited by Keith H. Basso and Henry A. Selby, pp. 221-237. Albuquerque: University of New Mexico Press.

Gilfillan, Joseph Alexander

"The Ojibways in Minnesota." *Minnesota Historical Society Collections* 9: 55-123.

Gill, Sam

1987 *Mother Earth: An American Story*. Chicago: University of Chicago Press.

1988 "The Power of Story." *American Indian Culture and Research Journal* 12, no.3: 69-84.

Graham, Elizabeth

1975 *Medicine Man to Missionary: Missionaries as Agents of Change among the Indians of Southern Ontario, 1784-1867.* Toronto: Peter Martin Associates.

Grant, John Webster

1984 *Moon of Wintertime: Missionaries and the Indians of Canada in Encounter since 1534.* Toronto: University of Toronto Press.

Gray, Susan E.

1994 "Limits and Possibilities: White-Indian Relations in Western Michigan in the Era of Removal." *Michigan Historical Review* 20, no. 2: 71-91.

Greenberg, Adolph M., and James Morrison

1982 "Group Identities in the Boreal Forest: The Origin of the Northern Ojibwa." *Ethnohistory* 29, no.2: 91.

Greenfield, Bruce

1995 "The Oral in the Written: The Irony of Representation in Louis Hennepin's *Déscription de la Louisiane.*" *Historical Reflections / Reflexions Historiques* 21, no. 2: 243-259.

Grim, John A.

1983 *The Shaman: Patterns of Siberian and Ojibway Healing.* Norman, Oklahoma: University of Oklahoma Press.

Hallowell, A. Irving

1934 "Some Emperical Aspects of Northern Saulteaux Religion." *American Anthropologist* New Series 36: 389-404.

1936 "The Passing of the Midewiwin in the Lake Winnipeg Region." *American Anthropologist* New Series 38: 32-51.

1942 *The Role of Conjuring in Saulteaux Society*. Philadelphia: University of Pennsylvania Press.

1960 "Ojibwa Ontology, Behaviour and World View." In *Culture and History*, edited by Stanley Diamond, pp. 19-52. London: Oxford University Press.

1967a "Ojibwa Personality and Acculturation." In *Beyond the Frontier: Social Process and Cultural Change*, edited by Paul Bohanannan and Fred Plog. 1949. New York: Natural History Press.

1967b *Culture and Experience.* Philadelphia: University of Pennsylvania Press.

1992 *The Ojibwa of Berens River, Manitoba,* edited with a preface and afterword by Jennifer S.H. Brown. Case Studies in Cultural Anthropology. Fort Worth, Texas: Harcourt Brace Jovanovich.

Ham, G. H.

1886 "Among the Indians." Toronto *Globe and Mail*, March 6.

Hamilton, James Cleland

1990 "Famous Algonquian Algic Legends." In *Canadian Institute Semi-Centennial Volume.* Also: *Transactions of the Canadian Institute* 6: 285-312.

Handbook of North American Indians.

1978 Vol. 15. *Northeast*, edited by Bruce G. Trigger. Washington, D.C.: Smithsonian Institution.

1981 Vol. 6. *Subarctic*, edited by June Helm. Washington, D.C.: Smithsonian Institution.

1988 Vol. 4. *History of Indian-White Relations*, edited by Wilcombe E. Washburn. Washington, D.C.: Smithsonian Institution.

Harrison, Julia D.

1982 "The Midewiwin: the Retention of an Ideology." Master's Thesis. University of Calgary.

Hennepin, Louis

1880 *Descriptions of Louisiana*; translated from the edition of 1683, and compared with the *Nouvelle découverte,* the La Salle documents, and other contemporaneous papers, by John Gilmary Shea. New York: J.G. Shea.

Henry, Alexander the Elder

1965 *Travels and Adventures in Canada and the Indian Territories between the Years 1760 and 1766*, edited by James Bain. 1901. Reprint edition, Edmonton: Hurtig.

Henry, Alexander the Younger

1988 *The Journals of Alexander Henry the Younger. 1799-1814.* Toronto: Champlain Society.

Hickerson, Harold

1962 *The Southwestern Chippewa: An Ethnohistorical Study.* American Anthropological Association Memoir 2.

1963 "The Sociohistorical Significance of Two Chippewa Ceremonials." *American Anthroplogist* 68: 67-85.

1974 *Ethnohistory of Chippewa in Central Minnesota*. New York: Garland.

1982 "Notes on the Post-Contact Origin of the Midewiwin." *Ethnohistory* 9, no. 4: 75-102.

1988 *The Chippewa and Their Neighbours: A Study in Ethnohistory*. With a review essay and bibliographical supplement by Jennifer S.H. Brown and Laura L. Peers. 1970. Prospect Heights, Ill.: Waveland Press.

Hickey, M.

1906 "A Missionary Among the Indians." In *Report of the Pioneer Society of the State of Michigan*, pp. 550-556. 1882. Reprint.

Highwater, Jamake

1981 *The Primal Mind: Vision and Reality in Indian America*. New York: New American Library.

Hindley, John Ingham

1885 *Indian Legends. Nanabush, the Ojibbeway Saviour. Moosh-kuh-ung, or the flood*. Barrie, Ontario.

Hinsdale, Wilber B.

1935 "The Midewin." *Indians at Work* 3, no. 6: 21.

1926 "Religion at the Algonquian Level." *Papers of the Michigan Academy of Science, Arts and Letters* 5: 15-27.

Hinsley, Curtis M.

1981 *Savages and Scientists: The Smithsonian Institution and the Development of American Anthropology, 1846-1910*. Washington: Smithsonian Institution Press.

Hirschfelder, Arlene B.

1992 *Encyclopedia of Native American Religions: An Introduction*, edited by Arlene Hirschfelder and Paulette Molin. New York: Facts on File.

Hobsbawn, Eric

1983 "Introduction: Inventing Traditions." In *The Invention of Tradition*, edited by Eric Hobsbawm and Terence Ranger, pp. 1-14. New York: Cambridge University Press.

Hoffman, Walter James

1888 "Pictographic and Shamanistic Rites of the Ojibwa." *American Anthropologist* 1: 209-229.

1891 "The Midewiwin or 'Grand Medicine Society' of the Ojibwa." Bureau of American Ethnology. *Seventh Annual Report to the Smithsonian Institution, 1885-1886*, pp. 145-300. Washington: Smithsonian Institution Press.

1896 "The Menomini Indians." Bureau of American Ethnology. *Fourteenth Annual Report to the Smithsonian Institution, 1892-93, Pt. 1*, pp. 3-328. Washington: Smithsonian Institution Press.

1899 "Notes on Ojibwa Folk-lore." *American Anthropologist* 2: 215-223.

Hoppál, Mihály

1992 *Northern Religions and Shamanism*. Budapest: Akadénuau Kiadó; Helsinki: Finnish Literature Society.

Howard, James H.

1977 *The Plains-Ojibwa or Bungi*. 1965. Reprint edition, Lincoln, Nebraska: J&L Reprint Co.

Hugolin, R. P.

1906 "L'idée spiritualiste et l'idée morale chez les Chippewas." *Proceedings of the 15th Session of the International Congress of Americanists* 1: 329-337.

Hultkrantz, Ake

1973 "A Definition of Shamanism." *Temenos* 9: 25-37.

1979 *The Religions of the American Indians*, translated by Monica Setterwall. 1967. Berkeley: University of California Press.

1980 "The Problem of Christian Influence on Northern Algonkian Eschatology. *Studies in Religion* 9, no. 2: 161-83.

1983a *The Study of American Indian Religions*, edited by Christopher Vecsey. New York: Crossroad Publishing.

1983b "The Concept of the Supernatural in Primal Religion." *History of Religions* 22: 231-253.

1987 *Native Religions of North America: The Power of Visions and Fertility*. San Franciso: Harper and Row.

1988a "Shamanism: A Religious Phenomenon?" In *Shaman's Path*, compiled and edited by Gary Doore, pp. 33-41. Boston: Shambhala.

1988b "Religion and Experience of Nature among North American Hunting Indians." In *The Hunters: Their Culture and Way of Life*, edited by Ake Hultkrantz and Ornulf Vorren. Oslo: Universitetsforlaget.

1992 *Shamanic Healing and Ritual Drama: Health and Medicine in Native American Religious Traditions*. New York: Crossroad Publishing.

Humphreys, Caroline, with Urgunge Onon

1996 *Shamans and Elders*. Oxford: Clarendon Press.

Illich, Ivan, and Barry Sanders

1988 *The Alphabetization of the Popular Mind*. New York: Vintage Books.

Jacobs, Peter

1858 *Journal of the Reverend Peter Jacobs, Indian Wesleyan Missionary, from Rice Lake to the Hudson's Bay Territory*. New York: Published by the Author.

Jameson, Anna

1835 *Winter Studies and Summer Rambles in Canada.* London: Saunders & Otley.

Jaenen, Cornelius J.

1976 *Friend and Foe: Aspects of French-Amerindian Cultural Contact in the Sixteenth and Seventeenth Centuries.* New York: Columbia University Press.

Jenness, Diamond

1935 *The Ojibwa Indians of Parry Island.* Department of Mines Bulletin 78. Ottawa: National Museum of Canada.

Johnson, Frederick

1929 "Notes on the Ojibwa and Potawatomi of the Parry Island Reservation, Ontario." *Indian Notes* 6, no. 3: 193-216.

Johnson, George

"Reminiscences." *Michigan Pioneer and Historical Collections* 12: 605-608.

Johnston, Basil

1976 *Ojibway Heritage.* New York: Columbia University Press.

1982 *Ojibway Ceremonies.* Toronto: McClelland & Stewart.

1995 *The Manitous: The Spiritual World of the Ojibway.* Toronto: Key Porter Books.

Jones, Dennis

1995 "The Etymology of Anishinaabe." *Oshkaabewis Native Journal* 2, no. 1: 43-48.

Jones, J.A.

1953 "The Political Organization of the Three Fires." *Proceedings of the Indiana Academy of Science* 63: 46.

Jones, Peter

1861 *History of the Ojebway Indians; with especial reference to their conversion to Christianity,* by Rev. Peter Jones (Kahkewaquonaby) Indian missionary. With a brief memoir of the writer; and introductory notes by the Rev. G. Osborne. London: A. W. Bennett.

Jones, William

1905 "The Algonkin Manitou." *Journal of American Folklore* 18: 183-190.

1916 "Ojibwa Tales from the North Shore of Lake Superior." *Journal of American Folklore* 29: 360-91.

1917 *Ojibwa Texts,* Part I, edited by Truman Michelson. Leyden, New York: Publications of the American Ethnological Society.

1919 *Ojibwa Texts,* Part II, edited by Truman Michelson. Leyden, New York: Publications of the American Ethnological Society.

Kasprycki, Sylvia S.

1990 "'A Lover of all Knowledge': Edwin James and Menominee Ethnography." *Native American Studies* 4, no. 1: 1-9.

Keating, William H.

1959 *Narrative of an Expedition to the Source of St. Peter's River, Lake Winnepeek, Lake of the Woods.* Preface by Roy P. Johnson. 1824. Reprint edition, Minneapolis: Ross & Haines Reprint Edition.

Keesing, Felix M.

1971 *The Menomini Indians of Wisconsin.* With a new introduction by Frank C. Miller. 1939. Reprint edition, New York: Johnson Reprint Corporation.

Keesing, Roger M.

1989 "Creating the Past: Custom and Identity in the Contemporary Pacific." *The Contemporary Pacific* 1, nos. 1 & 2 (Spring & Fall): 19-42.

Kehoe, Alice Beck

1989 *The Ghost Dance: Ethnohistory and Revitalization.* Chicago: Holt, Rinehart and Winston.

Kellogg, Louise Phelps

1917 *Early Narratives of the Northwest, 1634-1699.* New York: Charles Scribners.

1925 *The French Régime in Wisconsin and the Northwest.* Madison: State Historical Society.

Kidder, Homer H.

1994 *Ojibwa myths and halfbreed tales, of Charlotte Kobawgam and Jacques la Pique, 1893-1895.* Recorded with notes by Homer H. Kidder, edited by Arthur P. Bourgeois. Detroit: Wayne State University.

Kidwell, Clara Sue

1985 "Native Knowledge in the Americas." *OSIRIS*, 2nd series, no. I: 209-238.

Kidwell, Clara Sue, and Ann Marie Plane

1996 "Representing Native American History." *Public Historian* 18, no. 4: 9-18.

Kinietz, Vernon W.

1947 "Chippewa Village: The Story of Katikitegan." *Cranbrook Institute of Science Bulletin* 25.

1972 *The Indians of the Western Great Lakes, 1615-1760.* Ann Arbor: University of Michigan Press.

Kinnaman, J. O.

1911 "Chippewa History as told by themselves and French Documents." *American Antiquarian* 33: 32-40.

Klein, Kerwin

1995 "In Search of Narrative Mastery: Postmodernism and the People without History." *History & Theory* 34: 275-298.

Klostermaier, Klaus

1978 "The Creative Function of the Word." In *Language in Indian Philosophy and Religion*, edited by Harold Coward, pp. 5-18. Waterloo: Wilfrid Laurier University Press.

Knight, J.

1913 "Ojibwa Tales from Sault Ste. Marie, Michigan." *Journal of American Folklore:* 91-96.

Kohl, Johann Georg

1985 *Kitchi Gami: Life Among the Lake Superior Ojibway,* translated by Lascelles Wraxall. With a new introduction by Robert E. Bieder and additional translations by Ralf Neufang and Ulrike Bocker. 1860. Reprint edition, St. Paul: Minnesota Historical Society Press.

Kugel, Rebecca

1983 "Utilizing Oral Traditions: Some Concerns Raised by Recent Ojibwe Studies: A Review Essay." *American Indian Culture and Research Journal* 7, no. 3: 65-75.

1985 "Factional Alignment Among the Minnesota Ojibwe, 1850-1880." *American Indian Culture and Research Journal* 9, no. 4: 23-47.

1990 "Religion Mixed with Politics: The 1836 Conversion of Mang'osid of Fond du Lac." *Ethnohistory* 37: 126-157.

Kurath, Gertrude P.

1959 "Blackrobe and Shaman: The Christianization of Michigan Algonquians." *Papers of the Michigan Academy of Science, Arts and Letters* 44: 209-15.

LaFleur, Laurence J.

1940 "On the Mide of the Ojibway." *American Anthropologist* 13, no. 4: 706-708.

Laidlaw, G.E.

1922 "Ojibway Myths and Tales." *Wisconsin Archeologist.* New Series 1: 28-38.

Landes, Ruth

1968 *Ojibwa Religion and the Midewiwin.* Madison: University of Wisconsin Press.

1970 *The Prairie Potawatomi: Tradition and Ritual in the Twentieth Century.* Madison: University of Wisconsin Press.

Landon, R. Horace, ed.

1964 "Letters of Early Missionary Days." *The Minnesota Archeologist* 26: 55-63.

Larzelere, Claude E.

1933 "The Red Man in Michigan." *Michigan History Magazine* 17, nos. 3-4: 344-376.

Long, John

1971 *Voyages and Travels of an Indian Interpreter and Trader.* 1791. Facsimile edition, Toronto: Coles.

Lovisek, Joan A. M.

1991 "Ethnohistory of the Algonkian Speaking People of Georgian Bay—Precontact to 1850." PhD Dissertation. McMaster University.

Lytwyn, Victor P.

1986 *The Fur Trade of the Little North: Indians, Pedlars, and Englishmen East of Lake Winnipeg, 1760-1821.* Winnipeg: Rupert's Land Research Centre.

2002 *Muskekowuck Athinuwick: Original People of the Great Swampy Land.* Winnipeg: University of Manitoba Press.

Mallery, Garrick

1972 *Picture-Writing of the American Indians.* Two volumes. Foreword by J.W. Powell. In Smithsonian Institution, Bureau of Ethnology, *10th Annual Report, 1888-89.* 1893. Reprint edition, New York: Dover Reprint.

MacLeod, D. Peter

1992 "The Anishinabeg Point of View: The History of the Great Lakes Region to 1800 in Nineteenth-Century Mississauga, Odawa, and Ojibwa Historiography." *Canadian Historical Review* 73, no. 2 (June): 194-210.

Margry, Pierre

1879-88 *Découvertes et establissements des Francais dans l'Ouest et dans le Sud de l'Amérique.* Six volumes. Paris: Maisonneuve.

Martin, Calvin

1978 *Keepers of the Game.* Berkeley: University of California Press.

Martin, Calvin, ed.

1987 *The American Indian and the Problem of History.* New York: Oxford University Press.

Masson, Louis F. R.

1960 *Les Bourgeois de la Compagnie du Nord-Ouest.* Two volumes. 1889-1890. Reprint edition, New York: Antiquarian Press.

McKenney, Thomas L.

1972 *Sketches of a Tour to the Lakes.* 1827. Reprint edition, Minneapolis: Ross & Haines.

McMullen, Ann

1996 "Soapbox Discourse: Tribal Historiography, Indian-White Relations, and Southeastern New England Powwows." *Public Historian* 18, no. 4: 53-74.

McTaggart, Fred

1976 *Wolf that I am: In Search of the Red Earth People.* Boston: Houghton Mifflin.

Messer, R.

1982 "A Jungian Interpretation of the Relationship of Culture-Hero and Trickster Figure within Chippewa Mythology." *Studies in Religion/Sciences Religieuses* 11, no. 3: 309-320.

Meyer, Melissa

1994 *The White Earth Tragedy: Ethnicity and Dispossession at a Minnesota Anishinaabe Reservation, 1889-1920.* Lincoln: University of Nebraska Press.

Michelson, T.

1913 "Note on the Gentes of the Ottawa." *American Anthropologist.* New Series 13: 338.

Miller, Christopher L. and George R. Hamell

1986 "A New Perspective on Indian-White Contact: Cultural Symbols and Colonial Trade." *Journal of American History* 73, no. 2: 311-328.

Milloy, John S.

1988 *The Plains Cree: Trade, Diplomacy and War, 1790 to 1870.* Winnipeg: University of Manitoba Press.

Moodie, D. Wayne, A. J. W. Catchpole, and Kerry Abel

1992 "Northern Athapaskan Oral Tradition and the White River Volcano." *Ethnohistory* 39, no. 2: 148-171.

Morris, Alexander

1991 *The Treaties of Canada with the Indians of Manitoba and the North-West Territories.* 1880. Facsimile edition, Saskatoon: Fifth House Publishers.

Morriseau, Norval

1965 *Legends of my People the Great Ojibway*, edited by Selwyn Dewdney. Toronto: Ryerson Press.

Morse, Jedediah

1822 *Report to the Secretary of War of the U.S. on Indian Affairs, Comprising a narrative of a tour in the summer of 1820.* New Haven: Davis & Force.

Myers, Frank A.

1956 "1836 Mission Tour of Lake Huron by James Evans: Extract from *Gore Bay Recorder and Little Current Expositor.*" United Church Archives.

Nash, Roderick

1973 *Wilderness and the American Mind.* New Haven: Yale University Press.

Neill, Edward D.

1858 *The History of Minnesota, from the Earliest French Explorations to the Present Time.* Philadelphia: J.B. Lippincott.

1885 *History of the Ojibways, and their connection with fur traders, based upon official and other records.* In *Minnesota Historical Society Collections* 5: 305-510.

1891 "Memoir of William T. Boutwell, the first Christian Minister resident among the Indians of Minnesota." *Macalester College Contributions: Department of History, Literature and Political Science* No.1. St. Paul.

Nicollet, Joseph N.

1970 *The Journals of Joseph N. Nicollet: A Scientist on the Mississippi Headwater with Notes on Indian Life, 1836-37.* Translated from the French by André Fertey, edited by Martha Coleman Bray. St. Paul: Minnesota Historical Society.

Nichols, John D., and Earl Nyholm

1995 *A Concise Dictionary of Minnesota Ojibwe.* Illustrations by Earl Nyholm. Minneapolis: University of Minnesota Press.

Nute, Grace Lee, ed.

1942 *Documents Relating to the Northwest Missions, 1815-1827.* St. Paul: Minnesota Historical Society.

O'Meara, Frederick A.

1846-49 *Report of a Mission to the Ottahwas and Ojibwas on Lake Huron.* London: Printed for the Society of the Propagation of the Gospel.

Overholt, Thomas W., and J. Baird Callicott

1982 *Clothed-in-fur and other Tales: An Introduction to an Ojibwa World View.* With Ojibwa texts by William Jones and foreword by Mary B. Black-Rogers. Washington: University Press of America.

Paap, Howard Dorsey

1985 "The Ojibwe Midewiwin: a Structual Analysis." PhD Dissertation. University of Minnesota.

Paper, Jordan

1980 "From Shaman to Mystic in Ojibwa Religion." *Studies in Religion / Sciences Religieuses* 9, no. 2: 185-200.

Pecham, Howard H.

1947 *Pontiac and the Indian Uprising.* Princeton: Princeton University Press.

Peers, Laura

1994 *The Ojibwa of Western Canada, 1780 to 1870.* Winnipeg: University of Manitoba Press.

Peters, Bernard C.

1994 "John Johnston's 1822 Description of the Lake Superior Chippewa." *Michigan Historical Review* 20, no. 2: 26-46.

Pettipas, Katherine

1994 *Severing the Ties that Bind: Government Repression of Indigenous Religious Cermonies on the Prairies.* Winnipeg: University of Manitoba Press.

Pitezal, John

1901 *Life of Peter Marksman.* Cincinnati: Western Book Concern.

Podruchny, Carolyn

1996 "Shifting Identifies and Constructing Communities: Joseph Constant's Journey to the Pas, 1773-1853." Paper presented at the 28th Algonquian Conference, Toronto.

Pomedli, Michael M.

1986 "Mythical and Logical Thinking: Friends or Foes." *Laval théologique et philosophique* 42, no. 3: 377-387.

1987 "Beyond Unbelief: Early Jesuit Interpretations of Native Religions." *Studies in Religion* 16, no. 3: 276-287.

1998 "Ojibwa Healing and Ordering in Treaty Number Three." In *Sacred Lands: Aboriginal World Views, Claims, and Conflicts*, edited by Jill Oakes, Rick Riewe, Kathi Kinew, and Elaine Maloney. Occasional Publication No. 43, Canadian Circumpolar Institute. Edmonton: University of Alberta.

1998 "'Trick or Treaty'? Treaty #3, Rice and Manitous." *Papers of the Twenty-Ninth Algonquian Conference* 29: 252-263.

Quimby, George Irving

1960 *Indian Life in the Upper Great Lakes: 11,000 B.C. to A.D. 1800.* Chicago: University of Chicago Press.

Radin, Paul

1911 "The Ritual and Significance of the Winnebago Medicine Dance." *The Journal of American Folklore* 24: 149-208.

1928 "Ethnological notes on the Ojibwa of southeastern Ontario." *American Anthropologist* 30, no. 4: 659-668.

1956 *The Trickster: A Study in American Indian Mythology.* With commentaries by Karl Kerényi and C.G. Jung. New York: Philosophical Library.

no date "An Introductive Inquiry in the Study of Ojibwa Religion." *Ontario Historical Society Papers and Records* 12: 10-18.

no date *Medicine Dance.* 18 pp.

no date *Ojibwa, Ottawa Indians; customs, etc.* [n.d.] Typed D. ca. 175L.

Radin, Paul, and Reagan, A.B.

1928 "Ojibwa Myths and Tales." *The Journal of American Folklore* 41, no. 159: 61-146.

Reagan, A.B.

1927 "Picture Writings of the Chippewa Indians." *Wisconsin Archeologist* 6: 80-83.

1923 "Rainy Lakes Indians." *Wisconsin Archeologist*. New Series 2: 140-147.

1933 "Some Notes on the Grand Medicine Society of the Bois Fort Ojibway." *America Illustrated* 27: 502-519.

1992 "Medicine Songs of George Farmer." *American Anthropologist* 24, no. 3: 332-369.

Redsky, James (Esquekesik)

1972 *Great Leader of the Ojibway: Mis-quona-queb*, edited by James R. Stevens. Toronto: McClelland and Stewart.

Rhodes, Richard A.

1985 *Eastern Ojibwa-Chippewa-Ottawa Dictionary.* The Hague: Mouton.

Ricoeur, Paul

1967 *The Symbolism of Evil.* Boston: Beacon Press.

1995 "MYTH: Myth and History." In *Encyclopedia of Religion*, edited by Mircea Eliade. Vol. 10. London: Simon and Schuster and Prentice Hall International.

Ritterbush, Lauren Walker

1990 *Culture Change and Continuity: Ethnohistoric Analysis of Ojibwa and Ottawa Adjustment to the Prairies.* PhD Dissertation. University of Kansas.

Ritzenthaler, Robert E.

1953 "Chippewa Preoccupation with Health." *Bulletin of the Public Museum of the City of Milwaukee* 19: 175-258.

Ritzenthaler, Robert E., and Pat Ritzenthaler

1983 *The Woodland Indians of the Western Great Lakes.* Prospect Heights, Ill.: Waveland Press.

Rogers, Edward S.

1969a "Band Organization Among the Indians of Eastern Subarctic Canada. In *Contributions to Anthropology: Band Societies*, edited by David Damas, pp. 21-50. Anthropological Series 84, Bulletin 228. Ottawa: National Museum of Canada.

1969b "Natural Environment—Social Organization—Witchcraft: Cree Versus Ojibwa—A Test Case." In *Contributions to Anthropology: Ecological Essays*, edited by David Damas, pp. 24-39. Anthropological Series 86, Bulletin 230. Ottawa: National Museum of Canada.

1983 "Cultural Adaptations: The Northern Ojibwa of the Boreal Forest, 1670-1980." In *Boreal Forest Adaptations: The Northern Algonkians*, edited by A. Theodore Steegmann, pp. 85-141. New York: Plenum Press.

Rogers, Edward S., and Donald B. Smith, eds.

1994 *Aboriginal Ontario: Historical Perspectives on the First Nations.* Toronto: Dundurn Press.

Ross, Hamilton Nelson

1960 *La Pointe—Village Outpost.* St. Paul: North Central Publishing Co.

Ross, Rupert

1992 *Dancing with a Ghost: Exploring Indian Reality.* With a foreword by Basil H. Johnston. Markham: Octopus Publishing.

Rouf, Timothy G., and Larry P. Aitken, eds.

1984 *Information Relating to Chippewa Peoples from the Handbook of American Indians North of Mexico.* Edited by Frederick Webb Hodge. 1907/1910. Reprint edition, Duluth: Lake Superior Basin Studies Center.

Salisbury, Neal

1982 *Manitou and Providence: Indians, Europeans, and the Making of New England, 1500-1643.* New York: Oxford University Press.

Schenck, Theresa M.

1994 "The Cadottes: Five Generations of Fur Traders on Lake Superior." In *The Fur Trade Revisited: Selected Papers of the Sixth North American Fur Trade Conference, Mackinac Island, Michigan, 1991*, pp. 189-198. East Lansing: Michigan State University Press.

1997 *"The Voice of the Crane Echoes Afar": The Sociopolitical Organization of the Lake Superior Ojibwa, 1640-1855.* New York: Garland Publishing.

Schlesier, Karl

1990 "Rethinking the Midewiwin and the Plains Ceremonial called the Sun Dance." *Plains Anthropologist* 35, no. 127: 1-27.

Schmalz, Peter S.

1991 *The Ojibwa of Southern Ontario.* Toronto: University of Toronto Press.

Schoolcraft, Henry Rowe

1835 "Mythology, Superstitions and Languages of the North American Indians." *New York Theological Review* 2: 96-121.

1839 *Algic Researches, comprising inquiries respecting the mental characteristics of the North American Indians.* New York: Harper & Bros.

1848 *The Indian in His Wigwam, or Characteristics of the Red Race in America.* Buffalo: Derby and Hudson.

1851 *Personal Memoirs of a Residence of Thirty Years with the Indian Tribes on the American Frontier A.D. 1812 to 1842.* Philadelphia: Lippincott, Grambo & Co.

1851-57 *Information Respecting the History, Condition and Prospects of the Indian Tribes of the United States.* Six volumes. Philadelphia: Lippincott, Grambo & Co.

1962 *The Literary Voyageur, or Muzzeniegan*, edited by Philip Mason. Detroit: Wayne State University Press.

1973 *Summary Narrative*, edited by Mentor L. Williams. New York: Kraus Reprint.

1991 *Indian Legends*, edited by Mentor L. Williams. 1956. Reprint edition, East Lansing, Michigan State University Press.

1992 *Narrative Journal of Travels*, edited by Mentor L. Williams. 1953. Reprint edition, East Lansing: Michigan State University Press.

1993 *Expedition to Lake Itasca*, edited by Philip P. Mason. 1958. Reprint edition, East Lansing: Michigan State University Press.

Segal, Robert A.

1987 "Relativism and Rationality in the Social Sciences." *Journal of Religion*: 353-362.

Skinner, Alanson

1910 "A Visit to the Ojibway and Cree of Central Canada." *American Museum Journal* 10: 9-18.

1911 "Notes on the Eastern Cree and Northern Saulteaux." *Anthropological Papers of the American Museum of Natural History* 9: 1-177.

1914 "Political and Ceremonial Organization, Cults, and Ceremonies of the Plains-Ojibway and Plains Cree." *Anthropological Papers of the American Museum of Natural History* 11: 475-511.

1915 "Associations and Ceremonies of the Menomini Indians." *Anthropological Papers of the American Museum of Natural History* 13, no. 2: 191-200.

1919 "Plains Ojibwa Tales." *Journal of American Folk-lore* 32: 280-305.

1920 *Medicine Ceremony of the Menomini, Iowa and Wahpeton Dakota*. Indian Notes and Monographs, 4. New York: Museum of the American Indian, Heye Foundation.

Slight, Benjamin

1844 *Indian Researches: or Facts Concerning the North American Indians; including Notices of their present State of Improvement in their Social, Civil and Religious Condition, with Hints for their Future Advancement*. Montreal: J.E.L. Miller.

Smith, Donald B.

1975 "Who are the Mississauga?" *Ontario History* 67: 211-222.

1981 "The Dispossession of the Mississauga Indians." *Ontario History* 73: 67-87.

1987 *Sacred Feathers: The Reverend Peter Jones (Kahkewaquonaby) and the Mississauga Indians*. Toronto: University of Toronto Press.

Smith, G. Hubert

1946 "The Form and Function of the Midewiwin." *Minnesota Archeologist* 12, no. 3: 22-37.

Smith, H.I.

1896 "Certain Shamanistic Ceremonies among the Ojibwas." *American Antiquarian* 18: 282-284.

1906 "Some Ojibwa Myths and Traditions." *Journal of American Folk-lore* 19: 215-230.

Smith, James G.E.

1979 "Leadership Among the Indians of the Northern Woodlands." In *Currents in Anthropology: Essays in Honor of Sol Tax*, edited by Robert Hinshaw, pp. 306-24. The Hague: Mouton.

Smith, Theresa S.

1989 "Ojibwa Persons: Toward a Phenomenology of an American Indian Life-World." *Journal of Phenomenological Psychology* 20, no. 2: 130-144.

1995 *The Island of the Anishnaabeg: Thunderers and Water Monsters in the Traditional Ojibwe Life-World*. Moscow, Idaho: University of Idaho Press.

Smith, Wilfred Cantwell

1963 *The Meaning and End of Religion: A New Approach to the Religious Traditions of Mankind*. New York: Macmillan.

1972 *The Faith of Other Men*. New York: Harper & Row.

Speck, Frank G

1915 *Myths and Folk-lore of the Timis-Kaming Algonquin and Timagami Ojibwa*. Anthropological Series, no. 9. Memoirs of the Canadian Geological Survey of Canada, no. 71. Ottawa.

Spindler, George, and Louise Spindler

1971 *Dreamers without Power: The Menomini Indians*. New York: Holt, Rinehart and Winston.

Starkloff, Carl F.

1986 "New Tribal Religious Movements in North America: A Contemporary Theological Horizon." *Toronto Journal of Theology* 2, no. 2: 157-171.

Stevens, Michael E.

1974-75 "Catholic and Protestant Missionaries among the Wisconsin Indians: The territorial period." *Wisconsin Magazine of History* 58, no. 2: 140-148.

Stewart, James

1904 "Rupert's Land Indians in the Olden Time." In *Archaeological Report*. Toronto: Ontario Ministry of Education.

Stocking, George

1991 *Colonial situations: essays on the contextualization of ethnographic knowledge*. Madison: University of Wisconsin Press.

Swanton, John R.

1952 *The Indian Tribes of North America*. Bureau of American Ethnology, Smithsonian Institution, Washington, D.C.: Govt. Publications Office.

Talamantez, Ines M.

1985 "Use of Dialogue in the Reinterpretation of American Indian Religious Traditions: A Case Study." *American Indian Culture and Research Journal* 9, no. 2: 33-48.

Tanner, Helen Hornbeck

1992 *The Ojibwa.* New York: Chelsea House.

Tanner, Helen Hornbeck, ed.

1986 *Atlas of Great Lakes Indian History.* Cartography by Milos Pinther. Norman, Okla.: Published for the Newberry Library by University of Oklahoma Press.

Tanner, John

1830 *A Narrative of the Captivity and Adventures of John Tanner.* London: Baldwin & Craddock.

1956 *A Narrative of the Captivity and Adventures of John Tanner during Thirty Years Residence Among the Indians in the Interior of North America.* Prepared for the Press by Edwin James. 1830. Reprint edition, Minneapolis: Ross & Haines Reprint Edition.

1994 *The Falcon: A Narrative of the Captivity and Adventures of John Tanner during Thirty Years Residence Among the Indians in the Interior of North America.* With an introduction by Louise Erdrich. 1830. Reprint edition, New York: Penguin Books.

Taussig, Michael

1987 *Shamanism, colonialism and the wild man: Healing, terror and the space of death.* Chicago: University of Chicago Press.

Tedlock, Dennis

1983 *The Spoken Word and the Work of Interpretation.* Philadelphia: University of Pennsylvania Press.

Thomas, Nicholas, and Caroline Humphrey, eds.

1994 *Shamanism, History and the State.* Ann Arbor: University of Michigan Press.

Thompson, David

1962 *David Thompson's Narrative, 1784-1812.* Toronto: Champlain Society.

1971 *Travels in Western North America, 1784-1812*, edited by Victor G. Hopwood. Toronto: Macmillan.

Thwaites, Reuben G., ed. and trans.

1896-1901 *The Jesuit Relations and Allied Documents: Travels and Explorations of the Jesuit Missionaries in New France, 1610-1791.* Cleveland: Burrow Brothers.

1905 *New Voyages to North-America by the Baron de Lahontan.* Chicago: McClung.

Trigger, Bruce G.

1985 *Natives and Newcomers: Canada's "Heroic Age" Reconsidered.* Kingston: McGill-Queen's University Press.

Turner, Victor

1969 *The Ritual Process*. Ithaca, N.Y.: Cornell University Press.

U.S. Office of the Commissioner of Indian Affairs.

1850-58 *Annual Report*. Washington, D.C.

Vansina, Jan

1985 *Oral Tradition as History*. Madison: University of Wisconsin.

Vastokas, Joan M., and Romas K. Vastokas

1973 *Sacred Art of the Algonkians*. Peterborough, New Hampshire: Mansard Press.

Vecsey, Christopher

1983 *Traditional Ojibwa Religion and its Historical Changes*. Philadelphia: American Philosophical Society.

1984 "Midewiwin Myths of Origin." In *Papers of the Fifteenth Algonquian Conference*, edited by Willian Cowan, pp. 445-467. Ottawa: Carleton University.

1988 *Imagine Ourselves Richly: Mythic Narratives of North American Indians*. New York: Crossroad.

Veenstra, Jan R.

1995 "The New Historicism of Stephen Greenblatt: On Poetics of Culture and the Interpretation of Shakespeare." *History and Theory* 34, no. 4: 174-188.

Vennum, Thomas Jr.

1978 "Ojibwa Origin-Migration Songs of the *mitewiwin*." *Journal of American Folklore* 91: 753-791.

1982 *The Ojibwa Dance Drum: Its History and Construction*. Washington, D.C.: Smithsonian Institution Press.

1988 *Wild Rice and the Ojibwa People*. St. Paul: Minnesota Historical Society Press.

Verwyst, Chrysostom

1886 *Missionary Labours of Fathers Marquette, Menard and Allouez in the Lake Superior Region*. Milwaukee and Chicago.

Vizenor, Gerald

1965 *Anishnabe Adisokan*. Minneapolis: Nodin Press.

1984 *The People Named the Chippewa: Narrative Histories*. Minneapolis: University of Minnesota Press.

Voegelin, E.W.

1941 "Notes on Ojibwa-Ottawa Pictography." *Proceedings of the Indiana Academy of Science* 50: 44-47.

Waisberg, Leo G.

1978a "The Ottawa: Traders of the Great Lakes, 1615-1700." Master's Thesis. McMasters University.

1978b "An Ethnological and Historical Outline of the Rainy Lake Ojibwa." In *An Historical Synthesis of the Manitou Mounds Site on the Rainy River, Ontario.* Volume 1. Cornwall: Parks Canada Office, National Historic Sites Branch.

Waisberg, Leo G., and Marie-Ange Beaudry

1984 *Manitou Mounds: Historical Evaluation of the Mission Lot.* Prepared for Parks Canada, Ontario Regional Office.

Wallace, Anthony F.C.

1956 "Revitalization Movements." *American Anthropologist* 58: 264-281.

1966 *Religion: An Anthropological View.* New York: Random House.

Warren, William W.

1846a "A Brief History of the Ojibwas." *Minnesota Archeologist* 12, no. 3: 45-91.

1846b "Sioux and Chippewa Wars." *Minnesota Archeologist* 12, no. 4: 95-107.

1847 "Answers to Inquiries regarding Chippewas." *Minnesota Archeologist* 13, no. 1: 5-21.

1852 "Oral Traditions Respecting the History of the Ojibwa Nation." In *Information Respecting the History, Condition and Prospects of the Indian Tribes of the United States,* by Henry R. Schoolcraft. Volume 2, pp. 135-167. Philadelphia: Lippincott, Grambo & Co.

1984 *History of the Ojibway People.* With an introduction by W. Roger Buffalohead. 1885. Reprint edition, St. Paul: Minnesota Historical Society Press.

1986 "Traditions of Descent." In *Native American Folklore in Nineteenth Century Periodicals,* edited by William M. Clements. 1898. Reprint edition, Athens: Ohio University Press.

1923 "When the Indians Owned Manitoba." *The Winnipeg Evening Tribune,* March 10, p. 3.

Whipple, H. B.

1901 "Civilization and Christianization of the Ojibways of Minnesota." *Collections of the Minnesota Historical Society* 9: 129-142.

White, Richard

1991 *The Middle Ground: Indians, Empires, and Republics in the Great Lakes Region, 1650-1815.* New York: Cambridge University Press.

Widder, Keith R.

1981 "Founding La Pointe Mission 1825-1833." *Wisconsin History* 64, no. 3: 181-201.

Wilson, Rev. Edward Francis

no date *Autobiography and family history of the Rev. E.F. Wilson (1844-1915).* Ontario Archives. Microfilm Ms. 24.

Wilson, Edward Francis.

1886 *Missionary Work Among the Ojebway Indians.* London: Society for the Propagation of Christian Knowledge.

Woodsworth, Joseph F.

1908 "Indian Paganism." In *Acta Victoria.* Toronto: Victoria University.

Wright, Ronald

1992 *Stolen Continents: The "New World" through Indian Eyes.* Toronto: Penguin Books.

Young, Egerton R.

1903 *Algonquin Indian Tales.* New York: Eaton & Mains.

INDEX